Poetics and the Gift

Poetics and the Gift
Reading Poetry from Homer to Derrida

Adam R. Rosenthal

EDINBURGH
University Press

Edinburgh University Press is one of the leading university presses in the UK. We publish academic books and journals in our selected subject areas across the humanities and social sciences, combining cutting-edge scholarship with high editorial and production values to produce academic works of lasting importance. For more information visit our website: edinburghuniversitypress.com

© Adam R. Rosenthal, 2022

Edinburgh University Press Ltd
The Tun – Holyrood Road
12(2f) Jackson's Entry
Edinburgh EH8 8PJ

Typeset in 10.5/13 Bembo by
IDSUK (DataConnection) Ltd

A CIP record for this book is available from the British Library

ISBN 978 1 4744 8840 2 (hardback)
ISBN 978 1 4744 8842 6 (webready PDF)
ISBN 978 1 4744 8843 3 (epub)

The right of Adam R. Rosenthal to be identified as the author of this work has been asserted in accordance with the Copyright, Designs and Patents Act 1988, and the Copyright and Related Rights Regulations 2003 (SI No. 2498).

Contents

List of Figures — vii
Acknowledgements — viii
Preface — x

Introduction: 'Economimesis' after *Given Time*, or:
The Return of Helio-Poetics — 1

PART I: POETIC DIVINITY AND PATRONAGE

1. Poetic Donation from Homer to Kant — 41
2. Symbolic Economies of Poet and Patron — 58
3. Patronage and Poetic Election in Wordsworth — 83

PART II: BEING AND NAMING

4. Stein and the Concern of Poetry — 121
5. Heidegger and the *Stiftung der Wahrheit* — 127
6. Shelley and the Gift of the Name — 138

PART III: ECONOMY AND ANECONOMY

7. Emerson and the Flower of Commodities — 165
8. Thoreau on Poetic Purchase — 178
9. Baudelaire and the Gift of Pleasing — 213

PART IV: GIVENS

10. Poetry Lost and Found in Howe, Goldsmith, and Philip   245

Conclusion: The Birth of Lyric in *The Homeric Hymn to Hermes*   265
Appendix: Henry David Thoreau, 'A Poet Buying a Farm'   271
Bibliography   272
Index   294

Figures

10.1	By Susan Howe, from *CONCORDANCE*, copyright © 2019, 2020 by Susan Howe. Reprinted by permission of New Directions Publishing Corp.	255
10.2	Page 27 of *Zong!* © 2008 by M. NourbeSe Philip. Published by Wesleyan University Press and reprinted with permission.	258
10.2	Page 101 of *Zong!* © 2008 by M. NourbeSe Philip. Published by Wesleyan University Press and reprinted with permission.	259
A.1	Henry David Thoreau (1852), 'A Poet Buying a Farm', *Sartain's Union Magazine* 11: 127.	271

Acknowledgements

This book has been a long time coming. Along the way, I drew on the generosity of friends and family, colleagues and critics, and even the odd adversary. Their contributions often took the form of time, but also, on occasion, patience, attention, instruction, and discipline. Perhaps, now and again, I may even have taken advantage of their magnanimity. What is certain is that this book was forged in the give and take of these ties. For that, I am grateful.

Where would I be today without the support of Elissa Marder, Geoffrey Bennington, Deborah Elise White, and Cathy Caruth, my dissertation committee? Through the years, they have proven their value on more occasions than I can recall. My time at Emory University was also shaped by Shoshana Felman, Valéry Loichot, John Lysaker, Andrew J. Mitchell, Erik Butler, Moyukh Chatterjee, Luke Donahue, Carl Hughes, Christina León, Hannah Markley, Ronald Mendoza-de Jesús, David Ritchie, Matthew J. Roberts, Taylor Schey, John Steen, and Rodrigo Therezo. I consider myself fortunate to have grown up in their presence. I am also particularly thankful to the Departments of Comparative Literature and French at Emory, which nurtured all of my early academic endeavours. At Texas A&M, I have been supported by many colleagues from across the College of Liberal Arts and beyond: Maddalena Cerrato, Daniel Conway, Robert Griffin, Stefanie Harris, Daniel Humphrey, Craig Kallendorf, Claire Katz, Chaitanya Lakkimsetti, Vikram Manjunath, Alberto Moreiras, Robert Shandley, Apostolos Vasilakis, Teresa Vilarós-Soler, and Michael Portal have each helped me make a home for myself there.

I have been the recipient of extremely liberal and insightful feedback on this book. No recognition would be sufficient to pay the debts I owe to Branka Arsić, Emile Bojesen, E. S. Burt, Katie Chenoweth, Thomas Hays, Daniel Hoffman-Schwartz, Peggy Kamuf, Kir Kuiken, Brian McGrath, Martin McQuillan, Laliv Melamed, Thomas Clément Mercier, Michael Naas, Nicholas Royle, Kas Saghafi, Art Smith, Naomi Waltham Smith, Sergio Villalobos-Ruminott, and David Wills. I could not have done it without each of you.

I am also thankful to the editorial team at Edinburgh University Press, especially Ersev Ersoy, Susannah Butler, and the perceptive anonymous reviewers who helped turn this project into something more than I could have hoped for.

Research for this book was supported by a number of sources. The Thoreau Society funded trips to Concord, Massachusetts, so that I could romp about in Walden's hallowed woods. The Bill and Carol Fox Center for Humanistic Inquiry at Emory University not only provided me with a full year's support so that I could complete my dissertation, but also gave me the space in which to do so and a community from which I could learn. In the final stages of the project, Texas A&M's Melbern G. Glasscock Center for Humanities Research also provided me with generous funding as well as encouragement, for which I am extremely thankful. Finally, all of the images used below were expertly photographed by Bella Kirchner, to whom I am obliged.

With such a theme – with this my argument – of thee, Armando Mastrogiovanni, shall I be silent? No one has been so constant a star in the progress of this work, nor been so subject to the numerous iterations it has taken, as you. For this you shall be remembered.

Which brings me to my family. No part of this book would have been possible without the contributions of Janie and Eric Rosenthal, my parents and biggest backers. Over the last decade, Stephen Hannaford and Marion Faber, along with Rachel and Justin and Zachary and Beatrice, have become central parts of my life. I am thankful to have known each of you. A special place, finally, must be reserved for Dinah Hannaford and Charlotte Rosenthal. I would thank you, make you offerings, and lavish you with presents, if I didn't already count you as so many portions of myself. In this respect, to express gratitude for your daily benefaction would be as senseless as to do so for my own. What could the left hand give to the right? I can only renounce such a project and hope that, in doing so, some semblance of the sentiment is grasped.

A previous version of Chapter 6 was previously published in *Studies in Romanticism* 55.1.

Preface

> Yet, fellow poets, us it behooves to stand
> Bareheaded beneath God's thunder-storms,
> To grasp the Father's ray, no less, with our own two hands
> And, wrapping in song the heavenly gift,
> To offer it to the people.
> [Doch uns gebührt es, unter Gottes Gewittern,
> Ihr Dichter! mit entblößtem Haupte zu stehen,
> Des Vaters Stral, ihn selbst, mit eigner Hand
> Zu fassen und dem Volk ins Lied
> Gehüllt die himmlische Gaabe zu reichen.]
>
> Hölderlin, 'As on a holiday . . .'[1]

This book argues that the Western poetic tradition is in need of reappraisal. An essential element of its form has been under-theorised. From this lack of attention, what in fact constitute founding and interrelated features of poetry's history have been interpreted to be disparate, secondary, and merely contingent. This neglected element, I show, is the gift.

The archive of poetry is littered with gifts. A motley crew of presents, grants, and benefits, scattered here and there, span both its material history and its figural self-representations. These gifts have supplied rich material for poets, critics, and philosophers alike. They have stood as the ground of poetry's dismissal as well as its embrace, its commendation as well as its condemnation. It is poetry's status as divine gift, in the *Odyssey*, that makes it both more and less than a sellable good for Alcinous and Demodocus, just as it is poetry's god-given status, in the *Ion* and *Phaedrus*, that convinces Socrates and Plato that it could not possibly be a learned *technē*. It is the fact of the poem's gifting, by Horace, that makes it so compelling for his patron, Maecenas, while it is the poet's exemplary gift of genius, in the *Critique of the Power of Judgment*, that renders the skill for composition categorically unteachable, for Kant. Even as late as Heidegger, it is poetry's *endowing-and-founding* nature, its capacity to give being, that makes it, for the philosopher, the very essence of language and ultimate bearer of truth.[2]

With great persistence and variation, gifts populate the long history of Western poetry and poetics, supplying an essential element of theories of inspiration, genius, and imagination, material economies of patronage, and notions of poetic essence and work. Scholars have made note of these many claims. Nevertheless, they have rarely questioned what connects them, across languages, historical periods, and geographical regions, nor asked why, in the first place, poetry might be drawn to figures of donation to define the nature of poet and poem. What stands or falls on poetry's determination as given–gifted–giving?

At any moment of its history, most seem to agree that it would be good for poetry to be a gift. The gift, Lewis Hyde tells us, is what makes art art and poetry poetry. According to Sir Philip Sidney, poetry is the first giver of milk to men. These sentiments are both decisive for their authors and interrelated. For Hyde, the access of poetry and art to this gift is what distinguishes their mode of engagement from that of the mere commodity.[3] For Sidney, the access of poetry, and by extension literature, to this gift is what distinguishes the true poet from the mere 'poet-ape'.[4] It is the given–giving nature of poetry that makes it, for both men, something truly human and, ultimately, divine. Only as the memory of God's creation in the imagination of men may poetry break free from 'the narrow warrant of [Nature's] gifts', Sidney tells us.[5] Only as the expression of human 'creativity' may art be sure to exceed the commodity market's cold, reductive reach, says Hyde. The gift at work in poetry serves to distinguish man, its keeper, from his mirror image in the natural world and his mechanical other in the market. It serves to preserve his right to exclusively *human* forms of production, invention, imitation, generosity, divinity, and even economy.

Whether or not poetry in fact has a privileged relation to the gift – a question that, still too poorly formed, I hold in suspense – an image of this historical constellation now begins to come into focus: upon the possibility of establishing poetry's origin in a divine present, its circulation in a gift-economy, or its impact in an excess of generosity, rests the very hope of distinguishing imagination from folly, creativity from automation, art from commodity, and, by extension, divinity from mundanity, humanity from animality, true priest from false prophet, and speech as *logos*, from mere gesture and soulless writing. Whether or not poetry *is* a gift, then, from antiquity to the present, its status *as* a gift has helped it to establish its distinction as a field and to carve out its singular place both among the arts and for humanity at large. Indeed, to take the poetic tradition seriously is to believe that, were poetry ever able to establish this gift-status definitively, then not only would it cease its 'self-hatred' and stop 'resisting itself', but also it would finally fulfil its promise to establish the order of the heavens on earth, impose, at long last, a new generous economy for humankind, and reveal, for all time, the poet to be the true legislator of the world.[6] On this possibility rests, in other words, not only the hope of 'assert[ing] Eternal Providence and justify[ing] the ways of God to men', as Milton had it, but also of confirming *poetry* to be the vehicle for such a demonstration, and *poet* to be its guarantor, as Hölderlin did.[7]

The gift-status of poetry is bound up in the hegemonic project of establishing poetic distinction as a field and poetic privilege as the proper of humankind. Variations on this motif are virtually endless and may be found throughout the classical and modern periods alike. Even today, after the deaths of genius, creativity, originality, patronage, inspiration, and God, even in its apparently most secular, least expressive, and wholly language-oriented forms, poetry remains tied up with this project so long as it is determined as a 'free' or 'liberating' art whose nature is to be opposed to that of sheer information, or the paltry commodity of commercial exchange. It remains bound to this project, in other words, so long as it is affirmed as an 'excess', irreducible to other, purely functional uses of language:

> Poetry is language's excess: poetry is what in language cannot be reduced to information, and is not exchangeable, but gives way to a new common ground of understanding, of shared meaning: the creation of a new world.[8]

The desire to distinguish poetry from prose – as benevolence differs from self-interest, life from death, and excess from restraint – is as old as 'poetry' itself and remains inextricable from the most theologically oriented tradition of humanist poetics.[9] And yet, having said that, what reader could in good conscience simply reject Bifo's paradigm? Who could *simply* embrace a poetry without gift, without invention, and without creation? Who could *simply* embrace a 'robopoetic', 'unoriginal', or unexcessive poetry – without talent, art, inspiration, or beauty – and do so, moreover, without a hint of irony?

As we shall see, even for those who claim to reject creativity and originality, the matter is never as clear-cut as it seems. Between the gift and the non-gift there is, quite simply, no simple nor straightforward solution. The poetic archive is, therefore, in need of reappraisal. Even before it entered its current state of crisis, before it lost its traditional structures of patronage and became dependent on the book trade, before the rise of calculative reason put its value into question, and before it embraced principles of uncreativity and unoriginality, the gift modality of poetry was already a problem for it, silently sowing seeds of supremacy and exclusivity among many of its most treasured figures.[10]

Poetics and the Gift confronts this problem. It examines its limits, history, and necessity, in order to reappraise the meaning of poetry in its Western acceptation. Through its examination of the gift's role within the poetic archive, it then asks not only what poetry's future might yet hold, but also what its past may already have secretly sown, without a reader prepared to receive it. Though scholars have long studied the gift in poetry, they have yet to ask what unites each of its disparate figures; nor have they enquired into whether it possesses a foundational character therein.[11] I argue that the thinker whose work has come closest to posing these questions, however, and thus to thinking the limits of the poetry-gift complex, is the philosopher Jacques Derrida.

What lies at the root of poetry's attraction to the gift? Could one conceive of poetry – what we call 'poetry' – without this onto-theological kernel, which is also to say, without hegemony? Could poetry have been otherwise constructed? And how might the gift's own ambivalence – its well-documented pervertibility into poison – already contaminate these poetic determinations? Were one, finally, simply able to eliminate the gift from poetry's archive, as contemporary poets Christian Bök and Kenneth Goldsmith appear, at times, to wish to do, then would such an expulsion in fact be desirable?

These questions, I show, are opened anew by Derrida's writings, which displace the traditional anthropo-philosophical conception of donation and, in so doing, lay the groundwork for a novel examination of the gift and poetry's interrelation. What separates Derrida's work on the gift is, first and foremost, his refusal to reduce it either to a simple object of representation or to a mere form of exchange. As he explores in *Given Time*, what the work of phenomenologists such as Heidegger and anthropologists such as Mauss alike reveals, is the fundamental, structuring role that gifts play for the spacing of time, the thinging of the thing, and the becoming subject of the subject. 'The gift gives, demands, and takes time. The thing gives, demands, or takes time,' Derrida writes of Mauss's account of gift-giving in the *Essay on the Gift*.[12] By this he means that there is no pure, homogenous temporality, nor any stable subject or object of exchange, prior to the presentations of those 'things' that, in truth, structure the experience of each. Be it in the sphere of economics or of phenomenology, in that of art or of politics, gifts turn out to play organising roles that could not be reduced to more basic elements or purely 'objective' principles.

Crucially, if the gift is neither an object nor a form, but what Heidegger calls a 'thing' and Derrida calls an originary mode of 'marking', then it must be thought of first as trace, or writing, before it is considered in any of its sociological, phenomenological, or linguistic determinations. The gift is not simply *like* a text, which makes demands, gives orders, and structures certain 'gift effects'; it *is* a text. And the onus of any reading of it, therefore, is to account for the experience of its double, impossible, and even mad demand that it each time inscribes: to give *and* to obliterate any trace of the gift; to enter into the cyclical circuit of exchange *and* to annul this circuit; to give account of this impossible 'gift' *and* to fail to give account, which is the only condition upon which one could retain a trace of what, by its very nature, ought to defy all incorporation and memorialisation.

Insofar, then, as what the gift as text names is a certain sending or address without return, insofar as the act of giving intimates – in principle, if not in fact – a dissemination that would not come back to the father, to this extent a reversal in the ordinary way of identifying gifts is made possible, and it is this insight that interests us above all. The gift, Derrida shows, is not only, in each instance, *a trace*, but *all traces* must now already bear something of a *gift-character*, because what 'gift' names is just this exorbitant sending. Before there can be any objective determination of the difference between gift and non-gift, all traces, as forms of address destined to non-return, would bear the basic structure of the gift.[13]

How might such an approach, informed by both Heideggerian phenomenology and Maussian sociology, alter the classical image of poetic donation, as a play of gift exchanges functioning *within* the representational field of the poem, or one circulating *outside* it, among poets and their real-life patrons? At a minimum, what the above implies is that this millennia-old poetic orientation towards giving may itself be overdetermined. *To give poetry* cannot simply be a matter of subjective generosity, of socio-political conditioning, or even of hegemonic desire, but is also, always already, possibly a mode of remarking the giving structure of (poetic) textuality itself. If the gift is not simply 'outside' poetry – as a form to which poets appeal or a content that individual poems re-present – but is itself already 'inside' it, as one of poetry's basic, structuring conditions, then before or beyond each of these historical determinations there would be an underlying formal relation that, in a certain sense, pre-orients each on its course. The gifts of poetry, as we understand them today, would both speak from and speak to this fundamental condition.

The above is precisely what Derrida gives to think in *Given Time*. As he writes there, not only is the gift, 'as the marking of a trace', 'always . . . the gift of a writing, a memory, a poem, or a narrative', but more critically still, 'writing would [be] . . . "something" that is tied to the very act of the gift, *act* in the sense both of the archive and the performative operation'.[14] In other words, the structure of textual inscription *in general* would infer and require a certain condition of the gift, 'in the writing itself':

> Let us first of all not forget something trivially and massively obvious. It constitutes the elemental medium for what one is given to think here, namely, that this text – apparently finite, this bit of corpus title 'Counterfeit Money' – is for us a *given*. It is there before us who read it and who therefore begin by receiving it. If it has the structure of a given, it is not only because we are first of all in a receptive position with regard to it but because it has been given to us. From the moment he published it and even if he had not published it, from the moment he wrote it and constituted it by dedicating it to his 'dear friend' . . . from the moment he let it constitute itself in a system of traces, he destined it, gave it, not only to another or in general to others than his 'dear friend' Arsène Houssaye, but delivered it – and that was giving it – above and beyond any determined addressee, donee, or legatee . . . . The accredited signatory delivered it up to a dissemination without return. Why without return? What history, what time, and what space are determined by such a 'without return'? Whatever return it could have made toward Baudelaire or whatever return he might have counted on, the structure of trace and legacy of this text – as of anything that can be in general – surpasses the phantasm of return and marks the death of the signatory or the non-return of the legacy, the non-benefit, therefore a certain condition of the gift – in the writing itself [dans l'écriture même].
>
> That is why there is a problematic of the gift only on the basis of a consistent problematic of the trace and the *text*.[15]

The implications of this insight into the relationship between gift and text are far-reaching. For the moment, however, let us simply highlight the following: rather than a mere polarisation, toward something external to it, poetry's explicit draw to explanatory gift figurations may instead have to do with its own internal constitution, as text, and with what in this constitution already bespeaks the gift's disseminal structure.

The poetic archive has long been drawn to the gift as a privileged form of autonomy and exchange. Derrida suggests, however, that before any such explicit figuration may take place within poetry's archive, the gift may already be at work, implicitly, within poetry's fundamental constitution as text. There is gift in the very act of inscription. As soon as the poematic or narrative text is written, there is address and dissemination, and therefore also donation. Far from a mere figure, a haphazard representation, or even a strictly formal determination in the poem, the gift would thus become an ineliminable, foundational element of all (poetic) inscription, insofar as said inscription structurally implies disseminal sending and receiving, and does so irrespective of the 'generosity' or 'self-interest' of its author.

Once viewed from this perspective, the poetic drive to donation ceases to be simply accidental and contingent. It ceases, in other words, to be simply historical, be it as the product of individual giving poets, of culturally embedded ethics of generosity, or of socio-economically structured relations of disequilibrium and reciprocity. Instead, it becomes the historical expression of a structural entanglement. Poetry's self-remarking as gift may have as much to do with its *internal structure*, as text, as it does with any *external representation*, as present. This both clarifies and complicates the hegemonic drive of the 'poetic tradition' – a term that I use to refer not only to formally poetic works, but also to any text concerned with *the question of poetry*, be it philosophical, critical, or poetic in genre.[16] Poetic texts speak to the gift at work in all writing. They attend to and receive this gift, and they do so, *apparently*, in exemplary fashion, as poets and critics as diverse as Sappho, Sidney, Bataille, Celan, and Carson have each insisted.[17] And yet, insofar as this 'gift' cannot be said either to be the exclusive privilege of poetry, or to be as internally stable as would be required of a founding principle, it must also threaten the very claims that it helps to ground. The gift cannot but bring poetry face to face with the experience of its own impossibility. Everything thus rides on the value one gives to the exemplarity of *poetic* testimony within this story, and to the excessiveness of *its* excess, which time and again leads beyond anything still recognisable by the name 'poetry'.

In this book, I explore the consequences of the above interpretation of the gift and poetry's co-implication for the Western poetic tradition in general. I show how versions of this story play out, time and again, from the age of Homer up through contemporary conceptual poetics. On each occasion, poetry grounds itself in a gift that cannot but undermine it, and this *excess*, once recognised, is then either rejected, or re-inscribed as poetry's true essence. In revealing the structural homogeneity between trace and gift, Derrida's work, I argue, supplies the groundwork for this examination. He offers the opportunity for a fresh look at poetry's history as well as a reappraisal of its drive to establish the proper of man, human, or mortal. And I begin, for this reason, with an analysis of his writings on the subjects of the gift and poetry in the following chapter. I argue that despite the importance of these writings for work in philosophy, critical theory, and literary studies, the relation between them has not been well understood. For reasons that are, in fact, endemic to Derrida's corpus, one has rarely taken account of the impact of the one on the other. I propose that Derrida's most important work on the gift, *Given Time: 1. Counterfeit Money*, and his most important work on the history of poetry and poetics, 'Economimesis', collectively bring clarity to issues that have haunted the poetic tradition for thousands of years. And yet, because Derrida himself never pursued the connection between these two texts – or the trajectories they represent – the relation between them has, for the most part, remained unaddressed. The unclarified divide between these two works has inhibited comprehension of the full impact of his notion of the gift for the poetic archive.

I thus return, in the Introduction, to these texts, which I show are emblematic of Derrida's writings on poetry and the gift in general. The problem, in short, is that in taking up the question of the gift in *Given Time* (1978–9/1991), Derrida all but abandons the question of poetry, which he had only just treated in 'Economimesis' (1973–4/1975) as a matter of escalating gift exchanges.[18] Both texts treat *of gifts* and *of poems*. Yet they do so in antithetical fashions. In order to theorise the notorious 'impossibility' of the gift in *Given Time*, Derrida gives up the gift-economy of poetry of 'Economimesis'. The disparity in their treatments of poetry and gift goes so far that it gives the impression that the insight of the second text is purchased only at the expense of the insight of the first. Nevertheless, one will require both works, as well as clarity concerning the nature of their incommensurability, in order to address how the problem of the gift informs the archive of poetry. It is such a project that I take on in the chapters that follow. Adopting this newly problematised understanding of the relationship between gift and poetry as my starting point, I show how the poetic tradition is conditioned at one and the same time by the gift's *economy* and its *impossibility*: both by its drive for mastery and by its failure to ground itself in an impossible present. This is the legacy of the gift and poetry's co-implication. Yet it is only through the double vision provided by the perspectives of both 'Economimesis' and *Given Time* that the full scope of this conflict comes into focus.

As I demonstrate in the following chapter, *Given Time* is a text categorically unconcerned with poetry. Moreover, this lack of concern is organised by the text's own investment in a concept of the gift irreducible to exchange. To say this is not, of course, to deny that Derrida spends a great deal of time discussing *poems* in this seminar-turned-book. Rather, it is to acknowledge that, for him, there is a critical difference between the history of poetry and poetics, on the one hand, and poems and the poematic, on the other. The extended treatment of Baudelaire's 'Counterfeit Money', from which the first volume of *Given Time* takes its subtitle, serves as a case in point: never acknowledged by Derrida as a work of poetry, recognised for its place within poetic history, or even addressed as a 'prose-poem', 'La fausse monnaie' is treated throughout as an instance of *récit* (narrative), whose play in turn produces various 'gift' and 'literary effects'.[19] This distinction is both vital and symptomatic, yet it is far too often overlooked by discussions of the text. The question of poetry only ever emerges in *Given Time* either in passing, through its disavowal, or, in the posthumously published second half of the seminar from which it was taken, by way of Heidegger's notion of *Dichtung*. And this is because, as becomes clear in '*Che cos'è la poesia?*', Derrida considered poetry – in distinction to the poem or poematic – to be a distinctly metaphysical category, bound up with the very onto-theological determination of the gift against which *Given Time* strikes out.[20] As he put it in the follow-up interview to '*Che cos'è la poesia?*', '*Istrice 2: Ick bünn all hier*':

> The point would thus be to remove what I am calling the *poem* (or the *poiemata*) from the merry-go-round or circus that brings them back in a circular fashion to *poiein*, to their poetic source, to the act or to the experience of their setting-to-work in poetry or in poetics. By dissociating the poematic from the poetic, one removes it, one makes way for the experience during which it removes itself from the initiative of the setting-to-work, of *poiesis*.[21]

In contrast, then, to the progression of Derrida's own thought, *Poetics and the Gift* attempts to hold together these two counter-currents of the gift (*in poetry*, as source and circuit of exchange, and *in the poem*, as excess without return), so as to establish in what the relationship between them consists. I argue that any reading of the poetic tradition requires considering poetry's metaphysical, or heliotropic, orientation, as it is diagnosed in the earlier 'Economimesis', alongside the poematic traces that exceed this bent, and as are clarified in *Given Time*. And this is because such a troubled, double-inscription of the gift is precisely what poetic history, first of all, gives to think.

Derrida turned away from this project. His focus on the more originary poematic and more deconstructive gift led him to neglect questions of poetic history, let alone the struggle, internal to this history, over the gift itself. What is called for is thus both a more robust account of the relationship between poetry and poem in his work, and a more extensive analysis of the interplay between these impulses within the history of poetry itself. Practically speaking, this does not mean bringing all that Derrida did under the aegis of the poem, the poematic, the impossible gift, literature, fiction, and *récit*, back under the umbrella of an all-governing Poetry, *ars poetica*, or *Dichtung* – which is surely what he feared – but developing an analysis that carries these deconstructive insights back into poetry's archive, in order to see how poetry's logics, its histories, and its structures may already deconstruct this signifier, from within. This project is akin to reading Derrida's famous engagement with Mauss *back through* the problematics of 'Economimesis': a project, I argue, that is absolutely requisite, before one may apply the insights of *Given Time* to specifically, generically, 'poetic' texts. It is by way of this re-reading of 'Economimesis', through the detour of *Given Time*, that *Poetics and the Gift* opens a path for returning to the Western poetic archive, in order to interpret its onto-theological, heliotropic orientation otherwise.

In each of the subsequent four parts of this book, I pursue this trajectory, tracing, in each case, how the gift modality of poetry organises central conflicts of the poetic tradition. I do so by re-reading integral moments of poetic history, in order to show, on the one hand, the persistence of Western philosophical, poetic, and poematic determinations of poetry as gift and, on the other, how these determinations invariably lead to the *construction and deconstruction* of their objects. These chapters reveal the extent to which the archive of poetry needs the gift to shore up its field, to distinguish itself among the arts, to establish the privilege of humankind, and then, among humans, to establish the privilege of the few who may accede to its divine/human gifts, always at the expense of some inhuman, less than human, or merely human other. At the same time, they demonstrate how these determinations inevitably fail, and how at distinct moments of its history the poetic archive in fact already engages with, speculates upon, and draws into its web the impossibility of establishing the distinction of poetry, as the immediate consequence of the impossibility of the gift. Such a process of reflection and refraction is what we might call, in the language of late Derrida, poetry's 'auto-immunitary' play. Poetry, what is called 'poetry', in each instance bears out a *necessary* relation to the gift. Regardless of whether this relation is embraced or rejected, the persistence of its conflict confirms a structural resonance between poetic textuality and the disseminatory, giving trace. And it is this struggle, I show, that the history of poetry time and again unfolds.

STRUCTURE OF CHAPTERS

Poetics and the Gift is divided into four parts, which are structured both chronologically and thematically. It is comparative in scope, moving between multiple geographical, linguistic, and historical regions. In each of its parts, it explores how the gift conditions a distinct domain of poetic theory and history, alternately challenging, and being challenged by, the period's various economic, social, philosophical, and aesthetic concerns.

Part I focuses on how the gift permeates traditional notions of lyric subjectivity, from Homer up to Wordsworth. Part II examines the role of the gift within nineteenth- and twentieth-century notions of poetic essence, specifically in Stein, Heidegger, and Shelley. Part III turns to the gift's influence on post-Kantian notions of the poetic work, in Emerson, Thoreau, and Baudelaire, while Part IV examines how contemporary poets negotiate with the 'found', or the 'already given', in their work of composition.

In this way, the four parts of this book collectively show how these different aspects of poetry's history are interrelated, forming a continuous if malleable network, and how the gift's role in each invariably leads to crises of poetic definition. That being said, in contending that the above regions of poetic history form a continuous web, I in no way mean to infer that either the meaning of 'poetry', or that of the 'gift', is ever entirely stable, or fully translatable, from one period or idiom to the next.[22] Rather, my intention is to claim that the variable meanings of the one remain linked with those of the other, and through this linkage something like 'poetic authority', as John Guillory has termed it, is able to be transmitted.[23] The gift *structures* poetic conceptuality. But just as this allows for a certain poetic liberty, it also, invariably, leads to a questioning of that liberty's very possibility. In each part, then, I show both how the gift is a necessary component of poetic conceptuality and how it introduces fissures into the very fundaments that it helps to form.

The readings that follow examine texts from as early as the eighth century BCE and as late as the twenty-first century CE. Ultimately, however, they gravitate around a series of 'events', of poetry, in the nineteenth century, when the famed 'crisis of verse' was in full swing. If the poem's status as gift has always led to a degree of slippage between it and the world of commodities against which it is formed, then, it will be shown, this slippage is radicalised in the nineteenth century, when the decline of patronage and acceleration of the book trade render such a conception no longer materially tenable. Rather than a break, however, with the tradition preceding it – or following it – what comparative analysis shows is that the specificity of this nineteenth-century radicalisation is to intensify issues already at work, within the archive of poetry, since its birth.[24]

Part I, 'Poetic Divinity and Patronage', demonstrates the complicity between figural determinations of verse as god-given in inspiration, genius, and imagination, and material systems of patronal support. In readings that begin with the age of Homer and end with the Romantics, Chapters 1 and 2 show how the traditional lyric subject comes to be constituted through its role as giver/receiver, and how this role manifests both within theories of poetic subjectivity and in material economies of patronage, up through print culture.

In Chapter 3, following the surveys of the previous chapters, I turn to a culminating figure of this tradition, William Wordsworth, to show how, for him, this role is experienced as both curse and blessing. I argue that Wordsworth's insistent and at times acute reflections on his inability to verify Nature's gift of genius reveal fissures that haunt this entire tradition and that can already be seen to begin to fester in Horace and Shakespeare. The determination of the poet as receiver of inspiration and giver of verse achieves a cult-like status for him. Nevertheless, it is just this dependence on a divine alterity that also threatens to undermine the poet's position when this given authority is, sooner or later, brought into question.

Part II, 'Being and Naming', turns from the central figures of subject-oriented Western poetics in inspiration, genius, talent, and imagination, to examine a tradition of poetic conceptuality that generally opposes itself to this one: the ontological determination of poetry as source of being, world, and language. Though one can find traces of this understanding in far-reaching periods, its most famous proponent, who raised it to the level of theory, is the twentieth-century German philosopher Martin Heidegger. Heidegger, in understanding poetry – or, more precisely, *Dichtung* – to be giving-not-given, developed an understanding of the work as productive of the poet. In this way, he believed he was able to sever the essence of poetry from the metaphysical preconceptions inherent in traditional notions of lyric subjectivity. Heidegger also reversed the traditional relation between gift and poetry, arguing that *poetry gives giving*, instead of simply *being given*.

Reading Heidegger alongside modernist American author Gertrude Stein and British romantic poet Percy Shelley, I argue in Chapters 4 to 6 that this tradition of poetics in fact risks repeating many of the assumptions already visible in canonical authors such as Plato and Sidney. It risks repeating the division between the poetic and non-poetic, now, however, on the grounds that poetry should give the name, and in giving the name, give being. Mere prose, or lesser poetic works that are ultimately deemed unworthy of the title 'poetry', would, by contrast, be excluded from the gift and, as such, the gift of giving. Ultimately, however, insofar as this tradition must also come face to face with the possibility of poetry's failure to give – not only its failure to give the name but, more critically, its failure to give insight into this failure to give the name – one can also identify in it the traces of a step beyond poetry, or what I call a *pas de poésie*.[25]

Part III, 'Economy and Aneconomy', looks at the situation of poetry as an object of exchange after the eighteenth-century decline of patronage and rise of the book trade. It demonstrates the struggles, but also resolve, of a range of authors, to maintain the identification of poem with gift, now in the face of its growing circulation as commodity. Such an effort, I argue, ultimately forces a split among nineteenth-century authors. Whereas Kant and Emerson attempt to maintain the distinction between gift and commodity, for Thoreau and Baudelaire poetry begins to be conceived of through the suspension of this opposition. After examining Emerson's efforts to save the gift from its debasement in interested exchange in Chapter 7, in Chapters 8 and 9 I show how Thoreau and Baudelaire's visions of the gift culminate in notions of poetry that would remain undecidable between poetry and prose, gift and commodity, and calculability and incalculability. It is this suspension of difference, at the heart of poetry's definition, that can be traced, formally speaking, through the many prose poetries of the period.

Finally, in Part IV, 'Givens', I pursue the development of these structured moments of poetic undecidability in nineteenth-century European and American writing through their expansion into full-blown poetries of uncreativity and unoriginality in late twentieth- and early twenty-first-century poetics. How to understand the emergence of Web-based poetic forms, algorithmic poetry generators, Flarf and found poetry, and even Oulipo and constrained writing, in light of this tradition of gift poetics? Examining the collage poems of Susan Howe, the conceptual poetry of Kenneth Goldsmith, and the explosive compositions of M. NourbeSe Philip, I show how these authors might be said collectively to struggle with *the given* and, in this way, to carry out a certain inheritance of this tradition, even as they risk effacing the distinction of poetry, *as poetry*.

In each of its parts, *Poetics and the Gift* traces the broad nexus of figures through which poetry's intricate relation to the gift is founded, becomes translated, and undergoes transformation, in conceptions of (1) poetic subjectivity, (2) poetic essence, (3) the poetic object, and (4) the poetic given. The gift, I argue, plays a foundational role throughout, both allowing for the construction of poetry's various conceptions of itself and contributing to its failure ever fully to distinguish itself. As each part shows, it is by way of such gift figurations that poets, philosophers, and critics have tried to account for the origin of something that, even in its most basic textual materiality, somehow seems to remain a mystery, and even in its most vulgar instrumentalisation, in some way appears to resist commercialisation. Nevertheless, and whatever the original intention of such gestures may be, the designations of poet as giver, poetry as giving, and poem as gift invariably lead to the division of poet from non-poet and, along with it, all the coordinate distinctions between poetry and prose, human and animal, and poet and poetess that have so marked and marred this tradition.

What calls to be thought, then, in the wake of this situation, is not only the necessity of the gift for poetry, or simply the failure of the gift to present itself therein, but also the survival of this modality, in the wake of its impossibility. Even if one could not simply *endorse* the gift for poetry, nevertheless, it would be no less pernicious to *reject* what goes by these names, as though the failure of either the gift or poetry to distinguish itself absolutely led to the simple collapse of gift and non-gift, or poetry and non-poetry. In the final analysis, then, it is the task of *Poetics and the Gift* to reconsider both the meaning of this ambivalence and the necessity of remaining mired in it.

NOTES

1. Friedrich Hölderlin, 'As on a holiday . . .', in *Friedrich Hölderlin: Poems and Fragments*, trans. Michael Hamburger (London: Anvil Press Poetry, 2004), 464–7.
2. See Martin Heidegger, 'The Origin of the Work of Art', in *Off the Beaten Track*, eds and trans Julian Young and Kenneth Haynes (Cambridge: Cambridge University Press, 2002).
3. See Lewis Hyde, *The Gift: Creativity and the Artist in the Modern World* (New York: Vintage, 2007). Hyde puts the point succinctly in his introduction: 'It is the assumption of this book that a work of art is a gift, not a commodity. Or, to state the modern case with more precision, that works of art exist simultaneously in two "economies", a market economy and a gift economy. Only one of these is essential, however: a work of art can survive without the market, but where there is no gift there is no art' (xvi). On poetry specifically, see xii and 208–81.
4. Sir Philip Sidney, *An Apology for Poetry (or The Defence of Poesy)*, ed. R. W. Maslen (Manchester: Manchester University Press, 2002), 82; 116. Henceforth, *AAP*.
5. *AAP*, 85.
6. On the long history of poetry's self-hatred and self-resistance, see Ben Lerner, *The Hatred of Poetry*, James Longenbach, *The Resistance to Poetry*, Aleksandr Skidan, 'The Resistance of/to Poetry', and Georges Bataille, *La Haine de la poésie*. On the poet as originator of a new generous economy, see Hyde. On the poet as legislator, see Percy Bysshe Shelley, 'A Defence of Poetry', in *Shelley's Poetry and Prose*, eds Donald H. Reiman and Neil Fraistat (New York: W. W. Norton, 2002), 509–35.
7. John Milton, *Paradise Lost*, ed. Gordon Teskey (New York: W. W. Norton, 2005), 4.
8. Franco Berardi, *The Uprising: On Poetry and Finance* (Cambridge, MA: MIT University Press, 2012), 147.
9. The problem of excess – both in its opposition to restraint and as excess with respect to the excess/restraint opposition – will be a constant theme

in what follows. For further instances in the history of poetry, see Shelley, who, in his 'Defence', argues that 'Those in whom it [the faculty of approximation to the beautiful] exists in excess are poets, in the most universal sense of the word' (512), and Jonathan Culler, who asks whether 'the hyperbolic character of lyric [is] a fundamental constituent of the genre or simply a major possibility, a frequent poetic pretension?' (38). Jonathan Culler, *Theory of the Lyric* (Cambridge, MA: Harvard University Press, 2015). See also Scott Cutler Shershow, *The Work and the Gift* (Chicago: University of Chicago Press, 2005), 136–59, on the role of excess in defining the 'great work' as gift.

10. On poetry's current state of crisis, see Marjorie Perloff, 'Presidential Address 2006: It Must Change'. On the eighteenth-century schism among Literary or imaginative writing, economic, and monetary genres, see Mary Poovey, *Genres of the Credit Economy*, and Pierre Bourdieu, *The Field of Cultural Production*.

11. Literature on the gift in poetry is vast and is inherently interdisciplinary, drawing from work in sociology, anthropology, history, and philosophy. Much of the best work also remains invested in both historical analysis and literary interpretation, revealing the deep interconnections between material and fictional economies. However, for reasons of specialisation, these studies generally remain focused on specific historical or linguistic contexts, with little conversation between classicists and modernists. For some representative works on the gift in classical literature, see Deborah Lyons, *Dangerous Gifts*, Barbara K. Gold, *Literary Patronage in Greece and Rome*, and Phebe Lowell Bowditch, *Horace and the Gift Economy of Patronage*. For the gift in the early-modern period, see Felicity Heal, *The Power of Gifts: Gift-Exchange in Early Modern England*, Alison V. Scott, *Selfish Gifts: The Politics of Exchange and English Courtly Literature, 1580–1628*, Natalie Zemon Davis, *The Gift in Sixteenth-Century France*, and Stephen Murphy, *The Gift of Immortality: Myths of Power and Humanist Poetics*. For studies of the gift in modern European literature, see Sarah Haggarty, *Blake's Gifts: Poetry and the Politics of Exchange*, Matthew Rowlinson, *Real Money and Romanticism*, Dustin Griffin, *Literary Patronage in England, 1650–1800*, Anne-Emmanuelle Berger, *Scènes d'aumône: misère et poésie au XIXe siècle*, and Charles Rzepka, *Selected Studies in Romantic and American Literature, History, and Culture* and *Sacramental Commodities: Gift, Text, and the Sublime in De Quincey*.

12. Jacques Derrida, *Given Time: 1. Counterfeit Money*, trans. Peggy Kamuf (Chicago: University of Chicago Press, 1992), 41. References to the French are taken from *Donner le temps. 1. La fausse monnaie* (Paris: Éditions Galilée, 1991). Throughout, wherever appropriate, page numbers

will be given first to the English edition and then to the foreign language edition.
13. As he puts it in *Given Time*: 'Is that which is given, whether or not it is alms, the content, which is to say the "real" thing one offers or of which one speaks? Is it not rather the act of address to the other, for example the work as textual or poetic performance?' (57). Within the narrative arc of *Given Time*, the move from discussion of theoretical texts in Heidegger, Mauss, Benveniste, and Lévi-Strauss to literary ones in Mallarmé and Baudelaire may be partially accounted for by this suspicion. What distinguishes the *récit* of Baudelaire and 'Don du poème' of Mallarmé, like the 'Fable' of Ponge, is the inextricability of the *given* of the gift from the *giving* of it. In other words, (performative) act of address and (constative) subject of address are indissociably linked, such that the very difference between the one and the other becomes impossible to articulate. The deconstruction of the divide between *act* and *thing*, or text and referent, paradigmatically at work within self-referential literary texts, then allows for a more general account of 'gift effects', without reference to a giving subject. For the invagination, or folding back, of everything that one *says* about the gift, to the situation of *language itself*, and even to 'the text in general', see *Given Time*, 80–1. For the analogy between the general situation of text and the literary, see 99–100.
14. *Given Time*, 43–4/63.
15. *Given Time*, 100/130.
16. For an excellent recent volume that addresses the meaning of poetry for philosophy, see *Philosophers and their Poets: Reflections on the Poetic Turn in Philosophy since Kant*, eds Charles Bambach and Theodore George.
17. See, for example, Georges Bataille, 'The Notion of Expenditure', in *The Bataille Reader*, trans. Allan Stoekl, eds Fred Botting and Scott Wilson (Oxford: Blackwell, 1997), 167–81: 'The term poetry, applied to the least degraded and least intellectualised forms of the expression of a state of loss, can be considered synonymous with expenditure; it in fact signifies, in the most precise way, creation by means of loss. Its meaning is therefore close to that of *sacrifice*' (171). See also Anne Carson and Kevin McNeilly, 'Gifts and Questions – An Interview with Anne Carson', *Canadian Literature* 176 (Spring 2003): 12–25, where she speaks of poems as 'ideally' acting as gifts, and 'the beauty of an art object [as] part of the gift that you give to the receiver, the listener, the observer' (15; 19). For Carson's most extensive account of the gift in poetry, see *Economy of the Unlost (Reading Simonides of Keos with Paul Celan)*, as well as *Nox*, where she offers a virtuosic example of the gift of the poem.

18. Though Derrida published *Given Time* only in 1991, the text consists of the first five lectures of a seminar he gave at the École Normale Supérieure in the academic year 1978–9, with only slight revisions. The second half of that seminar focused on the role of gifts and giving in the writings of Heidegger, and has recently been published in a posthumous edition, *Donner le temps II*, eds Laura Odello, Peter Szendy, and Rodrigo Therezo (Paris: Éditions du Seuil, 2021). For a discussion of *Donner le temps II* and its relation to the issues addressed below, see my essay 'On Derrida's *Donner le temps, Volumes I & II*: A New Engagement with Heidegger'. Though I cannot engage with it at length here, my discussion of Heidegger in Chapter 5 is indebted to Derrida's analyses in part two, which I first read in the summer of 2013 at the Institut Mémoires de l'édition contemporaine (IMEC). 'Economimesis' was initially published in *Mimesis, Des articulations*, eds Sylviane Agacinski et al. (Paris: Aubier-Flammarion, 1975), 55–93 and then in English translation as 'Economimesis', trans. Richard Klein, *Diacritics* 11.2 (1981): 2–25. It probably emerged out of the 1973–4 seminar 'L'Art (Kant)', from which *The Truth in Painting* (1978/87) was subsequently also published.

19. Rather than being significant for its place within poetic history, 'Counterfeit Money' is judged by Derrida to be significant for its place within the European institution of literature, which establishes the possibility of its 'fiction'. On Baudelaire's narrative and literature, see *Given Time*, 86, 93–4, 97, 124–5, 150, and 169–70.

20. See '*Che cos'è la poesia?*', in *Points . . . : Interviews, 1974–1994*, trans. Peggy Kamuf, ed. Elisabeth Weber (Stanford, CA: Stanford University Press, 1995), 288–99; 296–7.

21. '*Istrice 2: Ick bünn all hier*', in *Points . . . : Interviews, 1974–1994*, 300–26; 304. See also 302–5 and 308–9. Later, towards the end of his life, Derrida would repeat the division, but in terms of 'poetics' and 'poetic signature', in his discussion of Paul Celan's work in 'Majesties': 'I do not say a poetics, a poetic art, or even a poetry; I will, rather, say a certain poetic signature, the unique signature of a unique poem, always unique, which attempts to express not the essence, the presence of what *is* there of the poem, but where the poem comes and goes, that attempts, then, to set itself free, through art, from art' (113–14). See 'Majesties', in *Sovereignties in Question: The Poetics of Paul Celan*, eds and trans Thomas Dutoit and Outi Pasanen (New York: Fordham University Press, 2005), 108–34. One observes a similar gesture in the less well known 1995 talk, 'How to Name', on the work of Michel Deguy. 'Michel Deguy, he who bears that name is also someone who, in these times, has called poetry – or even more so the

poem – a nomination, a naming, and someone who has been known to do this in order to put his being-poet to the test, his attribute of poet as responsible-being' (268). See Jacques Derrida, 'How to Name', in *In the Name of Friendship: Deguy, Derrida and Salut*, eds and trans Christopher Elson and Garry Sherbert (Leiden: Brill, 2017), 267–300.
22. For an excellent recent study of poetry's not only unstable, but also extrapoetic character, see Jahan Ramazani, *Poetry and its Others*.
23. On the problem of poetic authority, see John Guillory, *Poetic Authority*, as well as Chapter 1 below.
24. On the 'birth' of poetry, see especially the Conclusion. Throughout, I use 'birth' less in the sense of historical origin than in that of emergence. The 'birth' of poetry corresponds with the *question of poetry*, which is why it is both multiple and always to come, the point from which literary-historical 'dating' becomes possible.
25. Following the play on the French 'pas', which can refer either to the adverb 'not' or to the noun 'step', a *pas de poésie* is both the step of poetry and the negation thereof. It is the process, in sum, by which poetry brings itself to the point of its own exceeding.

Introduction: 'Economimesis' after *Given Time*, or: The Return of Helio-Poetics

The gift of the poem cites nothing, it has no title, its histrionics are over, it comes along without your expecting it, cutting short the breath, cutting all ties with discursive and especially literary poetry. In the very ashes of this genealogy.

[Le don du poème ne cite rien, il n'a aucun titre, il n'histrionne plus, il survient sans que tu t'y attendes, coupant le souffle, coupant avec la poésie discursive, et surtout littéraire. Dans les cendres mêmes de cette généalogie.]

Derrida, '*Che cos'è la poesia?*'[1]

Hearing me speak of the date and of circumcision, some might hasten toward the 'circumcised heart' of the Scriptures. That would be going too fast and along a path of too little resistance. Celan's trenchant ellipsis requires more patience, it demands discretion. Caesura is the law. Yet it gathers in the discretion of the discontinuous, in the severing of the relation to the other or in the interruption of address, as address itself.

Derrida, 'Shibboleth: For Paul Celan'[2]

In an influential essay on Kant's third *Critique* entitled 'Economimesis', first published in French in 1975, Derrida makes a single, fleeting reference to what he calls 'helio-poetics'. Helio-poetics (in the plural) refer to the specifically solar trajectories of a long tradition of Western writings on poetry. A 'helio-poetics' is drawn, as if unconsciously, towards the sun because it takes this star to be both the giving origin and receiving end of the poetic work. Once conceived as model of production, the sun thus silently vouchsafes a whole series of relays, or 'analogical chains', through which God becomes linked to King, King to Poet, and Poet back to God. Like so many other circles identified in Derrida's writings, the annular trajectory of the helio-poetic ultimately marks an Odyssean voyage. It describes a logic of poetic departure that is pre-oriented by the primal desire for repatriation and return.

Though Derrida's interest in the many solar trajectories of Western thought is well known, from the 'heliotrope' of 'White Mythology' (1971) to the 'heliopolitics' of 'Violence and Metaphysics' (1967) and the 'basileo-patro-helio-theological dictum' of 'Plato's Pharmacy' (1968), for reasons unknown, Derrida cast off the problem of the helio-poetic as soon as it was coined.[3] The helio-poetic never returns within his work, at least by name. It becomes a fatherless figure, one of many orphaned terms whose memory today marks a path not pursued. In this chapter, I will take up this abandoned figure, so as to see both why it was left behind and how it might have been recast, in the wake of *Given Time*, had Derrida chosen to return to it.[4]

As can be gleaned from the writings that immediately follow 'Economimesis', the turn away from the helio-poetic, even if itself unintentional or unconscious, probably had to do with a deliberate, strategic choice. That is, it probably had to do with Derrida's decision to pursue another concept of the gift, and one no longer bound to the analogical chain of circularity evidently at work in most philosophical discourses on poetry. The mark of the helio-poetic for Derrida *is* circularity. To explore another concept of the gift, one marked by non-return, thus intuitively required a change of focus. And this change of focus becomes evident as soon as one examines the text that comes closest to taking up the mantle of the helio-poetic, in the immediate wake of 'Economimesis'. *Given Time* addresses the very same themes of circle, economy, gift, poetry, and sun as 'Economimesis'. In doing so, however, it places itself at an infinite remove from its predecessor. First given as a lecture in the years just following 'Economimesis', at times *Given Time* comes so close to the 1975 text that it risks burning up. Trading Kant for Baudelaire and Frederick the Great for the Roi Soleil, *Given Time* marks a kind of return, but one in which nothing is the same. Where in 'Economimesis' the sun had marked a point of absolute clarity and seamless transference, in *Given Time* it is now a source of blindness and madness. Where in 'Economimesis' the helio-poetic had identified a poetic ideology shared by many of the West's most well-known thinkers, in *Given Time* the most extended textual encounter – a nearly hundred-page-long engagement with a prose poem by Baudelaire – is hardly ever even recognised as having a poetic lineage. And, just as the poem of 'Economimesis' becomes the *récit* (narrative) of *Given Time*, so too do the countless transferences of an infinity of poetic gift exchanges of the former become the *impossibility* of any gift, as such, in the latter. In short, in the brief span between these texts, the nature of the questions being asked has shifted so radically that the very same thematics are hardly recognisable any longer.[5]

In what follows, I would like to return to the problem that links and separates these two moments of Derrida's thought. In this way, I aim to raise the question of the helio-poetic again, but to do so *in the wake* of *Given Time* and its understanding of the gift's fundamental, structural impossibility. In moving on from 'Economimesis', Derrida will not turn back to the poetic tradition as a tradition. Save for a few notable exceptions, nearly all from the end of his life, he will not even return to questions of Poetry and Poetics, unless, that is, it is in order to problematise them in the work of others.[6] And that is because, as 'Economimesis' exemplarily demonstrates, Derrida found the whole paradigm and history of the *ars poetica* to be too metaphysical in their orientation. Turning instead to 'some poem', to *récit*, to literature, and to the poematic, he may in fact read poetry – and he may do so in inimitable and exemplary fashion – but his engagement with these poems is with them first and foremost *as texts*. That is, it is with them as 'the unique signature of a unique poem, always unique', in order to 'remove . . . the poem (or the *poiemata*) from the merry-go-round . . . that brings them back in a circular fashion to *poiein*, to their poetic source'.[7] What does this mean? What is at stake in such a distinction – between poem and literary poetry, or between text and genealogy – and can it simply be overlooked in speaking of 'poetry', after Derrida?

To clarify: I am not arguing either that Derrida does not read poetry, or that he is inattentive to what we call 'poetic language'. Any number of brilliant encounters with Ponge, Celan, Shelley, Jabès, Baudelaire, Mallarmé, Lawrence, Valéry, Artaud, Deguy, and Cixous – to say nothing of Joyce, Shakespeare, Camus, Poe, and Kafka – would immediately contradict such claims. What I am arguing instead is that, whereas any number of his works betray a clear investment in the institution of literature, the *débordement*, excess, or overflowing of *récit*, the unique singularity of the poem, and the fabular of fiction, there are few places where either the *tradition* or the *concept* of poetry is taken up, unless it is in order to reveal the metaphysical orientation of the one (Kant), or the participation of the other in a movement of gathering (Heidegger).[8] Derrida is above all suspicious of what is called 'poetry'. And he expresses this suspicion explicitly, on numerous occasions, and without ambiguity. Indeed, one already hears it in what is perhaps his most-cited and certainly most well-known text on the subject, '*Che cos'è la poesia?*':

> There is never anything but some poem, before any *poiesis*. When, instead of 'poetry,' we said 'poetic,' we ought to have specified: 'poematic.' Most of all do not let the *hérisson* be led back into the circus or the menagerie of *poiesis*: nothing to be done (*poiein*), neither 'pure poetry,' nor pure rhetoric, nor *reine Sprache*, nor 'setting-forth-of-truth-in-the-work.'

[Il n'y a jamais que du poème, avant toute poïèse. Quand, au lieu de 'poésie,' nous avons dit 'poétique,' nous aurions dû préciser: 'poématique.' Surtout ne laisse pas reconduire le hérisson dans le cirque ou dans le manège de la *poiesis*: rien à faire (*poiein*), ni 'poésie pure,' ni rhétorique pure, ni *reine Sprache*, ni 'mise-en-œuvre-de-la-vérité.']⁹

As we shall see, there are important resonances between Derrida's description of this exposed poem-hedgehog that severs all ties with 'discursive' and 'literary poetry', that 'cites nothing', that 'comes along without your expecting it', and that 'addresses itself' on the condition of 'the interruption of address', and the unconditional gift of *Given Time*. And it is no coincidence that the *destinerrance* of the 'gift of the poem', in 1984, 1988, 1990, 1995, or 2003, is markedly opposed to the repatriating destiny of solar poetics of 1975.¹⁰ After all, from the perspective of *Given Time*, the God-given gifts of the poet of 'Economimesis' are always already returned and, therefore, annulled. *It seems* that the only way to retain a trace of the gift (of poetry) would therefore be to sever it from this history, to treat it as a runaway, and to let it consume itself, *perhaps*, in the non-sacrificial blaze of a reading willing to risk that neither poetry nor the gift might ever come back fully intact. *It seems* that one could only ever speak of the gift of *the poem*, but certainly not that *of poetry*, at least if one wished, in speaking, to do so of what might possibly still be worthy of this name.

I say that *it seems* this way because the question remains as to what would happen, were we to choose to follow this hedgehog back into the circus, so to speak. This is not to say to revert back to the determination of '*reine Sprache*', but instead to pursue *what happens* with the experience of this hedgehog, within the circumference of what still goes by the name 'poetry'. In the chapters that follow, I pursue this trajectory by rereading the poetic tradition through the very problematics of the gift that spurred Derrida away from it. I propose that the structural impossibility of the gift that Derrida declares in 1978 and that contributes to his turning away from further engagement with the various Western helio-poetics in fact already determines this poetic history from within. The im-possibility of giving gives birth to a helio-poetics that is always already on the way to displacing its solar orbit. And it does so *in the name of poetry*.

To propose the above is not to put forward a thesis that Derrida necessarily would have denied. Indeed, he comes close to it, at the end of his life, in his reading of the 'poetic revolution' at work in Celan's 'Meridian', on the heels of affirming the importance of 'poetry' for a thinking concerning the animal.¹¹ Nevertheless, to follow the itinerary of this displacement, through the 'menagerie' of the poetic archive, and as a matter of its own unworking, is to pursue a trajectory that has largely gone untrekked, and certainly not at the scale that it would need to be followed, were one to wish to understand in what the structural and historical relation between poetry and gift consists. In what follows, I do not argue either that the essence of poetry *is the gift*, as Hyde might say, or that the essence of the gift *is poetry*, as a certain Heidegger can be understood to affirm. Rather, I ask what the implications are, for the past as well as the future of the poetic archive, given that this archive has been determined, from its birth, by way of a relation to the gift. My question, then, is not *What is the essence, or even experience, of poetry?* but rather *Of what does the inevitability of this determination, of essence, consist in the first place?* Each of the four parts of this book pursues this question, by reading how the poetic archive has responded to the uncertainty of its origin, nature, being, and end, by way of some recourse to the gift, giving, or giftedness. It is because 'there is never anything but some poem, before any *poiesis*', nor any gift of poetry, before the destining of the giving trace, that the movement of *poiēsis* arises, and with it the desire for a gift robust enough both *to account for poetry* and *to account for what is unaccountable in it.*[12] The story of this movement remains, however, as yet untold.

The task of the present chapter, then, is to formalise the relation between gift and poetry, as well as the *necessity* of their relation, by retracing Derrida's itinerary in the 1970s. The problem, as well as the interest, of this project is that the connection between the historical orientation of the various Western helio-poetics, as it is diagnosed in the essay 'Economimesis', and the structural determination of the impossibility and co-originarity of gift and *récit*, as are put forward in the seminar for *Given Time*, remains as yet unresolved. Though each of these texts provides a rationale for theorising the relationship between gift and poetry, they do so in wholly different, even contradictory, fashions. A prerequisite to formalising the poetry–gift complex as a structural as well as historical phenomenon will thus be the reconstitution of the connection between these texts and their insights. Only through the prism provided by both, which Derrida above all does not give us, can we get a handle on poetic history, in the full complexity of this term.

Thus, while *Given Time* was written and published *after* 'Economimesis', its insights into the structural im-possibility of the gift must, in fact, have priority with respect to the observations of the earlier text. They must be taken account of *within* any account of helio-poetic drift. Far from contradictory, one must read the historical emergence of helio-poetics as a possibility of an impossible gift without present. One must learn to read the historical relation between gift and poetry – including the emergence of various Western helio-poetics, the externalisation of the dedication, the institutions of patronage, and the eventual commercialisation and marketisation of the poetic work – in the wake of this structural entanglement.

I begin by examining the central arguments of 'Economimesis', concerning the onto-theological complicity of poetry and gift for Western helio-poetics. From there, I turn to *Given Time*, which I show *responds* to the problematics put forward in this earlier text, by offering a reading of the gift that would both account for and interrupt that laid out in 1975. Though Derrida never says so explicitly, the concepts of *récit* and gift advanced in *Given Time* can be read only as an effort to deconstruct the appropriative drive at work within the solar orientation of the poet's gift economy. This connection is imprinted, in implicit but undeniable fashion, throughout the 1978–9 lectures.

Whereas in the earlier essay poetry and gift are linked as co-constitutive expressions of the metaphysics of presence – the gift gives itself as poetry, poetry poetises the gift – in *Given Time*, the trace emerges as the mutual 'origin' of gift, *récit*, and poematic, with poetry all but left out of the account. In both texts, therefore, parallel relations can be observed: metaphysical gift is linked to metaphysical poetry, and deconstructive gift is linked to deconstructive *récit*. The question that remains unresolved, between these two works, is thus how the gift as trace, exemplified in a *récit* capable of re-marking the disseminatory textuality of the given, might culminate in the onto-theological association of poetry and present, but also, and no less critically: what, still under the name *poetry*, might yet speak to the unconditional gift that, for all intents and purposes, Derrida elects to search for elsewhere. Beyond the specific interest of this inquiry for the Derridean corpus, then, at stake in this question is the very meaning of poetry, and the possibility of a revolution under its name.

POETIC GIFT ECONOMY IN 'ECONOMIMESIS'

As he explains in the opening pages of 'Economimesis', Derrida's self-imposed task in taking up the secret alliance between *production* and *mimesis* in Kant was to identify 'the most pointed specificity' of an implied 'politics and political economy' within the philosopher's writings on aesthetics.[13] That is, beyond any comparativism, it was to establish the specificity of the *system*, through which these figures might be said both to be signed by Kant and to determine the matrix of the philosopher's signature. Far from an occasion to develop his own thinking of the gift, or even one for taking a closer look at the schizoid character of giving, at stake here was thus the (political–economic) architectonics of the Kantian discourse on beauty. And it is this motivation that, in turn, would come to determine the focus on paragraphs 43 to 51 of the third *Critique*, within which 'the whole Kantian theory of *mimesis* is set forth', between two comments on 'salary'.[14]

Given such a focus, it will not come as a great surprise if the concept of the gift operative within 'Economimesis', being still entrenched in its Kantian articulation, does not yet attain its eventual deconstructive specificity, such as was later made possible through increased focus on the gift's implicit demand for unconditionality, expressed in its structuring of *delay*. Indeed, it is in this respect particularly telling that, within 'Economimesis', at the heart of the system of production of the liberal artist who freely 'gives', instantaneity is one of this economy's principal markers:

> One ought to analyze closely the paragraph that exploits the false opposition between liberal art and craft. Liberal art is an occupation that is agreeable in itself. The liberal artist – the one who does not work for a salary – enjoys and gives enjoyment. Immediately.[15]

As I argue below, in Chapter 3, at stake in the question of poetry for Wordsworth is precisely this double temporality of the gift – *both* instantaneous *and* deferred – and thus, by extension, precisely the line that separates and conjoins 'Economimesis' and *Given Time*, in their collective, double inscriptions of *the gift*.

How, then, are poetry and gift here initially understood to relate, in their Kantian, heliotropic, 'onto-theological humanis[t]' orientation?[16] What joins the one to the other, in this, their Western, historical specificity? As we learn in the essay, the bond between poetry and gift is, essentially, sympathetic. Poetry *is* a gift, being the highest expression of God's benevolence to humankind. But, insofar as it is the highest expression of this divine bestowal, it is also the first example of what makes the gift *a gift*. In a motif that we will see repeated in Heidegger, to the extent that it is the *first* example of the gift, poetry turns out, in some sense, *to give this gift*. It is – to adopt a line from Sidney – 'first nurse, whose milk by little and little enabled [men] to feed afterwards of tougher knowledges'.[17]

The reason that poetry is first example of a 'free production' of the imagination is that its unimpeded play has been made possible through the 'mimesis' of no mere product of nature, but of nature's very capacity for production. And its presence, in Man, therefore testifies *both* to a divine bestowal *and* to this originary capacity for largesse, of *physis*. For the helio-tropic tradition that Kant reproduces and helps to redefine, there could be no poetry without gift, nor, if one follows the 'law of analogy' at work in this text, any gift without poetry, because poetry just names the essence thereof.[18]

The key to Derrida's reading of Kant lies, then, in the interpretation of 'gift', not yet as unconditional, incalculable, unforeseeable event, or im-possible – in other words, as something *irreducible* to exchange because other to it – but as the *apotheosis* of exchange, or 'trans-economic' point of passage. The gift vehiculates the 'immaculate commerce' of an 'inexchangeable . . . pure productivity'.[19] As such, it is opposed to the commercial, the mercenary, and the mechanical, but only insofar as it names their higher, sublated form. The free, liberal artist takes into himself, he incorporates into his work, the lowly productions of *Lohnkunst*, 'chang[ing] work into mere play'.[20] And poetry expresses, in this sense, the very summit of such pure productivity:

> Poetry, the *summit* of fine art considered as a species of art, carries the freedom of play announced in the productive imagination to its extreme, to the top of the hierarchy.[21]
>
> *At the summit* is the poet, analogous (and that precisely by a return of logos) to God: he gives more than he promises, he submits to no exchange contract, his over-abundance generously breaks the circular economy. The hierarchy of the Fine-Arts therefore signifies that some power supersedes the (circular) economy, governs and places itself above (restricted) political economy. The naturalisation of political economy subordinates the production and the commerce of art to a transeconomy.[22]
>
> This is a poetic commerce, because God is a poet. There is a relation of hierarchical analogy between the poetic action of the speaking art, *at the summit*, and the action of God who dictates *Dichtung* to the poet.[23]
>
> *At the summit* of the highest of the speaking arts is poetry. It is *at the summit* [*den obersten Rang*] because it emanates almost entirely from genius.[24]
>
> Everything is measured on a scale on which poetry occupies *the absolutely highest level*. It is the universal analogical equivalent, and the value of values. It is in poetry that the work of mourning, transforming hetero-affection into auto-affection, produces the maximum of disinterested pleasure.[25] (my emphasis throughout)

To be clear, in none of these passages is Derrida saying that poetry *is* the absolute summit of art, and therefore the highest expression of God's gift to humankind, as the human re-production of the former's benevolent faculty for production. It is *Kant* for whom this would be the case, and beyond Kant, to a certain extent, the whole Western, onto-theological humanist tradition. For the tradition of 'helio-poetics' that extends from Plato up through Bataille, poetry is unthinkable without gift, and gift without poetry.

Within the logic of Kant's aesthetics, poetry and the poet are thus at the summit. They name the absolute limit of the gift in its onto-theological trajectory. They name the place where the lowly economy of mimesis in mercenary exchange is transmuted into a generous exorbitance of free production. Poetry establishes this limit through its 'trans-economy', which joins economic to aneconomic, benevolent gift to commercial exchange, generosity to jealousy, God to Man, mimesis to imitation, and high art to lowly product. It reveals the apotheosis of this circularity of the circle, by revealing how that circle must invert itself to include also the aneconomic excess that is the genius for poetry: a capacity for giving that is itself given by God, through nature. The highest order of economy *is* the aneconomic that orients it. And this is what poetry names, Derrida argues, for Kant.

In similar fashion to what he will locate, some years later, in Heidegger's writings, notably in 'Heidegger's Hand (*Geschlecht* II)', the gift of the onto-theological humanist tradition, here exemplified by Kant, is essentially auto-affective. It is the auto-affective expression of the logos's self-affirmation, which seeds itself, through an extended analogical chain, from God to Man. The gift names the *form* of this passage, in a commerce without commerce, but it can do so only insofar as it already supplies the secret law, or principle, of its own possibility. Sun, God, King, Poet – each can give only because the unity of the logos is already given *as* generous liberality. The produced is already contained in the production, and the production in the produced.

Poetry and gift are thus here *joined*. The onto-theological movement of poetry requires the gift as its mode of passage, while the highest, most generous expression of the gift finds its clearest voice in that of the poet. And this is, finally, what Derrida calls 'helio-poetics':

> Frederick the Great, the 'great king,' is almost the only poet quoted by the third *Critique* – a sign of the servile precaution and bad taste on the part of the philosopher, it is often ironically noted. But these poetic lines, like the commentary that surrounds them, very rigorously describe the generous overabundance of a solar source. God, King, Sun, Poet, Genius, etc. give of themselves without counting. And if the relation of alterity between a restricted economy and a general economy is above all not a relation of opposition, then the various helio-poetics – Platonic, Kantian, Hegelian, Nietzschean (up to and including Bataille's) – form an apparently *analogical* chain. No oppositional logic seems fitted to disassociate its *themes*.[26]

From Plato, up through Kant, Hegel, Nietzsche, and Bataille, one could locate versions of this bond at work. It is what marks the historical determination of poetry as poetry, as well as that of gift as gift, within the most influential philosophical lineage. And yet, for all that, once each figure is determined through this logocentric co-determination, the deconstructive interest of both poetry and gift immediately becomes quite limited for Derrida. The true other of 'economy' is no longer to be located simply in the gift or poetry's 'aneconomy', which merely *appears* to oppose the former.[27] Both gift and poetry appear to transcend economy but only so that they may in fact enact a trans-economy that allows for a more complete, comprehensive, even infinite appropriation. '*Economimesis* is not impaired by it', Derrida explains, 'on the contrary':

> It unfolds itself there to infinity. It suffers that transeconomy in order to pass to infinity as 'Kantism' passes into 'Hegelianism.' An infinite circle plays [with] itself and uses human play to reappropriate the gift for itself. The poet or genius receives from nature what he gives, of course, but first he receives from nature (from God), besides the given, the giving, the power to produce and to give more than he promises to men. The poetic gift, content and power, wealth and action, is an add-on given as a [power] to give by God to the poet, who transmits it in order to permit this supplementary surplus value to make its return to the infinite source – this source which can never be lost (by definition, if one can say that of the infinite). All that must pass through the voice. The genius poet is the voice of God who gives him voice, who gives himself and by giving gives to himself, gives himself what he gives, gives himself the [power] to give (*Gabe* and *es gibt*), plays freely with himself, only breaks the finite circle or contractual exchange in order to strike an infinite accord with himself. As soon as the infinite gives itself (to be thought), the *opposition* tends to be effaced between restricted and general economy, circulation and expendiary productivity. That is even, if we can still use such terms, the *function* of the passage to the infinite: the passage *of* the infinity between gift and debt.[28]

Constrained to the infinite passage 'between gift and debt', economimesis, and with it the various helio-poetics that name its most extreme moments of auto-affection, remain limited in their interest. They *collapse* restricted and general economies, rather than fracturing the circulation that makes either possible. And this is why Derrida ultimately looks elsewhere for an interruptive moment of excess, turning, in the concluding pages of 'Economimesis', to disgust and the unrepresentable, inassimilable excess that vomit names for the philosophical system. Once determined as participants in the analogical circle that begins and ends with the logos, neither poetry nor gift seems to have much more to offer.[29]

The situation, of course, is wholly other by the time, just three years later, that Derrida begins to lecture 'Donner – le temps'. It is wholly other because, in the short span between these two texts, a Copernican revolution has taken hold of Derrida's thought vis-à-vis the gift. One result of this shift will be that the relationship between gift and poetry will be more difficult to discern. The majority of comments concerning their relation, in *Given Time*, are vague – at best suggestive and at worst evasive. Rather than gift and poetry, what calls to be thought is above all gift and *récit*, and through *récit*, poem and poematic.[30]

In this respect, two other texts from the period, 'Living On' (1979) and 'Psyche: Invention of the Other' (1984), will prove invaluable resources. They expand on the thinking of *récit* that *Given Time* develops and show why it would prove so critical there. In short, *récit* allows for the thought of a bond, a bind, or a contract, without a subject-author at its source. It displaces both mimetic referentiality and the privilege allotted to being, while rendering 'gift effects' thinkable without the logos. At the same time, *récit* does not simply show how gift-texts function *like* poematic-texts – or vice versa – but how, once considered as trace, both become indissociable. To speak of the ability either *to give* poems, or that of poetising *the gift*, thus runs the risk of obfuscating this more fundamental relation. It runs the risk of privileging a form that, historically speaking, has always been privileged, and doing so at the expense of a broader, more originary, and less metaphysical articulation. Before either the gift or the poem becomes recognisable as such – which is to say, 'a present' – it is the inscription of traces, destined to circulate without return and without present, that structures the possibility of either. One must therefore think through this originary interrelation of *récit* and gift, by way of the trace, before one may speak in any definitive way concerning poetry, the poem, or the historical sedimentation that links both to the problematics of donation.

IM-POSSIBLE GIFT IN *GIVEN TIME*

> To GIVE. *v.a.* preter. *gave*; part. paff. *given*
> 1. To beſtow; to confer without any price or reward.
>   Conſtant at church and change; his gains were fure,
>   His *givings* rare, fave farthings to the poor.   *Pope's Epiſtles*.
> 4. To pay as price or reward, or in exchange.
>   He would *give* his nuts for a piece of metal, and exchange his sheep for ſhells, or wool for a ſparkling pebble.   *Locke*.
>   Johnson, *Dictionary of the English Language*, 1755[31]

> The subject is clear. In Scandinavian civilization, and in a good number of others, exchanges and contracts take place in the form of presents; in theory these are voluntary, in reality they are given and reciprocated obligatorily.
>
> Mauss, *The Gift*[32]

> If we had to speak of disappointment here (which we don't believe we do), ours would not concern the fact that someone or other, at home or elsewhere, had been the first to discover what there is to be said about the gift, but rather that neither Molière nor Mauss, at bottom, has ever said anything about the gift *itself*. And what we are trying to explain here is why there is *no fault* in that.
>
> Derrida, *Given Time*[33]

If there is one thing that readers of Derrida's groundbreaking discussion of Mauss's *Essay* seem to have taken away from it, it is that, for the founding father of deconstruction, *the gift is impossible*. One cannot give because any gift that is recognised as such immediately enters into an infinity of calculations and, therefore, ceases to be one. To speak of 'gift exchange' is, therefore, to contradict oneself, because what one above all cannot do when giving is enter into a circuit of reciprocity. A gift worthy of the name would be unconditional, unanticipatable, and exempt from all economy. But given that the subject is *always* in the process of calculating – be it consciously or unconsciously, materially or symbolically – all pretensions to largesse, charity, generosity, altruism, selflessness, philanthropy, benevolence, or magnanimity are just that: *pretence*. We may believe that we give but, in point of fact, what we do is merely simulate giving while doing everything else under the sun. If ever there was a counterfeit, therefore, the gift is it.

As the third epigraph above demonstrates, there is some truth in this caricature. Derrida is sceptical – to say the least – of the entire anthropological discourse of donation, extending from Boas and Mauss, up through Lévi-Strauss and Bourdieu, and – why not? – as far back as Emerson, Locke, Seneca, and Aristotle. He is sceptical of this discourse, just as he is of the helio-poetic tradition extending from Plato up through Kant and Bataille. Derrida is intolerant – in *Given Time* anyway – of any hint of 'gift exchange'. Nevertheless, the hasty conclusion that one tends to reach from this – namely, that there is no such thing as a gift, for Derrida – misses the singular contribution of this challenging text, not to mention the critical importance of the gift, for him, in his subsequent work on pardon and forgiveness.[34] Moreover, for a long line of readers of *Given Time*, the central complaint concerning the gift's impossibility has less to do with this claim's actually validity than it does with the following, implicit accusation: Derrida *takes* something *away* from us. He appears to offer us a book about giving *but, in fact*, what he does is declare the gift to be impossible. He – and, by extension, deconstruction – act as if they give, when what they actually do is take. And, worst of all, now what they are taking is the very possibility of not taking, by denying the gift and giving![35]

As I argue below, the confusion begins with the precise status of the gift's so-called 'impossibility'. It increases when the question inevitably arises of Derrida's justification for defining gift in the way that he does. And it culminates when the virtuosic but at times frustrating reading of Baudelaire fails to proffer anything more definitive, on the gift, than a series of tantalisingly thetic propositions that (by design) never quite amount to a theory. In reading Derrida's arguments in *Given Time* as staged responses to the problematics laid out in 'Economimesis', we will see both why the above is a misrepresentation of this text and why the frustrations elicited by *Given Time* are, in a certain sense, inevitable.

To begin, then, Derrida does not exactly argue in *Given Time* that the gift is impossible. Rather, he contends that it names '*the* impossible': the perhaps thinkable, but not actualisable, point of excess of calculation, reason, and obligation that, for this reason, must be wholly excluded from any economy, be it of gifts or goods in exchange.[36] And this is because, as we saw in 'Economimesis', as soon as the gift is a matter of exchange, transference, or economy (be it restricted or general), it is implicated in an infinity of calculations and appropriated, in advance, by the logic of return. The possibility of the gift thus turns out, for Derrida, to be its impossibility, or, as he puts it some years later: 'Giving is impossible, and it can only be possible as impossible.'[37] This is not, as it has often been understood, to say that one simply cannot give. It is not to say that giving simply *is impossible*, a position that, as far as Derrida is concerned, is the one occupied by sociological accounts of the gift that can understand it only *as an element of exchange, apparently voluntary, but in fact obligatory*. From Derrida's point of view, by reducing the gift to a merely (possible) deferred or concealed exchange, an accusation that Lévi-Strauss, Bourdieu, Godelier, Godbout, Hénaff, Douglas, Sahlins, and Strathern would all be guilty of, one precisely denies *its* 'possibility'.[38] Instead, for him, to say that giving can be possible only as impossible is to acknowledge that if any gift were to exceed calculation – as a certain historical, archived conception as well as experience of 'the gift' appears to call us to think, and we will return to this in a moment – if any gift were to exceed calculation, then, for Derrida, one consequence of this would be that it would also have to exceed the logical distinction between 'possibility' and 'impossibility'. Only a gift that remained in a mode of ontological, logical, and phenomenological indecision, one that could be said to be neither possible nor impossible, could live up to this conception of radical incalculability, and – in another formulation that only later becomes associated with the gift – be called 'worthy of the name'.[39] A gift worthy of the name is one that, insofar as it must remain in excess of the logic of calculation, reason, and exchange, must also possibly *fail* to be what it is; it is one that can be 'worthy' of this distinction only to the extent that it defies the logic of distinction itself and, thus, can no longer simply be opposed to what is other to it. The gift, as the other of calculation, is not simply *incalculable*, in the sense of being *opposed* to the calculable, but is in-calculable, other to the logic of calculability, which, as we saw in 'Economimesis', can include incalculability as part of its underlying, oppositional scaffold. All of which is to say that, for Derrida, a 'gift' that is to be worthy of the name 'gift' must remain undecided, its arrival and non-arrival alike unheralded.

Now, if one accepts all this, then the problem becomes *why* Derrida would have chosen to pursue this concept of the gift, or rather, this aspect of what we call 'gift', since, as he states above, one has rarely, if ever, spoken about 'the gift *itself*'. What justifies privileging the gift's ostensible unconditionality, what Derrida argues is *its* demand that it be absolutely removed from exchange of any kind, and to do so above and beyond all other aspects of the gift, of which its inevitable entry into economies of exchange is certainly no less marked? What justifies this decision, in a scientific text, or one at least *about* the social sciences, especially given that this starting point produces a certain madness for the investigation and draws into question the very possibility of methodological justification in the first place?

If one is to understand Derrida's project in *Given Time* – and this includes its turn away from poetry and the helio-poetic – then one must first of all understand why it is that he 'decides' to privilege this aspect of donation and to proceed from it, and not any of those others taken up, for example, by the sociological, anthropological, or philosophical traditions. As will become clear below, Derrida's 'choice' to pursue this line of questioning is not a simple *matter of choice*. It is neither a mere instance of calculation nor an arbitrary act of will. It is not, that is, what we would call a 'voluntary decision', at least not in any simple or straightforward sense of this term, and even if the intention to pursue the gift's unconditionality is clearly expressed by him at the outset of the text:

> Even though all the anthropologies, indeed the metaphysics of the gift have, *quite rightly and justifiably*, treated *together*, as a system, the gift and the debt, the gift and the cycle of restitution, the gift and the loan, the gift and credit, the gift and the countergift, we are here *departing*, in a peremptory and distinct fashion, from this tradition. That is to say, from tradition

itself. [I note in passing the resonances, already apparent, between Derrida's insistence on the importance of cutting himself off from *tradition*, in dealing with the gift, and the Celanian-poematic-hedgehog that addresses itself on the condition of interrupting address, and that *establishes* tradition therefore on the condition of *departing* from it.] We will take our point of departure in the dissociation, in the overwhelming evidence of this other axiom: There is gift, if there is any, only in what interrupts the system as well as the symbol, in a partition without return and without division [*répartition*], without being-with-self of the gift-counter-gift.[40]

To follow Derrida in *Given Time* is to understand that this methodological 'decision' follows from an exigency no less inscribed in actual gift-giving practices than it is in the theoretical reflections of Mauss, and others, upon these practices. Indeed, it is largely following Mauss, and still in accordance with Derrida's contemporary, the sociologist Pierre Bourdieu, that he argues that isolating the specificity of 'gift' ultimately comes down to interpreting the 'delay' that, to all appearances, is the only stable marker of difference between 'gift (exchanges)' and 'market exchanges'.[41] It is in the interpretation of this delay, inscribed in the very act of giving, that Derrida can first be said to depart from these other thinkers of the gift. What must be exposed is therefore the *reason* or *cause* for departing in this fashion.

It is from the delay, then, inscribed right on or in the given of the gift, and not from the system of exchanges within which each given gift participates, that Derrida grounds his approach. And there are at least two reasons for this preference, the one having to do with what one assumes, or takes for granted, if one begins one's interpretation from the fact of exchange, the other having to do with the meaning, within exchange, of this delay. There is, strictly speaking, no delay without reference to some exchange, nor any gift-specific form of exchange without some delay. Both of these evidences go together. And yet, the whole problem posed by the gift, the whole difficulty of its doubled or duplicitous appearance, begins and ends with the importance one lends to – or that is called for by – these two paradigmatic features.

The reason, then, for focusing on the gift's delay, rather than on the system of exchanges in which it participates, would be as follows: as long as one interprets the temporal gap between gift and counter-gift *within* the already circular movement dictated by the logic of exchange, one will have already assumed that the gift *is merely a subset of exchange*, and in so doing, one will have abandoned any hope of defining 'gift' in the first place. Indeed, one will have given up on one's subject altogether. To interpret the gift in terms of its exchanges is to acknowledge that, in fact, *there is no such thing as a gift*, but only the appearance of gifts which, in the final analysis, remain so many pre-, proto-, or crypto- tokens of circular economy. Such an interpretive decision may be *justified*, it may prove *effective*, and it may, in fact, account for the accounting that actually takes place whenever *anyone gives anything to anyone else*. Yet it will cease to be an examination of this word or thing that we name when we say 'gift'. It will cease, precisely, to account for or to attest to what within the 'gift' has always seemed to pull away from the very model of exchange to which it is also magnetised, which is also to say that it will cease to account for what within the 'gift' appears most unaccountable. 'Gift' says, it appears to say, 'exchange' *and* 'non-exchange', *at the same time*. To reduce the gift to an 'exchange' that happens to be delayed is to reduce one of its poles for the sake of the other. This is always possible to do. Indeed, it is precisely what is 'possible' about the gift, precisely what happens when one pursues the gift's possibility. And this is why the decision in favour of, the preference for, or the reception of, what in the gift is polarised towards each of its poles – the one eminently possible, the other, as we shall see, eminently impossible; the one economical and accountable, the other aneconomical and unaccountable – can never be 'justified'. One can never, entirely, justify the 'decision' to pursue the gift of sociology or that of deconstruction, precisely because the gift also describes the line of demarcation that runs between the justified or justifiable, and the unjustified or unjustifiable, just as it does that of the possible and impossible, each of which determinations are no less at work in 'theoretical reflection' than they are in the 'phenomenon' to be analysed.

If the gift *might be* unaccountable, unexchangeable, and unconditional, then the 'decision' to remain within the logic of justifications is always already, in some sense, a decision against the gift, or at least, against what in the gift calls to its impossibility. It is a decision *for* calculation, which is itself ultimately just as groundless, just as abyssal, as is its opposite. But this is also why, to return to the epigraph above, Derrida says there can be 'no fault' in this. The logic of debt cannot yet be applied to a 'decision' that comes anterior to the difference between calculation and non-calculation, ground and abyss, conditionality and unconditionality.[42]

To decide for exchange is thus to decide, in advance, that the gift *should be possible*, that what the gift announces is ultimately *accountable*, and that the difference between the possible and impossible, or between the accountable and unaccountable, *is one that we may simply decide*, for example, analytically. Derrida's 'decision', if it remains describable in these terms, and if it remains *his*, his decision to give time to what in the gift is impossible, unaccountable, and unjustifiable, does not – indeed, *it cannot* – preclude what is done in the name of the gift's possibility, by Mauss and so many others. Rather, what *Donner le temps* does as a whole is, precisely, *give time to*, suffer, or remain in the opening that leaves undecided, the very possibility of deciding between the possible and impossible, the justifiable and unjustifiable, or the economic and aneconomic. The work is, therefore, in this respect also an act of affirmation.[43]

Thus, something in the gift, Derrida contends, is polarised towards, or calls to, what is impossible, incalculable, unaccountable; what would not simply return, in short, within the economy of an exchange; what is not a matter of 'exchange' or 'changed out' by another term, token, or present. The delay that appears to inhere to the giving of a gift, although only recognisable within the context of the circuit of gift/counter-gift, nevertheless seems to defy the very exchange within which it participates, *in principle if not in practice*.[44] How, then, to give account of that principle properly?

FROM POETRY TO *RÉCIT*

If, as I have been arguing, following Derrida, a gift that is worthy of the name is one that would adhere to a different logic from the calculating present of interpersonal *or* helio-poetic exchange, then the traces of such an 'offering' should be most visible where a law other than the economic principle of return is dominant. Thus, while all given gifts may be polarised away from exchange (even as they may actively participate in them), it nevertheless remains the case that the logic of the im-possible gift, of radical dissemination, or of an address without return, may be more explicitly apparent in some structures than others. Within *Given Time*, the exemplary site of such an experience of the gift is to be found in *récit*, a term that, while often translated as 'narrative' or 'story', corresponds, for Derrida, more accurately to a certain passion of narrative, as he clarifies in the near-contemporary text, 'Living On'. To be precise, in 'Living On', he proposes replacing the classical form of the question 'What is a narrative [*récit*]?' with another order of approach altogether, corresponding to '*the demand for/of narrative* [récit]':[45]

> What is a narrative – this thing that we call a narrative? Does it take place? Where and when? What might the taking-place or the event of a narrative be? [. . .]
>
> I suggest, for example, that we replace what might be called *the question of narrative* ('What is a narrative?') with *the demand for/of narrative*. When I say *demand* I mean something closer to the English 'demand' than to a mere request: inquisitorial insistence, an order, a petition. To know (before we know) what narrative is, the narrativity of narrative, we should perhaps first recount, return to the scene of one origin of

narrative, to the narrative of one origin of narrative (will that still be a narrative?)

[Qu'est-ce qu'un récit? cette chose qu'on appelle récit? A-t-elle lieu? Où et quand? Quel serait l'avoir-lieu ou l'événement d'un récit? [. . .]

Je suggère par exemple de remplacer ce qu'on pourrait appeler *la question du récit* ('Qu'est-ce qu'un récit?') par *la demande de récit*. J'entends *demande* avec la force que ce mot peut avoir en anglais plus encore qu'en français: exigence, insistance inquisitoriale, mise en demeure, requête. Pour savoir, avant de savoir, ce que c'est que le récit, l'être-récit du récit, peut-être devra-t-on commencer par raconter, revenir à la scène d'une origine du récit, au récit d'une origine du récit (sera-ce encore un récit?)]⁴⁶

Récit, from *réciter*, 'to recite or recount', derives etymologically from the Latin *citare*, 'to call or convoke'. Related to the English 'cite', in the senses of both quotation or mention, and that of summoning before a court of law, *récit* formally implies repetition, and usually the repetition of events, whether real or imagined. A *récit* summons certain events before an audience, before whom it may always be called to give further account. And this re-citing or re-presenting, which is to say, the internal necessity of a certain form of re-presentation, recitation, or re-petition, is also that in or through which, Derrida argues in *Given Time*, the gift arrives, *if* it arrives:

> The gift gives, demands, and takes time. The thing gives, demands, or takes time. That is one of the reasons this thing of the gift will be linked to the – internal – necessity of a certain narrative or of a certain poetics of narrative. That is why we will take account of 'Counterfeit Money' and of the impossible account that is Baudelaire's tale. The thing as given thing, the given of the gift arrives, if it arrives, only in narrative. And in a poematic simulacrum of narrative.
>
> [Le don donne, demande et prend du temps. La chose donne, demande ou prend du temps. C'est une des raisons pour lesquelles cette chose du don se liera à la nécessité – interne – d'un certain récit ou d'une certaine poétique du récit. Voilà pourquoi nous tiendrons compte de *La fausse monnaie*, et de ce compte rendu impossible qu'est le conte de Baudelaire. La chose comme chose donnée, le donné du don n'arrive, s'il arrive, que dans le récit. Et dans un simulacre poématique de la narration.]⁴⁷

The interest of this well-known passage lies in the specific form that the gift's ambivalence here takes. For Derrida, it is *récit* – and not poetry – that holds the key to thinking the conditions of possibility and impossibility of the gift. And yet, it is no mere coincidence that this *récit* is also drawn, as if by some still unaccountable force, to a 'certain poetics of *récit*' and to a 'poematic simulacrum of narration'. As he puts it on the prior page of *Given Time*, though only parenthetically, as if he cannot quite own up to, account for, or fully avow the question:

> What is a thing that one can talk about it in this fashion? Later we will have to encounter this question in or beyond its Heideggerian modality, but it seems to be posed in a certain way at the very opening of *The Gift*, right after the definition of a program and the quotation of a poetic text in epigraph. (Why must one begin with a poem when one speaks of the gift? And why does the gift always appear to be the *gift of the poem*, the *don du poème* as Mallarmé says?)[48]

For Derrida, the theorisation of the gift requires *récit*, which is itself often enough bound to 'some poem', though not to 'poetry', as it has been discursively defined, for all the reasons that we have already explored. The question, for us, is thus why *récit* should here take pride of place, and precisely *replace* – if not *re-cite* or *re-write* – the position classically held by poetry, in the longest and most influential philosophical determination of what we could call 'gift poetics'? And if, as 'Living On' makes clear, we can no longer simply ask 'what is a *récit*?' or 'what is *récit*?', because doing so would be to adhere to the classical, philosophical form of the question, and above all to presume some *being* or *presence* of *récit*, prior to the exigency (or 'demand') of the inscribed trace as it here confronts us – always already, perhaps, in some *récit* – then we must instead ask why *récit* itself puts us in touch with this demand in a manner that might otherwise be obfuscated.[49] Why *récit*, and what is the relation between *récit* and some poem – for example, Baudelaire's 'Counterfeit Money'?

> The text credited to Baudelaire, and which we have barely begun to read, belongs to a scene of writing and therefore to the scene of a gift unthinkable for any subject. It is within this exceeded and excessive scene, within its destiny and its destination without identifiable addressee and without certain addressor, that our corpus is carved out. But insofar as it tells the story of a gift, this corpus is going to say 'in' itself, 'of' itself the exceeding that frames it and that exceeds its frame. It is going to re-mark in a supplementary *abyme* that absolute dissemination that destines the text to depart in ashes or go up in smoke [en tant qu'il raconte une histoire de don, ce corpus va dire 'en' lui-même, 'de' lui-même le débordement qui l'encadre et qui déborde son cadre. Il va re-marquer en abyme supplémentaire cette dissémination absolue qui destine le texte à partir en cendre ou en fumée].[50]

Baudelaire's prose poem, what Derrida refers to, time and again, as a *récit*, and whose reading organises the structure of the first volume of *Given Time*, not only recounts the story of a gift, or simply is, itself, as a proffered text, a sort of present, but, at the limit, above and beyond supplying so many examples of gifts (thematically or materially), can also be said to 're-mark', in supplementary abyss, through the unresolvable play of its text and title, the drift of an absolute dissemination. This play between text and title, the differential network that 'La fausse monnaie' establishes, and that can have no definite addressor or determined addressee, has no referent prior to its inscription. It is a performance without precedent, an 'event' born of its own making, which, we could say, in a language that Derrida will employ in another, related text, 'gives itself to be read', only because every such relation has been cut off. *Récit* re-marks this textual drift. It remains visibly bound up with 'what' it re-peats, re-cites, or re-presents, but crucially, there is no 'what' prior to its re-marking. For this reason, we could say that *récit* re-enacts – in an originary repetition – a dissemination that is no longer simply *like* the one that the gift, too, gives to think, but one that must be endemic to the act of giving, itself.

At this point, it will be worthwhile comparing what Derrida says of *récit*, in 'Living On' and *Given Time*, to his comments concerning it just a few years later, in 'Psyche: Invention of the Other'. In 'Psyche', it is a question of the logic of invention, as exemplified by Ponge's 'Fable'. Ponge's verse *récit* displaces all the oppositions normally thought to be at work in a poem. Its 'event' cannot be isolated to what it tells, but concerns precisely the invagination of the telling and the told. By way of this specularity, whose tain, subject, or psyche 'should not be tolerated', the text contracts itself and, says Derrida, 'gives itself to be read':

> Not all performatives are somehow reflexive, certainly; they do not all describe themselves as in a mirror, they do not designate *themselves* as performatives while they take place. This one does just that, but its constative description is nothing other than the performative itself. '*Par le mot par commence donc ce texte.*' Its beginning, its invention, or its first coming does not come about before the sentence [la phrase] that recounts [raconte] and reflects precisely this event. The narrative [le récit] is nothing other than the coming of what it cites, recites, points out, or describes [cite, recite, constate ou décrit]. It is hard to distinguish the telling and the told faces of this sentence [la face récitée et la face récitante de cette phrase] that invents itself while inventing the tale [le récit] of its invention; in truth, telling and told are undecidable here. The tale is given to be read [Le récit se donne à lire]; it is itself a legend, since what the tale narrates [ce qu'il raconte] does

not occur before it or outside of it, of this tale producing the event it narrates [de lui qui produit l'événement qu'il raconte]; but it is a legendary fable or a fiction in a single line of verse, with two versions or two versings of the same. *Invention of the other in the same*—in verse, the same from all sides of a mirror whose tain could not, should not be tolerated. (translation slightly modified)[51]

So, what is *récit*? Or, again, in what consists the demand for or of *récit*? *Récit*, it is by now clear, displaces the question of being. The demand for *récit* is not anticipated by any subject. Its 'event' is born of text (*récit*) and takes place within text (*récit*). And yet, from out of this play, the very real differences between subject and object, text and title, telling and told, and addressor and addressee can first be constituted. *Récit* is exemplary for Derrida for speculating upon – indeed, for making a spectacle of – this process.

Let us now return to those comments, in *Given Time*, concerning the possibility of the 'arrival' of the gift in *récit*. The reason that 'the gift will be linked to the – internal – necessity of a certain *récit* or a certain poetics of *récit*' is not simply because storytellers and poets have any particular proclivity for thematising gifts in their works. The necessity at stake here is more categorical, and the future tense that Derrida employs more predicating than it is predictive. When gifts and things 'give, demand, and take time', they do not just happen to do so *in* narrative. Rather, the very capacity of either for such performances already bespeaks the structure of *récit*, internal to them. Gifts are not 'like' *récits*. They 'are' *récits*, in the originary sense of this word. And the *récits* of Baudelaire, Blanchot, Ponge, Nietzsche, and Shelley allow us to read this.

In light of the above, we may now reconsider Derrida's assertion, concerning the possibility of the arrival of the gift – if it arrives – in *récit*. 'The thing as given thing, the given of the gift arrives, if it arrives, only in narrative. And in a poematic simulacrum of narrative.' If the gift as given thing only arrives *in* – but could we not also now say *as*? – *récit*, then the force of this passage cannot be in opposing one gift (that arrives) to another (that does not). Such an 'arrival' would contradict not only everything that is said here of the gift, but also everything that we know about *récit* and text, which are each tragically 'overrun':

> a 'text' that is henceforth no longer a finished corpus of writing, some content enclosed in a book or its margins, but a differential network, a fabric [tissu] of traces referring endlessly to something other than itself, to other differential traces. Thus the text overruns all the limits assigned to it so far (not submerging or drowning them in an undifferentiated homogeneity,

but rather making them more complex, dividing and multiplying strokes and lines) – all the limits, everything that was to be set up in opposition to writing.[52]

If there is one thing that could not be expected from such a text, it is the gift of 'the gift', as a present. *Récit* and text instead force us to rethink the logic of arrival itself, in the wake of this 'differential network', this 'fabric of traces referring indefinitely . . . to other differential traces'. To say that the gift arrives, if it arrives, only in narrative, is thus neither to claim that it *does*, nor to claim that it *does not*. (And is what the 'gift', in its Derridean conception, first of all gives to be thought not precisely this 'perhaps' that no longer subscribes to the either/or of presence and absence?) To arrive in *récit*, once this latter term is understood as a writing (*écrit*) that, in being sent, cannot totalise itself, is thus to arrive *as* the non-arrival of an abyssal text without borders and without end, a text, in sum, that will never be (a) present. But to locate the primal scene of the gift in such a disseminatory textuality is also to place the originary site of its contract, promise, or demand, the dating of its dative, in the caesura of the circumcision of address, rather than the subjectivity of a psyche. The text – and exemplarily the poem or poematic text, here Baudelaire's prose poem – *performs* and *re-marks* this labor, which Derrida calls dissemination, but it does so without *presenting* it.

Although, then, strictly speaking, the structures of the trace and textuality are no more at work in abyssal narratives that bespeak their unaccountable origins than they are in the intersubjective relations that form the object of sociological research, it is because *récit* and literature are invested in re-marking the play of dissemination at work in them that they acquire a certain privilege, for Derrida.[53] But if it is *récit* that Derrida names, *récit* that, for Derrida, names the structure of this thing of the gift, what then to make of the place – or non-place – of poetry in this account? Can one simply sever *récit*, poem, and poematic from poetry and its circular, helio-tropic menagerie? And if so, what does one lose in the process?

Given everything that was said in 'Economimesis', the time given to *récit*, poem, and poematic in *Given Time* now appears to be both calculated and, to a certain extent, 'justified'. Strictly speaking, none of these terms would preclude what Derrida calls 'poetry', but instead, they should speak to a more originary experience of it. Indeed, they should speak to what of the unique singularity of the poem each time risks going up in smoke (or being run over, forgotten, or otherwise thrust into oblivion) *even as* it repeats, memorialises, inherits, and addresses. The iteration of 'the poem' is more robust, Derrida seems to be saying, than what the helio-tropic tradition of 'poetry and poetics' gives to think. And this is why he will have no difficulty speaking of 'the gift of the poem', or 'the gift of some poem', while he will remain strictly silent concerning 'the gift of poetry'.

As I said above, such a decision seems to be at once calculated and justified in light of everything at stake in it. One wonders, however, what Derrida's corpus might have looked like, had he instead chosen to work *through* the figure of 'poetry' – as he had that of 'gift'. In other words, by locating the deconstructive force of rupture and cut in *poem*, rather than *poetry*, more is at stake than a simple terminological choice. No serious interrogation of poetic history, let alone its enormous investment in the gift, any longer appears necessary. 'The gift of the poem' can become a free-floating figure, even a mantra, locatable within the work of a Celan, a Mallarmé, or a Deguy, without any questioning of the impact of thousands of years of *poetic interest* in just this configuration. Again, nothing prevents Derrida from focusing on this each-time-unique-inscription of the 'gift'. Nor would a more historically inclined approach to this problem be capable of simply overturning his conclusions. I am merely trying to indicate, on the one hand, a certain refusal, on his part, to inherit the tradition of poetry, and on the other hand, the persistence of this tradition's imposition, *through* the poem.

Through the poem. This is to say that the 'poem' – or, at least, 'the gift of the poem' – while 'cit[ing] nothing', while 'hav[ing] no title', and while emerging in 'the ashes of this genealogy', nevertheless also has an incredible tendency precisely to repeat and reaffirm the very genealogical tradition with which it breaks, a tendency to repeat and reaffirm this tradition *which was not one*, prior to *the poem's* cutting re-petition of it. Does every poem not also possibly secretly affirm a genealogy that never was, precisely by breaking from 'it': for example, the very poem with which *Given Time* ends? (And is it, after all, a mere coincidence that *Given Time* ends on a poem? Two poems, in fact, if one includes the text's concluding footnote, which gives the last word to Deguy's *Donnant Donnant*.[54]) If Mauss's quotation of a poetic text in epigraph spurred Derrida to ask why *one must* (il faut) begin with a poem when one speaks of the gift, and why the gift *always* (toujours) seems to be the gift of the poem, then should one not also ask why, in speaking of whatever, in the final analysis, Derrida is speaking of, *one must end with a poem*? Why, in other words, give the final word of this tour de force to two poets, and to two poems, which re-pose the ancient question of *poetry's* gift, at the moment of its decline, unless of course there is more to be said about the ashes of this genealogy?

> Therefore we could, looking for noon at two o'clock, read again, and this will be the end, the downfall [la chute], 'Les plaintes d'un Icare' (The Complaints of an Icarus), the end, the falling off – precisely – of the poem, its absolute humility, and just the lowest possible:

> [. . .]
> my consumed eyes see only
> Souvenirs of suns.
> [. . .]
> Beneath some unknown eye of fire
> I feel my wing breaking;
>
> And burned by the love of beauty,
> I will not have the sublime honor
> Of giving my name to the abyss
> That will serve as my tomb.
> [*mes yeux consumés ne voient
> Que des souvenirs de soleils.
> (. . .)
> Sous je ne sais quel oeil de feu
> Je sens mon aile qui se casse;*
>
> *Et brûlé par l'amour du beau,
> Je n'aurai pas l'honneur sublime
> De donner mon nom à l'abîme
> Qui me servira de tombeau.*]⁵⁵

The end of *Given Time* is to be found at the nadir of the poem ('le plus bas possible') with Baudelaire's sun-struck Icarus, this late figure for the poet who, precisely, cannot give his name there where his final resting place is to be found, in the oblivion of the abyss. This is, of course, the end of a *poetic* dream that is announced. The end of the dream *of poetry*, as that which memorialises and gives being to the name. It is the recognition, in Baudelaire, anyway, that 'naming' is perhaps today more a question of technical forces, of mechanical reproducibility and the *cliché* – that is, of Icarus's father, Daedalus – than it is one of starry-eyed boys and their delusions of grandeur and fame.

Setting aside the question of the specific purview of poetic naming, to which we shall return later on, does not this *pas de don*, and even this *récit* of this *pas de don*, of the poem, point us back in the most direct fashion possible to 'Economimesis'? To what links and separates these texts, *at the summit and the base*, and to the double-inscription of the gift that, in truth, already marks each? Is the story that this poem tells not that of the becoming poem of poetry, and also, therefore, that of the remainder of poetry in the poem, to which it cannot but respond? 'Les plaintes d'un Icaire' is a *pas de poésie*, a step (not) beyond this tradition that is not one.

Drawing away from this culminating scene and its still poetic figure for the death of helio-poetics – what, after all, should we make of the *multiplication* of suns in the poem, 'mes yeux consumés ne voient que des souvenirs de *soleils*'? – there are yet other questions that are raised by Derrida's approach to and departure from the tradition of sociology. For example: should the possibility of his dispute, vis-à-vis Mauss and Lévi-Strauss and their privileging of exchange, not also have forced him to turn back to what he had earlier diagnosed as poetry's own helio-tropic polarisation? In other words, if *Given Time*'s recovering of a deconstructive notion of the gift from the ashes of anthropo-philosophic discourse is possible, or possible as impossible, and if this more robust ambivalence of the gift is itself structured into the *différance* of the trace, then could one any longer be so sure about what exactly draws 'poetry' – now in contradistinction to 'the poem' – to this gift, at its heart? Could we be sure whether, indeed, what Derrida diagnoses as 'helio-poetics' can reasonably be treated without reference to other, more general or more radical, movements, embedded *tout contre* this tradition? Can we be sure any longer in what, truly, consists the impulse behind discursive poetry's identifications: for example, how to know that poetry's draw to gifts and giving is (1) to the latter as a deferred form of *exchange*, (2) to the gift as symbol of *excess or inexchangeability* (what, according to 'Economimesis', may amount to the same thing),[56] or, perhaps, (3) to what in the 'gift' would remain precisely *undecidable*, between the first and the second of these alternatives?[57] Is this, in the final analysis, decidable? And would Derrida's own account of this undecidability not force a kind of double reading of the very helio-poetic tradition he incriminates and then abandons, of the *suns* at work in any seemingly singular solar orbit?

GIVING TIME FOR THE GIFT OF POETRY

Far from simply levelling an accusation against Derrida – be it of negligence or of repression – I wish here to indicate that a still unresolved tension or tie to some trace of this poetic tradition remains in *Given Time*, and that it is above all *Derrida* who re-marks it, as remaining, in tension. Derrida's presentation of the *textual* nature of the gift – or the *giving* nature of text – squarely puts on notice every attempt to understand donation by way of the 'subject' and its 'gift exchanges'. Instead, *récit*, narrative, and the poematic become exemplary sites for the reading of a gift *digne de ce nom*, a gift that *is* text, and that therefore requires some text for its theorisation, be it a *récit* or a prose poem. Such an observation is, for all intents and purposes, the principal insight of *Given Time*. Having set his sights on the gift, Derrida identifies the imposition of some trace, text, or writing for its theorisation – but also, at times, parenthetically or supplementally, some poem or poematic thing – and asks, in sum, what the grounds for this imposition might be. The unconditional im-possibility of *the gift* gives birth to a radical dissemination of the *thing* called gift, eliciting a series of readings of parts or divisions of this word, whose whole, evidently, in each instance, calls to its own impossibility.

But nowhere, in discussions of poems such as Mallarmé's 'Don du poème', Baudelaire's 'La fausse monnaie', or his 'Plaintes d'un Icare', does Derrida raise the converse question, as to what the specific meaning of these gifts might be *for the poem*, or why, beyond a general structural coherence, the gift seems to impose itself whenever one poses the question *of poetry* – nowhere, that is, in *Given Time*. However significant this text's insights may be for the philosophical, anthropological, and sociological thoughts of the gift, Derrida's work simply never returns to the no less insistent imposition of the gift within the archive of poetry, or to poetry's appeal to, and appropriation of, this figure within its own self-conceptualisation. Persuaded that *récit*, a *poematic simulacrum of récit*, a *poetics of récit*, a *narrative poematic simulacrum*, or simply *some poem*, persuaded that any or all of these unaccountable textual accountings of text are necessary for the theorisation of the gift, Derrida never returns to the question of poetry, to the proper of poetry, as the proper of the gift, in order to see whether that tradition does not also, already, inscribe an *other* gift, without this helio-tropic, or onto-theological, hold.

Ultimately, had Derrida raised such questions in *Given Time*, they may not have radically altered his conclusions vis-à-vis the textual character of the gift. They may, however, have offered another kind of insight altogether, into one of the constitutive conflicts of this poetic tradition that he both dissects and draws from. From Homer and Hesiod, to Horace and Spencer, to Hölderlin and Shelley, the imposition of figures of donation calls for an inquiry into what can no longer simply be considered a mere poetic theme. It calls, therefore, for the reversal of *Given Time*'s trajectory, and for an investigation into the gift's significance for poetry, rather than the poem's significance for the gift. Why must one start with a gift when one speaks of poetry? How to account for the gravity of this figure within the history of poetry's evolving self-conception, its role both at the historical origin of the birth of Western poetics and at the theoretical origin of poetic inception, through the persistence of figures of inspiration, talent, genius, and imagination? And can it all simply be accounted for under the catch-all of a 'helio-poetic', or quickly worked around, through recourse to the primacy of 'some poem'? In each of the following parts of this book, I examine how the movements of the various Western helio-poetics not only already incorporate, respond to, and sublimate the im-possibility of the gift – which is to say, survive on its very condition – but also embrace it, to the point of exploding 'poetry' itself, through the non-dialectical steps of so many *pas de poésie*.

NOTES

1. '*Che cos'è la poesia?*', 296–7.
2. 'Shibboleth: For Paul Celan', in *Sovereignties in Question*, 1–64; 4.
3. See Jacques Derrida, 'White Mythology: Metaphor in the Text of Philosophy', in *Margins of Philosophy*, trans. Alan Bass (Chicago: University of Chicago Press, 1982), 245, 271, 'Violence and Metaphysics', in *Writing and Difference*, trans. and ed. Alan Bass (New York: Routledge, 2002), 111, and 'Plato's Pharmacy', in *Dissemination*, trans. Barbara Johnson (Chicago: University of Chicago Press, 1981), 134.
4. Though Derrida does not return to it, others have: most notably, Richard Klein, in his response to 'Economimesis', in 'Kant's Sunshine', *Diacritics* 11.2 (1981): 26–41. See also Susan Blood, 'The Poetics of Expenditure'.
5. The seeds of what I am calling 'another thought of the gift' can be located at least as early as *Clang* [*Glas*], where one finds passages such as the following: '[T]he gift, the sacrifice, setting everything on fire or putting it all into play, are potentially ontological. They carry ontology and overrun it but cannot fail to give birth to it. Without the holocaust the dialectical movement and the history of being could not open, start out on the ring of their anniversary, annul themselves in producing the solar course from East to West. Before, if one could count with time here, before every thing, before every determinable being, there is, there was, there will have been the irruptive event of the gift. An event which no longer has any relation to what is commonly designated by this word' (269). See *Clang*, trans David Wills and Geoffrey Bennington (Minneapolis: Minnesota University Press, 2021). Given that most of *Clang* emerged from Derrida's 1971–2 seminar 'La Famille de Hegel', while 'Economimesis', in all probability, came from the 1973–4 seminar on 'L'Art (Kant)', there can be no simple dating of Derrida's 'decision' to embrace a notion of the gift irreducible to exchange. Nevertheless, even if first formulated prior to 'Economimesis', this decision does not take strong hold in his writings until *after* the latter text's publication, notably in his extended engagement with Mauss, in 1978–9. 'Economimesis', we could say, does not yet bear the signature of this insight, even if it will have already been inscribed elsewhere.
6. The most obvious exception, where a clear priority is lent to *poetry*, is to be found in 1997, with the lecturing of *The Animal that Therefore I Am*

(More to Follow), ed. Marie-Louise Mallet, trans. David Wills (New York: Fordham University Press, 2008). There, Derrida opposes philosophical knowledge with poetic thinking, and argues that 'thinking concerning the animal, if there is such a thing, derives from poetry' (7), though he does not expand much on this thought from that point. Similarly, and though priority is still lent to the 'poem', above and before any and all 'poetics', in the 1995 lecture 'How to Name', Deguy is lauded as a 'poet thinker', just as Cixous had been in 1990. One of the most striking examples of Derrida's late willingness to embrace what is called 'poetry', and to do so under its name, is to be found in his discussion of Celan in *The Beast and the Sovereign, Volume 1*, where he takes up Celan's 'poetic revolution' in the 'Meridian'. As to his interest in classic topics of poetry and poetics, see especially *Geneses, Genealogies, Genres, and Genius: The Secrets of the Archive*, trans. Beverley Bie Brahic (New York: Columbia University Press, 2006). First lectured in 2003, during a symposium dedicated to the work of Cixous, *Geneses* does in fact present an effort to recover a concept of 'genius' that would retain a relation to the tradition of poetry and poetics while making space for the arrival of an event. The other clear exception is to be found within *'Che cos'è la poesia?'* (1988), where Derrida pursues the deconstructive potential of the poetic dictum 'apprendre par coeur' (to learn by heart). Nevertheless, as I discuss below, the consequences of this dictum are taken up as being endemic to *the poem*, to the precise extent that one extricates it from all *poetry*. For an earlier appraisal of the 'by heart', as relating to writing and opposing the animation of speech, see 'Plato's Pharmacy', 108–9.

7. 'Majesties', 113; *'Istrice 2'*, 304. On the poematic event of a unique signature, as cut-off poem-hedgehog, see also 'Shibboleth' and *Signéponge–Signsponge*, 24.

8. On this connection, see especially 'Heidegger's Hand (*Geschlecht* II)', in *Psyche: Inventions of the Other, Volume II*, eds Peggy Kamuf and Elizabeth Rottenberg, trans John P. Leavey Jr and Elizabeth Rottenberg (Stanford, CA: Stanford University Press, 2008), 27–62, as well as *Geschlecht III: Sex, Race, Nation, Humanity*. In *Given Time*, Derrida links the 'logic' or 'aporetics' of the gift to that of *différance*, during an analysis of the role of *physis* and production in 'Counterfeit Money' (127–8). Again, what is interesting to note is the absence of any recognition of the role of 'poetry' within this problematic, which, only a few years prior, *was marked through and through by its exemplarity*. Another essential text in this regard, from a few years earlier, would be 'White Mythology', where the problems of mimesis, solar orbit, natural genius, and the necessity of securing return structure

Derrida's reading of metaphor in Aristotle. On the problem of literary singularity in Derrida's work, see especially Timothy Clark, *The Poetics of Singularity*, and Derek Attridge, *The Singularity of Literature*.

9. '*Che cos'è la poesia?*', 296–7. It is worth noting that, while Derrida's emphasis on the poematic and the unique singularity of the poem is what, evidently, here separates his focus from that of the 'setting-forth-of-truth-in-the-work' of Heidegger, in the ninth session of the initial seminar for 'Donner – le temps' he proffers the term 'poematic' as a translation of *Dichtung*, precisely in order to capture the poem-centred focus of *Heidegger*'s mode of reading in 'The Origin of the Work of Art'. See *Donner le temps II*, 85.

10. For Derrida's use of this phrase, see 'Ants', trans. Eric Prenowitz, *Oxford Literary Review* 24 (2002): 17–42; 17 (first lectured in 1990), *Politique de l'amitié: suivi de L'oreille de Heidegger* (Paris: Galilée, 1994), 192, and 'How to Name', where the 'gift of the poem' is once more related to the 'origin of the work of art' (287). In 1984, Derrida first lectured 'Shibboleth: For Paul Celan', a text that offers an extremely rich discussion of the relation between the poem and gift, and that returns to the problem of the 'gift of the poem'. Again, for Derrida, on each occasion it is a matter of the gift of *the* or *some poem*, and not *poetry*, because only the unique singularity of 'the poem' gives itself over to the oblivion that marks a condition of the gift: 'Desire or gift of the poem, the date is borne, in a movement of blessing, toward ash' ('Shibboleth', 41). Nevertheless, the priority given to *the poem* allows it, in turn, to account for the appropriative movement of *poiēsis*, insofar as this movement becomes derivative with respect to its originary caesura. This is what one reads, much later, in 2003, in 'Rams: Uninterrupted Dialogue – Between Two Infinities, the Poem', also in *Sovereignties in Question*, 135–63: 'The blessing *of* the poem: this double genitive says well the gift of a poem that both blesses the other and lets itself be blessed by the other, by the receiver or the reader. But this address to the other does not exclude self-referential reflection, for it is always possible to say that the poem speaks *of itself*, of the scene of writing, of the signature and of the reading that it inaugurates. This specular and auto-telic reflection does not close upon itself. Without any possible return, it is simultaneously a blessing granted to the other, the giving of a hand, *at once open and folded shut*' (144). In what follows, I argue that Derrida's focus on poems and certain philosophical conceptualities of poetry leads him to neglect the deconstructive resources proffered by the self-recognised tradition of poetics.

11. See, above all, sessions 8, 10, and 11 of *The Beast and the Sovereign, Volume I*.

12. '*Che cos'è la poesia?*', 296. No one has been more attentive to the link between poem and gift in Derrida's work than Nicholas Royle. See especially his 'Poetry Break', in *Jacques Derrida* (London: Routledge, 2003), 129–42, and 'The Poet: *Julius Caesar* and the Democracy to Come', in *In Memory of Jacques Derrida* (Edinburgh: Edinburgh University Press, 2009), 1–20, where he shows how Derrida's writings work to displace, or 'meddle with', poetry, in the name of the poematic. On the problem of the poem as untitled, broken, or cut off, what 'n'histrionne plus', one should also return to Derrida's reading of Mallarmé's 'Mimique', in 'The Double Session' of *Dissemination*, concerning the *histrion* that 'produces himself here' (209). Finally, on Derrida's 'hedgehog' and the problem of the poematic, see Chiara Alfano, 'Porpentine', in *Derrida Reads Shakespeare*.
13. 'Economimesis', 2.
14. 'Economimesis', 4. With this in mind, it is also worth noting that Derrida's task, in this text of 1975, is itself overdetermined by at least two further contexts. On the one hand, it is printed in a volume co-edited by Sylviane Agacinski, Sarah Kofman, Philippe Lacoue-Labarthe, Jean-Luc Nancy, Bernard Pautrat, and Derrida himself. An investment, a suspicion, or a belief in a secret alliance between mimesis and production thus motivates the entire project, which, far from being unique to Derrida, is avowed as a shared concern by each of the volume participants. 'The choice of "mimesis" was deliberate – a little bit, if one wishes, as the choice of a theme that seemed to impose itself today and to impose itself in a number of fashions' (5, my translation). On the other hand, the issue of 'production' at stake in the essay, far from being unique to 'Economimesis', had been at the forefront of Derrida's work for some time. Between 1971 and 1978 Derrida gave a number of seminars interrogating the logics of production (and reproduction) within discourses of art, economy, pedagogy, and life. On the relation between these seminars and their mutual focus, see Thomas Clément Mercier, 'Re/pro/ductions: *Ça déborde*'.
15. 'Economimesis', 6.
16. 'Economimesis', 6.
17. *AAP*, 82.
18. 'Economimesis', 6.
19. 'Economimesis', 9.
20. 'Economimesis', 7.
21. 'Economimesis', 6.
22. 'Economimesis', 11.
23. 'Economimesis', 12.
24. 'Economimesis', 17.

25. 'Economimesis', 18.
26. 'Economimesis', 12.
27. This motif returns, much later, in Derrida's lectures on the death penalty. See session 6 of *The Death Penalty, Volume 2*.
28. 'Economimesis', 11.
29. The principle behind this lack of interest is hammered home in *'Che cos'è la poesia?'*: 'And if you respond otherwise depending on each case, taking into account the space and time which you are *given* with this *demand* (already you are speaking Italian), by the demand itself, according to *this* economy but also in the imminence of some traversal *outside* yourself, away from *home*, venturing toward the language of the other in view of an impossible or denied translation, necessary but desired like a death – what would all of this, the very thing in which you have just begun to turn deliriously, have to do, at that point, with poetry? Or rather, with the *poetic*, since you intend to speak about an *experience*, another word for voyage, here the aleatory rambling of a trek, the strophe that turns but never leads back to discourse, or back home, at least is never reduced to poetry – written, spoken, even sung' (289–91). And then: '*The heart*. Not the heart in the middle of sentences that circulate risk-free through the interchanges and let themselves be translated into any and all languages' (291).
30. The term 'poematic', which appears twice throughout the full lecture course for *Given Time*, and then becomes a point of emphasis in '*Che cos'è la poesia?*', first appears in English in Coleridge. It is used by him to refer to the adjective proper to 'the poem', which contrasts with 'poetic', as the adjectival form of 'poetry'. On the poematic in Coleridge, see Emerson R. Marks, *Coleridge on the Language of Verse*. For an excellent essay on the poematic in Derrida and Artaud, see Sarah Wood, 'Editorial: "It will have blood"'.
31. Samuel Johnson, 'To Give', in *A Dictionary of the English Language, Vol I* (London: W. Strahan, 1755), 903 (edited).
32. Marcel Mauss, *The Gift: The Form and Reason for Exchange in Archaic Societies*, trans. W. D. Halls (New York: Routledge, 1990), 3. References to the French are taken from *Essai sur le don: Forme et raison de l'échange dans les sociétés archaïques* (Paris: Presses Universitaires de la France, 2007).
33. *Given Time*, 114n.4.
34. See, for example, *The Gift of Death*, *Perjury and Pardon, Volume I*, and '*Shibboleth*'.
35. For some representative dismissals of Derrida's project, see, for example, Marcel Hénaff, *The Price of Truth*, 418n.49, Pierre Bourdieu, 'Marginalia – Some Additional Notes on the Gift', and Jean-Luc Marion, *Being Given*, 344n.12 and n.13.

36. On '*the* impossible', see, in particular, *Given Time*, 7–10.
37. 'A Certain Impossible Possibility of Saying the Event', *Critical Inquiry* 33.2 (Winter 2007): 441–61; 449. See also, on this motif, *Geneses*, 'Genius that is a gift of nature is not genius. Genius that gives out of natural generosity gives nothing. A gift that knows what it is giving to someone who knows what it is he is receiving is not a gift . . . Silent genius surpasses both the symbolic and the imaginary, it grapples with the impossible. Genius gives without knowing it, beyond knowledge, beyond the awareness of what it gives and of the fact, of the performative event that constitutes the gift, if there is one' (75), as well as 'Women in the Beehive: A Seminar with Jacques Derrida'. Finally, in 'Ants', Derrida offers a novel formulation: '"what does it mean to give the thing?", "what is it to give?", "what does one mean by 'to give'?", before the word or the thing, I propose the following thesis . . . : if there is such a thing as a gift [*don*], it must be given [*se donner*] like a dream, as in a dream' (20).
38. See, for example, Pierre Bourdieu, *Practical Reason* and *Outline of a Theory of Practice*, Jacques T. Godbout and Alain C. Caille, *The World of the Gift*, Maurice Godelier, *The Enigma of the Gift*, Marshall Sahlins, *Stone Age Economics*, and Marilyn Strathern, *The Gender of the Gift*.
39. On the motif of that which is 'worthy of the name' or 'digne de ce nom' in Derrida's writings, see Geoffrey Bennington's discussion in *Scatter 1: The Politics of Politics in Foucault, Heidegger, and Derrida* (New York: Fordham University Press, 2016), 238–82, as well as my brief comments on the idiom vis-à-vis the gift in 'Some Notes Toward the Dignity of this Pipe (which is not one)', where I address the marked absence of this figure within *Given Time*. In short, the only gift worthy of the name for Derrida is one that risks exploding the very concept of the gift, and thus one that bears a certain *unworthiness* or *indignity*. This ambivalence at the heart of the (un)worthy concept must nevertheless at least provisionally be differentiated from the 'philosophical' or 'anthropological' concept of the gift, which, for Derrida, disqualifies itself in advance, because by amounting to no more than an element of (deferred) exchange, it fails even to recognise the radical nature of the problem. Derrida does in fact appeal to this idiom later, specifically in a round-table discussion published as 'L'Esprit de l'argent. Autour des écrits de Jacques Derrida sur l'argent', in *L'Argent: croyance, mesure, speculation*, 222.
40. *Given Time*, 13.
41. See, in particular, from *Practical Reason: On the Theory of Action*, trans. Randall Johnson (Stanford, CA: Stanford University Press, 1998): 'Mauss described the exchange of gifts as a discontinuous succession of generous

acts; Lévi-Strauss defined it as a structure of transcendent reciprocity of acts of exchange, where the gift results in a countergift. In my case, I indicated that what was absent from these two analyses was the determinant role of the temporal interval between the gift and the countergift, the fact that in practically all societies, it is tacitly admitted that one does not immediately reciprocate for a gift received, since it would amount to a refusal . . . If I can experience my gift as a gratuitous, generous gift, which is not to be paid back, it is first because there is a risk, no matter how small, that there will not be a return (there are always ungrateful people), therefore a suspense, an uncertainty, which makes the interval between the moment of giving and the moment of receiving exist as such. In societies like Kabyle society, the constraint is in fact very great and the freedom not to return the gift is infinitesimal. *But the possibility exists and, for the same reason, certainty is not absolute. Everything occurs as if the time interval, which distinguishes the exchange of gifts from swapping, existed to permit the giver to experience the gift as a gift without reciprocity, and the one who gives a countergift to experience it as gratuitous and not determined by the initial gift*' (94, my emphasis). See also 76.

42. Derrida *opts* to pursue this other, im-possible gift. Far from discrediting the important work of sociologists, philosophers, and anthropologists on gift exchange, Derrida's contribution in *Given Time* might best be understood as a formalisation of the exclusion that makes possible these disciplines in the first place. His *decision* to break with this tradition is explicit, and is, by necessity, an *unjustified and unjustifiable* decision. *Given Time*, we might say, is offered *as a gambit*, even an experiment, with the intention of giving time to the possibility of this other gift that will never be susceptible to reason, justification, or proof. If Derrida is unapologetic in this regard, even this attitude must be read against his discussions of Mauss's self-expiation and the implied ethics of Baudelaire's prose poem.

43. 'We are going to give ourselves over to and engage in the effort of thinking or rethinking a sort of transcendental illusion of the gift. For in order to think the gift, a *theory of the gift* is powerless by its very essence. One must engage oneself in this thinking, commit oneself to it, give it token of faith [*gages*], and with one's person, risk entering into the destructive circle' (*Given Time*, 30). See also 30–1. For an excellent account of the gift and the irreducibility of its affirmation in Derrida, see Geoffrey Bennington and Jacques Derrida, *Jacques Derrida*, 188–203.

44. For an interesting critique of Derrida's position, see Simon Jarvis, 'The Gift in Theory', *Dionysius* 17 (Dec. 1999): 201–22. Jarvis argues that the notions of the 'free gift' and 'interested exchange' emerge only with the rise of political economy in the eighteenth century. By taking this distinction as a given,

Jarvis contends, Derrida treats a historical divide as a (quasi)-transcendental one. Without the space to respond adequately to Jarvis, I would counter only that the gift/exchange binary, while perhaps only formalised in these terms in the eighteenth century, may not, for all that, be susceptible to such neat historical dating.

45. Jacques Derrida, 'Living On: Border Lines', in *Deconstruction and Criticism*, trans. James Hulbert (New York: Seabury Press, 1979), 75–176; 87 (translation modified). References to the French are taken from 'Survivre', in *Parages* (Paris: Galilée, 1986), 117–218; 130. Far from an externally imposed exigency upon *récit*, Derrida here proposes that the marker of *récit* is already just the auto-positing of its demand, through the inscription (and demand) of its own origin. Compare to the description of the dialectical logic of philosophy for Hegel in 'Khōra': 'This teleological future anterior resembles the time of a narrative [récit] but it is a narrative [récit] of the going outside of narrative [récit]. It marks the end of narrative fiction' (101). See 'Khōra', in *On the Name*, trans. Ian McLeod (Stanford, CA: Stanford University Press, 1995), 89–130. On *récit*, see also Francesco Vitale's excellent discussion in *Biodeconstruction*.
46. 'Living On', 87/130.
47. *Given Time*, 41/60.
48. *Given Time*, 42/59.
49. See also 'Shibboleth', where Derrida speaks of the 'provocation' of the poem, from its dating, and thus gifting: 'Yet the poem speaks. Despite the date, even if it also speaks thanks to it, as of it, of it, toward it, and speaks always of itself on its own, very own behalf, *in seiner eigenen, allereigensten Sache*, in its own name, without ever compromising the absolute singularity, the inalienable property, of that which convokes it. And yet this inalienable must speak of the other, and to the other; it must speak. The date provokes the poem, but the poem speaks! And it speaks of what provokes it, *to* the date that provokes it, thus convoked from the to-come of the *same* date, in other words, from its return at *another* date' (8). See also '*Che cos'è la poesia?*': 'You will call poem from now on a certain passion of the singular mark, the signature that repeats its dispersion, each time beyond the *logos*, a-human, barely domestic, not reappropriable into the family of the subject' (297). In another text, more or less contemporary with 'Living On' and the *Given Time* lectures, Derrida speaks of the 'demand' for translation, and thus for survival, of the untranslatable text. See Jacques Derrida, *The Ear of the Other*, ed. Christie McDonald, trans. Peggy Kamuf (New York: Schocken Books, 1985), 103, 122, 148, 152, 153.
50. *Given Time*, 102/133.

51. Jacques Derrida, 'Psyche: Invention of the Other', in *Psyche: Inventions of the Other, Volume I*, trans. Catherine Porter (Stanford, CA: Stanford University Press, 2007), 1–47; 11. References to the French are taken from *Psyché: Inventions de l'autre* (Paris: Galilée, 1987), 11–62; 22–3. For a further related text, see especially *Life Death*, first lectured in 1975–6, in which Derrida pays great attention to the contractual structure of *récit* at work in Nietzsche's autobiographical writings.
52. 'Living On', 84.
53. On this point, see the following passage from the 1991 interview, 'A "Madness" Must Watch Over Thinking', in *Points . . . . : Interviews, 1974–1994*, 339–64: 'What counted for me [in literature] is the act of writing or rather since it is perhaps not altogether an act, the experience of writing: to leave a trace that dispenses with, that is destined to dispense with the present of its originary inscription, of its 'author' as one might say in an insufficient way. This gives one a way that is better than ever for thinking the present and the origin, death, life or survival . . . The possibility no doubt carries beyond what is called art or literature, beyond in any case the identifiable institutions of that name' (346). On Derrida's notion of literature, see especially 'This Strange Institution Called Literature', 'No Apocalypse, Not Now', and 'Psyche'. On the distinction between literature and poetry – on which he comments, in *On the Name*, that 'I have often found myself insisting on the necessity of distinguishing between literature and belles-lettres or poetry' (28) – see especially *Of Grammatology*, 59, and 'This Strange Institution', 37–41, 45–6; 48, and 'Before the Law', both in *Acts of Literature*, ed. Derek Attridge (New York: Routledge, 1992), where he admits that 'these distinctions remain highly problematical' (187), even as he continues to appeal to them (214). See also 'The Double Session', 177 and 183, where the problem is already the difference between *literature* and *truth*, in his reading of Mallarmé with Plato (185–6), and *Positions*, trans. Alan Bass (Chicago: University of Chicago Press, 1981), where he chides Heidegger for 'the privilege accorded, in a very classical fashion, to poetic speech (*Dichtung*) and to song, and the disdain for literature' (11).
54. On Derrida and Deguy, see Christopher Elson and Garry Sherbert, *In the Name of Friendship*, as well as Kas Saghafi, 'Incurable Haunting: Saluting Michel Deguy'.
55. *Given Time*, 171–2.
56. As he puts it in 'Economimesis': 'Just as everything in nature prescribes the utilization of animal organization by man, in the same way free man should be able to utilize, were it by constraint, the work of man insofar as it is not free. Liberal art ought thus to be able to use mercenary art

(without touching it, that is without implicating itself); aneconomy must be able to utilize (render useful) the economy of work,' (6).
57. This is the starting point of *Given Time*: 'If the figure of the circle is essential to economics, the gift must remain *aneconomic*. Not that it remains foreign to the circle, but it must *keep* a relation of foreignness to the circle, a relation without relation of familiar foreignness. It is perhaps in this sense that the gift is the impossible' (7).

PART I

POETIC DIVINITY AND PATRONAGE

> Then the herald approached leading the good minstrel, whom the Muse loved above all other men, and gave him both good and evil; of his sight she deprived him, but gave him sweet song [δίδου δ' ἡδεῖαν ἀοιδήν].
>
> Homer, *The Odyssey* (8.62–4)[1]

> There is something in poetry beyond prose-reason; there are mysteries in it not to be explained, but admired; which render mere prose-men infidels to their divinity.
>
> Young, *Conjectures on Original Composition*[2]

> Nevertheless, something prevents us from putting on equal footing a collection of poems and an industrial product.
>
> Hénaff, *The Price of Truth*[3]

As early as Homer and as late as Anne Carson, Western conceptions of poetry tend to account for the origin and circulation of the poem through acts of donation. From Ion's inspired madness to Maecenas' famed patronal largesse, Kant's concept of poetic *ingenium*, and Hyde's notion of artistic creativity, figures of inspiration, genius, talent, and patronage each locate a gift at the heart of the poetic work. In this way, poetry is removed from the vulgar money economy and set aside as a thing apart: as an offering of or to the Muse, a prophetic incantation, an irruption of nature, or a token of the *gift*-economy. These gifts thus allow poetry to circulate in the world while testifying to what may remain 'mysterious' in it and in 'excess' of commercial exchange and prosaic sense-making. In the following three chapters, I will ask how such variegated yet interconnected determinations function in the course of poetic history and at what point they may render impossible the very poetic thing that they had served to make possible in the first place.

In the previous chapter, we saw how Derrida, in diagnosing the various Western helio-poetics, had initially looked elsewhere for an exception to the cyclical system of auto-affective poem presents – notably to vomit. In the years that followed, he went on to identify *récit* as the site of such non-sacrificial poematic events, only then to distinguish between the unique singularity of the poem (as text, *récit*, or *écrit*) and poetry proper, in its genealogical attachment. By contrast, in what follows I ask in what way the *poetic discourse* of donation may itself, already, struggle with just this tension.

As a first step in the direction of this reading, the next two chapters offer a survey of some of the gift of poetry's most pervasive and influential figures. They offer an interpretation of the network through which these figures function. As we shall see, within the history of poetry and poetics, a certain dominant strand of poetic conceptuality has consistently differentiated 'poetry' from 'non-poetry' on the basis of the former's privileged relation to some gift. This relation has taken many forms. What is required is therefore an account of the plastic nature of the 'gift logic' common to these figures, and an analysis of the necessity of it for the formation of poetry's very sense of identity.

Before proceeding, a brief word on the term 'poetry' and its ostensible opposition to 'prose'. As Wlad Godzich and Jeffrey Kittay have shown in *The Emergence of Prose: An Essay in Prosaics*, our common narratives surrounding the origins of both terms are deeply flawed. Historically speaking, 'verse' almost always precedes 'prose'. Thus, the common, though by no means absolute, conceit that 'prose' is simply given, while 'verse' and 'poetry' represent a subsequent invention, betraying *an addition* overtop of the fundament of unrhymed language, cannot be taken at face value. Moreover, one would have to differentiate between *our* use of the term 'poetry', as it is employed in the wake of the apparent opposition between poetry and prose, and those 'poetic' forms that emerge prior to the invention of prose, as such. As will become clear, at stake in the present analysis is an effort less to determine an absolute sense of either of these terms than it is to follow their treatment within the milieu of their opposition. It is precisely *the concept* of poetry that is here at stake, and thus 'poetry' precisely insofar as it is caught up in the need to differentiate itself from figures of 'prose' or 'non-poetry'.

NOTES

1. *Odyssey. Volume 1: Books 1–12*, trans. A. T. Murray, revised George E. Dimock (Cambridge, MA: Harvard University Press, 1919), 276–7 (translation modified). Henceforth *Odyssey*.
2. *Edward Young's Conjectures on Original Composition*, ed. Edith J. Morley (London: Longmans, Green & Co., 1918), 14. Henceforth *Conjectures*.
3. *The Price of Truth: Gift, Money, and Philosophy*, trans. Jean-Louis Morhange (Stanford, CA: Stanford University Press, 2010), 10.

1

Poetic Donation from Homer to Kant

The figure of the poetic gift takes solidified form in the West at least as early the eighth century BCE. Though by no means exclusive to this tradition, in the oral culture represented by Homer to conceive of poetry as a gift was to understand it as being of divine origin.[1] It was to take it as a missive sent from above, and one that in turn served celestial and human ends alike. Later, in the classical period, to conceive of poetry as a divine bestowal was to establish its place within the polis. It was to secure its status against the other arts (*technē*), while distinguishing it from them in terms of nature, content, and importance.

The Greek terms for poetry (*poiēsis*) and poet (*poiētēs*), based in the verb *poiein* (doing, making, fabricating), first emerge in the fifth century BCE, while *poiētikē* (poetry) and *poiēma* (poem) appear no earlier than the fourth. Prior to this point, for Hesiod and Homer, the principal 'poetic' terms available were the song (*aoidē*) or hymns (*hymnoi*) of a singer (*aoidos*). For Hesiod, the role of the language (*epos*) of the singer (*aoidos*), who makes man 'forget . . . his sorrows' (l.102), could be opposed to that of the orator–king (*basileus*), who 'effect[s] persuasion with mild words' (l.90) – though both ultimately shared in the Muses' gifts of divine inspiration.[2] One of the principal differences between *poiēsis* and *aoidē* is that once the former term comes into use, it encompasses a much wider range of forms than the archaic *aoidē*/*aoidos* had. It includes, for example, both *melos*, or accompanied melodic poetry that was meant to be sung, and non-melic or metered poetry, which was instead recited (a distinction that did not exist for Hesiod), as well as all kinds of performers, including rhapsodes, actors, and singers, their various forms of expression, and works that we today would identify as both lyric and dramatic, including those in both verse and prose.[3] Throughout this chapter, it is less a question of delimiting the scope of the Greek notions of *aoidē* or *poiēsis*, of the Homeric or the classical, than it is of identifying a current of gift poetics that runs through each.[4]

In one of the most famous Homeric examples of the divinity of poetry, Alcinous, in book eight of the *Odyssey*, 'summon[s] the divine minstrel, Demodocus', explaining that 'to him above all others has the god granted skill in song [τῷ γάρ ῥα θεὸς πέρι δῶκεν ἀοιδὴν], to give delight in whatever way his spirit prompts him to sing' (8.43–5).[5] Likewise Hesiod, throughout the *Theogony*, affirms the divine origin of his words, declaring that

> such is the holy gift of the Muses to human beings. For it is from the muses and far-shooting Apollo that men are poets upon the earth and lyre-players . . . and that man is blessed, whomever the Muses love, for the speech flows sweet from his mouth. (ll.93–7).[6]

Bacchylides speaks of the 'countless paths of ambrosial verses [that] lie open for him who obtains gifts from the Pierian Muses [πάρεστι μυρία κέλευθος ἀμβροσίων μελέων, ὃς ἂν παρὰ Πιερίδων λάχῃσι δῶρα Μουσᾶν]' (ll.1–5), and Pindar of 'sending the poured nectar, gift of the Muses and sweet fruit of the mind, to men who win prizes [νέκταρ χυτόν, Μοισᾶν δόσιν, ἀεθλοφόροις ἀνδράσιν πέμπων, γλυκὺν καρπὸν φρενός]' (ll.8–9).[7] As divinely bestowed, 'poetry' bore an infallible aura for the Greeks and was often associated with, or considered another form of, prophecy.[8] In this way, to be given was a distinct mark of poetic singularity.

While early Greek poets such as Pindar see no conflict between the poured nectar of the Muses and the sweet fruit of the mind, with Plato, for the first time, a strict division emerges between poetic inspiration on the one hand and human poetic production on the other. Whereas Pindar freely mixes the two, Plato's polemic with his predecessors over the nature of *technē* and poetry's place among the arts leads him, most notably in the *Ion* and *Phaedrus*, to put forward a doctrine of inspiration that precludes human intervention. Precisely because inspiration comes to be seen as a 'kind of possession and madness [that] comes from the Muses [δὲ ἀπὸ Μουσῶν κατοκωχή τε καὶ μανία]' (245a), it becomes excluded from intervening in a human *technē* that, for Plato, must be entirely grounded in logos.[9] '[T]his is not an art in you', Socrates explains in the *Ion*, 'whereby you speak well on Homer, but a divine power, which moves you [ἔστι γὰρ τοῦτο τέχνη μὲν οὐκ ὂν παρὰ σοὶ περὶ Ὁμήρου εὖ λέγειν, ὃ νυνδὴ ἔλεγον, θεία δὲ δύναμις ἥ σε κινεῖ]' (533d).[10] In this way, inspired communication, or what would later be known as the *furor poeticus*, becomes severed from skilful labour. The division holds even when the same labour is itself recognised – as a product of *physis* – to be grounded in a divine gift of talent (εὐφυοῦς), as Aristotle often understands it.[11]

In the tradition that follows, one thus finds the divinely inspired word of poetic inspiration, or the sweet-flowing speech that Hesiod speaks of and that

Plato theorises, opposing all poetic composition with human contribution, regardless of whether that poetic ability is ultimately based, like Demodocus's 'god granted skill in song', in the divine bestowal of an otherworldly ability. After the *Ion*, to be 'gifted' like Demodocus with skill or talent may have been a sign of divine benefaction or *tuchē*, but it was no longer possible simply to conflate it with an inspired mode of production.[12]

It is nevertheless the case that, in spite of the Platonic division between divine power (θεία ... δύναμις), vehiculated through inspiration, and human *technē*, grounded in the self, the gift-modality of poetry continues to thrive, both throughout the classical period and beyond. Although they become conceptually severed, both accounts of inspiration and those of natural or inborn talent continue to resonate as vouchsafed grants, and even as the theological orientation of these endowments yields, from time to time, to apparently secular notions of genius and inspiration.[13] Rather than causing poetic givenness to recede solely into inspired poetics, in other words, Plato's challenge has the impact of bifurcating the poetic gift and reifying the double pathway of its transmission. Henceforth, the central conflict concerning the poetic gift will not be between inspiration and talent – both of which seamlessly integrate divine donation – but nature- or god-given talent (*physis, natura,* or *ingenium*) on the one side, and human-developed skill (*technē, ars, doctrina,* or *exercitatio*) on the other. The conflict emerges, in other words, in the difference between an 'ability' that is given at birth, and one that may be learned or taught.[14]

Traces of this dispute between the given and the man-made are visible as early as Homer and in slightly more pointed fashion in Pindar, who openly derides all that which is untouched by the gods.[15] By Ovid's time, however, and among post-Augustan poets such as Lucan, Seneca, and Martial, it was not uncommon to find appeals to human-born poetic skill as well as outright repudiations of the Muses and their presents. 'Pallas-fashion were my verses born from me without a mother', writes Ovid in *Tristia*; 'these are my offspring, my family' (3.14.13–15).[16] Likewise, for a poet like Propertius, the muse was more likely to be identified with a mortal beloved than a celestial deity. Nevertheless, and in spite of having shifted the discussion away from divine *afflatus*, the question of *natura* remained, and through it that of a gift of talent subtending an otherwise human-born skill. As Horace puts it in his *Ars Poetica*:

> Often it is asked whether a praiseworthy poem be due to Nature [Natura] or to art [arte]. For my part, I do not see of what avail is either study, when not enriched by Nature's vein, or native wit, if untrained [ego nec studium sine divite vena nec rude quid prosit video ingenium]; so truly does each claim the other's aid (ll.408–11).[17]

For Longinus, writing in *On the Sublime*, it is the very same opposition, between nature (*physis*) and art (*technē*), that allows him to differentiate between the capacity for producing properly sublime works and that for merely persuasive ones. And while, for Longinus, the sublime – or the ability of a work to transport one outside of oneself – may inhere no less in certain forms of prose than in those of poetry, by differentiating between works of genius (μεγαλοφυῆ), on the one hand, and those of art, on the other, he nevertheless maintains a similar opposition to that articulated by Horace, between that which is within the productive capacity of the human and that which requires some gift or natural endowment for its realisation.

The problem, for Longinus, thus becomes how, given a necessary bare minimum of inborn talent, one is to determine the additional conditions required for a poet or orator to produce 'marvellous [τὸ θαυμάσιον]' or transporting works:[18]

> Now, since the first, I mean natural, greatness plays a greater part than all the others, here too, even if it is rather a gift than an acquired quality, we should still do our utmost to train our minds into sympathy with what is noble and, as it were, impregnate them again and again with lofty thoughts.[19]

And what Longinus concludes, as he categorises the various ways in which one may miss the mark – be it through 'tumidity [τὸ οἰδεῖν]', 'puerility [μειρακιῶδες]', or 'emotion misplaced' – is that while learning (art or *technē*) is a positively necessary accessory for the 'genius', who 'needs the curb as often as the spur', an 'artist' would nevertheless be helpless to produce the sublime as long as the gifts of nature had not already underwritten their talents.[20] The privilege is thus, in Longinus, less of poetry (ποιητῶν) as such than it is of that form of poetry, shared with a certain version of prose (συγγραφέων), that elevates itself above the flat insipidity of mere scholarly or learned productions so as to create, not simply 'consummate excellence and distinction of language', but a 'flash of sublimity [that] shatters everything like a bolt of lightning and reveals the full power of the speaker at a single stroke'.[21] The latter alone is the mark of the sublime. This is a pattern that reappears throughout the tradition, whereby the merely, or only formally, 'poetic' is displaced by a 'Poetry' (here the sublime), more poetic than poetry, through the arrival of an irreplaceable gift.

During the Renaissance, the question of poetry's givenness became a source of tension for writers who struggled, like Horace and Longinus, to understand the role of human growth and learning within poetic production. Thus, while Thomas Lodge writes in his *Defence of Poetry* that, 'I reson not that al Poets are holy, but I affirme that Poetry is a heauenly gift, a perfit gift, then which I know not greater pleasure,' Philip Sidney, in his own *Apology for Poetry*, argues for the necessity of nurturing this inimitable endowment through education and exercise.[22] For both writers, the 'abuses' levelled against poetry – be they those of Plato or of Stephen Gosson – may be traced to a common error: namely, the confusion of what merely goes by the name 'poetry' with 'Poetry' properly understood. And it is by way of such an act of exclusion that, in each case, *true* poetic production can be considered to be the possession of the privileged, instead of a capacity either broadly shared or universally able to be learned.

In Ben Jonson's celebrated elegy, 'To the Memory of my Beloved, the Author Mr William Shakespeare', the familiar tension between nature and nurture emerges, with Jonson ultimately concluding, alongside Sidney, that poetic composition requires both nature's gifts and the poet's labours:

> Yet must I not give nature all: thy art,
> My gentle Shakespeare, must enjoy a part.
> For though the poet's matter, nature be,
> His art doth give the fashion. And, that he,
> Who casts to write a living line, must sweat,
> (Such as thine are) and strike the second heat
> Upon the muses' anvil [. . .]
> For a good poet's made, as well as born. (ll.55–64)[23]

Yet while both Sidney and Jonson emphasise the role played by experience and human art in poetic composition, their visions of poetry never fully abandon notions of poetic divinity, bestowal, and natural endowment, which remain indispensable for them in order to account for the difference between poetry's higher and lower forms, or between true 'poets' and mere 'poet-apes'.[24] 'For Poesy must not be drawn by the ears,' Sidney cautions:

> It must be gently led, or rather it must lead; which was partly the cause that made the ancient-learned affirm it was a divine gift, and no human skill; since all other knowledges lie ready for any that hath strength of wit; a poet no industry can make, if his own genius be not carried unto it; and therefore is it an old proverb, *orator fit, poeta nascitur*.[25]

And while Jonson appears to resist just such traditional thinking when he reverses the concluding proverb with his pithy 'a good poet's made, as well as born', in doing so he must nevertheless still acknowledge the ineradicable necessity of good birth, and thus of the passive reception of something in poetic production that may not be attained through learning and exercise: which is to say, must not be *taken* through willed acts of subjective mastery.[26]

On the whole, there is great divergence among early modern and Enlightenment notions of inspiration, enthusiasm, and imagination, as each of these figures was subjected to extreme polemic and redefinition. In his study of Renaissance poetic authority, John Guillory tracks the emergence of Literature and the rise of the imagination alongside the fracturing of the authority of the Bible and the proliferation of scriptural forms of writing, such as those propagated by Spenser and Milton. What follows the decline of inspiration, Guillory argues, is a transfer of authority and the surge of another figure, imagination, which had previously been denigrated by authors such as Bacon for its secular and lunatic character.[27] The later Romantic revival of imagination would, in this sense, completely miss this 'original' Renaissance meaning of the term. And yet, for Guillory, what proves more significant than such historical misunderstanding, or even the election of one mode of authority over another, is just the process by which the authority of poetry may remain relatively constant, even as it is transferred, passing from inspiration to imagination, or, in another context, from genius as tutelary god to genius as natural ability. Both cases testify to the survival of what Guillory calls 'scriptural' modes of writing, or the differentiated forms that religious authority takes, even and especially in the absence of an unquestioned religious authority. The fracturing of the dominance of the Bible (and, as a consequence, inspiration) thus announces, for Guillory, the eventual rise of a self-given poetic authority (or imagination):

> My hypothesis is that the authority of the imagination (which is almost never questioned by post-Renaissance critics) is completely implicated in the efflorescent death of inspiration; and this death, paradoxically, makes possible the survival of 'scripture,' always at the end of its era. The continuance of scripture is what we must now try to understand, as it is finally more important than the event announced in literary history as the internalization of the muse.[28]

What Guillory tracks in the work of Milton and Spenser is thus a hesitation, as each author attempts to render their work 'scriptural' through modes of self-begetting. The new meaning of the imagination that emerges incorporates its older, Aristotelian, sense – the mind's capacity to represent images to itself – with a new sense of feigning, which allows for the bringing forth of images that have never yet been seen. 'The only thing the poet imitates, in Sidney's view, is his own Idea, and this Idea is created *ex nihilo*.'[29] From receiver of divine gifts of vatic vision, the poet thus becomes, by way of the imagination, primary giver of beings themselves, though this is neither a simple nor a straightforward transition.

Recent work focusing on the role of secularisation for the transformation of enthusiasm in the seventeenth and eighteenth centuries has demonstrated the divisiveness of these topics for authors in the period.[30] Michael Heyd shows how extensive European critiques of divine inspiration were, extending to religious, scientific, literary, and political contexts. Sarah Eron, on the other hand, and in direct opposition to Guillory, argues that rather than doubling down on critiques of enthusiasm, Enlightenment writers from Shaftesbury to Pope and Barbauld can be read as reforming 'enthusiasm as a species of the secular' and working towards the 'establishment of a form of inspiration that conformed to the newly emerging standards of the Enlightenment'.[31] Eron thus contends that rather than dying out, inspiration simply became a secularised affair of worlding in the eighteenth century. And yet, though the secularising efforts of Augustan-era poets would succeed, for Eron, in redirecting inspiration to the public sphere, the rhetorical effect of these apostrophising invocations nevertheless remained just as 'self-begetting' as they had for Guillory's Milton and Spenser.[32] That is to say, for Eron, though Pope's and Barbauld's writings involved *modern* modes of origination, they nevertheless were still modelled on Biblical forms and remained invested in a self-authorisation grounded in 'genius'.[33]

What I am marking in the shared gift logic of these various tropes of enthusiasm, inspiration, genius, natural-born talent, and imagination is thus the survival of scriptural modes of writing: that is, the survival of modes that precisely betray our best efforts either to affirm or to deny them, to embrace, abandon, or supersede them, because that to which they respond may ultimately defy the secular/religious binary through which we attempt to cognise them. To mark the operation of a logic of the gift within Western poetics, and to mark it as being a constitutive attribute of this tradition, is thus also to recognise that within what Guillory calls the 'authority of the merely human', there might always remain 'mysteries . . . not to be explained, but admired', because at work within the 'human' is already a language and a trace that defy our mastery.[34] 'Merely human' language, or the inscribed trace, can never simply be opposed to forms of scripture. The gift (of poetry) survives at authority's edge, and it does so because it lives on the very non-presence of this trace that allows for something like 'scripture' to appear in the first place.

That the capacity for poetic composition, the capacity *to learn* poetic composition, must first be given, and also that this 'gift' is not one that is simply shared by each and every *zoon logon ekhon*, or rational, speaking being, but rather is a privilege of the few thus remains commonplace in pre-Enlightenment and Enlightenment thought. Writing in his treatise on education, Locke decries the fact that anyone should push a student without poetic talent to pursue the art, 'for if he has no genius to poetry, it is the most unreasonable thing in the world to torment a child, and waste his time about that which can never succeed'.[35] Similarly, Descartes, in his *Discourse on Method*, admits to a youthful belief in the givenness of poetic talent: 'I held oratory in high regard and was enamored of poetry, but I thought both were gifts of the mind, rather than fruits of study.'[36] But though Descartes and Locke admit to this belief, Kant goes a step further than either when he defines genius for art, in general, as being either 'gifted by nature [welchen die Natur für die schöne Kunst begabt hat]' or the 'talent (natural gift) that gives the rule to art [Genie ist das Talent (Naturgabe), welches der Kunst die Regel gibt]'.[37] And once the structure of genius is established in the *Critique*, it is none other than poetic ability that will stand as the exemplary, privileged case of a genius that must be nature-given:

> Thus everything that Newton expounded in his immortal work on the principles of natural philosophy, no matter how great a mind it took to discover it, can still be learned; but one cannot learn to write witty poetry, however exhaustive all the rules for the art of poetry and however excellent the models for it may be.[38]

The figure of 'genius', upon which Kant's arguments concerning poetry depend, turns poetic ability into a distinctly unlearnable and arguably inhuman trait. Beyond its specifically Kantian figuration, however, genius occupied an integral place in eighteenth-century conceptions of poetry generally, which conceptions would eventually contribute to the propagation of the poem's 'gift status' in the Romantic period that followed.

The modern notion of genius is derived from the two Latin figures of *genius* and *ingenium*. While the latter signified a natural or inborn talent, the former referred to a tutelary god or guardian spirit: hence, to an external source not to be conflated with one's own character or psyche. Such notions of poetic genius have, at least since antiquity, been tied to forms of inspiration, yet as Frederick Burwick shows, during the eighteenth century the predominance of rationalist and empirical thought led to an upheaval of classical and neo-classical notions of poetic creativity, which had until then been grounded in 'irrational' experiences of furor, rapture, and delirium. This led, Burwick argues, to the specific development of two distinct notions of genius during the Enlightenment: genius either became a sign of being directly inspired by a divine concept, where the poet, in Shaftesbury's language, became a 'second maker', or it was seen as the mark of 'an acute sensitivity to the dynamism of nature', elements of which we have just observed in Kant.[39]

Edward Young, one of the earliest and most influential eighteenth-century originators of the cult of genius, opposes its products to those of mere learning and imitation. For Young, genius itself is associated with divinity and its works with natural growths: 'An *Original* may be said to be of a *vegetable* nature', he writes in *Conjectures on Original Composition*; 'it rises spontaneously from the vital root of genius; it *grows*, it is not *made*.'[40] As to its divinity, he explains a few pages later that

> Learning we thank, genius we revere; That gives us pleasure, This gives us rapture; That informs, This inspires; and is itself inspired; for genius is from heaven, learning from man . . . genius is knowledge innate, and quite our own.[41]

The cults of genius that emerged in Germany, the UK, and France and that grew out of the works of Young, Lord Shaftesbury, and Joseph Addison attempted to reconcile what remained inhuman in genius – and consequently in the creative work itself – with the possibility of its rational interpretation.[42] At the same time, the experience of *furor poeticus*, initially revived by Marsilio Ficino's fifteenth-century Latin translation of the *Ion*, came to be construed more and more in the following century as a liberating malady of the psyche, instead of a simple act of divine intervention. Poetic furor thus, at times, goes from a public event to a private one, as the rise of poetic pathologising takes hold in such figures as Hölderlin, Nerval, and Poe.[43] And yet, in nearly all cases, regardless of whether genius was imagined to be a divine endowment, a bestowal of nature, or the internal discovery of an ever more enigmatic psyche, it continued to mark a site of incursion within the subject, in which the individual's creative acts remained dependent upon an external source or internal alterity. Just, then, as Plato's *enthousiasmos* fell asymmetrically from its divine source to the poet–rhapsode who passively received it, genius in the eighteenth and nineteenth centuries marked a site of receptivity that, no matter whether it originated from within or from without, bestowed on the elected something otherwise wholly unattainable to it and wholly unmasterable by it. The mark of genius, be it natural, psychological, or divine, signified the reception of a part or a portion, a *moira*, or gift of fate, that always arrived from the other and that established the economy of the subject as beholden to this external source.[44] In the words of Coleridge, 'there is in genius itself an unconscious activity; nay, that is the genius in the man of genius'.[45]

In the Romantic period, figures of the poetic gift abound, not only due to the growing cult of genius, but also because of the renewed fascination with Hellenic thought and emphasis on inspired poetics generally. 'Indeed, I should need the gifts of the greatest of poets if I were also to describe his expressive gestures, the harmony of his voice and the secret fire in his eyes, to any effect', writes an impassioned Werther to Wilhelm.[46] The poetic gift reappears in the elevated pitches of Hölderlin's, Blake's, Keats's, and Clare's invocations of the muses, in the visions of the 'chosen' poet of Wordsworth's *Prelude* and *Recluse*, in the distinctly Romantic writing of imagination, and in the proliferating, physical embodiments of poetic enthusiasm well known in the 'correspondent breeze' and aeolian harp.[47] In his *Biographia Literaria*, Coleridge too adopts the oft-quoted maxim, earlier exploited by Spenser and Jonson, as he joins the ranks of those arguing that '*poeta nascitur, non fit*',[48] and Landon, in her *Improvisatrice*, speaks of 'that great and glorious dower/ Which Genius gives', and in which 'I had my part:/ I poured my full and burning heart' (ll.26–8).[49]

As long as the question of poetry's origin has preoccupied Western thinkers and poets, relating it as something that need be 'given' or 'received', and not 'taken', 'learned', or simply 'willed', has been a constant refrain. Such appeals serve to affirm not only the alterity of poetry and its privileged, divine, inhuman, superhuman, or simply unlearnable character, but also the ineradicable element of chance or luck that allegedly inhabits poetic production, sets it apart, and stifles human agency in the process – doing so even if the latter *is also* necessary for the development of a given poetic talent. This logic persists whether one identifies the crucial component of poetic origination to lie in the figure of *euphuous*, *ingenium*, genius, *esprit*, furor, birth, talent, imagination, or inspiration. That is, it persists whether one locates it in a gift of the gods, of nature, of the psyche, or of biology, in an active 'gift' or passive 'given', and with or without intentional act. From Homer to Plato and up through at least Kant and Coleridge, a certain dominant line of thinking binds the essence of poetry to its divine or inhuman beginnings, and the form that this bind takes is that of the gift.

None of this is to say that poetry *must* be designated as gift. Rather, it is to observe that as long as poetry is to remain outside the purview of human action, or is to bear a privilege among the arts, to that extent, given words or a given, preternatural talent for poetic production, remain the most constant resources for establishing such distinctions.

NOTES

1. In what follows, I focus on the tradition of gift poetics within European literary history. One could also pursue this question within the Chinese,

Hebrew, Islamic, and Norse traditions. On the gift of poetry in Norse mythology, see Snorri Sturluson, the *Prose Edda*. On the gift in Islamic and Arabic poetry, see Samer M. Ali, *Arabic Salons in the Islamic Middle Ages*, as well as Suzanne Stetkevych, *The Poetics of Islamic Legitimacy*.

2. *Theogony. Works and Days. Testimonia*, ed. and trans. Glenn W. Most (Cambridge, MA: Harvard University Press, 2007), 10–11. Henceforth *Theogony*. On these distinctions, see Jeffrey Walker, *Rhetoric and Poetics in Antiquity* (Oxford: Oxford University Press, 2000), 3–17.

3. See Walker's discussion, 19–22. On melic lyric poetry, see Glenn W. Most, 'Greek Lyric Poets'.

4. On this development and its relation to lyric in antiquity, see Gregory Nagy, 'Lyric and Greek Myth'. As to the difference between *poiēsis*, in the sense that Heidegger reclaims, as a *technē* that produces by bringing to presence, versus *technē* as making or creation, again, my interest lies less in establishing the authenticity of the 'gift' implicit in the first, or inauthenticity of the second, than it does in their mutual reliance on a common standard.

5. *Odyssey*, 274–5.

6. *Theogony*, 10–11.

7. Bacchylides, 'Dithyrambs 19', in *Greek Lyric, Volume IV: Bacchylides, Corinna, and Others*, ed. and trans. David A. Campbell (Cambridge, MA: Harvard University Press, 1992), 232–3. Pindar, 'Olympian 7', in *Olympian Odes. Pythian Odes*, ed. and trans. William H. Race (Cambridge, MA: Harvard University Press, 1997), 120–1. Henceforth *Olympian Odes*.

8. On the performative aspect of such incantatory poetic speech, as the gift of second sight and memory, see Jean-Pierre Vernant 'Mythic Aspects of Memory', in *Myth and Thought Among the Greeks*, Bruno Snell, *Poetry and Society*, and Marcel Détienne, *The Masters of Truth in Ancient Greece*. On the subsequent secularisation of this speech with the transition to the polis, see Détienne, 107–34, and Hénaff, 1–22.

9. Plato, 'Phaedrus', in *Euthyphro. Apology. Crito. Phaedo. Phaedrus*, trans. Harold North Fowler (Cambridge, MA: Harvard University Press, 2005), 468–9.

10. Plato, *Statesman, Philebus, Ion*, 420–1. See also *Apology* 22a-c, *Meno* 99c-e, *Laws* 682a, 719c–d.

11. Though poetry, for Aristotle, usually bears the sense of drama, and is famously understood by him to be mimetic in nature – and thus, to a certain extent, to be learnable by all – at various points in both the *Poetics* and *Rhetoric* he refers to poets as enjoying the privilege of an unlearnable natural talent and a divine influence: 'Hence poetry is the work of

a gifted person, or of a manic: of these types, the former have versatile imaginations, the latter get carried away [διὸ εὐφυοῦς ἡ ποιητική ἐστιν ἢ μανικοῦ· τούτων γὰρ οἱ μὲν εὔπλαστοι οἱ δὲ ἐκστατικοί εἰσιν]' (1455a). See also *Poetics* 1459a, where he declares that the genius for metaphor is a rare gift that cannot be learned, and *Rhetoric* 3.7.11. *Poetics. Longinus: On the Sublime. Demetrius: On Style*, trans. Stephen Halliwell, rev. Donald A. Russell (Cambridge, MA: Harvard University Press, 1995), 88–9. Henceforth *Poetics. Longinus*.

12. Penelope Murray makes this point in 'Poetic Inspiration in Early Greece', *The Journal of Hellenic Studies* 101 (1981): 87–100, where she argues for the fluidity of inspiration and talent prior to Plato. These gifts, as Murray points out and as I shall discuss further on, can be parsed into the temporary gift of poetic inspiration and the permanent gift of poetic ability, or later genius (89). See also her 'Homer and the Bard', in *Aspects of the Epic*, on the commensurability of human and divine contributions to poetic production, as well as Alice Sperduti's 'The Divine Nature of Poetry in Antiquity', on the role of divinity in Greek poetry.

13. The theoretical underpinnings of such 'gifts of nature' vary drastically from period to period. Whether, indeed, they are thought to be subtended by a divine force such as Aristotelian *tuchē*, a Christian belief in election, or even a secular confidence in an inborn or genetic predisposition – which, as a figure of *automaton*, may lack the intentional quality of the former two – the passive receptivity of the endowed poet nevertheless holds. To be 'gifted' in the contemporary sense subscribes to the extended logic of gift poetics, even absent any notion of divine endower. One is thus privileged without being elected.

14. On this difference, see especially Cicero's *Pro Archia Poeta*, where he grounds poetry in an unlearnable divine attribute and makes use, in the process, of theories of both talent and inspiration: 'And yet we have it on the highest and most learned authority that while other arts are matters of science and formula and technique, poetry depends solely upon an inborn faculty, is evoked by a purely mental activity, and is infused with a strange supernal inspiration [poëtam natura ipsa valere et mentis viribus excitari et quasi divino quodam spiritu inflari]. Rightly, then, did our Ennius call poets "holy", for they seem recommended to us by the benign bestowal of God' (26–7). *Pro Archia. Post Reditum in Senatu. Post Reditum ad Quirites. De Domo Sua. De Haruspicum Responsis. Pro Plancio*, trans. N. H. Watts (Cambridge, MA: Harvard University Press, 1923). For an analysis of a similar split during the Romantic period, see Sara Guyer, *Reading with John Clare* (New York: Fordham University Press, 2015), where she argues

that 'The Romantic conflation of the formerly opposed supernatural and natural conceptions of poetry figures natural genius as opposed not to the supernatural, as an extrinsic power of inspiration or enthusiasm, but to the nonnatural (mechanical, rhetorical, learned, contrived)' (35). On the survival of Platonic inspiration up to the Renaissance, see E. R. Curtius, *European Literature and the Latin Middle Ages*.

15. As Murray points out, even Homer at times appears to embrace a human element in composition, albeit one that contributes alongside divine inspiration: 'I am self-taught, and the god has planted in my heart lays of all sorts, and worthy am I to sing to you as to a god' (*Odyssey* 12.347–8; pp.370–1). See also *Odyssey* 1.346–7 and 8.43–5. For Pindar, see, for example, 'Olympian 2': 'Wise is he who knows many things by nature [φυᾷ], whereas learners who are boisterous and long-winded are like a pair of crows that cry in vain against the divine bird of Zeus' (*Olympian Odes*, ll.86–9; pp.72–3) and 'Olympian 9': 'What comes by nature is altogether best. Many men strive to win fame with abilities that are taught, but when god takes no part, each deed is no worse for being left in silence' (*Olympian Odes*, ll.100–4; pp.160–1).
16. Ovid, *Tristia. Ex Ponto*, trans. A. L. Wheller, rev. G. P. Goold (Cambridge, MA: Harvard University Press, 1924), 152–3.
17. Horace, *Satires. Epistles. The Art of Poetry*, trans. H. Rushton Fairclough (Cambridge, MA: Harvard University Press, 1926), 484–85. See Steele Commager, *The Odes of Horace: A Critical Study* (Norman: University of Oklahoma Press, 1995), 1–41. Commager argues that, by and large, Latin poets rejected the gift-poetry dynamic of Muse-driven inspiration in favour of a poetics more focused on the subject and human agency (8). Even where the language of the Muses persisted, it was merely as a convention or appurtenance for Latin poets who adopt it either out of habit or for political reasons (16–20). Nevertheless, Commager explains that as Latin poets moved away from inspired poetics, the notion of poetic givenness persisted through figures of innate talent such as *natura* or *ingenium* (22–3). It of course also remained through the relays of patronage.
18. *Poetics. Longinus*, 162–3.
19. *Poetics. Longinus*, 182–5.
20. *Poetics. Longinus*, 165–8.
21. *Poetics. Longinus*, 163.
22. Thomas Lodge, *A Defence of Poetry, Music, and Stage-Plays* (London: Printed for the Shakespeare Society, 1853), 14. See also William Webbe's *A Discourse of English Poetrie* (1586), ed. Edward Arber (Westminster: A. Constable and Co., 1895): 'In all Artes nature is the beſt helpe, and learned

men vfe commonly to fay that *A Poet is as well borne as made a Poet*' (91). For a Spanish equivalent, see Calderón's *Panegyrico*.
23. Ben Jonson, 'To the Memory of My Beloved, the Author Mr William Shakespeare', in *The Complete Poems*, ed. George Parfitt (New York: Penguin, 1988), 265. For an analysis of Jonson's struggle to define the poet as giver of praise and his poems as gifts to his patrons, see Scott, *Selfish Gifts*, 15–18; 25–7; and 125–58.
24. *AAP*, 116.
25. *AAP*, 109.
26. On the preservation of inspiration in Renaissance humanist thought, see Craig Kallendorf, 'From Virgil to Vida: The *Poeta Theologus* in Italian Renaissance Commentary', *Journal of the History of Ideas* 56 (1995): 41–62, where he traces the tradition of *theologia poetica*, or the reinterpretation of classical poetry as revealing the truths of Christianity through monotheistic divine inspiration. For a discussion of early modern debates over the parable of the talents, as so many efforts to understand the relation between God-given gifts and human labour, see Shershow, *The Work and the Gift*, 140–51. As he puts it, 'The idea of work is thus doubly linked to the idea of the gift: first, because work is the necessary means by which divine gifts are developed and employed; second, because one's vocation in this specific sense is also conceptually linked to charity as an analogous form of what is sometimes called "spiritual usury"' (146–7).
27. For Dante, the imagination had named a mediating faculty whereby the poet could become inspired by a higher spiritual reality: 'O thou, Imagination, that dost steal us/ So from without sometimes, that man perceives not/ Although around may sound a thousand trumpets,/ Who moveth thee, if sense impel thee not?/ Moves thee a light, which in the heaven takes form,/ By self, or by a will that downward guides it', *The Divine Comedy*, trans. Henry Wadsworth Longfellow (Boston: Ticknor and Fields, 1867), 'Purgatorio', 17.13–18. By the time Montaigne would take it up in 'On the Force of the Imagination', it was already something like a psychogenic force capable of influencing corporeal experience. On the transformation of medieval conceptions of *inventio* by Renaissance critics for the purposes of consolidating the poetic imagination, see Murray W. Bundy, '"Invention" and "Imagination" in the Renaissance'. Bundy argues that for Ronsard, Daniello, Castelvetro, Gascoigne, Shakespeare, and Puttenham, the concept of *inventio* can be seen to help establish a poetic faculty out of the rhetoric of the Trivium, while, on the other hand, serving to differentiate poetic invention from the hallucinations and dreams of lover and lunatic.

28. *Poetic Authority: Spenser, Milton, and Literary History* (New York: Columbia University Press, 1983), ix.
29. *Poetic Authority*, 10. On the classical thought of fantasia and imagination, see Jean Starobinski, 'Jalons pour une histoire du concept d'imagination', in *La Relation critique* (Paris: Gallimard, 1970), 174–95. For Starobinski, it is with Longinus that one first finds an association between enthusiasm and fantasia, thereby setting up the possibility of reconciling Platonism with imagination, and the supersensible with the sensible for neo-Platonists such as Plotinus (181–2).
30. See Heyd, *Be Sober and Reasonable*, and Sarah Eron, *Inspiration in the Age of Enlightenment* (Newark: University of Delaware Press, 2014). For a history of eighteenth-century 'enthusiasts' in England, see also Lionel Laborie, *Enlightening Enthusiasm*, and for an examination of the role of poetic enthusiasm in the works of Edward Young and James Thomson, see Shaun Irlam, *Elations*.
31. Eron, *Inspiration*, 1.
32. See Eron, *Inspiration*, 6–9 and *Poetic Authority*, 172–8.
33. Eron, *Inspiration*, 19.
34. *Poetic Authority*, 178, *Conjectures*, 14.
35. John Locke, *The Works of John Locke, vol. 8 (Some Thoughts Concerning Education, Posthumous Works, Familiar Letters)* (London: Rivington, 1824), 167. This is not to say, however, that Locke supports such an education even for one *with* poetic genius, a choice that he merely finds to be 'the strangest thing in the world' (167).
36. René Descartes, *Discourse on Method and Meditations on First Philosophy*, trans. Donald A. Cress (Indianapolis, Indiana: Hackett, 1998), 4.
37. Immanuel Kant, *Critique of the Power of Judgement*, trans Paul Guyer and Eric Matthews, ed. Paul Guyer (Cambridge: Cambridge University Press, 2000), 186. References to the German are taken from *Kritik der Urteilskraft* (Frankfurt am Main: Suhrkamp, 1974), 241.
38. *Critique of the Power of Judgement*, 187/243–4 (translation modified). On the problems of art, poetry, and the gift in the third critique, see also Klein's 'Kant's Sunshine', especially 29–30.
39. Quoted in Frederick Burwick, *Poetic Madness and the Romantic Imagination* (State College: Pennsylvania State University Press, 2004), 22. Diderot's encyclopedia entry on 'Génie' also confirms this sense, calling genius 'un pur don de la nature'. *L'Encyclopédie, ou dictionnaire raisonné des sciences, des arts et des métiers*, 1st edn, vol. 7, eds Diderot and d'Alembert (1757), 582. On the coalescence of these notions of genius with the imagination, such as one finds in Coleridge, see also Starobinski, *La Relation critique*, 186–7.

40. *Conjectures*, 7.
41. *Conjectures*, 17. See also, in this respect, Johann Kaspar Lavater: 'Where there is activity, energy, deed, thought, feeling, which may not be learned or taught by men, there is genius! . . . Genius is not learned, not acquired, not to be learned, not to be acquired, it is our unique property, inimitable, divine, inspired. Genius flashes, genius creates; it does not arrange, it creates!' quoted in Roy Pascal, *The German Sturm und Drang* (New York: Philosophical Library, 1953), 138.
42. On the development of the concept of genius in the eighteenth century, see also Paul W. Bruno, *Kant's Concept of Genius*.
43. Seán Burke makes this argument in his introduction to *Authorship: From Plato to the Postmodern: A Reader*, ed. Seán Burke (Edinburgh: Edinburgh University Press, 1995), xviii. According to the *Oxford English Dictionary*, 'enthusiasm' first starts to become associated with emotional states, rather than divine intervention, in the 1700s. On this, see also Eron, 1–32. For an earlier genealogy of the interpenetration of divine inspiration with human pathologising, and in particular through the embodied experience of melancholy, see Carol V. Kaske and John R. Clark, 'Introduction', in Marsilio Ficino, *Three Books on Life* (Binghamton: CEMERS, 1989), 3–90, where they argue that '*De Vita* was the first work to give the Platonic notion of the four noble *furores* – itself restored to the West almost single handedly by Ficino – a medical basis in the melancholic humor or black bile' (23).
44. For a similar claim, see, for example, Owen Barfield, 'Imagination and Inspiration'. On the intersections of Romantic genius with the figure of the improvisor, see Angela Esterhammer, *Romanticism and Improvisation, 1750–1850*.
45. Coleridge, 'Essay on Poesy or Art', in *The Literary Remains of Samuel Taylor Coleridge, Volume 1*, ed. Henry Nelson Coleridge (London: William Pickering, 1836), 223.
46. Johann Wolfgang von Goethe, *The Sorrows of Young Werther*, trans. Michael Hulse (New York: Penguin Classics, 1989), 35.
47. On Romantic figures of inspiration, see M. H. Abrams, *The Correspondent Breeze*, Timothy Clark, *The Theory of Inspiration*, and Burwick. On the specificity of Romantic modes of performative speech, such as invocations, see Eric Lindstrom, *Romantic Fiat*.
48. The full passage in Coleridge runs: 'But the sense of musical delight, with the power of producing it, is a gift of the imagination; and this, together with the power of reducing multitude into unity of effect, and modifying a series of thoughts by some one predominant thought or feeling, may be cultivated and improved, but can never be learnt. It is

in these that "Poeta nascitur non fit"' (20). *Biographia Literaria*, eds James Engell and W. Jackson Bate, in *The Collected Works of Samuel Taylor Coleridge*, 7.2 (Princeton, NJ: Princeton University Press, 1983). This proverb has an illustrious and somewhat confused history, first appearing in Pseudo-Acro's commentary to Horace's *Ars Poetica*. It becomes a common cliché in the Renaissance, reappearing in one form or another not only in Sidney, Jonson, and Webbe, but also in *Don Quixote*: 'for it is a true opinion, that the poet is born one; the meaning of which is, that a natural poet comes forth a poet from his mother's womb, and, with this talent given him by heaven, and without further study of art, composes things which verify the saying, *Est Deus in nobis* [*the god is inside us*],' Miguel de Cervantes, *Don Quixote de la Mancha*, trans. Charles Jarvis, ed. E. C. Riley (Oxford,: Oxford University Press, 2008), 567. On the history of this motif and its adoption by the Romantics, see William Ringler, 'Poeta Nascitur Non Fit: Some Notes on the History of an Aphorism'. For an interesting discussion of its broader implications for 'biopoetics', see Guyer, 25–39.
49. *Letitia Elizabeth Landon: Selected Writings*, eds Jerome McGann and Daniel Ross (Ontario: Broadview Press, 1997), 52.

2

Symbolic Economies of Poet and Patron

—All those who thank the author of this gift, at least with words or with letters, will be found by Aeneas in the Elysian Fields, where they will be praised by Anchises. The others by chance will find themselves in Hell—by their own fault.
—The response should be addressed to the bookshop 'della Serena' in Venice.

dell'Anguillara, 'Book 1 of Virgil's *Aeneid*'[1]

My dear friend, I've asked you gently
    And pleaded with you repeatedly.
I turned to you as a tower of strength,
    A shield and buckler before my enemy –
a hot day's shelter against the sun,
    a stove on a day that's cold and wintery:
And like Eklanah remembering Peninnah –
    May the Lord take note – you remembered me,
and sent on, bless you, a piece of cheese.
    But what good is cheese when I'm thirsty?

Khalfoun, 'A Gift of Cheese'[2]

I've nothing Else – to bring, You know –
So I keep bringing These –
Just as the Night keeps fetching Stars
To our familiar eyes –

Maybe, we shouldn't mind them –
Unless they didn't come –

> Then – maybe, it would puzzle us
> To find our way Home –
>> Dickinson, 'I've nothing else – to bring, You know'[3]

Poetry's status as an endowment, at least as early as Homer and as late as Kant, serves to confirm its divine or inhuman origins and to distinguish it from other, profane arts. Far from an essential property of poetry, at stake in this association is precisely the establishment of a poetic essence. The history of this trope – of the translations and transformations of the poetic internalisation of giving – is thus grasped in part through this ongoing tension between human agency and poetic alterity, visible already in the *Iliad* and *Odyssey*. It is not, however, restricted to literary figures of poetic origination such as inspiration and talent, but encompasses as well the very modes of transfer of the poem to reader, patron, and public. One finds, in other words, the trope of the gift of poetry reflected not only in the poet's gifts *for* verse, in the inspiration, god-given talent, and genius that deliver poetry to the human world, but also in the poet's gifts *of* verse, his or her offerings or presents to readers, patrons, and listeners alike.

Whether one thinks of John Heywood's 'This gift alone I shall her give;/ When death doth what he can,/ Her honest fame shall ever live/ Within the mouth of man' (ll.53–6), Joachim du Bellay's dedicatory 'je te fay present de mon *Olive*', or Auden's elegiac 'your gift survived it all' in speaking of the departed Yeats,[4] the move to treat the poet as giver – and the work as gift – becomes no less significant for Western poetics than the divine or inhuman origins of verse itself.[5] The gift, in sum, fulfils the double function of accounting for the *archē* and *telos* of poetry, supplying the disposition and mode of address of this inhuman missive as it *should* arrive, to poet and listener alike.[6]

As the following discussion demonstrates, no analysis of the gift *in* poetry, or of the meaning of the gift *for* poetry, or of what we might more broadly call the gift *of* poetry, can suffice with poetic appropriations and internalisations of this 'gift', alone. At the same time, the importance of patronage, literary subscription, and 'gift books' within this story lies not only, or not simply, in their bearing on verse as economic, material, or historical structures. Far from representing the final or true cause of the phenomenon of poetry, patronage represents one more discursive component of poetic self-reflection. Indeed, as well as a common subject within poetic discourse, 'patronage' – understood in the broadest conceivable terms, as spectre of *support* – often comes to name the very site of the non-poetic within poetry, the moment of historical reference within the self-referential play of verse, or the incursion of the extra-textual, or paratextual, within the textual. It therefore gives access, as well as to a common poetic and historical topos, to the very question of the limit: the limit of poetry and the limit of the gift. This becomes important, practically speaking, as soon as one wishes to know what, in fact, one refers to in speaking of the 'poetic gift': a question of no less significance for theorists and historians of patronage than for those of poetic apostrophe and address. What, after all, does it mean *to give*, *to dedicate*, or *to address* a poem? In what way is *the thing* of the poem related to *the thing* of the gift? And to what extent are these very questions posed and imposed by the poetic tradition itself, not only at moments of lofty religious or existential questioning, such as one finds in Milton or Dickinson, but also in lowly reflections on the fiscal needs of the poet, such as in the comic appeals of dell'Anguillara and Khalfoun? The following attempts to formalise some of the difficulties surrounding these common conceits of poetic discourse and poetry criticism, while in Chapter 3 I will return to many of these issues, through an exploration of their *failure*, in Wordsworth's writings on patronage, genius, and talent in *The Prelude*.

Although any appeal to the poem as gift is bound to be overdetermined, the institutions of patronage and of modern authorship significantly contribute to the solidification of a discourse of poetic donation in the classical and modern periods, respectively. Through highly developed patronage systems, works of verse (alongside nearly all other artistic and intellectual productions) are rendered 'dependent' on the favours of benefactors. The work of poetry (though in no way exclusively the work of poetry) thus becomes dedicated, a 'gift' of devotion to a benefactor whose counter-gifts or grants, in turn, make the poet's livelihood possible.

The gifts exchanged between patron and poet vary widely. From a patron in the Greco-Roman period, they might include money, houses, food, services, or favours, while a poet, recognisant of such gifts or even solicitant of them, might offer presents of both a poetic and a non-poetic nature.[7] In the Augustan period, such non-poetic presents could consist in performing a *salutatio*, accompanying a patron to dinner, or aiding him or her in their own efforts at composition. Poetic gifts, on the other hand, might involve addressing a book of poems to a patron, composing encomia, invitation poems, or other works in honour of them, or in making them the dedicatee, or addressee, of one important poem in particular.[8] So prominent were these forms of recognition that Horace, in his 'Epistle to Augustus', speaks of the 'stupid gift [pingui donatus munere]' (2.1.267) of the maladroit poet unable to produce effective panegyric.[9] In spite of the prevalence of such presents, however, determining the precise nature of a poetic gift – not only whether it is well wrought, but also in what, exactly, it may consist – often proves a rather difficult task.

In her study of Horace's participation within Augustan-age patronage, Phebe Lowell Bowditch makes two distinctions between the orders of patronage presents that are critical for any study of the subject. On the one hand, Bowditch differentiates between those 'objectification[s] of poetry as a concrete good', such as gifted papyrus rolls of poetry or tablets with poems etched on them, and those concrete offerings 'embedded in the poem', such as dedications, *recusatio*, and invitation poems.[10] On the other hand, and as a further refinement of the latter category of poetic embeddings, she distinguishes between the 'generic conventions' of the dedication or invitation poem, and the mere 'theme of patronage' as it appears in verse. While, she contends, such 'conventions . . . display the "material trace" of the socioeconomic world', the non-conventional 'theme' does not, and thus, it may be extrapolated, should not properly be considered a gift.[11]

While the first distinction that Bowditch makes separates the non-poetic utilisation of poetry as a present from the self-reflexive inscription of a poem or work of poetry that bequeaths itself – distinguishing Keats's hypothetical presentation of a single copy of *Endymion* to Joseph Severn, for example, from his dedication of the text 'To the Memory of Thomas Chatterton' – the latter distinction attends to the difference between use and mention, between proper participation within an accepted convention and merely fictional reference to it. Bowditch's double distinction thus reveals the twofold problem faced by any study of literary patronage: that of distinguishing what is proper to literature or poetry, on the one hand, and that of identifying what does and does not qualify as a gift, on the other.

As far as the first difficulty is concerned, that of differentiating between the embedded dedicatory inscription and the mere presentation of a physical or concrete copy of a work, it is thus (presumably) self-evident that both, regardless of their differences, in fact constitute gifts.[12] The difference between them thus lies not in their quality as presents, but in the fact that, whereas an address or dedication is conventionally understood to form a part of the work itself (being that one cannot change it after the fact, without reprinting or reissuing the manuscript), in the latter instance of the gift of a physical copy of a work, the fact that one gives *this* work of poetry is wholly contingent and fails to touch the content of the work at all.[13] As far as the work is concerned, one could just as well give any other, or any other good, just as the work remains unaffected, whether one gives identical copies of it to one person or to twelve, genuinely or cynically, in earnest or with irony. The 'work' itself is (ostensibly) indifferent to the uses to which it is put as a concrete good: *Endymion* remains what it is, whether I choose to give it, or something else, to you, whether 'I', its giver, am its author or merely its purchaser. Only those embedded instances that alter our reading of the work, then, constitute properly 'poetic' gifts, at least as far as patronage is concerned.[14]

And yet, to this line of thinking, one could respond that even if the individual work is indifferent to the uses to which it is put once it is published, it follows neither that the (contingent) gift of poetry (as a 'good') is equivalent to the gift of any other kind, nor that 'poetry' – as a practice, an archive, or a self-reflexive discourse – is itself indifferent to the perpetual possibility of its disposal in contingent, hazardous, malicious, or beneficent manners, or, for that matter, to its subsequent susceptibility to becoming a token of gift exchange or commodity profit. One of its most conventional motifs, that of poetic immortality, hangs on the tension between the poem's embeddedness in an always-possibly errant written or oral text (hence its 'material' inscription), and the pretensions of the poetic work to a transcendent future inscription in the minds of humans, gods, or God (hence its ever-growing immateriality). Both the confidence of sonnet 55 in 'The living record of your memory' (l.8) and the unrest of 'When I have fears that I may cease to be' (l.1), or, to remain with Shakespeare, 'Thy gift, thy tables ... Which shall above that idle rank remain/ Beyond all date ... Or at the least so long as brain and heart/ Have faculty by nature to subsist' (ll.1–6), are equally informed by the poem's relationship with contingency.[15] This is a relationship that it may systematically avow or disavow. The gravity of this conflict, which casts its shadow over both the work (in general) and the copy (in particular), is one reason why the gift of a book of verse can never simply be *equivalent* to a gift of another kind: when I present you with a copy of Shakespeare's sonnets, through this ephemeral, weighty body, I in fact offer you access to something potentially immortal and divine – or so the story goes. Yet, at the same time, the existence of this conflict, between poetic apotheosis and material effacement, manifested through the contrast between divine memory and the flammable page, also offers evidence that the contingent *possibility*, if not the *fact*, of the work's (and copy's) future gifting is already at play within poetic discourse as one of the many probable destinies that may befall it, just as being sold, burned, archived, or forgotten also occupy what we could think of as the 'poetic unconscious'.[16] These contingencies haunt the poem: they are 'embedded' in it, though in a different fashion from that of the individual, inscribed, poetic dedication.

Ultimately, then, while distinguishing between properly poetic and non-poetic presents may be helpful for grasping the relatively regular and conventional operations of what is called 'patronage', such a distinction fails to comprehend the complexity of poetry's discursive struggles with its own status as a textual as well as a material body; its sensitivity to its own susceptibility to suffering unlikely and accidental, as well as probable and relatively foreseeable events; or its concern with its own reception and perceived sense of superiority with respect to presents of other kinds.[17] Any concept of the poetic gift must grapple with both of these orders (non-contingent and contingent; inherent and external) if it is to attempt to understand not only what 'poets' give, but also the *meaning* of the gift within what is called 'poetry'.

Turning to the second difficulty posed by Bowditch, between the conventional and non-conventional 'theme', it is in this case presumably self-evident that both are poetic. Thus, while the first distinction establishes the limits of poetry (while taking the gift for granted), the latter establishes those of the gift (while taking poetry for granted). The conventionality of the convention is here measured by its ability to bear what Bowditch calls 'socioeconomic weight', its convertibility, in other words, with gifts, commodities, and favours of another (non-poetic) order. Thus, while *recusationes*, dedications, and addresses are all established tropes, commonly exchanged for presents of 'material' value such as money, the 'mere theme' of the gift as it arises in verse, lacking this liquidity, would qualify at best as a fictional, and at worst as a counterfeit, gift. Poetic reference to the gift that does not bear socio-economic weight is, in sum, no gift at all. Or, put conversely: the poetic gift must be exchangeable, it must bear weight, value, or substance of some kind, if it is to be one.

As with the first distinction, the utility of grasping the latter for understanding the relays of patronage is without question. Certain articulations embedded within verse yield favours, money, and even property, while others do not. Yet one might wonder whether the line between the 'conventional' and 'non-conventional' is ever rigorously determinable. Does, for example, a conventional gift that *fails* to elicit a response still constitute a gift by these measures, or does it descend into virtuality? On the other hand, does the unreciprocated present remain dissociable from the merely fictional gift embedded in a text? Such questions force us to confront what the difference between the 'weight-bearing' and 'non-weight-bearing', or the 'binding' and 'non-binding', within the poetic text consists in – a problem that I will return to in Chapter 8. If the 'gift' must bear socio-economic weight, how then to grasp the difference between different degrees of the gifts of no-thing or of non-weight: that is, between orders of non-gift gifts? Among such presents, one would have to separate between the sheer absence of the presentation of a (fictional) gift and the (mere) fiction of a present, which, while not being exchangeable for other goods or services, may nevertheless be integral to the development of a conception of patronage within a given text. But also, one must be able to account for the difference – if there is any – between 'conventional' gifts made to (real) living people and those made to the deceased, which may nevertheless bear significant 'symbolic' weight, even if not, exactly, a readily identifiable socio-economic value.

How, moreover, to reckon with the vast array of dedicatory inscriptions, which span not only the living and the dead, but also fictional, inanimate objects, abstractions, and, of course, gods? When Lévi-Strauss dedicates *The Raw and the Cooked* 'À la musique' or when Aragon dedicates *Mouvement perpétuel* 'à La Poésie et merde pour ceux qui le liront', these are, by every conventional standard, 'real gifts'. Yet by addressing abstractions, they remove any possibility of reciprocation by their addressees, and thus become oddly 'weightless'.

Even if each of the above issues could be settled and we could determine the difference between the gift and non-gift – that is, between the real and virtual gift – as well as that between real gifts to real people that are not reciprocated or received and those to fictional people, concepts, ideas, and gods, one would still have to be able to account for what, in fact, any of these gifts (real or virtual, explicit or implicit) gives. What does the gift of the poem give? This is to ask both: What does it mean to bestow *a poem*, and what can a poem, in its turn, *bestow*?

Horace's invitation poem (*Odes* 1.20) to Maecenas, written in recognition of the gift of the Sabine farm, is a classic example of a 'conventional' gift that may offer insight into some of the issues just raised.[18] It opens thus:

> You will drink, dear knight Maecenas, cheap Sabine wine from small
> cups, which I myself stored away and sealed in a Greek cask
> [Vile potabis modicis Sabinum
> cantharis, Graeca quod ego ipse testa
> conditum levi
> (. . .)
> clare Maecenas eques][19]

The 'cheap Sabine wine', commonly understood to be a figure for the poem itself, makes an ironic show of Horace's largesse in writing the ode.[20] But what, exactly, does the poet, *or poem*, here give? While it is a simple enough matter to recognise a *quid pro quo* at work, identifying the precise terms of the exchange is a much more difficult task. Horace may be said to 'give' Ode 1.20 to Maecenas to the extent that he addresses the poem to him. Yet such attribution requires either that the gap between the poem's author and speaker be suspended, or that what Horace 'gives' is merely the *inscription* of a (silently dedicated) discourse, the pretensions of which to address Maecenas and give him wine (and, metaphorically, this very ode) can never be fully reconciled with those of the author himself. If the latter position is overstating the case, the following critical point nevertheless stands: we must reckon with the difference between the non-textual or extra-textual gift of the inscription of a poem – which may always be dedicated to someone who is never named within the work or never named at all – and the inscribed gifts of a poet speaker that may either double the acts of the author or depart from them. Once we acknowledge such a split, there is, however, a further difficulty: each of the opposing terms requires the other, without being reducible to it. On the one hand, the act of inscription is realised only with the written text, and on the other hand, the written text may reflect on the act of inscription; it may, as Horace's ode does, say to 'dear knight Maecenas', 'You will drink cheap Sabine wine', but in doing so it can never fully contain the act of inscription, nor be contained by it. There is always a gap between the act of inscription and the inscribed, even if the 'convention' of the poetic-patronage present requires that we conflate these roles. In any case, we may always ask what it is that the poet gives. Is the gift the writing of the poem, or the poem itself, which names or dedicates itself to the patron?

We might say that 'poetic gifts' necessarily traverse the border between inscription and inscribed, extra-textual and textual, or material–socio-economic relations and discursive, poetic, or fictional textual economies. The legibility of the poem-gift in patronage, whether it is realised through address or dedication, requires reading from the 'textual' to the 'extra-textual', across the abyss or chasm of the fiction of the text and the fiction of the *hors-texte*, or, in other words, the acceptance of the (problematic) modalities of what is commonly called 'autobiography'.[21]

Let us put aside for the moment the question of Horace's contribution. There is still the problem posed by the poem itself. The poem, as textual machine, makes an offering of wine. The wine stands metaphorically for the poem. The offering of wine does not merely re-present the gifting of the poem to Maecenas, however, but constitutes it as an originally metaphorical present.[22] There is no literal moment of the poem's presentation, to which this metaphor refers. The poem's gifting is never directly (a) present. It is as its act, and requires passing through a figural detour that never quite says what it means, and that could always not mean what it says. Beyond the gift of the poem itself, however, there is still the perhaps even more critical conferral of fame that it bestows. The gift of the poem (wine) to Maecenas occurs on the condition that, through its iterability, it propagate his name by being read (drunk) by others. In this way, what it grants Maecenas is not simply a 'draught' of wine, but his own indefinite consumability through the public's imbibing of the odes.

In the terms of speech-act theory, we could speak of the perlocutionary attainment of the gift of fame, in opposition to the illocutionary presentation of the wine (poem) that the poem's speaker effects. Indeed, while the gift of the wine and (metaphorically) the poem occurs through an illocutionary act (the announcement that *you* will drink the wine [*potabis*]), the locutionary inscription of Maecenas's name would already stand as perpetuating his fame without any further dedication of wine whatsoever, and would thus constitute a 'gift' of sorts through its perlocutionary, honorific effects – although not necessarily a gift of 'the poem'. As to the alleged gift of the poem (wine), then, there is no separation between *what* it gives and the *act* of giving it. In the case of the ode – or any ode, for that matter – the 'making show' of the gift *is* the gift, for there is never any outside, or literally present, present. (In this sense, the thing given is the performance of a gift, and thus the performative is the constative, and the constative the performative, as Derrida has pointed out concerning other poetic effects.[23]) Yet all this begs the question: what does 'give' mean here? Is it possible 'to give' a poem? And what, after all, is 'a poem'? As these four lines of Horace's ode demonstrate, in the case of a poem-gift, it is difficult, and perhaps impossible, to say exactly what one 'gives', either intentionally or otherwise. And yet such acts of donation constitute a significant element both of patronal structures and of poetic self-identification.

Perhaps, even before it is a matter of give-and-take, at stake in 'voicings' such as these is the basic establishment of poetic subjectivity, such that a 'give-and-take' might be possible in the first place. In other words, at stake in every 'gift of poetry' would not be so much *a gift* as the *capacity to give*, which the poematic address performs. To ask whether a gift was in fact given, or whether a poem participates in patronage or not, would in this sense be to miss the point. As Jonathan Culler puts it, concerning the traditional role of address in lyric:

> If we think of what the vocative represents in this process, we can see why apostrophe should be embarrassing. It is the pure embodiment of poetic pretension: of the subject's claim that in his verse he is not merely an empirical poet, a writer of verse, but the embodiment of poetic tradition and of the spirit of poesy. Apostrophe is perhaps always an indirect invocation of the muse. Devoid of semantic reference, the O of apostrophe refers to other apostrophes and thus to the lineage and conventions of sublime poetry.[24]

Apostrophes, such as Horace's, but also, by extension, the dedicatory addresses of works of all kinds, perform the (embarrassing) embodiment of a 'giver', as such, thereby allowing for the possibility of both failure *and* success, as well as the basic difference between gift *and* non-gift, in the first place. And this is why, for example for Claudia Rankine, speaking of Celan, 'the poem was no different from a handshake':

> *I cannot see any basic difference between a handshake and a poem* – is how Rosemary Waldrop translated his German. The handshake is our decided ritual of both asserting (I am here) and handing over (here) a self to another. Hence the poem is that – Here. I am here. This conflation of the solidity of presence with the offering of this same presence perhaps has everything to do with being alive.[25]

Before every give-and-take there is, at the heart of the poem, the conflation of presence with the offering of that presence. And this gift of the poem, Rankine tells us, has everything to do with the experience of being alive.

During the Renaissance, the newly printed poem or book of verse was frequently projected as a 'gift' by way of dedicatory epistles, the advent of which introduced into the work for the first time a formal divide between dedication and text.[26] Such inscriptions granted the work a mode of address and circulation that, in theory, distanced it from the processes of capitalist commodification. In practice, however, the work often participated in both of these modes simultaneously, being 'gifted' to a patron while it was marketed and sold by a publisher.[27] The continuation, or afterlife, of the poetry-gift configuration within the formalised space of the poetic dedication both confronted and resisted the new-found economic role of the work in nascent capitalism, and dedicatory epistles, preceding works of lyric poetry – alongside works of nearly all genres – formalised within the technology of the book a site of recognition and donation.[28] There are countless examples of such dedications, which were often written proleptically to prospective patrons so as to solicit the promise of future favours or money.[29] Variations on this motif include common dedications in prose as well as entire sonnet sequences, such as Spenser's dedicatory poems to the *Faerie Queene*. Here, as in other sixteenth-century works, one sees both gift modalities operative simultaneously, with the muse serving as poetic source – 'Most Noble Lord the pillar of my life,/ And Patrone of my Muses pupillage' (ll.1–2) – for a work that is in turn gifted to a worthy patron – 'Vouchsafe in worth this small guift to receaue,/ Which in your noble hands for pledge I leaue,/ Of all the rest, that I am tyde t'account' (ll.8–10).[30] As Dustin Griffin has shown with respect to the seventeenth and eighteenth centuries, authors exploited every variation permitted by the structure of the dedicatory inscription, be it like Dryden, in order to seek innovative ways to flatter prospective patrons, or like Pope, so as to resist the constraints patronage had imposed upon them.[31] It is thus that within this space one may find examples in which the patron is gratified as the true muse and author of the work, as well as those in which, conversely, he or she is stripped of all credit for its production.[32] Regardless of the particular tenor of any given response, however, as an institution, the space of dedication propagated the gift status of the poem and poetic work, which status made possible the refusals of recognition such as one finds in Pope and other authors dissatisfied with the economy of flattery.

As early as 1720s, the effects of a burgeoning print culture led to a deepening of the tension between notions of poetic vocation, on the one hand, and participation in literary markets, on the other. In Britain specifically, changes in copyright law, persistent population growth, expanding literacy and readership, shifts in the mode of valuation of commodities, and the perception, if not the fact, of patronage's declining influence all contributed to what, perhaps most famously in Wordsworth's case, but to some extent for all of the major and minor poets of the period, became a conflict internal to poetic production itself, newly defined through the possibilities and perils of professionalisation.[33] Whether figured as the intonation of a 'strange speech', as Susan Eilenberg has diagnosed the impact of literary property on the marketed text's new voice, or as the self-imposed alienation of a novel 'Literary writing', now cut off from economic value, as Mary Poovey traces the nineteenth-century fracturing of credit genres, the experience of poetic publishing became one of visible estrangement.[34] As Keats put it, in his dedication to Leigh Hunt of *Poems* (1817):

> Glory and loveliness have passed away;
>   For if we wander out in early morn,
>   No wreathed incense do we see upborne
> Into the east, to meet the smiling day:
> No crowd of nymphs soft voic'd and young, and gay,
>   In woven baskets bringing ears of corn,
>   Roses, and pinks, and violets, to adorn
> The shrine of Flora in her early May.
> But there are left delights as high as these,
>   And I shall ever bless my destiny,
> That in a time, when under pleasant trees
>   Pan is no longer sought, I feel a free
> A leafy luxury, seeing I could please
>   With these poor offerings, a man like thee.[35]

For Keats, it is not only possible, but also necessary to view the work of poetry through an at least double register, being as its circulation is at least double. It is, at once, an 'offering' to the friend and an object 'poor' in value. Indeed, it is just its relative poverty, as a commodity, that turns it into a 'leafy luxury', for, as Bataille might have pointed out, it is precisely the disparity between the investment poems represent for their authors and the profit that they yield that turns them into a social form of expenditure, or 'sacrifice', which is, according to him, the true meaning of 'luxury'.[36] A broadening of print publishing thus heightens the tension between the perception of poetic essence and the work's material circulation in a world in which 'glory and loveliness have passed away'.

To ask whether poetry could be given – to the poet, by the poet, as the poem, or from the poem – was thus to ask whether it was still possible to locate continuity not only among poetry's various and fragmented nineteenth-century determinations – as market commodity, religious vocation, inspired vision, or vessel of beauty – but also between these determinations and those of the poetic tradition at large. Moreover, as a hybrid form that allowed for the circulation of debt, goods, and services, yet without the social or legal constraints associated with modern commercial concepts such as economic individualism and the freedom of contract, gifts and instrumental gift giving supplied an integral component of nineteenth-century economic life, in general.[37] In this way, as Margot C. Finn has demonstrated, gift exchange made possible greater participation within market economies by agents who might otherwise be excluded from them, on the grounds of class and gender. Frequently allowing for greater flexibility than the modernising market system, whose tenets were still often met by resistance, and offering neither the same punitive threat nor venal appearance as did civil contracts, gifts, endowments, and loans could be both more reliable and more palatable for Romantic-period authors than monetary-based commercial transactions. To choose to give rather than to sell poetry could therefore also have been an expeditious means of negotiating a growing, but still highly variable, market economy.

One can trace at least two further associations of gift giving, around 1800, with significance for the literary context, and for poetry in particular. First and foremost, travel narratives, based in colonial and mercantile exploration, had by this time supplied extensive imagery of gift exchange in what were perceived to be 'primitive', pre-commercial societies encountered across the South Seas. Jonathan Lamb explains how these practices were entered into by European military explorers such as Cook and Bougainville, and perceived, particularly by the former, as a significant threat to his Lockean sense of private property.[38] Around the same time, in the *Groundwork for the Metaphysics of Morals*, Kant mobilises a Eurocentric view of these peoples when he asks whether one has a duty to cultivate one's 'natural gifts', or if it is permissible to let them lie dormant and merely 'to seek pleasure' instead. The ideal image of the pleasure-seeking, naturally gifted 'system of nature' is there supplied by these very same South Sea Islanders, whose wasted gifts are opposed by Kant to the 'culture' and 'reason' of a West that, precisely, works to put these givens *to work*:

> A third finds in himself a talent which with the help of some culture might make him a useful human being in many respects . . . He asks, however, whether his maxim of neglect of his natural gifts, besides agreeing with his inclination to indulgence, agrees also with what is called duty. He sees then that a system of nature could indeed subsist with such a universal law, although human beings (like the South Sea islanders) should let their talents rust and resolve to devote their lives merely to idleness, amusement, and propagation of their species – in a word, to enjoyment.[39]

One thus finds that the very terms, such as pleasure and leisure, that Keats and later Baudelaire would identify with poetic experience *par excellence* are, in the eyes of earlier Enlightenment writers, directly associated with the so-called 'natural' gift economies of peoples whose riches are so abundant as to permit their squandering. For authors as varied as Keats, Thoreau, and Baudelaire, the allure of the gift of poetry could thus not be dissociated from the dream of returning to pre-capitalist modes of production and exchange, and what their images still held of natural purity.

At the same time, within Great Britain, but also in France, the question of charity, the struggle with Poor Laws, numerous philanthropic efforts, and the growing visibility of rural and urban poverty (*la misère*) contributed to more and more frequent associations between poetic praxis and mendicancy, vagrancy, and pauperism.[40] For an author such as Blake, who found the idea of charity to be fraught, the problem of altruistic donation and the possibility of reconciling it with the free gift, gift exchange, and social obligation persisted throughout his career as writer and printmaker.[41] For Wordsworth, it would present a constant and explicit concern. In 1798, for example, he exhorted 'Statesmen!', in 'The Old Cumberland Beggar', not to 'deem . . . this man useless' (l.67).[42] Then later, when he returned some forty-five years after to reflect on the poem, he condemned 'the political economists' for their 'war upon mendicity in all its forms, and by implication, if not directly, on Almsgiving also'.[43] As Alexander Dick has pointed out, 'given Wordsworth's tendency to trope himself as a "wanderer," as an "idler," as a vagabond', in appealing to the political economists to 'grant his ambling vagrant a function . . . Wordsworth may well have been speaking of himself'.[44] Acts of self-identification such as these – as well as their correlate, in acts of self-distancing – abound in nineteenth-century poetry, with notable figures of gleaners and *chiffonniers* populating not only Wordsworth's writings, but also those of Clare, Baudelaire, and Mallarmé.[45]

Such associations of gift-giving, be it with pre-modern forms of exchange, with Christian beneficence, or with divine vocation, thus hung over Romantic and post-Romantic writings. Moreover, for nineteenth-century male poets in particular, whose pretensions to creative autonomy often contributed to an open – though not always private – disdain for the literary marketplace and the 'popular' reading public, to give and receive gifts of verse, loans, grants, subscriptions, and publishing sponsorships was commonly viewed as being greatly preferable to the sale of poems.[46] This is to say neither that the relay of presents was itself without tension – be it in the realm of publishing or within poetic figurations of alms-giving – nor that the unsavoury aspects of such commercial economies were themselves sufficient to prevent male poets from participating in them, or from profiting handsomely from them, as Byron and Scott certainly did. Rather, it is to indicate how a general preference, at least for the appearance of giving, impacted male poets in ways that it did not always impact female ones.[47]

The example of the short-lived 'gift-book', popular between 1825 and 1860, is in this respect a case in point, as well as evidence of the misogyny often implicit in authorial views of publishing.[48] Ironically named, as these annuals were often aggressively marketed to nineteenth-century audiences as ornate, luxury commodities, gift-books provoked great ambivalence in male authors such as Wordsworth, Charles Lamb, and Alfred Tennyson, who could bring themselves neither to refuse the lucrative fees that they offered, nor ever to embrace the form fully. One thus frequently finds participation in the annuals *alongside* public and private condemnation of them, as Kathryn Ledbetter and Laura Mandell show, particularly among male poets uncomfortable either with the transactional nature of their involvement or with the volumes' common associations as the marketplace of women writers and readers.[49]

Just, then, as exchanges between patron and client had always been composed of multiple, fluid, and frequently hybrid forms of transactions – from official, state-given sinecures, such as Wordsworth was awarded in 1813, to gifts of property from private patrons, such as Horace received from Maecenas, to recommendations to booksellers, such as was common in Great Britain throughout the eighteenth century – so too were practices of nineteenth-century poetic gift exchange, in their pretensions to sociality, generosity, and flexibility, both highly varied in their form and felt to be more fitting to the poetic vocation than openly commercial dealings.[50] For authors such as Wordsworth, De Quincey, Blake, Barbauld, Keats, Clare, and Landon, though their resistance to participation in the market was certainly not uniform, nor even consistent, over the course of their careers, nevertheless, as well as an often efficacious mode of negotiating print culture, the gift frequently held out the promise of reconciling frictions between personal poetic motives and material economic realities.[51] To put the latter point, once again, in the words of Keats, as he expresses this hope in a well-known letter on poetry, communal labour, and the beehive to John Reynolds:

> But let us open our leaves like a flower, and be passive and receptive; budding patiently under the eye of Apollo and taking hints from every noble insect that favours us with a visit—Sap will be given us for meat, and dew for drink.[52]

In a perfectly emblematic image of what Derrida diagnosed as the logic of economimesis, Keats here depicts the heliotropic passage of Apollo's gift of light as it is freely bestowed upon the poet-flower and seamlessly synthesised into 'sap' and 'dew'. Noticeably absent from this scene are the well-known traumas and turmoil that so marked Keats's own life in money matters, be it that of his struggle to sell or his difficulty balancing all of the credits and debits between family, associates, and friends.[53] The image is, in the words of Richard Klein, paraphrasing Derrida's own synopsis of Kant's ideal economy of fine art, that of 'an immaculate commerce, one which allows a certain profit to be made without falling into the venality of what Mauss calls the mechanical cruelty of money exchange'.[54] It is a way of talking about, and even of conceptualising, poetic labour that, alongside the complex interplay of the epistolary form itself,[55] the writing of dedications, the soliciting of literary subscriptions, the manuscript exchange of poems, the bestowal of small and large donations, the imparting of loans both meant and not meant to be repaid, and the development of new conceptions of giving grounded in disinterest,[56] collectively contributed to the Romantic literary scene and its participation in, reflection on, and propagation of dreams of poetic gift economies that might survive the fading flame of patronage and the harsh realities of 'the selfish and calculating principle', now feared to be at work in an Age of Gold.[57]

In distinction to the gift of song to poet that establishes the inhuman, sacred character of poetry for Homer, the poet's gifts of verse to reader and patron speak to a different set of political, social, and economic conditions. While the former figures address the relation of poetry as a foreign missive to humanity as a whole, the latter intervene in the passage of this missive from poet to reader, and thus in the ethical, economic, political, and social bonds between producer and consumer. Within this context, the poet's 'gifts' or 'offerings' of verse to patron, reader, and dedicatee serve to establish the work as an object outside the relays of mere monetary, market, or commodity exchange, and thus as a thing apart. As others have observed, the adoption of a language of the gift to describe poetic circulation among individuals is bound to the necessity of keeping a supposedly divine form elevated above a mundane economic sphere. Natalie Zemon Davis, for example, has argued that during the Renaissance the reliance of the book trade on patronage had directly to do with the medieval period's belief that knowledge was a gift of the gods, and that it was therefore not permitted to be bought and sold.[58] Barbara K. Gold argues for a similar taboo for Greco-Roman writers, albeit with a different socio-cultural basis.[59] Although the precise nature of the poem-present undergoes significant transformations – and innovations – as the conditions of literary production shift with each historical and socio-cultural–economic milieu, as Bourdieu has illustrated, the language and practice of the gift may always serve as an alibi for those wishing to partake of economic transactions without wanting to admit as much.[60] The discourse and practice of patronage, in sum, might always offer the possibility of ontologically distancing the patronised work from mere economic labour. By articulating the work's passage through the human sphere by way of 'presents' and 'gifts', rather than 'debits' and 'credits', it upholds the work's pretensions to a certain distinction, whether that be understood as divinity or simply gentility.

The structures of patronage, it should be noted, are in no way exclusive to poetry; nor have they ever been. Much as discourses of inspiration and genius mark poetic practice for classical and modern writers without, however, being exclusive to the domain of poetry, so too are the patronage structures and practices of dedication that turn works of verse into gifts shared by texts written across genres.[61] In the Renaissance, one would dedicate religious, historical, and scientific texts alongside literary ones, just as Homer might speak of one gifted with strength, or skill in painting. It is neither the exclusivity of these tropes to the field of poetry that lends them their significance; nor is it, for that matter, the fact of the poetic work's participation within actual, 'material' gift exchanges, such as Augustan-age invitation poems, Renaissance New Year's poetic dedications, or Romantic-era assistance with publishers. Rather, what makes an understanding of these figures critical to the study of poetry is the internalisation of these apparently 'contingent', 'historical', or 'inessential' forms *as essential*, within poetic discourse itself.

The formalisation of the site of dedication within works of verse is just one way that the poetic text does this by overwriting itself as a gift in print culture,[62] for as well as always potentially marking participation in 'actual' gift exchanges, the space of dedication, as an institution, marks a site of poetic self-inscription as gift, where the work both posits itself as a present and is able to reflect on this status.⁶³ This reflection on the gift-status of the poem may take negative or positive form. What makes Pindar's openly commercial reflections on the muse remarkable for his age, and partially obscene, is the fact that they run counter to this poetic commonplace, just as Baudelaire's wistful meditations on his muse's exhibiting of her charms, though a sign of the times, is seen as unbefitting to the poetic vocation precisely because it reveals its mercenary character.⁶⁴ In each instance, whether or not poetic patronage crosses over into the realm of artistic prostitution (or market exchange), or in classical terms, whether *praise* becomes *flattery*, is ultimately less important than the conception of the 'work' that makes the sustaining of such a difference at once vital and impossible to maintain. Instances of positive affirmations, or explicit internalisations of the gift within poetic discourse, also abound of course. Invitation poems like Horace's and dedicatory inscriptions such as Spenser's actively both *present* the poetic work as a gift and *represent* it as such. And even after the cordoning off of the dedication from the body of the text, thematisations and allegories of the work as gift (in Bowditch's terminology, as a 'theme') continue to make their way into the body of the poetic text, and potentially even to bear 'weight'. This is the case both for Milton, at the opening of *Paradise Lost*, calling forth his Muse to lend him support, so that he 'may assert Eternal Providence/ And justify the ways of God to men' (ll.23–6), and for Wordsworth, at the conclusion of *The Prelude*, imagining himself and Coleridge as 'Prophets of Nature' (1.442) working toward the redemption of humankind. Though no earthly compensation can likely be expected for such gestures, in each case the assertion of the text as divine and of the author as priest transforms the latter into benevolent benefactor and the former into celestial offering. Who could say with certainty that such gifts have not been reciprocated?⁶⁵

NOTES

1. Notices printed on the final page of Giovanni Andrea dell'Anguillara, 'Book 1 of Virgil's *Aeneid*', quoted in Craig Kallendorf, 'In Search of a Patron: Anguillara's Vernacular Virgil and the Print Culture of Renaissance Italy', in *The Papers of the Bibliographical Society of America*, 91 (September 1997): 294–326; 299.
2. *The Dream of the Poem: Hebrew Poetry from Muslim and Christian Spain 950–1492*, ed. and trans. Peter Cole (Princeton, NJ: Princeton University Press, 2007), 36.
3. *Emily Dickinson's Poems: As She Preserved Them*, ed. Cristanne Miller (Cambridge, MA: Harvard University Press, 2016), 124.

4. John Heywood, 'A Praise of his Lady', in *The Book of Elizabethan Verse*, ed. William Stanley Braithwaite (Boston: Herbert B. Turner & Co., 1907), 107. Joachim du Bellay, *La Défense et illustration de la langue françoise suivie de L'Olive et quelques autres œuvres poétiques, 1* (Paris: Revue de la Renaissance, 1903), 95. W. H. Auden, 'In Memory of W. B. Yeats', in *Collected Poems*, ed. Edward Mendelson (New York: Modern Library, 1976), 246.
5. Such figures appear at least as early as Pindar. See, for example, 'Olympian 7': 'As when a man takes from his rich hand a bowl foaming inside with dew of the vine and presents it to his young son-in-law with a toast from one home to another . . . so I too, by sending the poured nectar, gift of the Muses and sweet fruit of the mind, to men who win prizes, gain the favor of victors at Olympia and Pytho' (*Olympian Odes*, ll.1–10; 121). See also 'Pythian 2'. On the offering of the poem as gift in antiquity, see Jesper Svenbro, 'La découpe du poème. Notes sur les origines sacrificielles de la poétique grecque', and Sperduti. On the divine circuit of poetic inspiration, homage, and fame in Sappho, see Franco Ferrari, *Sappho's Gift*, especially 60–4.
6. Lewis Hyde makes this observation for art in general in *The Gift*. 'A work of art', he writes, 'can survive without the market, but where there is no gift there is no art' (xvi). Yet while he makes it as a normative claim, arguing for the essentialness of the gift within art as such, my aim is to demonstrate how the Western concepts of 'art', and especially 'poetry', emerge out of an internalisation of the gift. Thus, I do not take it for granted that 'poetry' is anything except for a self-reflexive discourse. Whereas Hyde believes that where there is no gift, there can be no art, I read the systematic grafting of each of these concepts on to the other as symptomatic. In this sense, Hyde's *Gift* propagates a poetic ideology that we can trace at least as far back as Greek antiquity. It also denies the integral role that ambivalence plays within the gift's functioning.
7. The limit between the 'poetic' and 'non-poetic', as the following discussion shows, is not so easily determined. Yet it remains an important distinction, if only because the difficulty of its determining becomes essential to poetry's reflection on itself, its exchangeability, and its translatability, as well as its aesthetico-economic character in general.
8. On these variations, see Gold, *Literary Patronage*, 3, Bowditch, *Horace and the Gift Economy of Patronage*, 25, and Barbara Pavlock, 'Horace's Invitation Poems to Maecenas: Gifts to a Patron'.
9. Horace, *Satires. Epistles. The Art of Poetry*, 418–19.
10. Bowditch, *Horace*, 25, n.54.
11. Bowditch, *Horace*, 25, n.54.

12. As Gérard Genette points out in *Paratexts*, this difference is captured by the two French verbs *dédier* (to dedicate) and *dédicacer* (to autograph). Genette goes on to describe the difference as that between the 'material reality of a single copy' and the 'ideal reality of the work itself', which can only be 'symbolic' (117). Gérard Genette, *Paratexts: Thresholds of Interpretation*, trans. Jane E. Lewin (Cambridge: Cambridge University Press, 1997).
13. Although the history of dedicatory inscriptions does not radically alter this distinction, it is worth noting that, from antiquity to modernity, the delimitation between work and dedication becomes increasingly pronounced. Classical authors like Pindar have no recourse to 'paratextual' markers, such as title pages, formal prefaces, or prefatory dedicatory epistles. Although we read invocations of the Muses and addresses to patrons as metatextual and 'prefatory', the earliest traces of a formal distinction between text and dedication emerge in the sixteenth century (Cf. Genette, 118). The increasing formalisation of paratextual spaces surrounding the literary text is, among other things, connected to the development of the notion of the 'work', and thus the presumed necessity of establishing its inside and outside. Moreover, the presumption of the difference between *dédier* and *dédicacer* also assumes that there is a relative stability *between* printings of a work. Erasmus, however, was known to have written different dedications for different *printings* of the same work, further problematising the assumption of a simple inside (or outside) of 'the text'. On this history, see Jean Hoyoux, 'Les moyens d'existence d'Érasme', *Bibliothèque d'Humanisme et Renaissance* 5 (1944): 7–59; 42–3.
14. Such 'embeddings' may include dedications of works that are not mentioned explicitly in the text, but which are nevertheless of public knowledge and thus part of the work's 'context'.
15. William Shakespeare, sonnets 55 and 122, in *The Complete Sonnets and Poems: The Oxford Shakespeare* (Oxford: Oxford University Press, 2008), 491; 625.
16. See, for example, book 5 of Wordsworth's *Prelude*, 'Books', where he reflects on the possibility of the total destruction of every material trace, including the archive of poetry. See also Shelley's 'Ode to the West Wind', which implores the wind to 'Scatter . . . my words among mankind!' (ll.66–7), *Shelley's Poetry and Prose*, 301, Keats's 'When I have fears that I may cease to be', or Whitman's 'In Cabin'd Ships at Sea'. In the words of Allen Grossman, 'No age prior to this age was ever so fully endangered by precisely that eventuality which poetry always contemplates, namely, forgetfulness or oblivion' (11). *The Sighted Singer* (Baltimore: Johns Hopkins University Press, 1992).

17. With respect to these issues, Shakespeare's sonnets represent a masterful exploration of all of the poem's ambivalences. On the gift in the sonnets, see Scott, *Selfish Gifts*, Heal, *The Power of Gifts*, and Sean Lawrence, *Forgiving the Gift: The Philosophy of Generosity in Shakespeare and Marlowe*.
18. Beyond 1.20, the entirety of the first three books of the *Odes* is dedicated to Maecenas, in recognition of this gift and his support generally. On Ode 1.20, see Pavlock.
19. The translation is Commager's (325).
20. See, in particular, Commager, who makes this case (324–6).
21. For a succinct analysis of the problems implicit in autobiography, see Paul de Man, 'Autobiography as De-facement', in *The Rhetoric of Romanticism* (New York: Columbia University Press, 1984), 67–82.
22. For a slightly less coercive variation on this theme, see Ode 3.29, also written to Maecenas. There the wine is merely 'for you [tibi]' (1), rather than forced down his throat, so to speak, as it is here.
23. See, in particular, 'Psyche: Inventions of the Other'.
24. Jonathan Culler, 'Apostrophe', in *The Pursuit of Signs: Semiotics, Literature, Deconstruction*, (London: Routledge, 1981), 149–71; 158. For a more developed version of this argument, see his *Theory of the Lyric*.
25. Claudia Rankine, *Don't Let Me Be Lonely: An American Lyric* (New York: Penguin, 2004), 130.
26. See Genette (118) on the history of this development. Up until the end of the eighteenth century, 'dedication' and 'dedicatory epistle' were synonymous terms (123).
27. On the paradoxes of the early modern publishing industry, see Arthur F. Marotti, 'Patronage, Poetry, and Print' and 'Shakespeare's Sonnets as Literary Property', as well as Dustin Griffin, 'The Beginnings of Modern Authorship: Milton and Dryden'.
28. On the role of the gift in the confrontation with capitalism, see Scott, *Selfish Gifts*, as well as Davis, *The Gift in Sixteenth-Century France*.
29. Though rare, there are even some instances in which virtually all the editions of a print run were distributed as gifts by their author, for this purpose of solicitation. Such was evidently the case for Giovanni Andrea dell'Anguillara's translation of the first book of Virgil's *Aeneid*, in 1564 in Padua. On the history of Anguillara's 'presentation copies', see Kallendorf, 'In Search of a Patron'.
30. Edmund Spenser, 'To the Lord Grey of Wilton', in *The Faerie Queene*, eds Thomas P. Roche, Jr and C. Patrick O'Donnell, Jr (New York: Penguin, 1978), 29.
31. See Pope's 1713 *Guardian* essay 'On Dedications' for his most extensive comments on the form, what he calls 'this prostitution of praise' (592), in

English Prose Selections, 3, ed. Henry Craik (New York: Macmillan and Co., 1894). He concludes the essay with a mock dedication entitled 'The Author to Himself'. See Griffin's entire chapter on it in *Literary Patronage in England, 1650–1800* (Cambridge: Cambridge University Press, 1996), 123–54.

32. See *Literary Patronage*, 131–2. Patricia Fumerton, in 'Exchanging Gifts: Elizabethan Currency of Children and Poetry', *ELH* 53.2 (1986): 241–78, offers an explanation of the phenomenon of identifying the patron with the muse or true author of the work: 'Because the patron on accepting the child gift becomes a kind of foster parent, and because givers in a sense become their gifts, the giving of dedications often conflates the "child" poem with Muse and poet. Samuel Daniel thus calls Lord Pembroke, "the fosterer of mee and my *Muse*," and Robert Greene, dedicating *Francescos Fortunes* (1590) to Thomas Burnaby in recompense for his "many friendly, nay fatherly fauours," signs his dedication, "Your Worships adopted sonne in all humble dutie to command"' (267).

33. On the expansion of English literacy, see Richard D. Atlick, *The English Common Reader: A Social History of the Mass Reading Public, 1800–1900*. On commodification, print culture, and the literary profession, see especially David Simpson, *Wordsworth, Commodification, and Social Concerns*, and Thomas Pfau, *Wordsworth's Profession*. The shift from a notion of value calculated in terms of labour time and use to one based in what Marx would call 'exchange value' is famously initiated by Adam Smith in his *Wealth of Nations* (1776). On changes in the patronage system, and the perception that it was newly in decline, see Griffin, *Literary Patronage in England*, 1–12. Scott Hess dates the print market's overtaking of patronage and coterie manuscript circulation to the 1720s in *Authoring the Self: Self-Representation, Authorship, and the Print Market in British Poetry from Pope through Wordsworth*. On the progress of literary professionalisation in nineteenth-century America, see Michael T. Gilmore, *American Romanticism and the Marketplace* (Chicago: University of Chicago Press, 1985). Gilmore dates the viability of becoming a professional writer in America to the 1820s.

34. On the effects of copyright law on Wordsworth and Coleridge, see Susan Eilenberg, *Strange Power of Speech: Wordsworth, Coleridge & Literary Possession*. On print culture and figures of audience, see Hess, Michelle Levy, *Family Authorship and Romantic Print Culture*, and Lucy Newlyn, *Reading, Writing, and Romanticism*. On the eighteenth-century schism among Literary or imaginative writing, economic, and monetary genres, see Poovey. Though I do not follow Poovey in her conclusions – and much of this book can be read, precisely, as attempting to problematise both the 'continuity' she locates prior to the Romantics and the sense of 'prestige'

that she laments Literary genres have lost in their wake – her vast study is extremely helpful in diagnosing the tension that runs through the period. Whereas she presents a return to the pre-Romantic continuity of value-mediating genres as preferable, I argue that her oversimplification of the Romantics precisely misses what is *irresolvable* in the conflicts that they bring to the fore, especially in figures of the poetic gift. For a classic articulation of the rise of *art as art* in Europe, or art as expression of Romantic autonomy, see Bourdieu, *The Field of Cultural Production*, 29–73.

35. 'Dedication. To Leigh Hunt, Esq.', from *Poems* (1817) in *Keats's Poetry and Prose*, ed. Jeffrey N. Cox (New York: W. W. Norton, 2008), 20.
36. On poetry, sacrifice, and luxury, see 'The Notion of Expenditure', in *The Bataille Reader*, 167–81.
37. Margot C. Finn, *The Character of Credit: Personal Debt in English Culture, 1740–1914* (Cambridge: Cambridge University Press, 2003), 2.
38. See Jonathan Lamb, *Preserving the Self in the South Seas, 1680–1840* (Chicago: University of Chicago Press, 2001), 132–62, and Simpson, *Wordsworth, Commodification, and Social Concern*, 54–82.
39. Immanuel Kant, *Groundwork for the Metaphysics of Morals*, ed. Lara Denis, trans. Thomas K. Abbott (Ontario: Broadview Press, 2005), 82.
40. On charity, alms-giving, and vagrancy in Wordsworth and Rousseau, see Celeste Langan, *Romantic Vagrancy*. On sympathy and the ethics of giving, see Adam Potkay, *Wordsworth's Ethics*, and Robert Mitchell, *Sympathy and the State in the Romantic Era*. On poverty, sympathy, and poetry, see David Simpson, *Wordsworth, Commodification, and Social Concern*, as well as his *Wordsworth's Historical Imagination*. On 'The Old Cumberland Beggar' specifically, see Dick, 'Poverty, Charity, Poetry: The Unproductive Labors of "The Old Cumberland Beggar"', *Studies in Romanticism* 39.3 (Fall 2000): 365–96. Finally, on the gift, poverty, and giving in nineteenth-century France, and its importance for the poetry of the period, see Berger, *Scènes d'aumône*.
41. Sarah Haggarty, *Blake's Gifts: Poetry and the Politics of Exchange* (Cambridge: Cambridge University Press, 2010), 84. In her chapter on 'Charity' in Blake, Haggarty demonstrates the tension, not only within Blake's writings on charity, but also within Derrida's, notably between *Given Time* and *The Gift of Death*. 'What we're again faced with', Haggarty writes, 'whether Derrida avows it or no, is a choice between genealogies' (207n.14). See 'Charity', 84–110.
42. *William Wordsworth: The Major Works*, ed. Stephen Gill (Oxford: Oxford University Press, 2008), 51.
43. William Wordsworth, *Lyrical Ballads, and Other Poems, 1797–1800*, eds James Butler and Karen Green (Ithaca, NY: Cornell University Press, 1992), 393.

44. Dick, 'Poverty, Charity, Poetry', 365.
45. On this, as well as Berger, see Patrick Greaney, *Untimely Beggar*.
46. On the position of the Cockney School, who viewed economic incentives as largely antithetical to poetic independence, see Jeffrey N. Cox, *Poetry and Politics in the Cockney School*. For Wordsworth's various and frequently contradictory positions, see Chapter 3 below.
47. For a well-known refusal of the gifts of patronage, see Griffin's discussion of Swift in *Literary Patronage in England*, 99–122. Some critics have tried to extend the conventional history of the Romantic opposition to the market, noting in particular the resemblances between Wordsworth and Pope. On this relation, see Hess and Robert J. Griffin, *Wordsworth's Pope*, 1–24.
48. As much recent work has shown, the politics of nineteenth-century gift poetics often fell along gendered lines, with the distinction between disinterested, 'high' poetic production and interested, 'low' mass-market publishing, corresponding to the distinction between 'poet' and 'poetess', or the perception of male autonomy and corresponding female dependence (on the reading public). On the problematic gendering of the gift and poet, see especially Anne K. Mellor, 'The Female Poet and the Poetess: Two Traditions of British Women's Poetry, 1780–1830', and *Women's Poetry: Late Romantic to Late Victorian: Gender and Genre, 1830–1900*, eds Isobel Armstrong and Virginia Blain.
49. On the gender of the gift-book, see Kathryn Ledbetter, 'Lucrative Requests: British Authors and Gift Book Editors', and Laura Mandell, 'Felicia Hemans and the Gift-Book Aesthetic'. As the work of Mandell and Rappoport has shown, Barbauld, Hemans, and Landon often subverted the opposition between gift and commodity in different ways from their male counterparts, frequently by working with market forces rather than rejecting them. On the gift in Landon, see Jill Rappoport, 'Buyer Beware: The Gift Poetics of Letitia Elizabeth Landon', as well as her *Giving Women: Alliance and Exchange in Victorian Culture*. On Hemans, see Mandell. For broader studies of the gift and gender in the long nineteenth century, see also Linda Zionkowski, *Women and Gift Exchange in Eighteenth-Century Fiction*, Daniela Garofalo, *Women, Love, and Commodity Culture in British Romanticism*, and Judith Still, *Feminine Economies: Thinking Against the Market in the Enlightenment and the Late Twentieth Century*.
50. For an excellent account of the history of patronage in England, see Griffin, *Literary Patronage in England, 1650–1800*. On patronage of the so-called 'natural poet' in the eighteenth century, see Betty Rizzo, 'The Patron as Poet Maker: The Politics of Benefaction'.

51. For other accounts of the gift in nineteenth-century literature, see Simon Jarvis, *Wordsworth's Philosophic Song* and 'Wordsworth's Gifts of Feeling', and Rzepka, *Sacramental Commodities* and *Selected Studies*. Though it precedes much of the contemporary critical reception of gift theory, Harold Bloom's *The Visionary Company* remains an excellent source on the role of gift poetics in Romanticism. For the gift within the Romantic discourse of hospitality, see Peter Melville, *Romantic Hospitality and the Resistance to Accommodation*. On Keats in particular, see Ronald A. Sharp, 'Keats and the Spiritual Economies of Gift Exchange', as well as Rowlinson, *Real Money and Romanticism*, 100–55. On the gift in Barbauld, see Angela Keane, 'The Market, the Public and the Female Author: Anna Laetitia Barbauld's Gift Economy', and Susan Rosenbaum, '"A Thing Unknown, without a Name": Anna Laetitia Barbauld and the Illegible Signature Author(s)'. On Shelley, see Nicholas Royle, 'Poetry Break', in *Jacques Derrida*, 129–42. Finally, on the gift in nineteenth-century America, see Hildegard Hoeller, *From Gift to Commodity: Capitalism and Sacrifice in Nineteenth-Century American Fiction*.
52. 19 February 1818, 'To J. H. Reynolds', *The Letters of John Keats: 1814–1821: Volume I, 1814–1818*, ed. Hyder Edward Rollins (Cambridge: Cambridge University Press, 2011), 232.
53. On Keats's money troubles and their complications for his poetry, see Robert Gitting, *The Keats Inheritance*, Cox, 187–225, Marjorie Levinson, *Keats's Life of Allegory*, and Rowlinson, 100–55.
54. Klein, 'Kant's Sunshine', 29.
55. On the letter as gift, see Alexander Regier, *Fracture and Fragmentation in British Romanticism* (Cambridge: Cambridge University Press, 2010), 119–40, as well as Michael Wetzel, 'Liebesgaben: Streifzüge des literarischen Eros', in *Ethik der Gabe: Denken nach Jacques Derrida*, eds. Michael Wetzel and Jean-Michel Rabaté (Berlin: Akademie Verlag, 1993), 223–47.
56. On the eighteenth-century origins of 'disinterest', and the polarisation of the disinterested gift away from interested exchange, see Jarvis, 'The Gift in Theory'. For a longer chronology of this development, see Jonathan Parry, 'The Gift, the Indian Gift and the "Indian Gift"', *Man* 21.3 (1986), 453–73, and Karl Polanyi, *The Great Transformation*. Shershow argues that Reformation discourse can itself be understood 'as a kind of obsessive attempt to imagine the absolute Gift' (149), and Scott contends that in the Elizabethan age, 'culturally, the gift conjured up an ideal not dissimilar to Derrida's notion of a "pure gift", yet in practice a proper gift relationship was paradoxically distinguished by timely and appropriate reciprocation' (18). The specificity of disinterest within this chronology, for Jarvis, would contribute to a further fracturing of the gift's double and contradictory tendency.

57. Shelley, 'A Defence of Poetry', *Shelley's Poetry and Prose*, 531. On the problem of the Golden Age for Romanticism, see especially M. H. Abrams, *Natural Supernaturalism*. On the opposition between the Golden Age and Age of Gold, in Keats, see K. K. Ruthven, 'Keats and "Dea Moneta"'.
58. Davis, *The Gift in Sixteenth-Century France*, 71.
59. See Gold, *Literary Patronage*, 1–10. She contends that this taboo was much greater for Roman writers than for Greeks such as Pindar, who at times spoke of payment in 'blatant terms' (8), albeit still within the parameters of gift exchange.
60. See especially his *Outline of a Theory of Practice*.
61. Socrates, for example, in the *Phaedrus*, includes prophecy, the art of purification by mysteries, and love, as so many inspired modes alongside poetic inspiration.
62. For another such inscription, or overwriting, see the introduction to *The Poet's Offering for 1850*, ed. Sarah Josepha Hale (Philadelphia: Grigg, Elliot, & Co., 1850), which reads: 'The publishers are resolved to try the experiment of giving a PERENNIAL for the Holydays – a book that will not lose its value when the season of gifts is over. We trust the plan will succeed – that The Poet's Offering will be warmly welcomed' (3). The irony of *marketing* the book of verse *as offering* requires no further comment.
63. Hence the importance of dedications to abstractions, fictions, and the memory of the deceased. See especially Genette and Griffin on these variations within the literary dedication.
64. See Pindar's 'Isthmian 2', where he laments the loss of poetry's previous freedom and the current state of the Muse's prostituted verse (ll.1–10), as well as 'Pythian 11', on the Muse's hiring of her voice for silver (ll.41–5). In *Literary Patronage*, Gold argues that although Pindar acknowledges the economic relations in which his verse is caught, he is always careful to maintain a necessary ambiguity (29–30). On this motif, see also Baudelaire's 'The Venal Muse', and Carson's *Economy of the Unlost*.
65. *Paradise Lost*, 4. Prelude, 482.

3

Patronage and Poetic Election in Wordsworth

Unthrifty loveliness, why dost thou spend
Upon thyself thy beauty's legacy?
Nature's bequest gives nothing, but doth lend,
And being frank she lends to those are free:
Then, beauteous niggard, why dost thou abuse
The bounteous largess given thee to give?
Profitless usurer, why dost thou use
So great a sum of sums yet canst not live?
For having traffic with thyself alone
Thou of thyself thy sweet self dost deceive.
Then how, when nature calls thee to be gone,
What acceptable audit canst thou leave?
  Thy unused beauty must be tombed with thee,
  Which usèd lives th'executor to be.

Shakespeare, *The Complete Sonnets*, 4[1]

This is my lot; for either still I find
Some imperfection in the chosen theme,
Or see of absolute accomplishment
Much wanting – so much wanting – in myself
That I recoil and droop, and seek repose
In indolence from vain perplexity,
Unprofitably travelling towards the grave,
Like a false steward who hath much received
And renders nothing back.

Wordsworth, *The Prelude (1805)*, (1:263–71)[2]

Perhaps the single greatest insight of Mauss's *Essai sur le don* is its discovery of the binding nature of the gift. One who receives is compelled to reciprocate in turn, and this bond that the gift bears as its burden engenders the circulation of goods constitutive of 'economics' in its most primordial form. The gift obliges, compels, and puts into debt and, in this sense, it supplies the unwritten origin of the contract.

To receive, then, is already a promise to reciprocate, or, in the words of Shakespeare, the gift *gives nothing, but doth lend*. Although Mauss makes use of this insight to theorise the origins of economy, as becomes clear in the sonnet, there is nothing distinctly 'economical' about the gift idiom, whose logic applies no less to the offerings of Nature than to those of human beings. Nature's bequest puts into debt to the precise extent that it distributes credit, yet the question of how to pay back such a grant remains an open one. For Wordsworth, just as for Shakespeare, it amounts to producing offspring of one kind or another, a counter-gift of life that survives, preserving the present for the future and paying untold dividends in exchange for Nature's generosity. Whether made to the Young Man or to the Poet, Nature's offerings must then eventually call forth an audit of the liberality of its beneficiary.

In the previous chapters, we saw how appeals to the gift function throughout the history of Western poetry, to the point of becoming determinative for it. Thus, we explored how this determination contributes to making poetry *poetry*: to grounding it conceptually, to separating it among the arts, and to elevating it among human forms of production. This was not to say – as Hyde does – that such gift figures ever actually reflect the conditions under which poetry is produced, or those through which it is disseminated. Rather, it was to contend *either* that these figures remain the ideals against which various fallen forms of verse are measured in their perceived aesthetic and economic declines, *or* that they become the rejected, yet ineliminable elements of so many poetic theorisations that can never quite wholly eradicate them. Poetry, insofar as it should not merely be prose, insofar as it concerns what one calls 'good poetry', insofar as it retains a trace of the divine, is not shared equally among members of humankind, or is not to be merely a matter of willed mastery, remains bound to the gift. This bond was visible both within the poetic work and in its critical reception alike, serving to distinguish it from mere mercantile goods, mundane works, and manufactured prose.

Turning now to Wordsworth, we will see how his writings take up each of the central elements of this tradition, only to reveal faults and fissures that have always haunted them. Wordsworth, we could say, radicalises the gift of poetry, and he does so by way of his very efforts to inherit it, as the self-proclaimed successor to Shakespeare and Milton. In his work, the question of the gift arises not simply as a concern with the poet's response to Nature's boon, but also as a worry over the very nature of Nature's gift, as it originally must have been bestowed on him. To raise the question of the gift in Wordsworth is for this reason to confront the problem of the poet's status as favoured heir, which is to say, his very status *as poet*, as well as the correlate transactions that this birthright engenders. For Wordsworth, whose concern with his place among the pantheon of English versifiers was a constant preoccupation, so much depended on the size of this endowment, his personal apportionment of poetic power as it was 'sown by Nature' (1:81) and then embraced by him.[3] It stands at the very centre of *The Prelude*, both as a recurring theme and as the aim, ultimately, with which the text was written. It played a formative role in his relationship with Coleridge, and it was considered the *sine qua non* of *The Recluse*, the great Philosophical Poem over which he obsessed for nearly forty years. And yet, to the precise extent that Wordsworth had been singularly favoured – or will have been such – so too did he become uniquely indebted. Nature's gifts, however intangible, obliged just like any other present. In each case, the questions of what, how, when, and how much to render haunted their donee.

As I shall show, Wordsworth's anxieties about what he was, or will have been given, and, consequently, what he should give back, betray a clear resemblance to Mauss's reflections on the gift and its essentially obliging character. One can and should, in reading Wordsworth, attend to this often explicit character of his autobiographical reflections, which affects his 'life' no less than his 'work' – indeed, which goes a long way in rendering 'life' and 'work' inextricable in the first place.[4]

At the same time, however, as soon as one attempts to calculate, in good Maussian fashion, the time between Wordsworth's presents, one encounters difficulties. It is never simply a matter for him of calculating the time between *reception* and *reciprocation*, or gift and counter-gift. In other words, it is never simply a matter for Wordsworth of taking the measure of Nature's boon and then comparing it to that of his proffered, published poems, so that he might at last be able to rest easy, knowing that whatever else one could accuse him of, one could never charge him with being a 'false steward'. The difficult, anxiety-producing problem that imposes itself on him, time and again, and that ultimately imprints a tiny, barely visible, perhaps even microscopic asterisk over everything he wrote, arises from the nature of Nature's gift itself, the foundation upon which all further structures, edifices, and facades should subsequently have been erected.

One cannot calculate the time between Wordsworth's presents without also reckoning with the deferred nature of this original endowment of 'genius'.[5] Or, to put it yet more concretely, as long as one wishes to follow the logic that Wordsworth's text itself constructs, the question of the deferred nature of Nature's gift remains a constant impediment. In the words of Derrida, we could say that Wordsworth's endowment from Nature would be a *don sans présent*, a gift without present, which his text everywhere re-marks.[6]

It will always be possible to ignore this gift's deferred present, and simply to analyse, for example, the time between the reception of the certified bank transfer and the grateful address of recognition that follows it in the post.[7] Yet in doing so, at least as far as the logic of Wordsworth's writings are concerned, one will miss everything that marks the specificity of these 'gifts', everything, or virtually everything, that Wordsworth says about them, the very contexts that make them the offerings that they are.

In what follows, I will be engaged in calculating the time between Wordsworth's presents, both given and received, which will include not only the delay between patronal offering and poetic counter, or the gift of Nature and subsequent poetic profusion, but also the deferral internal to Wordsworth's original reception of Nature's endowment itself, for this present may never have arrived in the first place. This is the conclusion that one must reach if one listens carefully to him and his circle. Yet once one takes Wordsworth's – which is to say, the text signed 'Wordsworth', the poetic as well as autobiographical and epistolary text that signs itself 'Wordsworth' – uncertainty vis-à-vis this gift into account, it risks altering the algebra of all his subsequent poetic presents. One interest of the Wordsworthian corpus will precisely be that, far from remaining blind to this difficulty, it takes it up, reflecting and even speculating on the constitutive incalculability of poetic genius's presence. And it is precisely at such moments of groundless speculation, upon the absence of a ground, that one finds his work's most generous moments of poetic redistribution.

The question of Wordsworth's 'power' or 'genius', as a divine gift bestowed by Nature, haunts his writings *as a question* from the moment that the great *Recluse* project enters into his sights in 1798. Its traces, which run throughout *The Prelude*, *Home at Grasmere*, and *The Excursion*, give way to numerous reflections on poetic mortality and immortality, as well as to a number of tributary economies that, originating in this pact with Nature, expand to encompass his more mundane relations with his patrons, friends, and family. Indeed, even before it becomes a matter of patronage *as such*, Nature's alleged sponsorship of Wordsworth's poetic labours could be said to constitute, for him, a type of patronal support *avant la lettre*. Not only does his rapport with Nature and its boon open the very possibility of patronage as he will later come to know it, by making him the poet that he is, but already his receptive submission to Nature's gifts gives rise to something that appears very similar to the patronal demand: the necessity of reciprocation or *quid pro quo*.

Ultimately, however, the question of the poetic gift takes its most extreme expression in *The Prelude*, where, I show, Wordsworth's very signature, the meaning and power of the name 'Wordsworth', and thus its very ability to give something *worthy of this name*, may be said to tremble. Yet, because the mark of the signature of *The Prelude*, the 'antechapel', 'portico', or 'preparatory poem' for what should have been his magnum opus, remains inextricably caught up with Wordsworth and his circle's confrontations with that opus, I will begin with *The Recluse* before I turn, by way of conclusion, to the 'poem to Coleridge'.

Finally, in what follows I read between and through Wordsworth's personal correspondence, the testimony of his friends and family, and his narrative, as well as autobiographical texts. The significance of these more 'personal' accounts is, however, less their testimonial character than their enactment of the same paradoxes that haunt the 'fictional' works. These documents do not simply comment on but in fact repeat *the same problem* as the fictional/autobiographical poetic texts. It is because the logic of the gift haunts equally the 'fictional' and 'non-fictional', both the 'poetic' and 'non-poetic', that one must read the traces of the Wordsworthian signature across all such borders.

ANXIETY AND *THE RECLUSE*

The story of *The Recluse*, 'Wordsworth's Great Failure', is well known.[8] Some time during the winter of 1798, while Wordsworth was living at Alfoxden with Dorothy and Coleridge, a plan was conceived for a poem of monumental purview. The earliest remaining clues as to the original scope of the project, located in two letters from March of that year from Wordsworth to James Tobin and James Losh, speak of the completion of 1,300 lines of a poem that concerns 'Nature, Man, and Society'[9] and whose further composition Wordsworth imagines will occupy him 'for at least a year and a half to come'.[10] Such positive sentiments, however, did not last, and by October–November of the same year the difficulties presented by his magnum opus had become so significant that he began work on what would eventually become the *Poem on the Growth of a Poet's Mind*, or *The Prelude*. In what, exactly, these difficulties originally consisted – whether they were temporary impediments or unyielding impasses relating to the structure of the poem – one could not say.[11] By September of the following year, however, real concerns about the promise and prospects of *The Recluse* had begun to surface. On 10 September 1799, Coleridge writes that he is 'anxiously eager to have [Wordsworth] steadily employed on "The Recluse"'; he 'entreats' him to go on with it, recommends against him publishing any 'small poems', and even proposes a new, engaging topic for the poem.[12] About a month later, another letter follows in which he pines, 'I long to see what you have been doing. O let it be the tail-piece of *The Recluse*.'[13] But in the roughly twelve-month period that had passed since the initial stoppage, instead of making advances on the philosophical poem it was the two-part *Prelude* that Wordsworth completed. By February of the following year – roughly two years from its inception – Coleridge can no longer sugar-coat his disappointment at *The Recluse*'s fate, writing to Wordsworth that he 'grieve[s] that *The Recluse* sleeps'.[14]

As William Minto rather bluntly put it in his response to the 1888 publishing of *The Recluse* fragments, the story of the text is largely the story of its failure. Yet it did not always seem that that would be the case, and in the course of the near forty-year period that Wordsworth would spend working on it one sees periods of intense activity and confidence followed by stretches of inactivity, frustration, and hopelessness. 'You will be glad to hear that I have been busily employed lately', writes Wordsworth to Sir George Beaumont on 8 September 1804. 'I wrote one book of *The Recluse*, nearly a thousand lines, then had a rest. Last week I began again, and have written three hundred more. I hope all tolerably well, and certainly with good views.'[15] But by the following June, writing to Beaumont again, now upon the completion of the thirteen-book *Prelude*, Wordsworth's outlook is bleak:[16]

> I was dejected on many accounts; when I looked back upon the performance it seemed to have a dead weight about it, the reality so far short of the expectation; it was the first long labour that I had finished, and the doubt whether I should ever live to write the Recluse and the sense which I had of this Poem being so far below what I seem'd capable of executing, depressed me much.[17]

By August of the next year Wordsworth is once again positive: 'Within this last month I have returned to *The Recluse*, and have written 700 additional lines. Should Coleridge return, so that I might have some conversation with him on the subject, I should go on swimmingly.'[18] But by the close of 1806 the tides had once again turned:

> I am going to the Press with a Volume . . . which I publish with great reluctance, but the day when my long work will be finished seems further and further off, and therefore I have resolved to send this Vol: into the world.[19]

On and on this cycle continued until the mid-1830s, the poem having become something that Wordsworth could neither finish nor forget.

The reasons for Wordsworth's particular cathexis to *The Recluse*, and the sources of not only his, but the entire Wordsworth circle's obsession with it, were at least twofold. There was, first of all, the hope that such a work – were Wordsworth actually able to write it – would have the greatest social and political ramifications for those who read it. 'A poem, in blank verse, addressed to those, who, in consequence of the complete failure of the French Revolution, have thrown up all hopes of the amelioration of mankind', as Coleridge would put it in 1799.[20] Wordsworth's own high expectations were firmly expressed on a number of occasions as well, including in *The Prelude*, *Home at Grasmere*, and *The Excursion*.[21] Nevertheless, alongside these ostensibly impersonal motives, a second, perhaps no less compelling, reason drove Wordsworth's writing of, and surely also his anxiety about, the text.

Of a more personal nature, this inducement concerned *The Recluse*'s presumed place within the English literary tradition. From the moment of its conception, the expectations for *The Recluse* were monumental. Already on 7 March 1798 Coleridge wrote to Wordsworth's publisher, Joseph Cottle, of 'The Giant Wordsworth – God love him! . . . he has written near 1200 lines of a blank verse, superior, I hesitate not to aver, to anything in our language which anyway resembles it.'[22] Again, on 15 January 1804, this time in a letter to Richard Sharp, Coleridge swoons over Wordsworth, 'a most original poet', who 'no more resembles Milton than Milton resembles Shakespeare – no more resembles Shakespeare than Shakespeare resembles Milton', and then he:

> prophes[ies] immortality to his *Recluse*, as the first and finest philosophical Poem, if only it be (as it undoubtedly will be) a Faithful Transcript of his own most august & innocent Life, of his own habitual Feelings and Modes of seeing and hearing.[23]

The stakes of the poem for Coleridge were thus immense, for were Wordsworth able to write it, *The Recluse*, Coleridge believed, would surely become not only the crowning achievement of his œuvre, but also a triumph of English literature, on a par only with *Paradise Lost*. Wordsworth's place within the tradition thus hung in the balance with its success or failure. As such, the text became a referendum not only on his career, but also, as years of Wordsworth and his circle's personal and public reflections on the poem testify, on his ability as a poet, the nature of Nature's gift to him, and his merit as a favoured heir.

A certain slippage between what Wordsworth actually produced of *The Recluse* and the nature of the poetic gifts which were believed to have subtended this production thus comes to mark the most haunting moments of his and his circle's reflections on his progress – or the lack thereof. It was not simply, then, that Wordsworth's confidence in the poem's eventual fruition fluctuated, but that the lack of progress and perceived incompletability of *The Recluse* bombarded him with doubt touching on all aspects of what he thought to be his *actual* poetic ability. The question thus became whether the origin of his difficulty lay in contingent matters of time, place, and opportunity, or an essential lack born of inadequacy and incompetence. Was Wordsworth a *chosen* poet who merely 'renders nothing back', or one who, indeed, never received such gifts in the first place, and thus who, *in fact*, had nothing to return? The growing reluctance with which Wordsworth approached *The Recluse* project beginning in 1800 gave way at first to apprehension and encouragement from members of his circle, then to fears that he would never find sufficient time for its completion, and finally to reticence and suspicion as to the very feasibility of the project *for him*. A looming figure of temporal finitude thus, from time to time, became supplanted by one of personal incapacity, but with no possible way to resolve such a dilemma Wordsworth and his coterie were left floundering between the two.[24]

This point is made as much in its denial as by its admission. Coleridge, who, in the wake of Wordsworth's publishing of *The Excursion* and the scathing reviews it received, repeats, time and again, that 'proofs meet me in every part of the Excursion, that the Poet's genius has not flagged',[25] that though it 'had disappointed my expectations . . . the Excellencies were so many and of so high a class, that it was impossible to attribute the inferiority, if any such really existed, to any flagging of the Writer's own genius'.[26] On each occasion, Coleridge attributes the blame for *The Excursion* rather to Wordsworth's ignorance of what, for others, seems commonplace, instead of any inherent failing in ability. In the *Biographia Literaria*, published two years later, Coleridge confirms this position, writing: 'How small the proportion of the defects are to the beauties, I have repeatedly declared; and that no one of them originates in deficiency of poetic genius,'[27] and proclaiming that 'What Mr. Wordsworth *will* produce, it is not for me to prophesy: but I could pronounce with the liveliest convictions what he is capable of producing. It is the FIRST GENUINE PHILOSOPHIC POEM.'[28] Thus, Coleridge's espoused confidence in Wordsworth's poetic genius never wavers, even if the compulsion to reaffirm such a conviction cannot but betray a looming doubt. Writing in the *Biographia* he acknowledges that his friend may never accomplish his monumental task, but he holds firm that, if he does not, it will not have been for essential, constitutive reasons.

Dorothy, for her part, struggles to explain and excuse Wordsworth's lack of progress. Relying at times on such justifications as the season,[29] lack of solitude,[30] the predominance of thought,[31] and Coleridge's absence,[32] and at others on Wordsworth's stubbornness and tendency to procrastinate, she nevertheless also eventually comes to doubt whether Wordsworth will ever finish *The Recluse*, though in doing so she rarely, if ever, addresses Wordsworth's talent, citing time, not ability, as the limiting factor.[33]

For his part, Wordsworth himself appears to hold out hope in the project until around 1836, when, as Beth Darlington observes, he removed the subtitle 'Being a Portion of the Recluse' from published editions of *The Excursion*.[34] Wordsworth had struggled in that very text with the relation between ability and output. Potential, after all, is such precisely because it is not always actualised:

> Oh! many are the Poets that are sown
> By Nature; Men endowed with highest gifts,
> The vision and the faculty divine,
> Yet wanting the accomplishment of Verse,
> (Which in the docile season of their youth
> It was denied them to acquire, through lack
> Of culture and the inspiring aid of books,
>   . . . these favoured Beings,
> All but a scattered few, live out their time,
> Husbanding that which they possess within,
> And go to the grave, unthought of.   (1:81–95)[35]

While the reception of Nature's 'endowment' and the 'accomplishment of Verse' are, in this passage, separated by a virtual abyss of contingency and experience, for Wordsworth himself, who, evidently, was weaned on the Derwent's 'ceaseless music' (1:9),[36] one wonders whether such an alibi remained acceptable. And, indeed, even if one allows that all those who are endowed with genius will not be able to realise their potential, nevertheless, if not through the works that one creates, how else is the presence of such an ability to be determined, measured, or otherwise assessed? How, in sum, is any given individual's 'potential' to be calculated, given that 'potential' involves, by definition, the presence of structures that *may not* manifest themselves?

As I have already mentioned, Wordsworth's initial confidence in his project quickly gave way to conditional statements that hedged on its eventual completion. At times they supply clear conditions upon which its success or failure will hinge:

> *The Recluse* has had a long sleep, save in my thoughts; my mss. are so ill-penned, and blurred, that they are useless to all but myself; and at present I cannot face

them. But if my stomach can be preserved in tolerable order, I hope you will hear of me again in the character chosen for the title of that poem.[37]

Often, however, they simply offer 'life' itself as such a condition: 'And if I live to finish these three principal works I shall be content';[38] 'the doubt whether I should ever live to write the Recluse . . . depressed me much'.[39] Such statements masterfully sidestep the question of cause, forcing their addressees to decide whether 'If I live to finish' indicates a mere temporal limitation or a personal inability, hence an external or internal barrier to completion. This is, moreover, the very question that Wordsworth puts to himself in the first book of the 1805 *Prelude* – without, however, answering it – in the dilemma between ability and indolence:

> Thus from day to day
> I live a mockery of the brotherhood
> Of vice and virtue, with no skill to part
> Vague longing that is bred by want of power,
> From paramount impulse not to be withstood;   (1:238–42)[40]

It was also a question that he returns to in book thirteen: 'Whether to me shall be allotted life/ And with life power to accomplish aught of worth . . . Is all uncertain' (13:386–90).[41] Nevertheless, if one believes George Ticknor, who dined with Wordsworth at Rydal Mount in 1838, such self-determined causes appear to have 'finally' won over:[42]

> On my asking him why he does not finish [*The Recluse*], he turned to me very decidedly and said, 'Why did not Gray finish the long poem he began on a similar subject? Because he found he had undertaken something beyond his powers to accomplish. And that is my case.'[43]

The determination of Wordsworth's gifts thus came to depend, at least as far as Wordsworth and Coleridge themselves were concerned, upon the success or failure of *The Recluse*. Set up as *the* testament to his poetic excellence, this demanding text would become *either* the source of justification for, *or* the cause of suspicion of, Wordsworth's self-identification as a poet and his coordinate claims to privilege in poesy's realm. And it would do so not only in the testamentary documents, letters, and opinions surveyed above, but also within the structure of all of Wordsworth's major autobiographical writings. Both what Wordsworth *will have been given* and, as a consequence, what he *must give in turn*, revolve, then, around this text.

Wordsworth's 'gift' will have been known, it will have been verified or grounded, it will have been gifted, only at the moment in which he will have presented so much conclusive evidence for it, by giving a poem *of* genius. But when and under what conditions, it bears asking, would such a presentation finally be able to be acknowledged?

THE PLACE OF *THE PRELUDE*

Although the conversations surrounding the drafting of *The Recluse* demonstrate the weight it held for Wordsworth, his family, and his friends, it is ultimately in and through the 'Poem to Coleridge' that the logic determining these displacements comes into clearest focus. From 1799 up to 1814, the place and importance of what would become *The Prelude* shifted alongside the prospects for *The Recluse*. Initially viewed as an entirely separate project and a mere means for Wordsworth to clear his throat, *The Prelude* slowly became more and more important for his philosophical poem, and did so in two separate but equally important ways. On the one hand, Wordsworth began to envision the *text* of the 'Poem to Coleridge' as forming an integral – if preliminary – portion of the total architecture of his Philosophical poem. From an independent project, to what Dorothy calls an 'appendix' to *The Recluse* in early 1804,[44] to a 'tributary' of it in March of that year,[45] to its 'portico' in 1805,[46] and finally as its 'Anti-chapel' in 1814,[47] it develops an ever more foundational role for the latter work. As such, Wordsworth determined that it should not be published during his lifetime or, at least, at any point prior to the publishing of *The Recluse*, which was esteemed by him as the only text capable of retroactively justifying *The Prelude*'s indulgences.[48]

On the other hand, considered as a performance, the writing of *The Prelude* was to prepare Wordsworth himself for the writing of *The Recluse*. As the conclusion to part one of the 1799 text makes clear, this form of preparation involved a process of growth and an acquisition of self-knowledge that could not simply be conflated with the timely completion of the written text. There is even a scenario, Wordsworth muses, in which he might succeed in the latter, while still remaining unprepared for the former:

> Meanwhile my hope has been that I might fetch
> Reproaches from my former years, whose power
> May spur me on, in manhood now mature,
> To honourable toil. Yet, should it be
> That this is but an impotent desire,
> That I by such inquiry am not taught
> To understand myself, nor thou to know

> With better knowledge how the heart was framed
> Of him thou lovest, need I dread from thee
> Harsh judgments   (1:450–9)[49]

The act of writing *The Prelude* was thus to be an event unto itself: an act through which Wordsworth would not only produce a written text, but also learn 'to understand myself'.[50] In the preface to *The Excursion* (1814), in which Wordsworth also makes his famous Gothic church analogy, he explains that: 'The preparatory Poem is biographical, and conducts the history of the Author's mind to the point when he was emboldened to hope that his faculties were sufficiently matured for entering upon the arduous labour which he had proposed to himself.'[51] Taken in the strong sense, by conducting such a history the Poem should not merely *report* a progression that would have already taken place, but *enact* the self-growth that it is due to recount. The journey through the growth of the author's mind 'emboldens' that mind, aids in its formation, and completes the transformation that it aimed to recount, in the very act of being written. The 'preparatory' poem thus prepares the poet himself for the writing of *The Recluse* and thereby serves the latter text not only as an introduction, addressed to the reader, but also as an undertaking for the poet, the completion of which should render its author capable, for the first time, of bringing his Gothic church to fruition. Like a *récit*, then, *The Prelude*'s 'event' is to be found in the relay between the telling and the told, where the true signature of 'Wordsworth' hangs in the balance.

Thus, if Wordsworth has, in fact, received the gifts of Nature, if he has been chosen, if his birth has been blessed, then so too should he be able to train his mind to the point of producing *The Recluse*. *The Prelude*, which takes up the question of Nature's gifts to Wordsworth and offers these reflections to Coleridge – the only reader equipped to understand them – should make *The Recluse* possible in advance, while *The Recluse*, in turn, should retroactively justify the apparent, but *only* apparent, 'indulgences' of *The Prelude*, those indulgences, so long as they appear as such, making the autobiography unpublishable. If *The Prelude* fails, so too does *The Recluse*, but, ultimately, the success of the former will have been determined only by that of the latter. As such, *The Prelude* is written as an attempt to testify to the possibility of its own writing, by interrogating and making manifest Wordsworth's chosen or elected status.

RECEIVING AND GIVING IN *THE PRELUDE (1799)*

> When, as becomes a man who would prepare
> For such a glorious work, I through myself
> Make rigorous inquisition, the report

>   Is often chearing; for I neither seem
>   To lack that first great gift, the vital soul,
>   Nor general truths which are themselves a sort
>   Of elements and agents, under-powers,
>   Subordinate helpers of the living mind.
>
>   *1805 Prelude* (1.157–64)[52]

The determination of Wordsworth's gift – both what he receives and gives back – thus comes to depend upon the dialectic between *The Recluse* and *The Prelude*. It is perhaps not then surprising that, of all of Wordsworth's writings, none is so overwritten by the figure and logic of giving than the 'Poem to Coleridge'. Addressed to his friend, *The Prelude* reads as an extended exercise in the trials of poetic endowment, inspiration, dissemination, and above all reciprocation. The two-part text of 1799, which works to establish Wordsworth's status as a favoured poet, opens and closes with acknowledgements of the greater-than-human gifts bestowed on him by Nature. In part one, through the apostrophised figures of 'Beloved Derwent!' (1:16), 'Gentle Powers!' (1:35), 'quiet Powers!' (1:73), 'ye Beings of the hills!' (1:130), 'Ye Powers of earth!' and 'ye Genii of the springs!' (1:186),[53] we learn how these spirits:

>   when they would form
>   A favored being, from his very dawn
>   Of infancy do open out the clouds
>   As at the touch of lightning, seeking him
>   With gentle visitation; quiet Powers!
>   [. . .]
>   They guided me   (1:69–73; 81)[54]

In similar fashion, the conclusion to the second part of the 1799 text closes with images of Natural spirits, this time apostrophised as

>   ye mountains! and ye lakes
>   And sounding cataracts! ye mists and winds
>   That dwell among the hills where I was born. (2:470–2).[55]

Now with 'grateful voice' (2:469), the poet addresses them so as to acknowledge – and thereby return with interest – the gifts given him:

>   If, in my youth, I have been pure in heart,
>   If, mingling with the world, I am content
>   With my own modest pleasures, and have lived

> With God and Nature communing, removed
> From little enmities and low desires,
> The gift is yours: if in these times of fear,
> This melancholy waste of hopes o'erthrown,
> If, 'mid indifference and apathy
>   . . . if in this time
> Of dereliction and dismay I yet
> Despair not of our nature, but retain
> A more than Roman confidence, a faith
> That fails not, in all sorrow my support,
> The blessing of my life, the gift is yours,
> Ye Mountains! thine, O Nature!   (2:473–92)[56]

Two things stand out in this culminating scene, which will be repeated on another occasion in the 1805 text. On the one hand, Wordsworth makes use of the conditional to acknowledge the evidence for the gifts he was sent: '*If . . . I have been pure in heart . . . the gift is yours*'. In this way, he remains diffident before these higher powers. Yet if it is tempting to read his modesty *as modesty*, which is to say, as mere rhetorical posturing, it is no less accurate to say that this posturing – the expression of uncertainty concerning gifts sent and received, and his distinction as a favoured heir – also corresponds to his yet-to-be-determined status as a poet, which constitutes the very impetus for, and matter at stake in, the writing of the two-book *Prelude*. In other words, '*if . . . I have been pure in heart . . . the gift is yours*' corresponds to and even speaks for the structural relation between *The Prelude* and *The Recluse*, the closure for which is here, *now*, at the moment of putting pen to ink, in the process of being sought.[57]

On the other hand, the expression of gratefulness or thanks is here performed in a speech act, itself inseparable from the very acknowledgement of the present. To declare that 'the gift is yours' is both to accept this gift as given – notwithstanding the fact that he implies that it might not be in the same breath – and to express gratitude for it. Reception and reciprocation are thus conjoined, just as to name a patron *as patron* is both to affirm the patronal relation and to begin to repay him or her. Nomination, the declaration of receipt, goes some way toward indemnifying the debt. Yet debt there may or may not be, and it is this tension that marks the specificity of Wordsworth's inscription, as well as the passage from a mere gift exchange to something else, more difficult to name.

It is moments like these in the Wordsworthian corpus that always force one to wonder, moreover, whether Wordsworth's desire to write *The Prelude* and *Recluse* in fact emerges out of a sense of obligation – to 'render back', as he puts it in 1805, for the gifts he had received from Nature – or, to the contrary, whether his desire to compose these texts materialises because writing his great philosophical poem would be the greatest evidence of these gifts and would first and foremost testify to their reception. Paradoxically, to accept the latter position would be to understand Wordsworth as giving or paying back his debt prior to its very receipt. It would be to take him as returning to the bank of Nature money he had not yet been credited – which also, perversely, turns the entire text of *The Prelude* into one grand gambit of counterfeit currency.[58] In spite of the paradox, perhaps this is the only possibility. Understood in this way, the dread he expresses over his 'lot' in book one would serve as a cover or lie, allowing him to shame himself only on the condition of an (as yet undeserved) confidence in an ability he yet seeks to prove that he possesses. Wordsworth takes it upon himself, he orients his work as poet, and above all as chosen poet, through the return of a present he may never have been awarded. Yet assuming the debt before its arrival appears to be the very condition upon which the economy of his labour can begin its traffic in poetic production. The question, of course, is: given such an abyssal origin, whither poetry?

Like the 1799 text, the 1805 *Prelude* opens with an act of donation, this time offered in the present of the narrative rather than recalled from the poet's past. Inspiration, in the form of a 'blessing in this gentle breeze' (1:1) or 'gift that consecrates my joy' (1:40), signals a propitious beginning for poetic freedom. When the poet 'breathe[s] again' and that freedom is immediately troubled by '[t]rances of thought and mountings of the mind', he is saved when '[a]s by some miraculous gift 'tis shaken off' (1:19–22). The opening verse paragraphs track the tension between poetic aspirations towards 'some work/ Of glory there forthwith to be begun' (1:86–7) (that is, *The Recluse*) and 'present gifts/ Of humbler industry' (1:143–4), which Wordsworth is unused to pursuing, yet which, on this singular occasion, occupy him until he is met with stultifying '[u]nmanageable thoughts' (1:149).[59]

In this way the 1805 *Prelude* establishes its particular subject, turning from Wordsworth's presently defrauded harp back to those encouraging childhood scenes of the 1799 text that most effectively betray the '[s]everer interventions' and 'ministry more palpable' which '[Nature] dealt with me' (1:370–1). In the absence of an inspired present or of knowledge of how to weave his philosophical poem, Wordsworth turns to the clearest evidence of his own gifted nature in the story of his life and offers it to Coleridge, the 'honoured friend', to whom he hopes '[t]his labour will be welcome' (1:674).[60]

Although assertions of his poetic endowment and of Nature's cultivation are constant refrains throughout the text that follows, re-emerging in the blessed babe scene in book two (2:297–310), during his time at Cambridge in book three (3:82–4), and in travels through France and England in books ten (10:904–40) and twelve (12:1–14; 278–312), in what follows I will focus on the concluding thirteenth book. It is in book thirteen that the possibility of *The Prelude*'s narrative closure, and along with it the prospects for *The Recluse*, come to depend explicitly on issues of poetic donation, debt, dissemination, and patronage. Not only does Wordsworth there reflect openly on the poem's status as a 'gift to Coleridge' (13:411), but also, confronted with the necessity of bringing the poem to a close so that he may finally begin his true work, he also broaches the inescapable question of his debts in writing it. Truly to finish the *Prelude* would be at once to realise the reception of the gift of genius that Wordsworth should have had all along, and to be capable, for the first time, of paying off his coordinate literary debts, to Nature and friend alike. It would be both to receive and to give, with interest, and in so doing to join the ranks of immortals Shakespeare and Milton.

RECEIVING AND GIVING IN *THE PRELUDE (1805)*

Initially, book thirteen appears simply to take Wordsworth's story up where twelve left off, with his excursions in England and Wales. Following his tour through the Salisbury plain in twelve, thirteen begins with his ascent of Mount Snowden, that 'universal spectacle . . . shaped for all admiration and delight', in which 'Nature [had] lodged/ The soul, the imagination of the whole' (13:60–5). In this way, the ascent of Snowden finally achieves the restoration of Wordsworth's imagination and faith in humankind that had been building in the prior two books, and does so as a culminating scene of election, of visible 'power . . . which Nature thus/ *Thrusts forth* upon the senses' (13:84–6, my emphasis). Nature's 'exhibiting' (13:75) of the sublime image of the imagination at daybreak thus confirms, not only that '[s]uch minds [as possess a similar glorious faculty] are truly from the Deity' (13:106), but also that the experience itself was nothing less than a divine presentation, tendered forth by Nature *for* Wordsworth.[61]

Having in this way reached the apex of celestial poetic confidence, brought forth through the memory of this scene of visitation, Wordsworth turns, in the concluding verses of *The Prelude*, to a final series of tributes to friends and family, along with the aforementioned reflections on his poetic debts. And this is what one finds in the last 250 lines of the poem: a concern with his outstanding obligations and so many attempts to settle them, beginning, naturally, with those to Dorothy and Coleridge:

> Child of my parents, sister of my soul,
> Elsewhere have strains of gratitude been breathed
> To thee for all the early tenderness
> Which I from thee imbibed.
> [. . .]   With such a theme
> Coleridge – with this my argument – of thee
> Shall I be silent?   (13:211–12; 247–9)

Wordsworth is, at last, winding down. The story of his mind's progress has been told, and now the two most formative figures of that journey have been recognised. Nevertheless, he is not yet quite ready to stop talking. Everything that needs saying has not yet been said. Or rather, having said too much, he needs to go on just a bit more, lest the ultimate justification for it all be left obscure.

Beginning a new paragraph, Wordsworth acknowledges that he has already gone on too long. As though he were some kind of literary debtor, writing on borrowed time, he makes a final appeal for indulgence to his reader: 'Let one word more of personal circumstance–/ Not needless, as it seems – be added here' (13:332–3). Though it *seems* needless, a mere extravagance or excess, as becomes clear a few paragraphs later, everything in *The Prelude* in fact depends on the revelation of the true value of such 'personal circumstance' as being, in fact, absolutely essential. The apparently needless or indulgent must, in fact, be totally justified, or else this gift that is *The Prelude* will turn from a panacea into a poison, a blessing into a curse – a *pharmakon*, in the worst sense of the word.

Unlike the recognition allotted to Coleridge and Dorothy for their contributions to Wordsworth's development – and thus to the writing of *The Prelude* – this 'one word more' names a debt of more concrete, and evidently more calculable, order. Who could ever say the worth of a friend, a soulmate, or 'a sister of my heart' (13:339), for the production of a work of literature? And who, for that very reason, could ever claim to expunge the charge, to demonstrate *adequate* gratitude, for such a good turn? Wordsworth acknowledges that something remains forever unresolved and incommensurate in bonds such as those shared with dearest friend and sister. Sister and friend may, indeed, be such only by virtue of the incalculability of what passes from the one to the other.[62] Yet if Wordsworth cannot return just what he has received, at the very least he can acknowledge such an imbalance in order to compensate for what payments he necessarily leaves delinquent:

> Three years, until a permanent abode
> Received me with that sister of my heart
> *Who ought by rights the dearest to have been*
> *Conspicuous through this biographic verse –*
> Star seldom utterly concealed from view –   (13:338–42, my emphasis)

According to the most classic understanding of gift exchange, it is nothing less than the function of the gift to maintain relationships between indebted parties, by allowing for a continuous flow of presents without resolution. In this regard, it is the *imbalance* that is essential, for this is what drives the continued exchange of presents, rather than bringing it (and the relationship) to a quick and definitive end. A quick and definitive end would, by contrast, be the function of commercial exchanges, such as one finds in capitalism, which allow for the appearance of immediate and absolute compensation, and thus the dissolution of the bonds between participating parties. All of this is to say: Wordsworth's recognition of his sister's immaterial, intellectual, and even inspirational role for his development is, in this passage, *exemplary*.

To his sister's immaterial contribution and to Wordsworth's recognition of his henceforth unpayable debt to her is, then, immediately juxtaposed – in the very same paragraph and under the very same banner of 'one word more' – the ostensibly straightforward grant of a material offering of a legacy. Wordsworth goes on to explain how, during the three-year period after his return from France but before the move to the permanent abode with Dorothy, while he 'led an undomestic wanderer's life' (13:343), he befriended a young man whose bequest would in turn allow him to perambulate at his own pace:

> Let one word more of personal circumstance –
> Not needless, as it seems – be added here.
> [. . .]
> I led an undomestic wanderer's life.
> In London chiefly was my home, and thence
> Excursively, as personal friendships, chance
> Or inclination led, or slender means
> Gave leave, I roamed about from place to place,
> Tarrying in pleasant nooks, wherever found,
> Through England or through Wales. A youth – he bore
> The name of Calvert; it shall live, if words

> Of mine can give it life – without respect
> To prejudice or custom, having hope
> That I had some endowments by which good
> Might be promoted, in his last decay
> From his own family withdrawing part
> Of no redundant patrimony, did
> By a bequest sufficient for my needs
> Enable me to pause for choice, and walk
> At large and unrestrained, nor damped too soon
> By mortal cares. Himself no poet, yet
> Far less a common spirit of the world,
> He deemed that my pursuits and labours lay
> Apart from all that leads to wealth, or even
> Perhaps to necessary maintenance,
> Without some hazard to the finer sense,
> He cleared a passage for me, and the stream
> Flowed in the bent of Nature. (13:332–67)

Unlike his sister, whom we learn ought to have been conspicuous throughout this biographical verse, Raisley Calvert played a comparatively short, but very sweet, role in Wordsworth's life. A patron in the strict sense of the word, Raisley bequeathed £900 to Wordsworth, directly enabling him to pursue his poetic vocation. Despite the relative transparency of Raisley's contribution, however – especially in contrast to Dorothy's – Wordsworth's counter-gift in this instance proves much more difficult to measure. As we shall see, his recognition of Raisley is anything but exemplary.

The story of Raisley Calvert, brother of William Calvert, Wordsworth's Hawkshead schoolfriend, is well known. Beginning in October 1794, Wordsworth became the primary caretaker for Raisley, who was then suffering from tuberculosis. Although the two were friendly, as Wordsworth himself later admits, they were not quite friends.[63] Nevertheless, they esteemed one another and developed a mutually beneficial relationship. Wordsworth took care of Raisley for four months, until his death in January 1795, and Raisley promised Wordsworth a portion of his legacy so that the latter – then a fledgling poet in dire need of steady income – could 'promote some good'.[64] As Kenneth R. Johnston points out in his chapter 'Legacy Hunting', some element of self-interest surely contributed to Wordsworth's taking on this charge.[65] Many critics also note that Wordsworth appears to have struggled with guilt for what came to pass, in part because securing his inheritance required Raisley to die, but also for fear that he would never succeed in the promotion of good that alone would justify receiving the patrimony.[66] Whether or not guilt drove Wordsworth, his unpublished tribute in the 1805 *Prelude* and subsequent sonnet to Calvert published in 1807 testify to a lingering sense of obligation, and one that, evidently, required an offering of poetic praise to be made in addition to the physical and emotional labour that Wordsworth had already invested in caring for Raisley on his deathbed.

While, then, it was Wordsworth who solicited the gift of £900, in the end he received it with at least some trepidation. Moreover, although the gift took the form of money, as is made clear in the passage above, what Raisley ultimately, *really*, gave Wordsworth was his autonomy, by granting him power over his own movement:[67] 'A youth . . . did/ By a bequest sufficient for my needs/ Enable me to pause for choice, and walk/ At large and unrestrained'. Liberating him from restraints as well as immediate pressure from 'mortal cares', Calvert 'cleared a passage for me, and the stream/ Flowed in the bent of Nature'. This stream is, of course, the very one now culminating in the narration of these reflections, at the moment of the writing of this scene, in the concluding book of the 'Poem on the Growth of the Poet's Mind'. Raisley's gift has thus led, as though inexorably, to its own recounting, and thereby marks both an origin for and an end to the poet's progress: a point at which autonomy and necessity seemingly coincide, one in which the promise of the present should finally pay, and *be paid*, off.

It is, however, just such a moment of simultaneous and reciprocal achievement that Wordsworth forcefully draws into question, at the very instant that he attempts to acknowledge it. Similar to what he writes in part two of the 1799 text, Wordsworth cannot help but put into doubt the status of what he has received – and now gives back – at the very moment of its bestowal: 'A youth – he bore/ The name of Calvert; it shall live, *if words/ Of mine can give it life*' (my emphasis). In the two-part *Prelude*, it was, of course, the *reception* of Nature's gifts that was subjected to the uncertainty of the conditional. Now, however, it is the poet's own counter-offering. Nevertheless, the same tension emerges in both instances: Wordsworth cannot but imbue with uncertainty the character of the gift – or counter-gift – at the moment of its acknowledgement. In so doing, he raises the implicit question as to whether there was (or is) any gift at all.

The form of the gift to be bestowed on Calvert, as on Dorothy and Coleridge, is *the word*. Wordsworth makes an offering, in words, of 'life', and of a life, precisely, *in language*. In doing so, he offers the prototypical poetic present, which, from Horace to Spenser to Shakespeare and beyond, is bestowed on the lover and patron as the promise of immortality.[68] The word – and by way of the word, the poem – may bear the promise of such a gift because, unlike the organic life of the individual, or even the inorganic 'life' of a stone temple, the written or spoken word need only be archived, either in the minds of human beings, or on the technically reproducible sheet of paper. The poem, or word, is thus free from the physical wear and tear that threatens even the most stable of monumental, material substances, such as brass and marble. '[T]he word lives longer than deeds,' says Pindar, and the word, as name, may confer 'immortality' on the deceased by bestowing the departed with fame[69] – a fame that lasts as long, of course, as the poem itself remains in circulation. Even, then, for non-rhyming or virtually unmemorisable works such as *The Prelude*, because the poem still only requires that it be written, it may promise 'life' to all it holds, for, as Ovid puts it, 'as long as men read me thy fame shall be read along with me'.[70] That is, as long as the poem is read, or recalled, it promises at least *de facto* immortality for those it names, whether they be the Young Man or Calvert.

What is critical for our reading of Wordsworth, then, is that before it even becomes a matter of conferring praise or blame through exposition – and, to a certain extent, regardless of which is ultimately employed – the poetic word bestows a certain tribute already at the moment of nomination, as soon as someone or something is named or otherwise inscribed: which is to say, as soon as the minimal conditions for memorialisation are met, something, however slight, is granted. And yet, just as Wordsworth's cautionary hedge of 'one word more' opening the verse paragraph signalled a strange, supplementary logic to be at work, so too does his conditional qualification here indicate a disruption within the logic of praise- or gratitude-giving speech, and thus of patronage. The tribute, strictly speaking, is performed at the moment that *the name of* 'Calvert' is inscribed. What follows, including Wordsworth's self-referential allusion to 'the name of' at the moment of this name's enunciation, serves not only to bring into doubt the character of his tribute, but also to question the nature of the poetic present as such.

On the surface, Wordsworth's eulogy of Calvert appears merely to mirror the latter's sacrifice. Having, in some sense, died for Wordsworth and having thereby freed the latter from 'mortal cares', Calvert requires a complementary oblation. Hence the poet's solution – which is not merely Wordsworth's, but the poet's *par excellence* – of bestowing life upon Calvert's name, supplementing the latter's loss of mortality, in death, with a potentially superior life-form: a monument or an epitaph that could last forever. The 'gift of life' of words does not merely give back what Calvert gave up, but replaces it – potentially – with a life without death, or at least a life *in* death no longer haunted by mortal cares. If this is what Wordsworth promises on the surface – without however promising it, at best promising to promise it – in the context of paean it cannot be forgotten that every word of reflection serves merely to distract from the text's ostensible object (Calvert) and to draw it back to its speaker (Wordsworth), when truly *to name* Calvert, rather than to name naming Calvert, would have sufficed to grant him his life after life.

Yet such reflections, in addition to simply turning our attention to their true subject (Wordsworth), may also here succeed in drawing our attention to what – even in giving this gift, or in trying to give this gift, or in giving one gift while taking or holding back from giving another – may haunt each and every gift Wordsworth *actually*, or merely *virtually*, or even only *almost*, gives. At the moment of bestowal – for to name, in poetic terms, is already to give, that is the point – Wordsworth cannot but draw our attention to the indeterminacy of *his* word: which is to say, his signature, *qua* poet. 'Wordsworth' signs every word that he writes. Every word 'he' writes is silently signed by this name, 'Wordsworth', and thereby imbued – or not – with whatever genius, fame, or power *it* possesses. This is, however regrettable a figure, *Wordsworth's word's worth*. And 'Wordsworth' – this name which, even now, at the time, at *each* time, of the reading and/or writing of *The Prelude*, still remains suspended upon this poem – in giving or almost giving this gift of 'his' word, cannot help but remind us that, even insofar as 'he' is now giving this gift, it may not, or at least may not yet, be his to give. The text signed 'Wordsworth' performs this reminder every time it gives this gift. He will give it, the text that signs 'Wordsworth' and whose power still hangs in the balance will give it, but only on the condition of acknowledging that what he/it gives will never simply be a matter of what he/it might wish to give, which is another way of saying that *it may not be given*. Put otherwise, what this text 'gives' will always already be bound up with the value of Wordsworth's word, the value of which remains, at least at present, at least at every present moment of *The Prelude*'s presentation – and therefore of the inscription and repetition of this Wordsworthian conditional – still to come, unknown and unknowable. By placing a condition on his gift of life, Wordsworth acknowledges the implicit claim of every such gift: that it may or may not attain to its promise because, to speak truthfully, immortality, or 'life', is not a thing that one can promise to give.

Nor is the presence, or absence, of this life-giving power a mere matter of chance. At least, according to Wordsworth, it is not a simple question of contingent matters of remembrance, archivisation, and popularity. More or other than a mere matter of contingency, or *de facto* life, within the context of *The Recluse* project this giving power of the poetic word emerges as an ontological matter: there would be a divine, *immortal* poetic language and a common, *mortal* one. By Wordsworth's own avowed standards, the bestowal of his gift of life on Calvert should depend, not upon the fickle preferences of any future readership, but upon the actual, life-giving power of his word, once – or if – it attains to the same character as that of those other 'labourers divine', the producers of 'immortal verse', Shakespeare and Milton (5:164–5).[71] Everything depends, that is, on the worth of this name or signature that signs 'Wordsworth'.[72]

That the association between poetry and life, or more specifically, between the poetic word and immortality, is at the very heart of Wordsworth's vision for *The Recluse* is stated by him over and over again. In book one of *The Prelude*, when the poet dreams of composing this 'philosophic song', it is imagined as 'immortal verse/ Thoughtfully fitted to the Orphean lyre' (1:230–4). Later, in book thirteen, the poet conceives of it as a 'monument' (13:430) and a 'work that should endure' (13:278). Yet, as he indicates time and again, to become the architect of this work and to produce this Gothic church requires first traversing the path imposed by *The Prelude*. It is only now, at its conclusion, that

> we may (not presumptuously, I hope)
> Suppose my powers so far confirmed
> . . . as to make me capable
> Of building a work *that should endure*.   (13:275–8, my emphasis)

To construct the right kind of monumental structure, one capable of indifferently suffering the affronts of time, requires the right kind of contractor, which is why not just anyone, and not even any 'Wordsworth', is capable of such a feat.

Wordsworth reprises the language of monumentality – and self-doubt – of *The Prelude* in the 1814 dedicatory epistle to *The Excursion*, where he presents this portion of *The Recluse* to Lonsdale as '[a] token (may it prove a monument!)'.[73] Again, in the 'Preface', he speaks of 'being enabled to construct a literary Work that might live'.[74] Yet unlike the 'life' that Wordsworth and Dorothy fear that Wordsworth himself may come to lack for the construction of this monument, the well-built work, cathedral, or monument 'lives' otherwise, as only immortal, eternal, or timeless verse can. Such is the sentiment, once again, in *Home at Grasmere*, which reproduces both the materialist language of monumentality and the metaphysical discourse of immortality, as well as the now signature Wordsworthian diffidence:

> Possessions have I that are solely mine,
> Something within, which yet is shared by none –
> Not even the nearest to me and most dear –
> Something which power and effort may impart.
> I would impart it; I would spread it wide,

> Immortal in the world which is to come.
> . . .
> Love, Knowledge, all my manifold delights –
> All buried with me without monument
> Or profit unto any but ourselves.
> *It must not be, if I divinely taught*
> *Be privileged to speak as I have felt*
> *Of what in man is human or divine.* (686–702, MS.D, my emphasis)[75]

With astounding consistency, Wordsworth leaves suspended the monumental, living, immortal character of his words and work. His hope is just that – a hope – as unverifiable, ultimately, as the very gift of Nature which, he hopes, subtends it. And this situation, in its entirety, as we have already seen, is openly reflected in the character of this gift to Calvert at the very moment at which he attempts to present it. If words of his can give the name of Calvert life, then so too shall they be able to endow *The Recluse* with it. Yet, strictly speaking, it is the inverse that is the case. It will only have been because *The Recluse* has a life of its own that Wordsworth's signature, his style, and his name – like those of Shakespeare and Milton, whose company he will have joined – will retroactively be imbued with the gift of life that he here doles out in advance, that he doles out without doling out. This is a promissory note promising to pay, not *when*, but *if* he should be fortunate enough to have the only goods worth delivering. This is also to say: only if Calvert's gift itself will prove to have been well spent, then, and only then, on the condition of *its* success, shall it in turn be recompensed, and along with it every word of this too-long – but *only apparently* too-long – text, which will have taken on the necessary and no longer contingent character that Wordsworth fears it appears to have, and that he fears it simply has.

The arrival of Wordsworth's gift of words to Calvert thus depends on the coming of a time when one could definitively say that not only *The Recluse*, but also *The Prelude* has become the pure present whose auto-justifying nature would no longer require supplementary excuse or pardon, and whose time of reading – and publishing – would no longer need to be deferred. But it is just such a time that appears to be excluded from the outset. When, after all, and under what conditions could one ever recognise that such a poetic apotheosis had taken place? Wordsworth himself famously admits in book five of *The Prelude* that even the immortality of his models, Milton and Shakespeare, is ultimately a contingent one, beholden, like all traces, to the survival of a material substrate. The point is that Wordsworth's 'gift of life' may be doomed from the moment of its enunciation, and necessarily so.

Ultimately, the specificity, even the wonder, of the Wordsworthian text lies, not in its establishing of this hope of life, but precisely in its speculations against it. It is as if Wordsworth, the text titled 'Wordsworth', had composed itself as insurance against its own capital wager, rendering *The Prelude*, from the very beginning, a testament to its own internal impossibility. Such a hedge is inscribed into the very pronouncement of the present offered to Calvert, through the conditional 'if', which puts the poet-speaker in the awkward position of being, at once, the most grateful and the least appreciative client, the most giving and the most mean. 'Wordsworth', we could say, responds to the ultimately unpresentable character of Nature's endowment by constructing an automated gratitude-giving machine: a textual time capsule capable of doling out perfectly proportionate presents to his patrons. The gift of life is modulated to be disbursed only on the condition that Calvert's original £900 will have finally been realised in the culminating apotheosis of a poetic-text capable of bestowing the life that is here produced without knowledge of whether it is actually produced. Were this offering never to realise itself in the poet, then neither would the latter's inscribed counter-gifts themselves exceed his abilities; neither would they expend or bestow more than he might reasonably pretend or promise to give.

The above situation, in its structure as well as its mode of articulation, resembles that of the entire 'Poem to Coleridge', which likewise holds itself back, waiting for its publication a date when its value will already have been shored up by the prior completion of *The Recluse*. Yet unlike the situation of publication in general – which merely makes more accessible a text that is already, in principle, 'published' at the moment it is inscribed – in the case of the conditional gift of life, it is ultimately not up to Wordsworth, or *anyone*, or even any text, whether this gift should be given. Wordsworth inscribes, 'Wordsworth' inscribes, as the explicit subject of the poem, the situation of a poetic gift that no one gives. And, in this way, he/it interrupts the economy of client–patron give-and-take, projecting this relation otherwise, through the time of a present that will perhaps always be still to come.

RECEIVING AND GIVING *THE PRELUDE*

> If poems are like wine which time improves, I should like to know what is the year that gives to writings fresh value.
>
> Horace, 'Epistle I' (2.1.34–5)[76]

There is, finally, one last debt that Wordsworth acknowledges in the concluding lines of his autobiographical poem. In contrast to the retrospective nature of his obligations to kith and kin, this final debt is essentially prospective and regards none other than the public. 'Whether to me shall be allotted life', Wordsworth reflects:

> And with life power to accomplish aught of worth
> Sufficient to excuse me in men's sight
> For having given this record of myself,
> Is all uncertain. (13.386–90)[77]

The Prelude itself, at the moment of its writing, requires 'excuse', and for no other reason than the fact that it is given: a lumbering, onerous gift, a white elephant for all those who are unable to recognise its true value. In the uncanny instance of the gift of *The Prelude*, giver is indebted to recipient until, that is, *The Recluse* shall be realised and may reveal to all the former text's true worth. For now, however, *The Prelude* can be offered only on credit.[78] The sole exception that Wordsworth locates to this perverse logic is Coleridge, who stands opposed to the obstinacy of 'men's sight' (women, it seems, need not apply), precisely because the 'belovèd friend',

> hast before thee all which then we were,
> To thee, in memory of that happiness,
> It will be known – by thee at least, my friend,
> Felt – that the history of a poet's mind
> Is labour not unworthy of regard:
> To thee the work shall justify itself. (13:390; 405–10)[79]

The Prelude, gift to Coleridge as well as gift to humankind, here hangs in the balance, suspended between the future presents of two incommensurate figures of the reader: its private and public addressees. Depending on one's perspective, the text may appear to be either auto-justifying or unjustifiable, either a blessing or a curse, either radically understood or radically misunderstood, or all of these at the same time. Like the gift of life to Calvert, offered a moment ago, this one also forces us to ask in exasperation: *What, after all, does it give? How are we to understand this gift's present?* And, in both cases, this is as much a question of time as it is of substance. Not just *what*, then, but *when*? When, exactly, does Wordsworth, or *The Prelude*, give what he/it gives? When does this gift of life arrive, if it arrives? When does *The Prelude* give itself as a present, not only to Calvert, Coleridge, or the public's sight, but also to 'Wordsworth', as the climax of the gifts (of Nature, of Calvert, and yes, of Wordsworth too, who gives his time, if nothing else) that will have made it possible?

Instead of forcing us to take sides in such a debate, the above questions allow us to see just how each of these gifts refuses, precisely, to take sides. Far from awaiting a decisive, future time to come, these gifts are given on the condition of their own deferral. They are inscribed in such a way as to perpetuate, with each repetition of the text and each repetition of the Wordsworthian signature, the still unsettled scenes of their not-quite-proffered presentations. Inscribed in the gap between mortality and immorality, or ignorance and understanding, they are the offerings of a poetry that knows no ground, and one whose gambit lies precisely in its struggle to shore itself up against the absence that conditions it.

Poetry, in Wordsworth, in the text that calls itself 'Wordsworth', constitutes itself in the wake of an origin that is not given, and as the attempt to consolidate itself against the possibility of its constitutive impossibility. The gifts of the word, the poem, or *The Prelude* may therefore be there for all to see, but so soon as one tries to grasp them, one learns that they 'give nothing, but doth lend'. Such a 'lending' should now, however, be understood to haunt the Wordsworthian gift within the very imprinting of its textual being, for, long before there can be any question of a weight-bearing give-and-take *between* subjects, this lending-inscription threatens to interrupt and dissolve *the very matter of exchange*, through the writing of a gift that knows that it may not be one. What is revealed to be 'lent', therefore, is no longer simply the ontic being of a 'present', but the being of that being, as a knowable, graspable totality.[80]

NOTES

1. *The Complete Sonnets and Poems*, 389.
2. *Prelude*, 42.
3. William Wordsworth, *The Excursion*, eds Sally Bushell, James Butler, and Michael Jaye (Ithaca, NY: Cornell University Press, 2007), 50.
4. The importance of the gift for Wordsworth has been touched on in a number of important critical contexts. Raimonda Modiano has shown to what extent a logic of gift exchange and sacrifice regulates the narrative progress of *Home at Grasmere*, and Simon Jarvis has argued that the emphatic references to donation in *The Prelude* betray an attempt by Wordsworth to think the incommensurate and to undermine the strict binary between interestedness and disinterestedness that emerges in the eighteenth century. See Modiano, 'Blood Sacrifice, Gift Economy and the Edenic World: Wordsworth's "Home at Grasmere"', and Jarvis, *Wordsworth's Philosophic Song* (Cambridge: Cambridge University Press, 2006),

as well as David P. Haney, *William Wordsworth and the Hermeneutics of Incarnation*, and Mary Jacobus, 'This Distressful Gift', in *Romantic Things: A Tree, a Rock, a Cloud*, 94–113. As Jarvis points out, 'the continual references to Nature's gifts, to the poet's gifts, and to the hope of establishing a living relation between poet and readers . . . run through Wordsworth's poetry and poetics like a red thread' (99). Work by these authors demonstrates just how critical the figure of the gift is to Wordsworth's poetics, not only for the frequency of its recurrence, but also for its employment at critical junctures of poetic self-reflection. In a now canonical reading of 'Resolution and Independence', Charles Rzepka has demonstrated how Wordsworth's economic difficulties, especially between 1798 and 1802, forced a confrontation between his conception of his poetic vocation and the realities of the literary marketplace, which valued shorter, commodifiable lyrics over the longer, unprofitable epics for which he believed Nature had gifted him. Work like Rzepka's 'A Gift that Complicates Employ: Poetry and Poverty in "Resolution and Independence"', in *Selected Studies in Romantic and American Literature, History, and Culture* (New York: Routledge, 2016), Alan Liu's *Wordsworth: The Sense of History* (Stanford, CA: Stanford University Press, 1989), Kurt Heinzelman's *The Economics of the Imagination* (Boston: University of Massachusetts Press, 1980), Pfau's *Wordsworth's Profession*, and Eilenberg's *Strange Power of Speech* has shown how such references to the gift may thus also relate to Wordsworth's specific experience of and anxieties over the economic situation of his day. They point to an implicit but no less deniable confrontation between the meaning and role of donation, on the one hand, and the structures and impositions of economic life, on the other. In what follows, I in no way seek to deny either the importance of gift exchange in Wordsworth's literary and personal life, or the significance of said economic structures in the long nineteenth century. Nor do I wish to try to resolve, as Rzepka does, the tension between the poles of art and economics in Wordsworth's life, or to decide whether Wordsworth's calculations on the literary marketplace should take precedence over his attempt to 'give' a work to the public. I take these contradictions in his character, work, and life as a given. What I try to show, however, is another structure that haunts all of the above relations and that does so even despite Wordsworth's express intentions, either to give or to profit.

5. The term 'genius' is one favoured by Coleridge, while Wordsworth usually speaks of the 'powers' or 'faculty divine' that Nature ought to have bestowed on him. In what follows, I refer interchangeably to these figures, not because there are not significant differences between them,

but because within the context of the reflections on Wordsworth's poetic powers, each participates in and contributes to the same general logic of the 'gifted'.
6. See *Given Time*, 51–95/34–71.
7. This is not to say that there are not deferrals that also haunt the bank transfer. On the symbolic character of money and the struggle with its effacement in the nineteenth century, see especially Rowlinson.
8. This is William Minto's phrase in his 1889 essay, 'Wordsworth's Great Failure', *Nineteenth Century* 26 (September 1889): 435–51.
9. 6 March 1798, *The Letters of William and Dorothy Wordsworth, 2nd Edn, vol. 1: The Early Years 1787–1805,* eds Ernest de Selincourt and Chester L. Shaver (Oxford: Clarendon, 1967), 212. Hereafter *EY*.
10. 11 March 1798, *EY*, 214. See also Coleridge's corresponding letter to Joseph Cottle from 7 March 1798, in *Collected Letters of Samuel Taylor Coleridge, (vols. 1–6)* ed. Earl Leslie Griggs (Oxford: Clarendon, 1966), I:391. Hereafter *STCL*.
11. On the various possibilities, see Richard Gravil, 'The "Recluse" Project and its Shorter Poems', in *The Oxford Handbook of William Wordsworth*, eds Richard Gravil and Daniel Robinson (Oxford: Oxford University Press, 2015), 345–64.
12. *STCL*, I, 527.
13. 12 October 1799, *STCL*, I, 538.
14. February 1800, *STCL*, I, 575.
15. William Wordsworth and Dorothy Wordsworth, *Letters of the Wordsworth Family from 1787 to 1855, Volume 1*, ed. William Angus Knight (Boston: Ginn and Company, 1907), 171.
16. See also the following passage from the 1805 *Prelude*: 'But from this awful burthen I full soon/ Take refuge, and beguile myself with trust/ That mellower years will bring a riper mind/ And clearer insight' (1:235–8; p.40).
17. 3 June 1805, *EY*, 594.
18. Wordsworth to Sir George Beaumont, 1 August 1806, in *The Letters of William and Dorothy Wordsworth, 2nd Edn, vol. 2: The Middle Years, Part 1: 1806–1811*, eds Ernest de Selincourt and Mary Moorman (Oxford: Clarendon, 1967), 64. Hereafter *MY*.
19. Wordsworth to Sir Walter Scott, 10 November 1806, *MY*, 96.
20. 10 September 1799; *STCL*, I, 527.
21. See 1805 *Prelude*, 1.228–71 and 13.428–52, *Home at Grasmere*, 775–852, MS.D, and the 'Preface' to *The Excursion*.
22. *STCL*, I, 391.

23. *STCL*, II, 1034. See also, for example, Robert Southey's letter to Daniel Stuart from 14 March 1814: 'Wordsworth is about to put his great poem "The Recluse" to the press; which has been the great work of his life. Sooner or later, it will no doubt place him in his proper rank among the English poets. If I were to supply him with a motto for it, it should be *Parturiunt Montes*, without any fear that the remainder of the line could be added; and in defiance of it' (410). *Letters from the Lake Poets: Samuel Taylor Coleridge, William Wordsworth, Robert Southey, to Daniel Stuart* (London: West, Newman and Co., 1889).
24. The reasons offered for Wordsworth's failure are numerous. Early on, Coleridge fears that Wordsworth will waste all of his creative energies on the writing of short, more remunerative poems, a fear that Wordsworth evidently also shared. On this, see Rzepka's 'A Gift that Complicates Employ'. In 'Wordsworth's "Tuft of Primroses": "An Unrelenting Doom"', *Studies in Romanticism* 14.3 (Summer 1975): 237–48, James A. Butler proposes that, in 1808, a symbolic ravaging of the vale of Grasmere rendered Wordsworth unable to take up the poetic voice necessary for the completion of parts one and two (243–8). Kenneth R. Johnston, by contrast, argues that internal contradictions in *Home at Grasmere* rendered it incompletable in '"Home at Grasmere": Reclusive Song', *Studies in Romanticism* 14.1 (Winter 1975): 1–28. In 'A Poet's Progress: Wordsworth and the "Via Naturaliter Negativa"', *Modern Philology* 59.3 (February 1962): 214–24, Geoffrey Hartman imagines the difficulty to lie in an 'unresolved antagonism between Poetry and Nature [that] prevents him from becoming a visionary poet' (217). The point is that the same problems that haunted Wordsworth and his contemporaries *continue* to haunt later generations of critics because of the nature of the questions being asked and the structure of the 'archive' able to be probed.
25. Coleridge to Lady Beaumont, 3 April 1815, *STCL*, IV, 564.
26. Coleridge to Wordsworth, 30 May 1815, *STCL*, IV, 573.
27. *Collected Works of Samuel Taylor Coleridge*, 7.2: 158.
28. *Collected Works of Samuel Taylor Coleridge*, 7.2: 155–6. Later, in *Table Talk* (21 July 1832), Coleridge repeats this position, though with a different excuse: 'I think Wordsworth possessed more of the genius of the great philosophic poet than any man I ever knew, or, as I believe, has existed in England since Milton; but it seems to me that he ought never to have abandoned the contemplative position which is peculiarly, perhaps I might say exclusively, fitted for him. His proper title is *Spectator ab extra*', *Specimens of the Table Talk of the late Samuel Taylor Coleridge*, vol. 2 (New York: Harper & Brothers, 1835), 38–9. In each of these instances Coleridge may be seen

to be responding to the criticisms of Francis Jeffrey, whose November 1814 review of Wordsworth's *Excursion* in the *Edinburgh Review* comes very close to diagnosing the poet as both inherently flawed and incurable: 'Inveterate habit must now have given a kind of sanctity to the errors of early taste; and the very powers of which we lament the perversion, have probably become incapable of any other application,' *Contributions to the Edinburgh Review by Francis Jeffrey* (London: Longman, Brown, Green, and Longmans, 1855), 585–6.

29. See, for example, Dorothy's letter to Lady Beaumont on 29 November 1805: 'My brother has not yet begun fairly with his great work; but I hope he will after his return from Park house. We shall then in right earnest enjoy winter quiet and loneliness; besides starlight walks and winter winds are his delight – his mind I think is often more fertile in this season than any other' (*EY*, 650).

30. 7 August 1805, Dorothy to Lady Beaumont: 'My brother has not resumed his great work since the finishing of the poem on his own life, and he now begins to be anxious to get forward again; but till we are alone I do not think that he will do much' (*EY*, 617).

31. 19 January 1805, Dorothy to Lady Beaumont: 'my Brother though not actually employed in his great work, is not idle, for he almost daily produces something and his thoughts are employed upon the Recluse' (*MY*, I, 2).

32. 26 December 1805, Dorothy to Lady Beaumont: 'He is very anxious to get forward with The Recluse, and is reading for the nourishment of his mind, preparatory to beginning; but I do not think he will be able to do much more till we have heard of Coleridge' (*EY*, 664).

33. 27 March 1821, Dorothy to Catherine Clarkson: 'William is quite well, and very busy, though he has not looked at The Recluse or the poem on his own life; and this disturbs us. After fifty years of age there is no time to spare, and unfinished works should not, if it be possible, be left behind. This he feels, but the will never governs *his* labours,' *The Letters of William and Dorothy Wordsworth, 2nd Edn, vol. 4: The Later Years, Part 1: 1821–1828*, ed. Alan G. Hill (Oxford: Clarendon, 1978), 50, and 13 December 1824, Dorothy to Henry Crabb Robinson: 'My brother has not yet looked at the Recluse; he seems to feel the task so weighty that he shrinks from beginning with it – yet knows that he has now no time to loiter if another great work is to be accomplished by him' (*LY*, I, 292).

34. William Wordsworth, *Home at Grasmere: Part First, Book First, of The Recluse*, ed. Beth Darlington (Ithaca, NY: Cornell University Press, 1977), 31. See also Wordsworth's statement to Aubrey de Vere in 1841: 'the Recluse has

never been written except a few passages – and probably never will [be]' (quoted from a letter of 25 June from de Vere to his sister, in Wilfred Ward, *Aubrey de Vere: A Memoir Based on His Unpublished Diaries and Correspondence* (London: Longmans, Green, and Co., 1904), 66.
35. *The Excursion*, 50–1.
36. *The Prelude, 1798–1799*, ed. Stephen Parrish (Ithaca, NY: Cornell University Press, 1977), 43. All citations from the two-part *Prelude* are taken from this edition. Hereafter *1799 Prelude*.
37. 20 April 1822, Wordsworth to Walter Savage Landor, *LY*, I, 126. See also 29 March 1804, Wordsworth to Coleridge: 'I cannot say what a load it would be to me, should I survive you and you die without this memorial left behind. Do for heaven's sake, put this out of the reach of accident immediately' (*EY*, 464).
38. 6 March 1804, Wordsworth to Thomas de Quincey, *EY*, 454.
39. 3 June 1805, Wordsworth to Sir George Beaumont, *EY*, 594.
40. *Prelude*, 40.
41. *Prelude*, 478–90.
42. Wordsworth also began preparing *The Prelude* for posthumous publication around this time, ostensibly because he now believed that there was no point in putting it off for *The Recluse*. See 'The Texts: History and Presentation', in *Prelude* on this (522), as well as Isabella Fenwick's letter to Henry Taylor, 28 March 1839, in *Correspondence of Henry Taylor*, ed. Edward Dowden (London: Longmans, Green, and Co., 1888), 117–18.
43. *Life, Letters, and Journals of George Ticknor, vol. II*, ed. George Hillard (Boston: James R. Osgood and Company, 1877), 167. The question as to Wordsworth's fitness for the construction of a work of enduring value continues to haunt his readers, as Kenneth R. Johnston points out in 'Wordsworth and the Recluse: The University of Imagination', *PMLA* 97.1 (1982): 60–82: 'Wordsworth criticism is haunted by a rhetorical tradition that assumes a connection between the decline in the poet's creative powers and his failure to finish *The Recluse*' (60). Making such an observation does not, however, stop Johnston from taking sides. In *The Hidden Wordsworth* (New York: W. W. Norton, 2001) he writes: 'Wordsworth's failure to advance *The Recluse* in March was not a failure of poetic power. On the contrary, it was a triumph of poetic power unleashed but uncontained' (416). Stephen Gill, in his introduction to *William Wordsworth's The Prelude: A Casebook*, ed. Stephen Gill (Oxford: Oxford University Press, 2006), 3–42, raises and answers the question as follows: 'But Wordsworth never completed the task he had set himself – to write *The Recluse*. The noble duty invoked at the close of *The Prelude* had been at best only partially fulfilled, it seemed.

Had he been mistaken, then, in concluding that Nature and Education had fitted him for his special task? Surely not' (5–6).

44. 13 February 1804, Dorothy to Catherine Clarkson: 'William, which is the best news I can tell you, is cheerfully engaged in composition, and goes on with great rapidity. He is writing the Poem on his own early life, which is to be an appendix to the *Recluse*' (*EY*, 440).
45. 6 March 1804, Wordsworth to Thomas de Quincey: 'This Poem will not be published these many years, and never during my lifetime, till I have finished a larger and more important work to which it is tributary' (*EY*, 454).
46. 3 June 1805, Wordsworth to George Beaumont: 'This work may be considered as a sort of portico to the Recluse, part of the same building, which I hope to be able erelong to begin with, in earnest' (594).
47. 'Preface' to *Excursion*, 38. For what it is worth, when Coleridge describes what he imagined the relation should be in 1815, he puts it as follows: 'the Poem on the growth of your own mind was as the ground-plant and the Roots, out of which the Recluse was to have sprung up as the Tree – as far as [there was] the same Sap in both, I expected them doubtless to have formed one compleat Whole' (*STCL*, IV, 573).
48. See also Wordsworth's letter to Richard Sharp, on 29 April 1804: '[*The Prelude*] will never be published, (during my lifetime I mean), till another work has been written and published, of sufficient importance to justify me in giving my own history to the world' (*EY*, 470).
49. *1799 Prelude*, 54.
50. On this journey, see Abrams, *Natural Supernaturalism*, and Jacobus, *Romanticism, Writing and Sexual Difference*.
51. *Excursion*, 38.
52. *Prelude*, 36.
53. *1799 Prelude*, 43–7.
54. *1799 Prelude*, 44–5.
55. *1799 Prelude*, 66.
56. *1799 Prelude*, 66.
57. One seeming exception to this self-effacement is in book three of the 1805 *Prelude*: 'I was a chosen son./ For hither I had come with holy powers/ And faculties, whether to work or feel' (3:82–4; p.96). Nevertheless, by 1850 he tempers these remarks considerably, cutting references to being 'chosen' and claiming only that 'hither I had come ... endowed with holy powers/ And faculties, whether to work or feel' (3:87–9, p.97). For the extension of this conditional logic of the gift into the lyrical works, see also 'Lines written a few miles above Tintern Abbey': 'Nor less, I trust,/ To them *I may have owed* another gift,/ Of

aspect more sublime; that blessed mood' (ll.36–8) and '*If this/ Be but a vain belief,* yet, oh!' (ll.50–1).
58. This was, in point of fact, a common strategy of many earlier poets who, in an effort to solicit the patronage of a wealthy aristocrat, would from time to time dedicate works to them prior to securing any commitment.
59. *Prelude*, 28–32; 36.
60. *Prelude*, 48; 64.
61. *Prelude*, 460–4.
62. On the friendship between Coleridge and Wordsworth, see Modiano, 'Coleridge and Wordsworth: The Ethics of Gift Exchange and Literary Ownership'. In *The Gift*, Hyde analyses the importance of leaving implicit the passage of goods among family members for the building of familial bonds (72–95). For Mauss and his readers, it is precisely the indefinite nature of the circuit of gift exchanges that renders them powerful tools of community building. For each of the above authors, what remains undeniable is the nature of some 'bond', tying together participants in their unspoken 'gift exchanges'. While the existence of such ties is, to a certain extent, undeniable – and I do not wish to bring it into question here – what nevertheless remains debatable is that this model of give-and-take is adequate to the Wordsworthian text, which refuses, time and again, to acknowledge the presence of the present. Wordsworth, the text signed 'Wordsworth', holds the gift in suspense, and this suspension affects the very 'economy' of his text, as well as the nature of the 'bond' itself.
63. See *EY*, 546.
64. Far from embellishment, Calvert's legacy did indeed enable Wordsworth 'to pause for choice' and to pursue his poetic vocation. At the time, in addition to pressures from his extended family to take up a profession, he was in need of money to send to Annette Vallon, as well as to finance his marriage to Mary Hutchinson, and to support Dorothy, who was not likely to marry. Wordsworth wrote to Sir George Beaumont on 20 February 1805 that 'I should have been forced into one of the professions by necessity, had not a friend left me £900' (*EY*, 546).
65. Johnston, *The Hidden Wordsworth*, 308. In letters to William Mathews it becomes clear that, whatever Wordsworth's initial motivations, he ultimately remained with Raisley out of a sense of obligation. See letters from 24 December 1794 and 7 January 1795, *EY*, 136–9. Wordsworth also became increasingly worried that Raisley might die before signing the will.
66. See Richard E. Matlak, *The Poetry of Relationship: The Wordsworths and Coleridge, 1797–1800* (New York: St Martins Press, 1997), 45–51, who

claims that Calvert's legacy led Wordsworth into a 'muddle of self-interest, money and death' (39).
67. This is how Wordsworth interprets it, anyway. As Liu points out, Raisley wrote out his will in such a way as to assure against the use of it for claims upon Wordsworth by his cousins for the debt he owed them for his education. It was thus removed from the normal cycle of capital. At the same time, Wordsworth later used part of it to support his own friends' projects, charging them an unreasonably high interest rate in the process (335). This makes identifying a single, univocal meaning for his gift all but impossible.
68. On this, see especially Murphy, *The Gift of Immortality*.
69. Pindar, 'Nemean 4', in *Nemean Odes. Isthmian Odes. Fragments*, ed. and trans. William H. Race (Cambridge, MA: Harvard University Press, 1997), 37.
70. Ovid, 'To His Wife', *Tristia. Ex Ponto*, 5.14, p.259.
71. *Prelude*, 160.
72. See also *Prelude* 11.328–43. See Heinzelman for an alternative reading of the Calvert relationship. Although Heinzelman offers a lucid account of the meaning of Wordsworth's tribute, he never entertains the possibility that Wordsworth's words might not actually be capable of such a gift (199). Ultimately, even if one wishes to take Wordsworth less literally and to read his claim, rather than ontologising this difference, as indicating that fame is a fickle business, the critical force remains the same. This gift that Wordsworth gives is ultimately out of his hands, and as a result, various paradoxes ensue.
73. *Excursion*, 37.
74. *Excursion*, 38.
75. *Home at Grasmere*, 95–7.
76. *Satires. Epistles. The Art of Poetry*, 399.
77. *Prelude*, 478–80.
78. Wordsworth's view on this, and the value of this wager, must of course have changed when he finally prepared *The Prelude* for posthumous publication after he had accepted that *The Recluse* would never be completed.
79. *Prelude*, 480.
80. Such a conclusion must finally be contrasted, in closing, with the tribute Wordsworth belatedly offered Calvert, just a few years later, in his sonnet 'To the Memory of Raisley Calvert'. Although Wordsworth here retains his hesitation in reference to his own abilities, as if to make amends for a tribute that had perhaps been something both more and less than a gift, he here attempts to offer the inscription of 'the name of Calvert' with as little mediation as possible, thundered forth without qualification and with as clear a

statement of purpose as one will find in his work: 'CALVERT! it must not be unheard by them/ Who may respect my name, that I to thee/ Owed many years of early liberty' (ll.1–3). Uttered outside the tensions of deferral, ingratitude, and denial surrounding the 'Poem to Coleridge', the name of 'CALVERT!' is, Wordsworth surely hopes, at last free to be heard. Indeed, though it falls to those who respect 'my name' to hear it, it is Calvert himself who is addressed, called forth as if to bear witness to his own poetic afterlife. Nevertheless, and somewhat sadly, Wordsworth's earlier lofty aspirations of 'life' have themselves passed away and been replaced by the modest injunction that 'CALVERT!' must be *heard*, or at least must not *go unheard*: a feat difficult for anyone who so much as looks at a poem whose exclamatory debut functions as much like an advertisement as it does a sonnet. Absent the glorious gambit that is the promise of poetry in *The Prelude*, Wordsworth can here offer Calvert hardly more than a token. Not quite a gift, then, 'To the Memory' is closer to what Emerson would call an 'apology for a gift': that is, a trinket or a token more meretricious than heartfelt. In attempting, at last, to re-enter the common circulation of poetic commerce and to close the book on Calvert, Wordsworth may, alas, have spoken too soon.

PART II

BEING AND NAMING

In following the gifts of poetry through their most deeply embedded tracks, the previous chapters aimed to establish as fundamental to the basic understanding of 'poetry' the constellations through which the logic of the gift functions in the widest reaches of the poetic tradition. In doing so, these chapters operated largely through the traditional opposition between poetry's *archē* and *telos*: its historical and conceptual origins, on the one hand, and its ethical, material, and self-determined ends, on the other. In spite of the efficacy of focusing on these modalities of poetic postality – which tendency can be found at work no less 'within' the poetic text's various projections than 'without', in extra-poetic or meta-discursive theory – something, however, remained missing. Indeed, one might suspect that by focusing on questions of origin and end, we ultimately touched on everything *but* poetry, assuming that there is such a thing. While examining how the tradition accounts for the possibility of the poem – by way of figures of genius, inspiration, and imagination – and for its social and material import – through patronage and poetic evangelising – were each important tasks, by attending exclusively to questions of origin and end we may have risked losing sight of the thing itself: that is, of the work *in its being*, enigmatic though it may be. This is not to say that we could merely have done otherwise, for such a problem, the problem of poetry, or poetry's imposition of itself *as a problem*, may indeed be one of its most undeniable features.

The task of Part II will now be to see what may heretofore have been evaded, even if this evasion was dictated by some necessity of the object itself. That is, it will be to ask how poetry might already be determined, *in its being*, as gift, before or beyond any subsequent historical or ontic determinations, such as one finds in tropes of inspiration, genius, and talent, or in the material relays of patronage and the literary market. Why, after all, appeal to figures of inspiration, or genius, unless something internal to the object already called to this, its alterity, unless poetry already phenomenalised something fundamentally foreign and 'beyond prose-reason', 'mysteries . . . not to be explained, but admired', and to which these 'gifts', in fact, respond? Understood in this way, the examples of poetic donation that we have already examined would allow something to circulate, but only on the condition of retaining a trace of that which *is not* and that which *is never presented*. As we saw in the previous chapter, for Wordsworth, the gifts of the poem, the word, and the name are ones that initially appear to be given by the poet, and are only latently recognised to be constitutive effects of text. In turning now to Shelley, Stein, and Heidegger, we will see how each prioritises the originary, giving essence of the word as productive of what we call 'poetry', and the various modalities of what Paul de Man calls its 'lyricization'.[1] It is only because the nature of the word is already that of 'gift' – in a radical sense of this term – that its reified form as 'poetry' in turn requires patronage presents and figures of genius, which would *re-present* its true ontological character, now through so many linguistic and material remainders.

NOTE

1. See Paul de Man, 'Anthropomorphism and Trope in the Lyric', in *The Rhetoric of Romanticism*, 239–62. For de Man, lyric is 'not a genre, but one name among several to designate the defensive motion of understanding, the possibility of a future hermeneutics'. 'What we call the lyric [is] the instance of represented voice, [and] conveniently spells out the rhetorical and thematic characteristics that make it the paradigm of a complementary relationship between grammar, trope, and theme' (261).

4

Stein and the Concern of Poetry

> Nouns are the name of anything. Think of all that early poetry, think of Homer, think of Chaucer, think of the Bible and you will see what I mean you will really realize that they were drunk with nouns, to name to know how to name earth sea and sky and all that was in them was enough to make them live and love in names, and that is what poetry is it is a state of knowing and feeling a name. I know that now but I have only come to that knowledge by long writing. So then as I say that is what poetry was and slowly as everybody knew the names of everything poetry had less and less to do with everything. Poetry did not change, poetry never changed, from the beginning until now and always in the future poetry will concern itself with the names of things. The names may be repeated in different ways and very soon I will go into that matter but now and always poetry is created by naming names the names of something the names of somebody the names of anything. Nouns are the names of things and so nouns are the basis of poetry.
>
> Stein, 'Poetry and Grammar'[1]

In 1934, during a one-year speaking tour of America, Gertrude Stein presented a lecture on poetic naming entitled 'Poetry and Grammar'. Amidst discussions of her shifting focuses in writing *The Making of the Americans* and *Tender Buttons*, she there outlines a deceptively simple account of the history of poetry, in which the name and noun are emphasised as poetry's central and timeless concerns. In so doing, Stein gives what we might today call an ontological account of poetry: one that does not simply address poetry as a genre or form, but that instead relates it back to the originary role of the word and language in bringing beings to presence.

In this way, Stein anticipated a number of elements now recognisable as commonplaces of Heideggerian poetics. Stein's essay locates the 'basis' of poetry in its ability to name and, in naming, to give the being of beings. Thus, prior to any question of its divine or psychic source, or of its import within political or economic relays, Stein identifies poetry with this essentially *grammatical* concern. Poetry begins by giving out all the names. When it is done giving out the names – because there are none left to be given – it gives instead the things themselves by taking the names back, so to speak. In this way, she explains, poetry's 'concern' remains constant, even as its socio-historical function shifts.

As we shall see, for a certain tradition of poetics, the gift of poetry is to be located first of all here: in language, in the relation between word and thing, and in the excess that marks each, for before there can be any matter of the tangible present, poetry must first give the gift that language is. Poetry gives language, which itself gives beings, being the condition of their presence. What we call the gift of the name thus both repeats and recalls this more originary gift of being, which is always its secret or implicit concern.

Poetry, it is worth noting, remains strange on this account – just as it was for the Greeks, just as it was for Kant. It remains strange, however, no longer as worldly vestige of divine source – as vatic vision or voice of nature – but as the strangeness of being itself, as only the most extreme proximity to language's ungraspability now allows us to experience. Poetry brings forth the strangeness of language by giving the name in its non-presence, by bringing to presence its non-presence. In what follows, we will pursue this tradition of poetics in Stein, and then see how she anticipates central elements of the Heideggerian thinking of *Dichtung*. By emphasising poetry's essential relation to the name, both thinkers offer decisive accounts of the survival of its gift modality, as that which persists in spite of the most varied historical and culture shifts.

Thus, argues Stein, poetry has *always* been concerned with nouns. What changes is not this concern, then, but instead the specific role and function of the noun, in a given society:

> Poetry is concerned with using with abusing, with losing with wanting, with denying with avoiding with adoring with replacing the noun. It is doing that always doing that, doing that and doing nothing but that. Poetry is doing nothing but using losing refusing and pleasing and betraying and caressing nouns. That is what poetry does, that is what poetry has to do no matter what kind of poetry it is. And there are a great many kinds of poetry.[2]

Poetry, Stein tells us, is by its very nature concerned with nouns. Yet if it has always been marked by this attention, or even care, for the noun, then one way of accounting for its diversity of forms will be through analysing society's shifting relationship to its own vocabulary. Thus, while 'early poetry' was 'drunk with nouns',

> Think of all that early poetry, think of Homer, think of Chaucer, think of the Bible and you will see what I mean you will really realize that they were drunk with nouns, to name to know how to name earth sea and sky and all that was in them was enough to make them live and love in names.

Thus, while early poetry could lose itself in its near-rapturous frenzy of naming all those names that were not yet given, well, 'slowly as everybody knew the names of everything poetry had less and less to do with everything'.[3] To understand what she herself had done in writing *Tender Buttons*, one must therefore first of all understand that the essential function of poetry, for Stein, writing in English in the twentieth century, could no longer merely be *to give* the names for things, nor even to give these things *new* names. Yet if poetry is not to concern itself with giving names, what is it to do?

> And then, something happened and I began to discover the names of things, that is not discover the names but discover the things the things to see the things to look at and in so doing I had of course to name them not to give them new names but to see that I could find out how to know that they were there by their names or by replacing their names.[4]

Poetry *had* a function: it was essentially Adamic in nature. It gave names to things and in so doing it profited from near-universal approval. Subsequently, all the things having received their names, poetry had to seek out a new role or else suffer extinction. This retrenchment resulted in another kind of poetic labour: one in which poetry did not simply give any more, but engaged in the presentation of things *as the things that they are* – which is to say, the re-presentation of the thing in non-representative fashion, no longer through the name-signifier, but so many disruptive processes of material repetition or nominative abstraction. Poetry loses its function as giver (of names), only to gain a role as giver (of things), precisely by denying or withholding the given name.

For Stein, the essence of poetry is thus identified with its concern for the name. But 'naming' – or, to be specific, poetry's present engagement with naming – names for her neither simple creation, nor mere nomination of what, even if nameless, is already a present. The singularity of poetry, we might say, consists in its ability to re-name, or even to un-name, that which has, through no fault of its own, become the reified object of past acts of nomination. This is why poetry '[does] not discover the names but discover[s] the things the things to see the things to look at'. The 'discovery' of poetry is of the things the things, of the things *as things*, in their thingness. And, for this project, the name must cease to be conceived of as a mere vehicle of transmission or sense. It must instead become prized in its own right, as a thing, a thing a thing, no longer simply dissociable from that which it names.

In this way, Stein both accounts for the long history of poetry in the West as unified in its nature and accounts for what, given the shifting conditions of lived language, has evidently changed in its focus. Poetry has always been and will always be occupied with names. This used to mean that it gave names. What has changed, as all the names have been given out, is therefore not poetry's essentially giving nature – which survives, though reborn – but only the lack that remains to be supplied by its bountiful presents. Where there are names, what remains to be given are now the things themselves: which is to say, the name-things themselves, the names as things and things as names, names as nouns. 'I had of course to name them not to give them new names but to see that I could find out how to know that they were there by their names or by replacing their names.'

As we shall see, far from being idiosyncratic, the formal structure of this narrative reappears in almost identical fashion in Heidegger. Moreover, it follows the same basic structure as anthropological narratives of economic development, in which the height of gift-giving in general is to be found in 'archaic societies', which, in passing over to money-based economies, see the gift gain a relatively niche or marginal role within an economic system now dominated by market exchanges. One's attachment to the gift (*or* to poetry) under such conditions, whether one theorises either term as Stein, Mauss, Heidegger, or even Agamben does, then becomes the gift's (or poetry's) disruptive or liberatory role *for* the thing, in the face of its linguistic, technological, and economic reification.[5] The merely given, or objectively known, moribund, and calculated present of modernity, becomes given otherwise – *saved*, as it were – through a gift of poetry that restores non-presence to the present.

Although I will be critical of the developmental structure of these narratives, as well as their exclusionary character – for they often require that one identify a strict limit between poetry and non-poetry, or gift and non-gift, a task that is difficult, if not impossible, to accomplish, and one that is always problematic in its implications – such narratives cannot simply be dismissed. Derrida perhaps goes as far as one can in attempting to suspend, without, however, simply effacing, the limits between gift and non-gift, or poetry and non-poetry, by embracing first of all the structure of *récit*. And, like him, I too will bear a certain ambivalence, being both critical of, yet nevertheless beholden to, some iteration of both of these terms, which I can neither fully abandon, nor fully embrace. It is precisely the meaning of this ambivalence, or what we might think of as the turn, away from and back to the gift, or away from and back to poetry, that has been a central motif of this book, and one that Stein, Heidegger, and Shelley's writings will help us to consider, now on ontological grounds.

The question, then, that is already posed by Stein's lecture is what this ontological tradition of poetics – which does not simply originate in the nineteenth and twentieth centuries, but whose flourishing perhaps has to do with the acceleration of processes of secularisation, modernisation, and capitalism – what this ontological tradition of poetics, concerned above all with the poetic word, actually dictates about 'poetry' and its alleged 'giving' nature. In other words, for this tradition of poetics, poetry's gift is to be found nowhere other than in its linguistic character. For Stein, it is poetry's concern with names and nouns that makes it *essentially* generous. This generosity is first expressed through explicit acts of donation and then, later, in its ability to exceed the given. For Heidegger, there is a certain, excessive generosity to be found already in the word. The word, or language, as giving source, is the ur-form of poetry, before anything explicitly goes by that name. But if, in both cases, one starts with the word, with this trace or this text that we call 'the word', will it henceforth be possible to delimit something called 'poetry', a domain or an activity proper to this name, at least insofar as it is to be opposed to some non-poetic other? Does the delimitation of poetic essence to the word not force one to risk abandoning this very term, *in its own name*? It is such a necessary possibility that we will confront through a reading of Shelley's 'Hymn to Intellectual Beauty'. Shelley's poem, I argue, gives us something like the poematic experience of the hedgehog, within the very menagerie of poetry.

NOTES

1. 'Poetry and Grammar', in *Lectures in America* (Boston: Beacon Press, 1985), 208–46; 233. Henceforth *PG*.
2. *PG*, 231.
3. *PG*, 233.
4. *PG*, 235.
5. See Giorgio Agamben, *The Man Without Content*, trans. Georgia Albert (Stanford, CA: Stanford University Press, 1999), where he theorises the 'extreme destiny of *poiēsis*, by which it dispenses its power only as privation

(though this privation is also, in reality, an extreme gift of poetry, the most accomplished and charged with meaning, because in it nothingness itself is called into presence)' (64). On the transition from gift-based economies to commodity- and money-based ones, as well as the co-existence of both forms, see Sahlins and Gregory. One might also compare this argument to eighteenth-century narratives of *Naturpoesie* and *Volkslied*, in which the first languages are understood as being originarily poetic. The birth of 'poetry' (in the restricted sense) occurs only with the loss of language's original vivacity, through a mechanical repetition of use that obscures the word's inherent metaphoricity (Rousseau) or character as song (Herder). 'Poetry' – now opposed to a 'non-poetry' – thus becomes a mode of recapturing the true being of the word, though now by other means. See Rousseau's 'Essay on the Origin of Languages' (12) and Herder's 'Essay on the Origin of Language' (136) in *On the Origin of Language*.

5

Heidegger and the *Stiftung der Wahrheit*

> For all essential poetry also poetizes 'anew' the essence of poetizing itself. This is true of Hölderlin's poetry in a special and singular sense. No calendrical date can be given for the 'Now' of his poetry. Nor is any date needed here at all. For this 'Now' that is called and is itself calling is, in a more originary sense, itself a date – that is to say, something given, a gift [ein Gegebenes, eine Gabe]; namely, given via the calling of this vocation [gegeben nämlich durch die Berufung].
>
> <div align="right">Heidegger, <i>Hölderlin's Hymn 'The Ister'</i>[1]</div>

Though Heidegger is today well known as a thinker of the gift, having been instrumental for the phenomenological tradition taken up by Jacques Derrida, Jean-Luc Nancy, and Jean-Luc Marion, and though his writings on poetry are among his most widely read works, nevertheless, one would not necessarily identify him as a greater thinker of the *poetic gift*, per se. This is at least in part because his writings on poetry dispense with the traditional tropes of gift poetics – modelled as they are on the lyric subject – such as inspiration, genius, and imagination. Moreover, Heidegger took little to no interest in the relays of patronage. Such economic structures were too ontic in nature, missing, on each occasion, what of poetry is truly historical. To be sure, Heidegger would have considered the better part of what we have analysed to this point as being far too metaphysical and overly subjective in its orientation.

And yet, in many ways, I will argue, Heidegger remains this tradition's most extreme proponent. At least as early as 'The Origin of the Work of Art' (1935) and as late as 'The Essence of Language' (1957–8), the exigency of conceiving of poetry as a gift is a visible motif in his work. It is a theme, moreover, at the very centre of his conceptions of language, art, and being, as *Dichtung* becomes, on the one hand, the essence of both art and language, and on the other, that through which the granting of being may not only be brought forth, but also be given otherwise.[2] Far, then, from being a mere topos in his writings, what I am calling the 'gift of poetry' was a dominant conceptual figure: To think poetry as a gift was, for Heidegger, a matter of pure ontological necessity, and one that testified to what, in fact, is most essential in art. It testified to what, of art, is most worthy of the name.[3]

The gift of poetry, or the conception of poetry as gift, was thus no mere figure for Heidegger, but the expression of what in art and language bears being and performs the labour of philosophy before even the philosopher may take up the task.[4] We could even say, as Heidegger at times insinuates, that there is nothing particularly 'poetic' about this 'gift of poetry', considered in its essential sense, for what we call 'poetry' (or *Poesie*, discursive poetry) ought, in fact, to be defined on the basis of *Dichtung* (the poetising essence of language), and not the other way around.[5] Rather, then, than being a matter of presents proffered by poets, or gift economies circulating apart from, yet alongside so many commercial transactions, the gift of poetry becomes, in his work, the very mode by which language gives its own essence by poetising the giving-not-given being at its heart. We may learn of such a process by way of what is commonly called 'poetry', but that which is thereby proffered – the *Dichtung* behind these *Gedichte* and this *Poesie* – is never simply reducible to what goes by this name.

The question remains, in following this motif in his work, of what is at stake, for Heidegger, in defining the essence of language *as a poem* that *gives the truth*. Does such a conception of *Dichtung* succeed in breaking free from the menagerie that otherwise keeps poetry penned up, or does it instead open up on to something more radical, for which we do not yet have an adequate name? Is Heidegger's turn to *Dichtung* simply a continuation of the most classical Western topos – always invested in some version of *man* – or does it announce a thought of language capable of breaking with such hegemonic thinking? It is in 'The Origin of the Work of Art' that Heidegger first explains in what, exactly, poetry's 'endowment [Stiftung]' consists, or more precisely, in what sense poetry may be said 'to give [stiften] the truth':

> The essence of art is poetry. The essence of poetry, however, is the founding of truth. 'Founding' is understood, here, in a threefold sense: as bestowing, as grounding, and as beginning.
>
> [Das Wesen der Kunst ist die Dichtung. Das Wesen der Dichtung aber ist die Stiftung der Wahrheit. Das Stiften verstehen wir hier in einem dreifachen Sinne: Stiften als Schenken, Stiften als Gründen und Stiften als Anfangen.][6]

To repeat what is already the condensation of a much longer argument: Poetry [*Dichtung*], for Heidegger, which is itself the essence of art and as such one of the principal fashions by which truth brings itself to light in beings, is in turn revealed to have as its essence the establishment of truth, in the mode of an endowing. The nature of this endowing is then broken down into three specific roles: bestowing, grounding, and beginning. The work can be considered a bestowing, a *Schenken* or *Schenkung*, Heidegger explains, to the extent that the truth it puts to work pushes forward [stößt auf] the extra-ordinary [Un-geheure] while overturning [stößt um] the ordinary [Geheure]: that is, to the extent that it introduces [stiftet] an unverifiable overflowing with respect to that which is.[7] It is a grounding, a *Gründen* or *Gründung*, to the extent that it never merely projects an arbitrary or indeterminate demand, but in its imposition is always already addressed to a historical people [einem geschichtlichen Menschentum zugeworfen]. Moreover, as the very opening of the earth, the self-closing ground [seine Erde, der sich verschließende Grund] into which Dasein is already thrown, the *Stiftung*, or 'poeticizing projection of truth [dichtende Entwurf der Wahrheit]', becomes the latter's very 'bearing ground [tragende Grund]'. It is, finally, an *Anfang* or *Anfangen*, in the sense of a 'leap [Sprung]' or 'incitement [Anstiftung]', insofar as both the bestowal and grounding of poetry bear the abruptness or non-mediated nature [Unvermittelte] of a 'beginning'. And a true beginning, Heidegger clarifies, does not preclude, but in fact necessitates, that its bestowal be predetermined by the historical, or sent [geschichtliches], essence of the work.

The gift of poetry, understood as 'die Stiftung der Wahrheit', is thus the privileged form of the setting-to-work of truth, upon which the unconcealment of being may be said to depend. This labour falls to *poetry*, because '[l]anguage itself is poetry in the essential sense [Die Sprache selbst ist die Dichtung im wesentlichen Sinne]', and it is 'language' that first brings beings into being.[8] It is a *gift* because the truth thereby set to work is never simply a truth of correspondence – which would merely relate to that which already is – but is the abrupt incitement, we could also say event or *Ereignis*, involved in supplying the very ground upon which that which *is not* may come *to be* (given).

In a contemporary text, 'Hölderlin and the Essence of Poetry' (1936), the same schema of poetry as endowment returns, though now with the focus on its character as 'verbal endowment of being [worthafte Stiftung des Seins]'. Beginning with Hölderlin's suggestion that 'what remains is founded by the poets [Was bleibet aber, stiften die Dichter]', Heidegger returns once more to the question of how, exactly, to understand this poetic 'Stiftung':[9]

> Poetry is verbal endowment of being . . . But because being and essence of things can never be calculated and derived from what is present at hand, they must be freely created, posited, and bestowed. Such free bestowal is a founding.
>
> [Dichtung ist worthafte Stiftung des Seins . . . Weil aber Sein und Wesen der Dinge nie errechnet und aus dem Vorhandenen abgeleitet werden können, müssen sie frei geschaffen, gesetzt und geschenkt werden. Solche freie Schenkung ist Stiftung.][10]

What was characterised as 'bestowing, grounding, and beginning' in the poetic act of endowing in the realm of the work of art has now become the 'creating, positing, and bestowing' of the being and essence of things through the *Stiftung der Dichtung*. This threefold gesture, whereby what remains [das Bleibende] comes to remain [bleiben], is a 'free bestowal' because, as Heidegger tells us, in the poetic naming of 'things' their being and essence always remain incalculable and irreducible with respect to that which is present [aus dem Vorhanden]. And this might further be broken down into the following two points: on the one hand, because the named 'thing', that which becomes poetically endowed, is *no thing* prior to the naming gesture, it is therefore derivable from (*abgeleitet*, able to be deduced or even drawn out of) nothing present. And, on the other hand, because of this, its originary non-derivativeness, even in being named, the 'thing' 'is' in the mode of remaining: which is to say, remains radically non-present, unable to be known in the mode of calculation.

Thus, once more, poetry [Dichtung] stands as the name for that which furnishes, grounds, posits and so on the being of what is never preceded in being, and what, in remaining, is never calculable or computable. At the same time, and just as in 'Origin', poetic *Stiftung*, Heidegger reminds us, cannot simply be understood as a 'freie Schenkung', but is always also the concomitant gesture of firmly grounding human existence in its ground.[11]

As Derrida cautions in his own reading of 'Origin', in *Donner le temps II*, given what is at stake in Heidegger's text, there is some danger in simply translating poetising *Dichtung* as 'poetry'. *Dichtung* is not poetry – it is not a matter of 'poems', 'poets', or even 'poetics' – but gives each of these formations life. It is the source from which poets may be the poets that they are, as the *worthafte* ('verbal', but also 'word-ly', or linguistic) endowment of being. It thus exceeds every poetics while naming what, of the poet and the poem, *may* yet give this gift of being, irreducible to every present. It is because 'poetry' puts us in touch with what of language may always exceed the given that its highest calling lies in this event that we call *the gift*.

As part of his effort to respond to the problem posed by translating *Dichtung* – which problem inhabits the German text no less than the French or the English – Derrida offers a number of translations in the course of his reading, including 'le *poiein* de la langue', 'poème de la langue', 'langue comme poème', and even 'essence poématique de la langue'.[12] *Dichtung*, like the *Gedicht* of Heidegger's subsequent 'Die Sprache im Gedicht', which Derrida examines a few years later, does not conform to any traditional concept of *poésie*. Nevertheless, by pointing us back to the work of a few privileged poets (*große Dichter*), whose experiences of language's essence remain singular and exemplary, Heidegger risks repeating the ageless exclusion of non-poet and non-man, now however on the grounds that the latter would lack access to this essential lack, which is to be found above all in the 'don du poème'.[13]

Although one could look to any number of texts to see how Heidegger continues to pursue and modify these motifs, I want to examine briefly, as a final example, 'The Essence of Language' (1957/8). While it was written some twenty years after 'Origin', its value does not lie simply in its comparative chronological distance from these other treatments of poetic endowment. More than that, it rests in how Heidegger here reprises the problem of the poetic word as that which first gives being to the beings thereby named. Whereas in 'Origin' and 'Hölderlin' the *Stiftung* of *Dichtung* was treated in its affirmative, even triumphal instance of bestowing, grounding, beginning, creating, and positing, the point of departure of 'Essence' is precisely the experience of the poet's failure, in not being able to give what he wishes to give. Although, in the final analysis, the failure of Stefan George's poet to grasp the thing 'where word breaks off' becomes the positive condition for a true, poetic experience with language (which is also to say, the failure of one kind of gift and the opening of another, more originary, one), because of the essay's emphasis on the necessity of a certain poetic collapse, in its tenor as well as its theoretical wager, it comes as close as possible to the kind of poetic event that we saw addressed by Stein, and that we will see staged by Shelley.[14] The word, in each case, must *fail*. But upon the interpretation of the consequences of this failure, of the nature of its parting gift, so to speak, lies all the difference in the world.

In 'The Essence of Language', the role of the poet appears, at first, to be precisely to receive a 'treasure [Kleinod]' without name – that 'delicate gift [zierliches Geschenk]', as Heidegger glosses it – and then to offer it in turn to his country, once the right word is bestowed [schenkt] by the Norn, goddess of fate [Schicksalsgöttin].[15] Although this poetic gift might appear to mirror Hölderlin's, for whom what remains is endowed by poets, unlike Hölderlin's 'founding' poetic gesture, George's bestowal of the prize [zierliches Geschenk] via the sent [schenkt] word differs from it to the precise extent that it still treats, according to Heidegger, what it gives as a mere thing.[16] By operating as though there are 'prizes' to be found prior to the naming gestures that render them graspable *as things*, the poet misconstrues both the nature of the relation between word and thing, and the nature of the very gifts that he himself has to offer. Or perhaps it would be better to say: The poet misconstrues not only the nature of *what* he gives, but also of *who* gives this gift, for it is ultimately not the poet, but language, or the 'word', that makes possible what is truly generous in poetic experience.

It is, then, only at the moment of the failure of this initial circuit of poetic gift exchanges (reception of the prize, then the corresponding word, which the poet gives, in turn, to his fellow citizens) that the poet experiences the true relation of word to thing, and along with it, what we might think of as poetry's true gift, as *Dichtung*. This is what 'Das Wort' recounts: the renunciation, and even abandonment [Verzicht], of one conception of the gift, as a present that might simply be given and taken, and the reception of another, infinitely more unwieldly one, because it is the gift of being itself. Or, put another way: because the poetic experience with language exposes us to the giving nature of the word, which furnishes the originary relation between being and language, the poem no longer gives any determinable, graspable, or calculable thing, but only and especially the originary giving being of language itself, which is therefore also a withdrawal:[17]

> What, then, does the poetic experience with the word show as our thinking pursues it? . . . It shows what is there and yet 'is' not. The word, too, belongs to what is there – perhaps not merely 'too' but first of all, and even in such a way such that the word, the nature of the word, conceals within itself that which gives being. If our thinking does justice to the matter, then we may never say of the word that it is, but rather that it gives – not in the sense that words are given by an 'it,' but that the word itself gives. The word itself is the giver. What does it give? To go by the poetic experience and by the most ancient tradition of thinking, the word gives Being. Our thinking, then, would have to seek the word, the giver which itself is never given, in this 'there is that which gives.'
>
> [Was zeigt die dichterische Erfahrung mit dem Wort, wenn ihr das Denken nachdenkt? . . . Sie zeigt solches, was es gibt und was gleichwohl nicht 'ist.' Zu dem, was es gibt, gehört auch das Wort, vielleicht nicht nur auch, sondern vor allem anderen und dies sogar so, daß im Wort, in dessen Wesen, jenes sich verbirgt, was gibt. Vom Wort dürften wir, sachgerecht denkend, dann nie sagen: Es ist, sondern: Es gibt – dies nicht in dem Sinne, daß 'es'

Worte gibt, sondern daß das Wort selber gibt. Das Wort: das Gebende. Was denn? Nach der dichterischen Erfahrung und nach ältester Überlieferung des Denkens gibt das Wort: das Sein. Dann hätten wir denkend in jenem 'es, das gibt' das Wort zu suchen als das Gebende selbst, aber nie Gegebene.][18]

The gift of the word, which is also the gift of 'The Word', the poem that goes by that name, is to allow us to suffer the loss of one concept of the gift in the experience of another. The 'gift' of the word is, in other words, to give us giving otherwise, to give us another, more originary, concept of giving itself, and one that no longer, strictly speaking, adheres to the category of the 'concept' because it precedes conceptual thinking, making it possible in turn. The 'word', Heidegger tells us, can no longer be considered as something given [Gegebene], but only as the giving itself [Gebende]: indeed, as the 'es' of the 'es gibt', by which not only things, but also being itself are given. Poetry, therefore, does not simply give beings, nor even being, but gives the very experience of the originary giving relation of being: which is to say, it gives giving. This is why such a gift must be suffered in a 'poetic experience with language'. Language, and *Dichtung*, its essential mode, give us another concept of the gift, and one that may no longer be treated as a thing to be given and taken. And poetry, as that which puts us in touch with the relation between word and thing (language and being), therefore *must give*, even and especially at the expense of what we already understand by this figure, because it is the unconcealment of the 'es gibt'.

As should now be clear, from 'Origin' to 'Essence', Heidegger's conception of *Dichtung* breaks free from the longstanding insistence on thinking the poetic gift merely in terms of (1) alternative forms of economic transactions in patronage, (2) the absolute outside of economic, moral, or historical circulation, as one finds in post-Kantian aesthetic movements such as art for art's sake, and (3) the subjective grounds of poetic potential in genius and inspiration. Heidegger 'elevates' *Dichtung* to what, for him, is the highest function of art and language, and what is inseparable from the highest task of philosophy. As 'inciting' and 'extra-ordinary', moreover, this conception of poetising *Stiftung* could be said to anticipate what Derrida will subsequently theorise as the gift's *event*, from the non-arrival of its present in *récit*. And what is 'Das Wort', if not, precisely, a *récit*, in Derrida's sense of this term: a *récit*, precisely, that recounts the passage from gift *exchange* to the gift *of being* (or text) that must subtend it, and that always, therefore, signs itself in its telling?[19]

For Heidegger, it is necessary to think this originary endowment of *Dichtung* as the essence of art. This endowment happens through language as it gives itself to be experienced. Far from taking 'poetry' for granted, then, *Dichtung* articulates a certain 'generous' capacity of language itself, to bend and even transcend its own limits. As he explains in the 1942 lecture course on 'The Ister', 'all essential poetry also poetizes "anew" the essence of poetizing itself'. From one angle, then, to champion such an 'essential poetry' is to champion, precisely, the interruptive, eventful, and incalculable force *of language*, as it comes to (give) itself otherwise. It is also to affirm a vision of language that risks, precisely, losing its grasp on itself. This is not the only angle, however. At the same time, Heidegger's account also risks repeating many of the restrictions commonly associated with poetic privilege, as well as blinding itself to its own contexts. No concern with poetry's merely ontic side – that is, either with the historical role that figures of the poem-present play or with the embodied notion of the poem as a material good – seriously enter into his account, as he himself admits.[20] He excludes these dimensions of the poetic gift as mere elements of the 'literature industry' or as so many merely material functions of the work. Thus, while on the one hand, by considering the poeticised as giving-not-given Heidegger avoids the most common pitfall of poetry criticism – the reduction of the poem to an element circulating within already established economies of exchange – on the other hand, by excluding poetry's 'historical', 'literary', or 'material' side, he nevertheless becomes incapable of identifying how its numerous forms of circulation within these economic, intellectual, artistic, and material domains may themselves become sites for events in their own right. Even more critically, however, by categorically dismissing these poetic provinces, Heidegger prevents himself from perceiving how his own language of poetic endowment [Stiftung] and free bestowal [freie Schenkung] may already be indebted to them, and especially to what they constantly remind us of: namely, that the gift of poetry, even and especially when it is irreducible to exchange, may always already be participating in it.

Beyond what he excludes, however, it is ultimately Heidegger's emphasis on *Dichtung* as endowment of truth, or historical address, that is most worrisome, for what poetry gives [stiftet] for Heidegger, by bestowing, grounding, and beginning, is always predetermined by a sending, addressed to a particular, preserving, historical people. And even if we could look past the troubling question of *which* people, language, society, and so on, the problem would remain of how he could account for the possibility that this address might always miss its mark, that the work, poem, or word might fail, precisely, *to fail*: which is to say, to give being in its most essential sense, through its denial.[21]

NOTES

1. Martin Heidegger, *Hölderlin's Hymn 'The Ister'*, trans William McNeill and Julia Davis (Bloomington: Indiana University Press, 1996), 9.

2. 'Language itself is poetry in the essential sense [Die Sprache selbst ist die Dichtung im wesentlichen Sinne]' ('The Origin of the Work of Art', 46/62). On art and being, see also the following passage: 'Truth, as the clearing and concealing of that which is, happens through being poeticized. *All art*, as the letting happen of the advent of the truth of beings, is, *in essence, poetry* [*Alle Kunst* ist als Geschehenlassen der Ankunft der Wahrheit des Seienden als eines solchen *im Wesen Dichtung*]. The essence of art, on which both the artwork and artist depend, is truth's setting-itself-into-work. From out of the poeticising essence of art [Aus dem dichtenden Wesen der Kunst] it happens that an open place is thrown open, a place in which everything is other than it was . . . [The effecting of the work] lies in a transformation of the unconcealment of beings which happens from out of the work, a transformation, that is to say, of being' (44–5/59–60). See also 45/60–1. Martin Heidegger, 'The Origin of the Work of Art', in *Off the Beaten Track*, eds and trans Julian Young and Kenneth Haynes (Cambridge: Cambridge University Press, 2002), 1–56. References to the German are taken from Martin Heidegger, 'Der Ursprung des Kunstwerks', *Gesamtausgabe I. Abteilung: Veröffentlichte Schriften 1914–1970. Band 5. Holzwege* (Frankfurt am Main: Vittorio Klostermann, 1977), 1–74. Henceforth *OWA*.
3. For an excellent account of the gift in Heidegger's work, see Andrew J. Mitchell, *The Fourfold: Reading the Late Heidegger*.
4. 'One essential way in which truth establishes itself in the beings it has opened up is its setting-itself-into-the-work. Another way in which truth comes to presence is through the act which founds a state . . . A still further way in which truth comes to be is in the thinker's questioning, which, as the thinking of being, names being in its question-worthiness' (*OWA*, 37).
5. See, for example, the following passage from 'Origin': 'If the essence of all art is poetry [Dichtung], then architecture, the visual arts, and music must all be referred back to poesy [Poesie]. That is completely arbitrary. Certainly it is, if we mean that these arts are branches of the art of language [Sprachkunst] – if we may be allowed to designate poesy [Poesie] with a title easily capable of misunderstanding. But poesy [Poesie] is only a mode of the illuminating projection of truth, of, that is to say, poeticizing [des Dichtens] in this broader sense. Nonetheless, the linguistic work, poetry in the narrower sense, has a privileged position among the arts as a whole' (*OWA*, 45/60–1).
6. *OWA*, 47/63.
7. The full passage reads: 'Das Ins-Werk-Setzen der Wahrheit stößt das Ungeheure auf und stößt zugleich das Geheure und das, was man dafür hält,

um. Die im Werk sich eröffnende Wahrheit ist aus dem Bisherigen nie zu belegen und abzuleiten. Das Bisherige wird in seiner ausschließlichen Wirklichkeit durch das Werk wiederlegt. Was die Kunst stiftet, kann deshalb durch das Vorhandene und Verfügbare nie aufgewogen und wettgemacht werdern. Die Stiftung ist ein Überfluß, eine Schenkung' (*OWA*, 47/63).
8. *OWA*, 46/62.
9. *Elucidations of Hölderlin's Poetry*, trans. Keith Hoeller (Amherst, NY: Humanity Books, 2000), 58. References to the German are taken from *Gesamtausgabe I. Abteilung: Veröffentliche Schriften 1910–1976. Band 4. Erläuterungen zu Hölderlins Dichtung* (Frankfurt am Main: Vittorio Klostermann, 1981), 41. Henceforth *EHP*.
10. *EHP*, 59/41 (translation modified).
11. *EHP*, 59/42.
12. *Donner le temps II*, 48, 49, 73, 85.
13. On 'große Dichter', see 'Die Sprache im Gedicht: Eine Erörterung von Georg Trakls Gedicht', *Gesamtausgabe I. Abteilung: Veröffentlichte Schriften 1910–1976. Band 12. Unterwegs zur Sprache* (Frankfurt am Main: Vittorio Klostermann, 1985), 31–78; 33.
14. The final line of Stefan George's 'The Word' reads: 'Where word breaks off no thing may be [Kein ding sei wo das wort gebricht],' quoted in 'The Essence of Language', in *On the Way to Language*, trans. Peter D. Hertz (San Francisco: Harper & Row, 1982), 57–110. 'Das Wesen der Sprache (1957/58)', *Gesamtausgabe I. Abteilung: Veröffentlichte Schriften 1910–1976. Band 12. Unterwegs zur Sprache*, 147–204. Henceforth *EL*.
15. *EL*, 79/173. 'But when the issue is to put into language something [etwas zur Sprache zu bringen] which has never yet been spoken, then everything depends on whether language gives or withholds the appropriate word [die Sprache das geeignete Wort schenkt oder versagt]' (*EL*, 59/151–2). 'Schicksalsgöttin' is Heidegger's gloss of George's Norn (*EL*, 67/160).
16. Heidegger makes this comparison himself: 'Wonders and dreams on the one hand, and on the other hand the names by which they are grasped [die greifenden Namen], and the two fused – thus poetry [Dichtung] came about. Did this poetry do justice to what is the poet's nature – that he must found what is lasting, in order that it may endure and be? [Genügte sie dem, was des Dichters ist, daß er nämlich stifte, was bleibet, damit es währe und sei?] But in the end the moment comes for Stefan George when the conventional self-assured poetic production suddenly breaks down and makes him think of Hölderlin's words: But what endures is founded by poets' (*EL*, 68/161).

17. Although Heidegger's German always resists translation, in the following passage it is barely intelligible, in English, without further commentary. Because the gender of the German word for 'word' is neuter, 'das Wort', it is possible to read each instance of the phrase 'es gibt' – meaning 'there is' – as 'es [das Wort] gibt'. 'Das Wort' is, of course, also the title of George's poem, which Heidegger has been reading throughout the essay, as well as the title of the next essay that follows this one in *On the Way to Language*. The conflation of the normally impersonal 'es' of the German expression 'es gibt' (there is) with the neuter singular pronoun has the effect not only of drawing attention to the generally overlooked 'gibt', but also of inserting language, or the word, in the place of the giver, within the expressions *es gibt Zeit*, *es gibt Sein*. Language, or the word, thus may be said to *give* being to what comes into being. At the same time, and no less critically, it also becomes impossible to read the obverse sense of the 'es gibt' – 'the word gives [es, das Wort, gibt]' – without now conflating *it* with the expression 'there is'.
18. *EL*, 87–8/182.
19. For an excellent account of some of the central differences between Heidegger's approach to poetry and Derrida's reading of literature, see Timothy Clark, 'Being in Mime: Heidegger and Derrida on the Ontology of Literary Language', as well as his *Derrida, Heidegger, Blanchot: Sources of Derrida's Notion and Practice of Literature*. See also Yue Zhuo, 'Derrida and the Essence of Poetry', for an interesting account of Derrida's reluctance ever simply to reject Heidegger's privileging of the poetic work.
20. On the problem with the approach of aesthetics, see, for example, in *OWA*, 18, 50–2. On that of the history of literature and aesthetics, see the two prefaces to *EHP*, 21. On the literature industry, see '. . . Poetically Man Dwells . . .', in *Poetry, Language, Thought*, 211–12.
21. Heidegger's confidence in the ultimately affirmative nature of the poetic experience is visible, for example, in 'The Essence of Language': 'But his poetry has learned renunciation, yet has lost nothing by the renunciation' (*EL*, 88/183).

6
Shelley and the Gift of the Name

For both Stein and Heidegger, the greatest gifts of poetry are not to be found either in inspired songs or in proffered poems. Turning back, *perhaps*, to the very source of those conventions, their writings illuminate a gift at work within the texture of the word itself. Nor does poetry simply give by presenting the word, name, or noun, as though there were some 'poetry' present prior to this act. Instead, reduced to its most essential essence, *Dichtung* would name the word's own rediscovery of its giving nature. Where 'there is word', we could say, there is poetry and there is gift.

Thus, for Heidegger, the move to recognise the word as giving source of being displaces poetry's privilege from its locus within the metaphysics of the subject to an experience of language, in each instance productive of what we call 'poetry'. And does Heidegger not theorise, in this way, and by way of George, an insight that Wordsworth's writings had also, already, *put to work*, even if they could never fully admit to it? The Wordsworthian experience of the predicament of the gift of poetry puts him face to face with the fragility of his own word, whose bestowals can no longer be delimited by way of temporal figures of before and after, or spatial figures of presence and absence, but which call, time and again, to a time and a place still to come, beyond any present.

While, then, Wordsworth may ultimately have tried to skirt this insight, alternately doubting its validity, attempting to work around it, and denying it outright, for George, Heidegger, and Stein, it would name that which is most essential *of poetry*. And this is why, for each of these authors, more ultimately stood to be gained than lost *through this loss*. Real *Dichtung*, great poets, and truly essential poetry, always have the final word, for Heidegger. They give access to a linguistic being that lesser poets, or minor works, simply lack. They give access to a poetry worthy of the name.

In turning now to Shelley and his 'Hymn to Intellectual Beauty', the question remains that of the word and its gifts. For Shelley, as for these other authors, what poetry does is put us in touch with some mystery, whose grasp is ever fleeting. Yet, whereas Heidegger remained confident in the ultimate success of this failure – in the loss of one form of apprehension and the birth of another – Shelley, I will argue, offers a more measured outlook, and one that ultimately puts him in greater proximity to Derrida.[1] Rather than a matter of loss, then gain, the experience of the word in the 'Hymn' forces one to confront what makes the back-and-forth between insight and obscurity inescapable, in the first place. Poetry, for sure, *can* lay bare the non-givenness of the origin, of language, and of the divine, but as is proper to such an insight, it can do so only in fleeting and ultimately ungraspable moments of poetic reflection.[2] *Like* an unrepeatable event of inspired revelation, then, insight into the frailty of poetic language strikes in the 'Hymn', but it does so with this decisive difference: in striking, it confounds the gift logic – the *presence* – by which revelation, classically considered, is thought to function. Through the 'Hymn', we will witness why the gift of the name always risks not revealing itself, and why the chance of the word is, therefore, no less its risk.

For early readers of 'The Hymn to Intellectual Beauty', the subject of the poem was evident: either it offered an autobiographical instance of poetic conjuring, linked to a moment of revelation experienced by the young poet, or it was a testament to Shelley's Platonism. In each case, such accounts grounded the poem in prior referential relations, at times linking it to a moment within Shelley's own life, while at others to the poem's classical sources.[3] And while a number of critics have – correctly – argued that the hymn problematises and even rewrites these sources (be they Christian, Platonic, Rousseauist, or Wordsworthian),[4] nevertheless, due to the time of its composition and its openly theological character, it was rarely seen as offering a vision of poetry, or of language, anywhere near as radical as what one finds in Shelley's subsequent work.[5]

This is for good reason. Written in praise of a divine spirit in high lyric style, the 'Hymn to Intellectual Beauty' is structured as a poetic *cri de cœur*, which cycles between quasi-philosophical contemplation of an 'unseen Power' (l.1) and personal reflection on the difficulties presented by this power's disappearance.[6] To follow the narrative arc of the poem, moreover, is to read a story of redemption: of loss followed by gain, of sorrow followed by hope, and of the death of one notion of presence followed by the birth of another.

The poet opens the 'Hymn' confidently, with a series of declarations (stanza 1), only to succumb to the doubt (3–4) inevitably raised by his existential–ontological questioning (2). At this point, he evidently palliates his angst and apprehension by recalling a moment of personal revelation (5) and poetic self-dedication (6), all of which culminates in a renewal of faith and the rebirth of hope in general (7). Unlike at the opening of the poem, these latter feelings now emerge in the wake of, and with open eyes to, the pain and suffering that necessarily come from knowledge of the failure of the spirit to hold 'firm state' within his heart. Like Coleridge's 'Dejection: An Ode' or Wordsworth's 'Immortality Ode', or any number of other greater Romantic lyrics, the 'Hymn' thus appears to go to the brink of despair, only to come back renewed with 'love' for 'all human kind' (l.84). And, by this point, the 'love' espoused would not simply be the poet's, but the closest thing we get to evidence of the actual workings of the spirit, whose mysterious presence it would disseminate. Only because Shelley, the poet, was touched by 'thy power, which like the truth/ Of nature on my passive youth/ Descended' (ll.78–80) would he now, at the moment of writing the 'Hymn', be able to compose *this* poem, which composition would, in turn, now bestow *on us* those traces of the Spirit of BEAUTY's mystery.

Taken as a story of doubt and redemption, the 'Hymn' would thus repeat, albeit on its own terms, the many tropes of the poetic present already visible in Wordsworth and later questioned in the *Defence of Poetry*. Indeed, it would appear to repeat, in almost classical fashion, the dialectical process through which the loss of one gift (of presence) gives birth to another (of faith, in the wake of absence). Yet, as I will show, Shelley's beloved hymn is far from univocal in this respect and offers an at least double account of poetic origination. In doing so, it performs the limit of any deconstruction of the poetic gift.

Against the narrative positing of the birth of the poet's vocation through his encounter with an inspiring, otherworldly force, one may thus glimpse the traces of a critique of the very lyric voice that recounts this narrative and, along with it, the poetic presents that it receives, bears, and proffers in turn. What I am provisionally calling a 'critique' of the gift-receiving-and-giving voice of lyric is *also* inscribed in the 'Hymn'. It stands alongside the former narrative, but it is constituted through a non-narratable unwriting of the name – and with it the poet's role as name-giver – located at the origin of its gift circuit: *Intellectual Beauty*. By systematically proffering and rescinding this name, by drawing into doubt the presence of this name and with it that of language itself, the 'Hymn' undermines the very foundation upon which its narrative comes to be constituted. And this insight, in turn, into the non-presence of the poetic gift – which is to say, into the non-presence of the very poem that 'presents' this non-presence – is no longer something that one could simply 'receive' or 'give' in turn.

Ultimately, poetry's gift, for Shelley, lies in its ability to recall this non-present at its origin: to reveal the memory of a linguistic remainder that, as remainder, may always suffer effacement. This is a 'gift of poetry' that is irreducible to the classical modalities of inspiration, genius, talent, and patronage, and one that therefore changes poetry's very function. At the same time, however, the 'frailty' of this insight prevents it from ever becoming a firm object of knowledge, of ever keeping 'firm state within [the] heart' (l.41). Poetry is, for this reason, destined to be caught between these versions of itself, in the gap between two notions of the present, and as a force of rupture as well as one of origination. The critical force of the 'Hymn' rests in the gap between these two propositions and in the ways in which the text accounts for this gap without, however, moving on to a third term.

In the wake of Heidegger's 'Essence of Language', this is now a familiar story. For Heidegger, the role of poetry is not to give any thing, but to grant the very being of Being, through its event. Critically, this happens in the failure of the gifts of poetry to be present(s), which failure yields a second order of reflection and a new kind of insight into non-presence. One could therefore read Shelley's 'Hymn' as anticipating Heidegger's ontological approach to *Dichtung*. I will argue, however, that there remains at least one crucial difference, as Shelley's work forces us to entertain the possibility of a suspension of poetry, at the very moment it reaches its poetising summit.

GIVEN NAMES

For a long time, the most pressing question facing readers of the 'Hymn to Intellectual Beauty' concerned identifying exactly where its oddly compelling titular term first sprang forth, as if for Shelley, that singularly talented lyricist, master of Italian rhyme schemes, and savant of ancient languages, the crafting of the phrase 'Intellectual Beauty' was a step too far. As if, for Shelley, who left this world more legend than man, it was nevertheless not quite within his power to name 'Intellectual Beauty'. He would not have been able to give this name, which others, evidently, had already given, and if he did, it was due only to the aid of these kindred classical, early modern, and contemporary spirits, whom he alternately was found to have translated, rewritten, or simply plagiarised, whether wittingly or not.[7] The central problem of the 'Hymn' was thus whether Shelley, the poet, had *given or taken* this name: whether – to put it in the language of Young – he was an *Original* or an *imitator*.

What was first treated as a philological inquiry, however, could not but become a hermeneutic one – and not simply because the two modes of questioning are inherently interdependent. Whether or not Shelley authored the term, the 'Hymn' itself proffers Intellectual Beauty (or *non-material* beauty, as it is usually glossed) as an unknown, the true meaning and origin of which would lie beyond the scope of human knowledge. Beginning with its first stanza, Intellectual Beauty (now addressed as 'some unseen Power') is regarded as a mystery, whose inscrutability would suffice to render it a fetish objects for poets, theists, and critics alike:

> The awful shadow of some unseen Power
>   Floats though unseen among us, – visiting
>   This various world with as inconstant wing
> As summer winds that creep from flower to flower. –
> Like moonbeams that behind some piny mountain shower,
>   It visits with inconstant glance
>   Each human heart and countenance;
> Like hues and harmonies of evening, –
>   Like clouds in starlight widely spread, –
>   Like memory of music fled, –
>   Like aught that for its grace may be
> Dear, and yet dearer for its mystery.   (ll.1–12)[8]

Intellectual Beauty, being unseen, is, by its very nature, enigmatic. Though present in its absence by way of awful shadows, though floating among us and a visitor to this various world, it remains, like moonbeams behind some piny mountain, or hues and harmonies of evening, dear – and yet dearer, we learn, *for its mystery*. What we cherish in 'Intellectual Beauty', Shelley thus tells us – but this is no less a diagnosis than it is a declaration – *is just its* evasiveness, its ungraspable, unmasterable, ungiven nature, which keeps us in a state of perpetual longing and leaves us yearning to know, to experience, and to understand.[9] To read the 'Hymn' is to succumb to this wonder.

However satisfying diagnosing a quasi-clinical obsession may be, it nevertheless may do little actually to ameliorate it, and in spite of Shelley's early warning, readers of the 'Hymn' have remained guessing as to the nature of 'Intellectual Beauty'. Indeed, given its epistemological instability, it is no surprise that such interrogations have attempted – and failed – to identify its elusive essence from both philological and exegetical angles. Each approach assumes that 'Intellectual Beauty' – as a phrase, a name, or a title – holds the key to understanding Shelley's 'Hymn', and that the solution to its riddle is to be located in ever-more rigorous historical or contextual understandings of this phrase's meaning: which is to say, they treat the poem and its erratic subject exclusively as a question of sense and reference.

Before, however, one can begin to answer what, exactly, is named by this spirit, and thus in what the significance of its possible ties to Plato, Plotinus, or Spenser may consist for the purposes of interpretation, Shelley's poem itself raises a different, no less critical question, and one that pertains to the status of 'Intellectual Beauty', as a name, within the work: not what does this spirit name, but rather who, within the play of the poetic text, names it? Is 'Intellectual Beauty', in other words, a name given by the higher power it apparently names, or is it one bestowed by the poet? Is it a self-given and therefore divine name, or is it a merely human moniker, proffered by a poet-speaker and thus representative of a mundane offering rather than celestial gift? But what, in either case, does it mean to be a 'given name'? And if poets are traditionally considered to be the true originators of language, then how to understand the difference between their name-offerings and those of the gods? As Shelley puts it in the *Defence*:

> [Poetry] creates anew the universe, after it has been annihilated in our minds by the recurrence of impressions blunted by reiteration. It justifies the bold and true word of Tasso – *Non merita nome di creatore, se non Iddio ed il Poeta*.[10]

All of this is to say that, insofar as the question of Shelley's role as creator or reproducer of the title of the 'Hymn' presumes an opposition between 'give' and 'take', for the poet, it also presumes that names themselves, as objects to be handled, may simply be doled out, stolen, accepted, or rejected: a presumption that the 'Hymn' itself will ask us to question.

As becomes evident in the course of the poem, 'Intellectual Beauty' is a name given by the poet to the personified subject of his verse, and not vice versa. But it is not the only one, and therein will lie the problem. As the source of beauty and truth, this unseen Power embodies that which must itself be beyond all appearance, knowledge, and representation, and therefore also beyond the order of the concept.[11] 'Intellectual Beauty' is the first name that the poet gives for this unnameable non-being. It is the first name, but it is one that is never repeated, only replaced and displaced, through the introduction of a series of equally un-iterated names for 'the name'.[12] In this way, by accumulating names for the nameless and then reflecting upon this necessity of accumulation, the 'Hymn' becomes legible as a poem about naming: about the necessity and impossibility of giving names, and the economy of name-giving that results thereby.

In all, the poet gives five names for the unnameable: 'Intellectual Beauty', 'Power' (l.1), 'Spirit of BEAUTY' (l.13), 'LOVELINESS' (l.71), and 'SPIRIT' (l.83). As we learn in the third stanza, these names are spoken on the condition of the absence of the 'Spirit', whose denial of any gift of a name for itself constitutes the position from which the poet speaks. These uttered names therefore serve both to supply this absence and to recall it. As so many name-supplements, they mark and re-mark this absence, and with it, the function of name-giving in general. Although, then, 'Intellectual Beauty' is the first name given, it does not simply name what it names. Or rather, let us say, it does not name what it names *as* the univocal, given name for it. It is not, simply, a *given* name, for though it is given by the poet, it cannot be taken for a given. It must rather be read as anticipating its replacement by other (ever-inadequate) names. We could say that Shelley inscribes each of the given names for 'Intellectual Beauty' – including 'Intellectual Beauty' itself – as the 'trace' of every other, meaning that each name is made to stand only provisionally as one, being inscribed as the supplement of every other.[13] Without the (divine) gift, the name cannot be present to itself. It must instead give way to an indefinite process of re-naming, without final term or end.[14]

The naming of 'Intellectual Beauty' and, as a consequence, the name 'Intellectual Beauty' therefore inaugurate another order of naming and another order of gift from within the poem. In a certain sense, what 'Intellectual Beauty', in its mysterious indefinability and tantalising untraceability, comes to name is just this process of un-naming and re-naming – but also of un-gifting and re-gifting – to which the poem's subsequent naming-acts testify. What the gift of the name of 'Intellectual Beauty' gives (and names) is a concept of the gift *as* something not given, something that is given despite and on the condition of its absence, something made possible on the condition of its impossibility. The gift of 'Intellectual Beauty' thus marks both the necessity and the impossibility of giving names, a double condition that falls to the poet and that determines the economy of his relation with this other that, not giving its name, yet remains, and remains *to be named*.

If 'Intellectual Beauty' can therefore no longer be read as a given name, but must instead be taken as a name for that which gives naming as a gift that will never be present, then it may pose problems for any reading hoping to determine the precise meaning of the phrase, or the exact reference of its source text. To say this is not, of course, to deny that one could establish, to a reasonable degree of certainty, the sense that 'Intellectual Beauty' bears within the context of the 'Hymn', and then, on this basis, analyse the extent to which it may or may not cohere with its Platonic, Godwinian, or Wordsworthian antecedents. Rather, what becomes difficult is reducing the inscription of 'Intellectual Beauty' to any mere signification or signifying function. It becomes difficult to delimit, at the expense of what we might call its naming function, its signified without remainder. Something remains in 'Intellectual Beauty' *as a name* that will not be reduced to philological, hermeneutical, or exegetical determinations. Or, as Shelley's poet proclaims:

> No voice from some sublimer world hath ever
>   To sage or poet these responses given –
>   Therefore the name of God and ghosts and Heaven,
> Remain the records of their vain endeavour,
> Frail spells – (ll.25–9)

The name remains. Names *remain*. Being given nothing, all that remains is a remainder of the name. But in the wake of this vacancy, how do we read such frail spells?

RE-NAMING / REMAINING

> First, then, human beings were formerly not divided into two sexes, male and female; there was also a third, common to both the others, the name of which remains, though the sex itself has disappeared. The androgynous sex, both in appearance and in name, was common both to male and female; its name alone remains, which labours under a reproach.
>
> *The Banquet*[15]

It is in the second and third stanzas of the 'Hymn' that the most explicit account of the name is given: not simply of what the name *is*, but of how it has come to pass that names *are*; or, as the poet explains, how it is that the name *remains*. What is thought here is not, then, simply a critique of a few particular appellations, nor even an historical or genealogical account of them, but an exploration of the ontological bearing of the name as remainder, by way of a certain sending – or lack thereof – that precedes being, and in preceding being opens it. While in the second stanza the poet addresses the 'Spirit of BEAUTY' in order to question its being and bearing on the world, in the third he responds to his own questioning stance and the meaning of the spirit's failure to offer any more perceptible response to these and similar queries.

2.
Spirit of BEAUTY, that dost consecrate
   With thine own hues all thou dost shine upon
   Of human thought or form, – where art thou gone?
Why dost thou pass away and leave our state,
This dim vast vale of tears, vacant and desolate?
      Ask why the sunlight not forever
      Weaves rainbows o'er yon mountain river,
Why aught should fail and fade that once is shewn,
      Why fear and dream and death and birth
      Cast on the daylight of this earth
      Such gloom, – why man has such a scope
For love and hate, despondency and hope?   (ll.13–24)

The second stanza, addressed to the 'Spirit of BEAUTY', opens much as the first did: by positing this spirit's singular nature as that which 'consecrates'. This time, however, the uttered qualities do not merely participate in an act of veneration, but become the grounds for an interrogation. 'Where art thou gone?/ Why dost thou pass away and leave our state,/ This dim vast vale of tears, vacant and desolate?' (ll.15–17). Though these questions are addressed to the spirit and are structured explicitly as questions, posed in the interrogatory mood, the poet immediately shifts register when he continues: 'Ask why the sunlight not forever/ Weaves rainbows o'er yon mountain river' (ll.18–19). The poet begins by calling to the spirit to answer, but he pursues his questioning by rendering overt its already coercive nature, by calling for it not to answer, but now *to ask*. In doing so, the reference of his address shifts. From an apostrophe to the spirit, his exhortation opens to include anyone who is willing to pick up the line of questioning itself. The poet no longer asks, but commands to ask.

One could well read the final seven lines of the stanza as a form of self-exhortation, as the poet, shaken, must steel himself against the futility he feels in posing such questions in the first place. In this way, rather than asking, he would command himself to ask, and rather than calling, he would call himself to call. He must do so because, the spirit being absent, it is no longer evident why he should address it at all. Why call to an absent spirit whose very existence is in question? Why risk an address that threatens to fall on vacant ears? What if these questions only question themselves, only return in the repetition of their pronouncement to their own sounding, never arriving outside or beyond the linguistic gesture?

In order to put an end to such questions, the third stanza does not respond to them, but rather responds to the lack of response they have elicited:

> 3.
> No voice from some sublimer world hath ever
>   To sage or poet these responses given –
>   Therefore the name of God and ghosts and Heaven,
> Remain the records of their vain endeavour,
> Frail spells – whose uttered charm might not avail to sever,
>   From all we hear and all we see,
>   Doubt, chance, and mutability.
> Thy light alone – like mist o'er mountains driven,
>   Or music by the night wind sent
>   Through strings of some still instrument,
>   Or moonlight on a midnight stream,
> Gives grace and truth to life's unquiet dream. (ll.25–36)

These questions, which the poet is not the first to ask, have received no response from the voice of some sublimer world. 'Some sublimer world', if and when it does reach out, does not do so through the 'voice', the medium of articulate speech proper to *humans*. Some sublimer world, whatever its offerings may look like, do not resemble those of poet and sage.

In this way, the poet severs his own vocation – with its proffered vocalisations – from the being and mode of address of the spirit. Voices, with their names – both given and received – are the things of sages and poets.[16] To name, to call – in short, to voice and to give voice – are the poet's givens.

Whatever, then, the spirit ultimately may be, wherever it may reside, it is only from the radical denial of its voice that something like human language can first be said to take shape. And it is this that is announced, immediately thereafter, in the poet's 'Therefore', which establishes a relation of consequence between the voice's absence and the state of the name as remainder: 'Therefore the name of God and ghosts and Heaven,/ Remain the records of their vain endeavour,/ Frail spells –' (ll.27–9). Denied the voice and coordinate response of some sublimer being, it falls to poet and sage to endeavour to respond to these questions, but also, to endeavour to name. In the absence of these sublimer gifts, poet and sage must supply this lack by giving names themselves.

But this is a vain endeavour, the poet tells us. It is vain, empty, or idle to utter these frail spells. Why? It remains a question how we are to understand the transition from the absence of a sublimer response to the circumstance of the sage and poet's endeavour. Although it is clear that what is missing is some firmer knowledge concerning the being of this spirit – or concerning the metaphysical conditions contributing to such a high variance of worldly events and experiences – it is less evident how this corresponds to a poetic or sage-worthy endeavour, or even what 'endeavour' itself here means. This being *their* endeavour, it is both what they strive for and what binds them: what puts them in a state of responsibility to which they respond by endeavouring. 'Endeavour', from the French *en-devoir*, means first and foremost to be in a state of obligation. It is from out of this state of being obliged that the colloquial sense of 'endeavour', as a striving, emerges. 'Their vain endeavour', in short, names not the endeavour that they possess or will, but the endeavour, indebtedness, or duty that possesses them, and to which they can respond only by *endeavouring*. What exactly, then, is the poet's vain task?

With respect to this question, the events of the fifth and sixth stanzas may prove instructive. There, it is also a matter of poetic debt, which the poet, flashing back to his youth, reflects on as the origin of his poetic vocation. This latter debt is also one of the main sources for traditional interpretations of the 'Hymn', as it evidently recounts the autobiographical experience of a divine visitation. Supported by accounts of Shelley's youth and a reported moment of epiphany that he underwent while a student, this experience, along with the phrase 'Intellectual Beauty', stand as two of the more stabilising elements used to interpret the poem:[17]

5.

While yet a boy I sought for ghosts, and sped
   Through many a listening chamber, cave and ruin,
   And starlight wood, with fearful steps pursuing
Hopes of high talk with the departed dead.
I called on poisonous names with which our youth is fed;
     I was not heard – I saw them not –
   When musing deeply on the lot
Of life, at that sweet time when winds are wooing
     All vital things that wake to bring
     News of buds and blossoming, –
     Sudden, thy shadow fell on me;
I shrieked, and clasped my hands in extasy!

6.

I vowed that I would dedicate my powers
   To thee and thine – have I not kept the vow?   (ll.49–62)

While yet a boy and all too eager to meet ghosts of the dead, 'thy shadow', the poet recalls, 'fell on me'. From that moment on he was fixated on the spirit and he reports in the following stanza how he 'vowed that I would dedicate my powers/ To thee and thine –'. Although the poet immediately thereafter asks, 'have I not kept the vow?', as though acknowledging a lingering doubt that may have arisen between the moment narrated and the narrating moment, this gesture does not generate any real uneasiness, as the 'Hymn' itself stands as a monument to his experience and vow, affirming each through its sheer presence. The 'Hymn', which bears the poet's experience inscribed, as it were, on its very body, would itself be the culmination of his vow – a vow that should have made the 'Hymn's' writing possible in the first place, by supplying the conditioning moment of poetic conception.

And yet, if the depicted relation between recounted experience and occasion of recounting appears felicitous, it nevertheless cannot entirely mollify the ambivalence of the encounter thereby described. Access to divinity is nothing short of rending, as the shadow's fall results in a less than poetic shriek: 'Sudden, thy shadow fell on me;/ I shrieked, and clasped my hands in extasy!' (ll.59–60). If the clasping of hands 'in extasy!' indicates an exuberant rapture, the shriek that precedes it less easily conforms to this joyful, lyrical tone. Certainly, one can shriek with joy, but as an expression of the shock of visitation, the shriek sounds and resounds the uncertainty and unaccountability of what is occurring prior to its reflection as positive or negative, and prior to the clasping of hands that signals the rejoining of self with itself. The encounter with the other that interrupts the speaker's communion with 'life' and 'All vital things' takes him by surprise and it makes him shriek, and it is precisely this rupture that in turn opens the experience of poetry. The shriek here recounted represents the origin and end of poetic praxis, whose limits the 'Hymn' embodies and recounts, achieves yet falls short of, circumscribes yet is also excluded from.[18]

It would be tempting, then, to relate the poetic and sagacious endeavour of the third stanza to the vow of the sixth. In the sixth, we find both a vow and a dedication: the origin of a debt, and one that can be repaid, if at all, only through a lifetime's work. The poet here does not dedicate any *thing* to the spirit – nothing, that is, that could be simply or immediately paid back – but rather his 'powers' themselves. Yet as these are still his ('my') powers, they remain of a personal nature, a possessed or possessive power that is extended to the spirit through the vow. The debt, in sum, is the debt of a self, an 'I', a voice, who claims it through the performance of a speech act reported in the poem. As a consequence, this latter, autobiographical, account, aligning the poem's composition and its poetic origins along a temporal axis, must be read against, and not with, the impersonal account of poetic obligation offered in the third. For the endeavour of the third stanza, by contrast, is born out of the denial of a sublimer voice. The consequence of the endeavour is not, merely, some thing – nor even a disposition of the poet – but is the name itself and the being of the name as what remains: 'Therefore the name of God and ghosts and Heaven,/ Remain the records of their vain endeavour'. The poet here contracts nothing. He takes nothing on himself. He finds only that he is already oriented by the prior absence of a sublimer voice, which absence conditions the 'name' in the first place. Nor is the endeavour here vain because it fails to name. To the contrary, its futility lies in the fact that naming succeeds. Succeeding in naming, the endeavour fails. That the endeavour results in the name *is* the failure, and it is one born out of the absence of some sublimer gift, as becomes evident in the fourth stanza.[19]

The scope of the endeavour, then, should be understood to comprehend not only the questions the poet poses in the second stanza, but also, and more fundamentally, the very necessity of speech, question, and knowledge that underlies these queries and eventually leads to them. The endeavour is not any specific endeavour – just as it is not to write any particular poem, to make any specific offering, to give any specific name – but rather describes being, life, and existence as so many consequences of the spirit's denied presence. The absence of the spirit opens life as endeavour and, as such, the question and the name, responding to this fundamental lack and therefore emblematic of it, become possible in the first place.

Names, therefore, remain. These names: the name of God and ghosts and Heaven, remain. But as every reader of Shelley's poem must remark, the poet's grammar is at odds with the line's most clearly intelligible sense. One must misread, ever so slightly, or at least neglect the ambiguities of the phrasing, in order to come away with the simple assimilation of *God*, *ghosts*, and *Heaven* to names, which then would serve as the collective subject of the verb *remain*, in the next line. The problem is not insoluble, but it is challenging enough to require comment. Simply put, whereas 'name' is singular and clearly refers to 'God', the verb 'Remain' requires a plural subject, which must then be understood to be the collection of 'name of God', 'ghosts', and 'Heaven'. However bizarre an assemblage it creates, given the singular form of 'name', the most direct way to understand the line would be as the *name* of God, followed by the *beings* ghosts and Heaven. Moreover, both the earlier version of the 'Hymn' published in the *Examiner* (1817) and that published in *Rosalind and Helen* (1819) read: 'Therefore the names of Demon, Ghost, and Heaven,/ Remain' (ll.27–8). Whereas these earlier versions both explicitly name 'Demon, Ghost, and Heaven' *as names* and give each in capitalised, singular form, just as if they were proper names, the later, corrected, draft drops the plural 'names' and in addition to replacing 'Demon' with 'God', pluralises and de-capitalises 'Ghost', as though reinforcing the divided being of the phenomena, rather than the singular, idealised form of its nominalisation.[20] Everything Shelley altered, in other words, serves only to problematise the direct assimilation of the line to a mere assemblage of names.

This is not to say that reading 'God and ghosts and Heaven' as names is simply incorrect. Despite the ambiguity, it would be entirely possible to take the form 'name of' as implicitly repeated for each item listed. This reading is further reinforced by the second half of the sentence, which calls these subjects 'Frail spells' and again refers to their 'uttered charm'. However, even if the force of the line ultimately pulls towards this interpretation, the phrasing's striking ambiguity calls for another approach.

The problem, of course, amounts to knowing what the difference between a name and a being is, and thus to understanding how it could be that both might 'remain', and do so as similar consequences of the non-event of the absence of the spirit's gift. As I have already indicated, if the endeavour is vain, it cannot be because poet and sage fail to name, but, conversely, because naming happens; because – perhaps – not only the name of God, but also ghosts and Heaven, remain. But what is the remaining of the name of God, this 'frail spell'? The endeavour, which results from the absence of the spirit's gift, voice, or presence, leaves as its records these traces, and it is the being of these traces *as remaining* that Shelley's hymn enables us to think. That is, it enables us to think the history of a certain routing of the traces of God, ghosts, and Heaven, as they come to be through the problematic figure of the name.

The name of God remains. This means, first and foremost, that God, or God's name, persists, idles, or hangs on. As the record of the poet's vain endeavour to respond to the question of being – to the gloom of death and birth, and the scope of despondency and hope – this name of God is the poet's gift. Of all names, however, that of 'God' identifies what is both most and least bound to the word. For the *name* of God names an origin, and a conception of origin, which presents a condition of possibility for naming as such. To name God is to name the origin of the poet's ability to name. The gift of the name of God gives not only *a* name, but a conception of naming that exceeds the word and derives it from the presence of this transcendent being whose words the poet, in his turn, would only relate. What the name of God names, then, is already in excess of the domains of the name and of language. The name of God posits an entire conception of language and, in so doing, a relation of word to thing, and of being to non-being.

That the name *of God* remains, moreover, is not simply because it is the first name given, but because the 'name of God' names language in general, or more precisely, because language in general *names it*. The endeavour, responding to the absence of the spirit, does not result in the proper name of God, but begets language and therefore also poets. There is no poet without the denial of the spirit's gift, Shelley tells us, and likewise no language. But language, insofar as it is then given, gives the name, and in each name it gives it gives the name of God as the ineluctable consequence of the word. The name of God 'names' the excess of name (or word), with respect to the purely linguistic.[21] The name cannot remain what it is because it cannot but also give being *and* the difference between beings and language. That the name of God remains, then, points to the persistence of name *and* Heaven *and* ghosts, the latter two of which are bound to the word (of God), yet irreducible to it, no longer *simply* words. They are in a state of undecidable difference from the word and from the theological system that the word posits even before the articulation of theology as such – that is, before signifying *God*, *ghosts*, or *Heaven*.

Remaining, then, articulates the resistance of name to be what it *is*. It articulates a restlessness, but also a remnant. The name of God, however outmoded, outdated, and even surpassed, remains and is ever again *re*named. Remaining, we might say, is – but also names – the being of being as the consequence of the absence of the spirit's gift (of its voice).

In commenting on the character of these 'Frail spells – whose uttered charm might not avail to sever,/ From all we hear and all we see,/ Doubt, chance, and mutability', Forest Pyle has observed the ambivalence of the poet's judgement.[22] These lines, he notes, do not simply articulate a dismissal of the power of these spells, as would be the case were the poet to have said that they *do not avail to sever*. They instead call for a critique of this power. That they '*might not avail to sever*' highlights the danger posed by the word, which can always fail to be read as spell (or word), and be taken instead for a god (or another present being). And this danger too remains, as long as does language and the name(s) of God it bears with it.

What thus distinguishes the 'Hymn's' disposition towards poetry and donation, setting it aside from the tradition of gift poetics, and making it interruptive of the order of the present, is not simply the fact that 'Intellectual Beauty' is itself a name that Shelley probably took from some other source, only then to reinvest and renew it palimpsestically within his poem, in the mode of what Marjorie Perloff calls 'unoriginal genius'.[23] Nor is it merely that the poem's serial re-namings of this already citational name, as 'unseen Power', 'Spirit of BEAUTY', 'LOVELINESS', and 'SPIRIT', is the textual equivalent of *unnaming*, or re-inscribing 'Intellectual Beauty', as a name-ruin that would constitutively remain *to be given*. More so than either of these evidences, what distinguishes the 'gift' of the 'Hymn' from those of either George or Heidegger, is that when the moment comes, within the poem, for the poet to theorise the divine gift of the name (of the divine) – this auto-poietic present that should have birthed name *and* gift in one fell swoop, and that would thereby have already guaranteed, in advance, the poet's own name-giving power – the poet, while denying the presence of this revelatory present, nevertheless cannot, for all that, simply deny the possibility of its effects, as the consequence of another logic of donation entirely.

The name of God, the very name 'God', has never been given by any voice that might live up to this name's concept. It is therefore a mere name-shell, or name-spell. Nevertheless, despite the absence of such divine name-presents, what remains, according to the poem, *is the name*, itself then a technology of sage or poet, inaugurated by the absence of the divine gift/given, which gives the name and gives giving as a form of remaining. As such, we learn, and due to this absence, what one is left with are so many 'frail spells', the 'vain endeavours' of poets who would in turn aspire, through the names that they give, to something that they cannot hope to attain: the one true proper name, in the full presence of revelation.[24] But if such frail spells are frail because they are not subtended by any divine, grounding gift, then the result of this 'frailty' is less a simple incapacity than it is a veritable potential or restlessness of the name *either* to unveil its own mutability, *or* to cover this mutability over, by way of some spellbinding name for the name, precisely as 'God' has historically done. Poetry – the vain endeavour of poets – thus becomes in Shelley the space where the name *might not avail to sever from all we hear and all we see, doubt, chance, and mutability*, or the space where *it might*. And the ambivalence, or back-and-forth, between these two poles would not be a mere matter of thesis and antithesis, awaiting synthesis, but the constitutive, unsublatable condition of the word, which remains undecided and, as undecided, remains.[25]

The spells of poets have the capacity to appear as stable presents, severed from doubt, chance, and mutability (and we might add 'frailty' to this list), as well as to appear *not* like this, as fraught with uncertainty and happenstance, all while betraying the mundanity of their origin and frailty of their being. And yet, regardless of whether we determine the telos of poetry to be presenting a present (God), presenting the non-presence of the present (frailty), or presenting the instability of any presentation hoping to perform either the first or the second (or even the third) of these operations, what we (evidently) learn in the 'Hymn' is that poetry's spells remain helpless to decide their own fate. Such helplessness infiltrates every mark of the word and renders unstable every certainty concerning its gifts.

Is not, then, to conceive of the spells of poets as frail in this way (which is to say, as being frail in their frailty) also to turn poetry into something that always may or may not be worthy of its name? Something, indeed, that is constituted by this uncertainty, and is so even if it also, apparently, holds a privileged relation to the experience of this, its undecidable frailness? What could such a 'poetry', as Shelley here depicts it, finally be said 'to give'? And who or what would be capable of giving it?

NOTES

1. One could map the difference between these two conceptions of poetry and word – initially as a present object, then as a giving thing – to that between the claw of the animal and hand of the human, as Heidegger explores in *What is Called Thinking?* At stake is precisely a conception of the 'die greifenden Namen' giving itself over to a *Wort* that *es gibt*. See Martin Heidegger, *What is Called Thinking?*, trans. J. Glenn Gray (New York: Harper & Row, 1968). On this logic, see also 'Heidegger's Hand (*Geschlecht* II)'.
2. The traditional understanding of Shelley's work as a struggle between scepticism and idealism generally forces one to conclude either that he succeeded in breaking from a redemptive transcendence, or that he succumbed to this transcendentalising motif. Among recent efforts to read Shelley as non-recuperative or non-transcendentalising, see Kir Kuiken, *Imagined Sovereignties*, Jerrold E. Hogle, *Shelley's Process*, Jean Hall, 'The Divine and the Dispassionate Selves: Shelley's *Defence* and Peacock's *The Four Ages of Poetry*', and Hugh Roberts, *Shelley and the Chaos of History*, as well as 'Chaos and Evolution: A Quantum Leap in Shelley's Process'. My principal interest in what follows is in Shelley's ability to think the conditions of possibility (and impossibility) of the transcendent, which remains even and especially because it is impossible. This can be compared to what Colin Jager argues, in *Unquiet Things*, concerning reading 'Mont Blanc' *after* atheism and *after* secularism. See Colin Jager, *Unquiet Things: Secularism in the Romantic Age* (Philadelphia: University of Pennsylvania Press, 2014).
3. On the 'Hymn' as an instance of conjuring, see Susan J. Wolfson, 'Byron's Ghosting Authority', 788–9n.8. For autobiographical readings of it, see Earl Wasserman, *Shelley: A Critical Study*, 192 and Kenneth Neil Cameron, *Shelley: The Golden Years*, 236–43. As an expression of Shelley's Platonism, see William Temple, 'Plato's Vision of the Ideas', Benjamin Kurtz, *The Pursuit of Death*, C. H. Grabo, *The Magic Plant*, 179, and James A. Notopoulos, *The Platonism of Shelley*. On the many possible classical and modern sources for the 'Hymn', see Notopoulos's 'The Platonic Sources of Shelley's "Hymn to Intellectual Beauty"', and Burton R. Pollin, 'Godwin's "Memoirs" as a Source of Shelley's Phrase "Intellectual Beauty"', 14–20, as well as my own discussion of this criticism in an earlier version of this chapter: 'The Gift of the Name in Shelley's

"Hymn to Intellectual Beauty"', and Cian Duffy's discussion in *Shelley and the Revolutionary Sublime*, 97–111.
4. On the 'Hymn's' rewriting of Christian themes, see Spencer Hall, 'Power and Poet: Religious Mythmaking in Shelley's "Hymn to Intellectual Beauty"', and Richard Cronin, *Shelley's Poetic Thoughts*. For its relation to the classical hymn, see John Knapp, 'The Spirit of the Classical Hymn in Shelley's "Hymn to Intellectual Beauty"'. As a revision of Plato, see Wasserman, 190–6; as a revision of Wordsworth, see Harold Bloom, *The Anxiety of Influence*, 108, Judith Chernaik, *The Lyrics of Shelley*, 33–4, Hogle, 60–4, and Angela Leighton, *Shelley and the Sublime*, 49–51. As a reclamation of Rousseau, see *Shelley's Process*, 71–2.
5. See in particular *Shelley's Process*, where Hogle argues of the 'Hymn' that 'Shelley is not yet at the point he reaches in the *Defence*, where the "invisible influence" reviving a "fading coal" is clearly a turning of old figures for divine inspiration toward the sudden recurrence of some interplays in the memory and vice-versa. Instead, this earlier poem makes possible that relatively nonchalant exchange of metaphors by seeking to defy Wordsworth, draw the hymn back to its primordial sense of estrangement, and substitute a movement in memory for a divine dictation' (65). Roberts, for his part, leaves the 'Hymn' almost entirely out of his account in *Shelley and the Chaos of History*. Tillotama Rajan, in *Dark Interpreter: The Discourse of Romanticism*, (Ithaca, NY: Cornell University Press, 1980), 83–8, reads the 'Hymn' as still propagating the myth of the ideal that 'Mont Blanc' would, in turn, revise. What distinguishes it from 'Mont Blanc' or the 'Ode to the West Wind' 'is a certain resistance to its own conclusions, which is reflected in the neotheological and therefore sentimental tendency of hymn: the tendency to believe in salvation by a pure and unambiguous Meaning that is outside life and therefore immune to it' (85).
6. All citations and line references to Shelley's 'Hymn to Intellectual Beauty' are taken from the corrected *Examiner* text (1817), as printed in *Shelley's Poetry and Prose*, unless otherwise noted. When indicated, *SDN* refers to the Scrope Davies Notebook variant of the 'Hymn', dating from August 1816.
7. Research by N. I. White, McNiece, Notopoulos, Pollin, and Duffy has shown the prevalence of the term in Shelley's day. It was, as Notopoulos indicates, a 'leitmotif of Platonism', although, to all appearances, it does not actually appear in the dialogues of Plato (198). See James A. Notopoulos, *The Platonism of Shelley* (Durham, NC: Duke University Press, 1949). In his attempts to locate the origins of Shelley's title, Notopoulos identifies a number of prior occurrences of 'Intellectual Beauty', both within the English

tradition and beyond it. The most obvious source, although one that does not actually contain the phrase, is Spenser's 'An Hymne of Heavenly Beautie', which Mary Shelley, at least, is known to have read in 1818, and Percy to have purchased in Spenser's *Works* in 1812. For the first actual occurrence of the phrase, however, one must look to Plotinus, who entitles section v, viii of his *Enneads* 'Concerning Intellectual Beauty'. While Notopoulos does not condone the assumption of a hypothetical reading of Plotinus by Shelley – for which, he admits, there is no evidence – he nevertheless identifies the repetition of the phrase in a number of works Shelley would have read prior to the summer of 1816 that he finds 'sufficiently attractive in presentation to influence Shelley's choice of the title of a poem embodying a personal Platonic experience' (197). These sources include Lord Monboddo's *Of the Origin and Progress of Language*, Wieland's *Agathon* in Pernay's French translation, *Histoire d'Agathon*, where it appears twice as 'Beauté Intellectuelle', and in Robert Forsyth's *The Principles of Moral Science*, where it appears as the title to Chapter xvi and once more on page 514. See also N. I. White, *Shelley*. Additional research by McNiece notes that it appears not only in the first edition of Godwin's *Memoirs of Mary Wollstonecraft* (an observation Pollin also makes), but also in Blake's 'Descriptive Catalogue', as well as Coleridge's notebook, as 'perfect Intellectual Beauty or Wholeness'. See Gerald McNiece, 'The Poet as Ironist in "Mont Blanc" and "Hymn to Intellectual Beauty"', *Studies in Romanticism* 14.4 (Fall, 1975): 311–36; 328n.30. Duffy, in *Shelley and the Revolutionary Sublime* (Cambridge: Cambridge University Press, 2009), believes himself to have located its proper referent by understanding that 'the *Hymn*, in effect, is an apostrophe to the "cultivated imagination" and its products', which emerge in Godwin's *Memoirs* (98–101). Matthews and Everest, finally, in their annotations to the poem in the Longman edition of *The Poems of Shelley*, identify the phrase in Opie's *Adeline Mowbray*, evidently read by Shelley in 1811, and in Mary Wollstonecraft's *A Vindication of the Rights of Woman*.
8. *Shelley's Poetry and Prose*, 93.
9. There is some debate as to whether 'Intellectual Beauty' and the 'unseen Power' of the first stanza may be equated. Of course, such uncertainty surrounding the naming of, repetition, and difference among, intellectual beauty's parts is inscribed into the 'Hymn' as one of its defining features. While some have argued for their absolute separation, most take the more modest position that they are related but not identical. For the former position, see Duffy, 100–1, and Cameron, 236–43, who understand 'intellectual beauty' to refer specifically to the beauty of the mind, and who for this reason differentiate it from both the 'Power' of the first stanza

and the 'Spirit of BEAUTY' of the second. For the latter position, see Rajan, 84–5, who begins by differentiating between 'Power' and 'Intellectual Beauty', but ultimately folds them together as different aspects of the same, and Leighton, 54–5, who likewise concludes that the 'Power . . . originates [the spirit of Beauty]'. I read each figure as a non-synonymous substitute for the other – as acts of address projected at a transcendent power of which they necessarily fall short.

10. *Shelley's Poetry and Prose*, 533.
11. This theme is particularly prominent in the first and fourth stanzas. The visitations of the 'Power' in the first stanza are at a double remove – the shadow of some unseen Power being itself unseen –highlighting that apprehension of this force is possible neither as a sensible nor as an intelligible entity. In the fourth stanza, the spirit's resistance to keeping 'firm state within [the] heart' (l.41) again figures its incomprehensibleness.
12. On the problem of 'Intellectual Beauty's' relation to 'the name', or the name of God, see Richard Isomaki, 'Interpretation and Value in "Mont Blanc" and "Hymn to Intellectual Beauty"', Cronin, 227–30, and McNiece, 330. Isomaki, following Cronin, takes 'Intellectual Beauty' as a substitution for the '"poisonous names" of "God and [Holy] ghosts and Heaven"'. But this is not entirely accurate. From the perspective of Christian theology, 'Intellectual Beauty' does indeed substitute for the name of God, hence for *the name*. Nevertheless, insofar as the 'Hymn' circumscribes the very appearance of the name of God within its more originary movement, it cannot simply be considered a substitution.
13. Compare to Carol Jacobs's understanding of the poem's opening lines: 'Like the figures in the "Medusa," those [series of similes] of the hymn mark the refusal of language to define by affirming an identity. Intellectual beauty, its inconstancy, is nothing if not this refusal, a denial then of those conventional concepts of language as naming and invocation, the "frail spells" and "poisonous names" of the later lines' (171n.16). See Jacobs, 'On Looking at Shelley's Medusa', *Yale French Studies* 69 (1985): 163–79.
14. Deborah Elise White, in her treatment of the name in Shelley's dedication and first canto of *The Revolt of Islam*, has identified a similar problem at work within that text. In 'Shelley and the Proof of History: Canto I of *The Revolt of Islam*', in *Romantic Returns: Superstition, Imagination, History* (Stanford, CA: Stanford University Press, 2000), 129–64, White argues for the centrality of the name within the passage from 'eye to star', a passage that allegorises the allegedly transcendent, pre-linguistic communion of 'kindling' or 'speechless beauty' (133). Similar to 'intellectual beauty', then, this 'speechless beauty' lies at the edge of phenomenality and in

fact makes the experience of beauty (or any experience *tout court*) possible in the first place, through the communion of its intuition. What White shows, however, through her reading of the Dedication ('To Mary–') and its thematisation of names, is that the passage from 'eye to star turns on the name. The perfected aesthetic communion that kindles the encounter between text and reader thus includes a perfected language: the language of names' (137). This 'perfected', symbolic language of names nevertheless is confronted with its own partiality in Canto I as names become distorted by 'the deceptive variability of signification. Abstracting or particularizing, they remain merely allegorical . . . The world in which evil triumphs . . . is one in which appearances deceive because unified identities have been dispersed into a multiplicity of forms. Names become multiple as well, at once excessive and insufficient for their task . . . Even the holiest name, when mediated by particular, historical names (Greece, France), risks partaking of evil's metamorphic powers unless those names are understood correctly to be *mere* names – signs that derive from and point toward the power of holiest name, but are themselves no more than the bare remainder, "–," of a kindling *that has occurred*' (137–8). When 'intellectual beauty' can be read as just such a 'bare remainder', it will be possible to put into perspective its relationship both to signification and to naming.

15. Translated by Shelley, in *The Platonism of Shelley*, 429.
16. *SDN* here reads: 'To wisest poets these responses given' (1.26).
17. As is not surprising with respect to an experience of this nature, critics are conflicted over the precise date of its occurrence. Most believe it took place while Shelley was a student either at the Syon House Academy or at Eton. See Notopoulos, *Platonism*, 15, and James Bieri, *Percy Bysshe Shelley: Youth's Unextinguished Fire, 1792–1816*, 75, for representatives of each position.
18. This structure is also visible in the final lines of the sixth stanza: 'They know that never joy illumed my brow/ Unlinked with hope that thou wouldst free/ This world from its dark slavery, That thou . . ./ Wouldst give whate'er these words cannot express (ll.67–72). Just as the 'Hymn' puts us in touch with the *origin* of poetic conception that is the scene of visitation of stanza five, so too does it present its *end*, which is the expression beyond expression of words, the 'gift' that the 'Hymn' identifies as the culmination it yearns for, but that it cannot attain on its own. Although origin and end are staged in linear chronological fashion in these two stanzas, with the grammatical opposition of past to present, and the conditional 'Wouldst give' marking futurity, the earlier stanzas, I will show, bring into question the narrativisation of these 'events', and their separation into diachronically linked moments.

19. This is the sense of those cryptic lines: 'Man were immortal, and omnipotent,/ Didst thou, unknown and awful as thou art,/ Keep with thy glorious train firm state within his heart' (ll.39–41). This 'firm state', like the presence of a voice from some sublimer world that would give the gift of its response, is not contingently denied, but constitutively so. That the spirit does not make firm state in the heart (does not make itself present there) is what separates mortality from immortality, or the poet's name (gift) from the spirit's. For an alternative reading of the 'firm state', see Forest Pyle's excellent reading in '"Frail Spells": Shelley and the Ironies of Exile'.
20. *SDN* shows the corrected *Examiner* edits, with the sole exception being that both 'God' and 'Ghosts' are capitalised there.
21. Christopher R. Miller, in 'Shelley's Uncertain Heaven', *ELH* 72.3 (Fall, 2005): 577–603, unearths a letter, written in 1811 to Elizabeth Hitchener, in which Shelley appears to make a similar point: 'What then is a "God"? It is a name which expresses the unknown cause, the suppositious origin of all existence. When we speak of the soul of man, we mean that unknown cause which produces the observable effect evinced by his intelligence and bodily animation, which are in their nature conjoined and . . . inseparable. The word God then, in the sense which you take it analogises with the universe, as the soul of man to his body, as the vegetative power to vegetables, the stony power to stones . . . In this sense I acknowledge a God, but merely as a synonime [sic] for *the existing power of existence* . . . I do not in *this* (nor can you do, I think) recognize a being which has created that to which it *is* confessedly annexed as an essence, as that without which the universe would not be what it is. It is therefore the essence of the universe, the universe is the essence of it. It is another *word for* the essence of the universe,' *The Letters of Percy Bysshe Shelley*, vol. 1, ed. Roger Ingpen (London: Sir Isaac Pitman & Sons, 1909), 92–3.
22. See Pyle, '"Frail Spells"', as well as his *Art's Undoing*, for his exploration of the implications of this reading for what he calls 'radical aestheticism' – the ability of a work, in reflecting on its aesthetic character, to undermine the very possibility of an autonomous aesthetic domain.
23. On this, see *Unoriginal Genius*.
24. Compare the 'Frail spells' of poet and sage to the 'frail Form' (l.271) of *Adonais*, commonly taken to be Shelley's description of himself. Though this self-portrait is disputed (see Cox, 213–14), whether one takes this portrait as being of Shelley or, as Curran and Cox propose, as a composite of 'the nineteenth-century philosophical poet or the archetype of the young poet doomed to death' (213), it remains marked by a similar

weakness: 'A pardlike Spirit beautiful and swift −/A Love in desolation masked; − a Power/ Girt round with weakness; − it can scarce uplift/ The weight of the superincumbent hour;/ It is a dying lamp, a falling shower,/ A breaking billow; − even whilst we speak/ Is it not broken?' (ll.280–6). See Curran, '*Adonais* in Context', 174–5, and Timothy Clark, *Embodying Revolution*, 214–23.

25. Compare also to the 'Ode to Heaven' (1820): 'Even thy name is as a God,/ Heaven! For thou art the abode/ Of that Power which is the glass/ Wherein man his nature sees; −/ Generations as they pass/ Worship thee with bended knees −/ Their unremaining Gods and they/ Like a river roll away −/ Thou remainest such − alway! −' (ll.19–27, p.296).

PART III

ECONOMY AND ANECONOMY

Throughout the previous chapters, in spite of Wordsworth's implicit critique of poetic donation and Shelley's deconstruction of onto-poetics, the central questions that both poets sought to respond to remained: *What gives poetry?* and *What does poetry give?* As I have been arguing, far from being Romantic in origin, such questions haunt poetic discourse as a structural feature of its own self-reflexivity. For Derrida, this feature can be traced back to the cut implicit in every mark, which births address. For Heidegger, it amounts to the poetising essence of language, which 'gives' being as the condition of any present, as such. For Kant, Young, Longinus, and Plato, it is evident right on or at the present of the poem, which would be unaccountable, lest one have recourse to some inhuman, mysterious, or divine origin for it. As soon as 'poetry' begins to ask after its *archē* and *telos*, its being and structure, or its sense and orientation within the theological, political, aesthetic, and economic fields, the question of its givenness necessarily emerges. What we call 'poetry', or at least what we have called 'poetry', would be a certain attunement to this givenness.

Nevertheless, as Mauss has demonstrated with respect to the gift and its social significance, such theological, political, aesthetic, economic, and theological fields were themselves originally tightly interwoven. Their dissolution into distinct spheres and institutions is, in this respect, a distinctly modern innovation, if not the very sign of 'modernity'.[1] As a 'total prestation' or 'total social phenomenon', the gift reflects and enacts the *cohesion* of the economic, juridical, political, religious, familial, and social fabrics of society.[2] Thus, while one could not simply assume on these grounds that such prestations were originally offered in wholly unfragmented, or quasi-mythic states of totality, what separates the *responses* of poets such as Wordsworth, Shelley, and Stein from those of their classical antecedents would nevertheless be their particular experiences of the fragmentation of social life and its many contexts in the nineteenth and twentieth centuries, be it through print culture, the experience of rural poverty, transitions in legal tender, modern war, or political upheaval.

Thus, to confront the question of the gift of poetry is, for Wordsworth, to do so amidst the rise of political economy, at a historical moment when the social worth of lyric hangs in the balance, in an era of shifting tastes and expanding readerships, and in a period in which publishing offers distinct economic incentives that directly contradict the generosity thought to be at work in a divine-oriented poetic vocation. The specificity of the nineteenth-century response to poetry's imperative is to bring to bear upon this 'ancient' poetic discourse all the complications implicit in such a 'modern' sensibility, which must include a newfound scepticism toward not only the possibility of poetry, but also that of the gift itself.

Traces of such a scepticism are not hard to find. In the text that spurred Shelley's writing of his well-known *Defence of Poetry*, Thomas Love Peacock's *The Four Ages of Poetry*, it is just the reduction of poetry to a *commodity*, and the labour of poetic production to the *work* necessitated by supply and demand, that distinguish Peacock's caustic, if satirical, vision. 'The successful warrior', Peacock writes,

> becomes a chief; the successful chief becomes a king: his next want is an organ to disseminate the fame of his achievements and the extent of his possessions; and this organ he finds in a bard, who is always ready to celebrate the strength of his arm, being first duly inspired by that of his liquor. This is the origin of poetry, which, like all other trades, takes its rise in the demand for the commodity, and flourishes in proportion to the extent of the market.[3]

In this passage, Peacock translates the traditional understanding of Homeric epos, as a relay of divinely given gifts passing from poet to auditor and back to the gods, into the nascent language of nineteenth-century economism. He intimates that what we call 'gift' might always not be one; that what appears *now* as a gift might reveal itself to have never actually operated according to this logic; and that, to refer to the products of the labour of poets as presents and offerings may prove, in the light of day, to be just another effort to cover up the actual conditions that underlie poetry's dissemination and circulation, as so many commodities, in the market.

The possibility that Peacock announces is that the whole language of inspiration, as well as the apparent gift economy of poetic patronage, might be so many *ruses*; that the gifts of poetry are therefore *counterfeits*; and that what we call 'gift' is in fact a 'commodity', and what we call 'inspiration' in fact 'inebriation', being that the same object cannot be both, at the same time. Such a vision is, of course, to a certain extent, always possible. It is part and parcel of the very structure of the gift which, as soon as it appears, enters into circulation and becomes economised, risking annulling what within its own concept calls to the other of exchange, quid pro quo, and the market. Nevertheless, the possibility of such a threat is not uniformly felt, nor is it uniformly internalised. One need not respond to such a possibility by *reducing* gift to commodity, or poetry to non-poetry, as Peacock does. The following chapters of Part III explore responses, in Europe and America, to the threat posed by such a reduction. They examine how the gift survives, in the wake of its apparent impossibility, now in the era of the market.

NOTES

1. See *The Gift*, 30; 46; 63. For a similar argument concerning the emergence of distinct literary and economic genres in the eighteenth century, see Poovey.
2. In the W. D. Halls translation of Mauss's *The Gift*, the French term 'prestation' is translated as 'total services'. Jonathan Parry offers a useful gloss of Mauss's use of the term 'prestation', which, he argues, Mauss selects precisely because of the difficulty of translating it into contemporary figures of gift, debt, and transaction. 'The whole ideology of the gift, and conversely the whole idea of "economic self-interest", are *our* invention', 'and the text explicitly acknowledges the difficulty of using these terms for societies such as the Trobriands where *prestations* – the word itself must have been chosen for its connotations of constraint – are a kind of hybrid between gifts, loans and pledges' ('The Gift, the Indian Gift and the "Indian Gift"', 458).
3. *Peacock's Four Ages of Poetry. Shelley's Defence of Poetry. Browning's Essay on Shelley*, ed. H.F.B. Brett-Smith (Boston: Houghton Mifflin Company, 1921), 4.

7

Emerson and the Flower of Commodities

> I respect not his labors, his farm where every thing has its price; who would carry the landscape, who would carry his God, to market, if he could get any thing for him; who goes to market *for* his god as it is; on whose farm nothing grows free, whose field bears no crops, whose meadows no flowers, whose trees no fruits, but dollars; who loves not the beauty of his fruits, whose fruits are not ripe for him till they are turned to dollars.
>
> Thoreau, *Walden*[1]

> Fruits are acceptable gifts, because they are the flower of commodities, and admit of fantastic values being attached to them. If a man should send to me to come a hundred miles to visit him and should set before me a basket of fine summer-fruit, I should think there was some proportion between the labor and the reward.
>
> Emerson, 'Gifts'[2]

Can one give? Is it still possible to present a present, today, and has it ever been? And if, by contrast, there has never been such a thing as a pure gift, *worthy of the name*, then how *best* to give, in the wake of this impossibility? These are the questions that haunt Emerson's 1844 essay, 'Gifts', to which I now turn. As becomes clear from its opening lines, the reason, impetus, or justification for writing an essay *on* gifts arises, for Emerson, in an experience commonly felt, at the time of its writing, of the fraught nature of giving. One no longer knows how to give, which means that one gives poorly, or perhaps not at all. One has forgotten the nature of giving and one must therefore learn to give again, which is to say, learn once more to separate out the gift from the non-gift, now in an age in which debt has become the law.

'Gifts' begins with four lines of verse – a short poem. We will thus have to ask, in reading it, whether, in doing so, it does not respond to some imperative dictated by its very subject: whether, as Derrida has observed, one *must* begin with a poem, when one speaks of the gift. Emerson's essay commences thus:

> Gifts of one who loved me –
> 'T was high time they came;
> When he ceased to love me,
> Time they stopped for shame.

It is said that the world is in a state of bankruptcy; that the world owes the world more than the world can pay, and ought to go into chancery and be sold. I do not think this general insolvency, which involves in some sort all the population, to be the reason of the difficulty experienced at Christmas and New Year and other times, in bestowing gifts; since it is always so pleasant to be generous, though very vexatious to pay debts. But the impediment lies in the choosing.[3]

The point from which Emerson writes, the problem to which he responds, is *akin* to that articulated by Peacock. Indeed, far from being satire, the reduction of gift to commodity, or of the order of 'bestowal' to that of 'bankruptcy', seems here to be a mark that threatens 'all the population', for all the population is implicated in the world's 'general insolvency'. Nevertheless, far from simply denying the validity of this insolvency, or of the perception thereof, Emerson here sets himself the task of parsing out the order of debt from that of gift. In distinction to Peacock, who conflates gift and commodity, for Emerson, one may 'owe' and yet 'give' at the same time. The risk, for Emerson, is precisely *confusing* the one with the other. It is believing that the situation of the first precludes that of the second, when, *in fact*, one should instead speak of two altogether distinct orders of circulation.

The difficulty that interests Emerson, experienced at Christmas, New Year, and other times, in bestowing gifts therefore has nothing to do with any purely theoretical impossibility of giving, such as Derrida diagnoses and Emerson elsewhere admits to.[4] It may in fact be impossible to give – and I hold this question, at least as it concerns Emerson's 1844 text, in suspense for the moment – but even if it is, what marks the experience of giving, for Emerson, here concerns a particular difficulty that he now claims is historically novel. For 'the impediment', as he puts it, 'lies in the choosing'. That is to say, it lies in how one approaches giving, today, now as a matter *of choice*.

One has forgotten how to give. We moderns know not what 'giving' any longer means, and *in giving*, in attempting to give, we either stop, from sheer frustration, or fail, in the final analysis, to give, because we have come to rely on strictly commercial concepts to do so. It is as if giving, though once an intuitive practice, has now, through frequent misuse and inattention, fallen into disrepair. And this is why 'if at any time it comes into my head that a present is due from me to somebody, I am puzzled what to give, until the opportunity is gone'.[5]

One no longer knows how to give. Whether we know it or not, we have all become like Peacock, believing we give when in fact we do something altogether different. As a result, if one does somehow manage to overcome one's initial experience of puzzlement and to extend an offering, what one gives turns out to be a mere token of persuasion, something 'barbarous' or an 'apolog[y] for gifts', rather than truly 'a portion of thyself'.[6] The gift, in other words, as a product of (economic) choice, rather than one of love, or the lover (as the introductory verse already intimates), easily turns out to betray the baser economies of the subject instead of the higher ones, and thus to fail to live up to its very name. The task, for Emerson, in offering 'Gifts' to his readers, is thus to return, or give back, the gift for giving. It is to offer a propaedeutic for giving, so as to cleanse this practice once more of the flavour of 'black-mail' it acquires for 'kings, and rich men who represent kings', and their 'false state of property'.[7] But is this not, in the final analysis, just the task, or *Aufgabe*, of every discourse on the gift, be it Emerson's, Mauss's, Heidegger's, or even Derrida's?

The problem with the gift, for Emerson, in the one text at least that he explicitly dedicates to the topic, is thus that it can so easily turn out to be a 'symbolical sin-offering', instead of a pure present, either because one no longer knows how to proffer gifts concordant with one's better intentions, or because one's intentions have themselves become degraded.[8] The ideal, then, as is already indicated in the essay's poematic opening, would be always to give from love, which Emerson later calls 'the genius and god of gifts'.[9] 'Gifts', in fact, is bookended by love, which is always here opposed to the economy of self-interest.

The model situation of giving, for Emerson, is thus provided by love, and it should also resemble something like the situation of friendship, as Emerson, and before him Montaigne, understands this term.[10] That is, one must give *without* giving; one must give without betraying that giver and receiver are, in fact, two.

> The gift, to be true, must be the flowing of the giver unto me, correspondent to my flowing unto him. When the waters are at level, then my goods pass to him, and his to me. All his are mine, all mine his. I say to

him, How can you give me this pot of oil or this flagon of wine when all your oil and wine is mine, which belief of mine this gift seems to deny? Hence the fitness of beautiful, not useful things, for gifts.[11]

The trick to giving lies, for Emerson, in doing so without presenting any visible change in property; in making 'flow', without betraying the presence of any interpersonal obligation, calculation, or inequality; of allowing the other to receive, then, but without their 'independence [being] invaded', for, ultimately, 'some violence I think is done, some degradation borne, when I rejoice or grieve at a gift'.[12]

How, then, is one to give without provoking joy or grief? Or, to put it in a Kantian language that Emerson does not use but which nevertheless underlies the logic of his argument: how to give without recourse to *subjective interest*, without the provocation of desire, and, thus, the entire economy of excitement and disappointment that necessarily follows in its train? How to give, in sum, *without giving*, at least if one understands this term in its common acceptation, as the sociological tradition, from Mauss and Lévi-Strauss up to Bourdieu and Godelier takes it, as necessarily 'bearing weight'?[13]

The answer, for Emerson, is that one should give beautiful things because only the beautiful may be received without betraying the preponderance of property, or value, that *in fact* underlies every relation between donor and donee. One should give only the beautiful because only beauty may succeed in transcending the value (and interest) that otherwise threatens to foil every giving of every gift:[14]

> Flowers and fruits are always fit presents; flowers, because they are a proud assertion that a ray of beauty outvalues all the utilities of the world. These gay natures contrast with the somewhat stern countenance of ordinary nature: they are like music heard out of a work-house. Nature does not cocker us; we are children, not pets; she is not fond; everything is dealt to us without fear or favor, after severe universal laws. Yet these delicate flowers look like the frolic and interference of love and beauty. Men use to tell us that we love flattery even though we are not deceived by it, because it shows that we are of importance enough to be courted. Something like that pleasure, the flower gives us: what am I to whom these sweet hints are addressed?[15]

The enemy of the gift, for Emerson, is value because value – whether conceived of through labour, use, or exchange – threatens to reify the gap between individuals and to pervert the natural relation between them with the 'false state of property' that currently exists.[16] That the ideal forms of the gift (here beauty and love) stand opposed to the market is, moreover, a position common throughout Emerson's writings, from his two-line takedown of Daniel Webster – 'Why did all manly gifts in Webster fail?/ He wrote on Nature's grandest brow, *For Sale*' – to his essay on 'New England Reformers', where, once again, recourse to the market represents a perversion of what the gift, left to circulate in its natural environment, truly has to give: 'He was a profane person, and became a showman, turning his gifts to a marketable use, and not to his own sustenance and growth.'[17] Flowers, therefore, make for the ideal gift. They do so, however, not because they lack value, but because their beauty manages to transcend the value that they may always possess, by rising above both the material, natural world and the social one, and offering to the spirit a form of aesthetic beauty that 'outvalues' mere use- or exchange-value. In wholly Kantian fashion, one finds that the ideal aesthetic pleasure of the beauty of the gift – 'Something like that pleasure, the flower gives us' – stands opposed to the economy of profane subjective desires, whose joys and griefs are always bound up with the actual presence of material objects in use.

(Let us note, in passing, this first figure for the gift of the poem, on the side of the aesthetic: the 'addressed flower' whose 'sweet hints' force me, their recipient, to ask *what am I?* We will return to the problem of self-identity, as it is elicited by the gift, in the following chapter. For now, I want to retain only the poematic force of a floral address that prompts questioning.)

If the ideal gift is the flower, for Emerson, it is because only beauty manages to outvalue value and thus to transcend utility and want. Beauty names the essence, or ideal form, of the gift, whose transcendental economy would remain opposed to that of the profane market, which is still bounded by interest. Yet Emerson, above all, knew that this idealisation of floral-flowing – of the flowing flower's beauty, which should culminate in a two-way 'flowing of the giver unto me, correspondent to my flowing unto him' – was a far cry from the actual state of affairs. And he betrays this realisation everywhere, including at those very moments when he appears to be least aware of it.

For example: this realisation is apparent, already, when he first acknowledges, not that *flowers outvalue all the utilities of the world*, but instead that *they are a proud assertion that a ray of beauty outvalues all the utilities of the world*. In other words, even for the beautiful present of the flower, which is the best gift that Emerson can muster, even in this case, the gift can only ever *assert* its ideal economy, exempt from interest and valuation, in which it *should* participate. It asserts this economy outside economy, without actually putting it into practice. To put this in Kantian terms: when it comes to giving, because bestowal still relies on the actual existence of the object given, aesthetic judgement can never fully suspend the economy of desire that threatens the purity of aesthetic pleasure. Such a difficult, downright vexatious situation of course raises a number of questions.

How is one to give in the wake of this realisation? When one knows full well that the interest against which the gift was to be immunised haunts even its purest manifestations? How to give when one is faced with the difficult, downright puzzling situation of a gift, which always threatens to betray itself, *but also* when even the gift of beauty cannot escape the material relations in which it is proffered? For Emerson, such a starting point is, of course, his very point of departure and the only point from which one may begin to give. As long as property relations are what they are, as long as there is inequality, one must simply resign oneself to doing the best that one can. Therefore, says Emerson:

> The only gift is a portion of thyself. Thou must bleed for me. Therefore the poet brings his poem; the shepherd, his lamb; the farmer, corn; the miner, a gem; the sailor, coral and shells; the painter, his picture; the girl, a handkerchief of her own sewing. This is right and pleasing, for it restores society in so far to the primary basis, when a man's biography is conveyed in his gift, and every man's wealth is an index of his merit.[18]

It may be impossible to give, after all. It may be impossible because even flowers, even very beautiful flowers, may ultimately only ever intimate, through their beauty, the outvaluing of utility that alone would allow the gift to exit the economy of the market, marked by interest, and enter instead into the pure pleasure of weightless, free-flowing, value-less interchange, in which the difference between self and other is dissolved – which is, of course, why Emerson will deem 'love' to be the god and genius of the gift. This all may be impossible. Therefore, one should settle for the next best thing, which is to give a portion of oneself, *beginning with the poet*, who brings his poem. This restores society to its primary basis. The poet here thus finds his place *alongside* the farmer, the miner, the sailor, and the girl, each of whom fulfils his or her particular social function, giving what each has to give, even if, in doing so, what they may accomplish can at best be considered a compromise, with respect to the ideal announced earlier, by the beautiful gift. (Second gift of the poem: now within economy but an economy of blood – without alienation.)

This is, if not exactly a solution, then, at least, a form of response to a puzzling problem of modernity: how to give? How to give when, as Jarvis has shown, the opposition between non-interested gift and interested exchange had become so polarised?[19] How even to begin to articulate the place of giving when, as Emerson points out, 'it is said that the world is in a state of bankruptcy; that the world owes the world more than the world can pay, and ought to go into chancery and be sold'?[20] And how, finally, to give when, as 'Gifts' makes clear, one can *neither* maintain as absolutely separate the world of the gift, of beauty, of the aesthetic, and of poetry from that of debt, of bankruptcy, and of the market, *nor* simply collapse the one into the other? It is, as David Foster Wallace puts it some 150 years later, 'a paradox':

> It may be that the only way in America to produce pure art would be to remove oneself from the public sphere and produce that art only as gifts, where there's no money involved and no attempt at publicity or publication involved. The problem is that if everyone does that, then there is no public arts here. So it all becomes really a paradox that I've spent a lot of the last years thinking about, and I don't have an answer.[21]

If, in responding to questions such as these, Emerson appears content to compromise on the gift, negotiating with conditions as they are to find the most suitable middle ground, then the writings of Thoreau and Baudelaire, in the following chapters, will be of interest precisely to the extent that they resist any such reconciliation. At once more troubling and more obscure, Thoreau's writings situate the place of the gift – and above all the gift of the poet, who in 'Gifts' ultimately brings his poem *like* the farmer, the shepherd, and the girl, who each bring what is proper to them – neither absolutely apart from the world of the commodity, *à la Kant*, nor absolutely united with the world of the commodity, *à la Peacock*, nor even in the best of all possible conjunctions of these worlds, *à la Emerson*. Instead, as with Shelley, the gift of poetry will be found to appear in *Walden* in a moment of failure and indecision, when neither separation, nor union, nor compromise of the aesthetic and the economic will any longer prove possible.[22]

Before turning to *Walden*, however, there remains one last gift of the poem to be read, in 'Gifts', which may serve as a final point of contact – and parting – between these two one-time friends. For Emerson, the impossibility of transcending value meant that the only choice was to embrace those values that offered the best hope of restoring, to the greatest degree possible, 'society [to its] primary basis'. This led him to conclude on the fitness of beautiful presents, above all, followed by 'things of necessity' and then things 'that . . . properly belonged to [one's] character'.[23] And yet, of all of the examples of gifts that he gives, the one that is perhaps most emblematic of the compromise that he situates at the heart of giving – between the transcendent and the material, or the pure gift and the adulterated one – is proffered at the first moment of the transition away from the beauty of the flower's free-flowing blossom. As soon as one is drawn away from the beauty of the (apostrophic poem) flower to the mere, gustatory thrill of (haptic, graspable) fruits, the crux of the problem takes shape:

> Something like that pleasure, the flowers give us: what am I to whom these sweet hints are addressed? Fruits are acceptable gifts, because they are the flower of commodities, and admit of fantastic values being attached to them. If a man should send to me to come a hundred miles to visit him and should set before me a basket of fine summer-fruit, I should think there was some proportion between the labor and the reward.[24]

Fruits, 'the flower of commodities', are acceptable gifts. They are acceptable because, though they are commodities, they nevertheless represent, from within this realm, that which is furthest from it: that is, the (beauty of the) flower. Moreover, to call fruit 'the flower of commodities' is necessarily to designate it in ambiguous – if sublime – fashion. Neither simply a commodity, nor simply a non-commodity, fruits would stand at the border of the two. They would come as close as possible to articulating, from within the commodity world and all that it entails of use- and exchange-value, of grasping and taking (for that is what 'acceptable' means, *ad* + *capere*, to grasp, seize, or otherwise receive, in hand) that which transcends utility. And while they are *the flower* of commodities, they would nevertheless perform this indecision otherwise than the flower does. Instead of 'outvaluing' utility, as the flower at least asserts, fruits would transcend utility *through value*, by admitting, precisely, of 'fantastic values'. Fruits are so valuable, Emerson tells us, that they manage to pervert value itself, admitting not simply of worth, but of something *fantastic* in worth. Through their excessive value, and like a Bataillean expenditure, fruits re-inscribe *within the commodity* the very imaginative element that is never reducible to pure utility, but that underlies its allure in the first place. In so doing, might not the poem that is fruit also remind us that use and the market are, themselves, 'social facts', defined through symbolic relationships that are produced in the interactions between things?

'Fruits', of course, never simply name what one commonly calls 'fruit', be it for Emerson or for Thoreau. And here, above all, as the exemplary figure for what lies *between* beauty and value, they threaten to take on a life of their own. Fruits are, moreover, what in the epigraph above necessarily stood for Thoreau between 'God' and 'the market', insofar as they could always go either way, be carried to or fro, be taken as something *to be taken*, or received as that which *must be given*, from above. 'Fruits', therefore, name the crux, the point of crossing, and perhaps even the crucifix, of an experience of the gift in crisis. They are 'acceptable gifts' and articulate – evidently in a way that flowers never could – the explicit point of contact and tension between the free bestowals of Nature and the restricted economies of (market) culture(s).

While Thoreau too, and just like Emerson, experienced the 'fantastic values' able to be admitted by property, nevertheless, the former's imagination carried him far beyond any experience that might still assert the ultimate value of 'beauty'. What follows this insight, for Thoreau, is instead a rending moment of generous indecision: a sudden surge of poetic sublimity that risks confusing the identities of poet and farmer alike, and with them, the circuits of gift- and commodity-exchange that ought to hold them apart. The experience of this risk names in *Walden* what of poetry can be neither abandoned, nor, any longer, simply embraced. It names another gift of the poem that, precisely, suspends the difference between each of these orders.

NOTES

1. Henry David Thoreau, *Walden, Civil Disobedience and Other Writings*, ed. William Rossi (New York: W. W. Norton, 2008), 134–5. Henceforth *Walden*.
2. Ralph Waldo Emerson, *The Complete Essays and Other Writings of Ralph Waldo Emerson*, ed. Brooks Atkinson (New York: Random House, 1950), 402–5; 402. Henceforth *Complete Essays*.
3. *Complete Essays*, 402.
4. In 'Uses of Great Men' (1845), Emerson writes: 'Gift is contrary to the law of the universe. Serving others is serving us. I must absolve me to myself' (6). See Ralph Waldo Emerson, *The Collected Works of Ralph Waldo Emerson, Volume IV: Representative Men*, eds Wallace E. Williams and Douglas Emory Wilson (Cambridge, MA: Harvard University Press, 1987), 1–12. Indeed, in the estimations of his son, Edward, writing in the notes to 'Gifts', '[Emerson] held that there was no such thing as giving' (323). See *The Complete Works of Ralph Waldo Emerson: Essays 2nd Series, volume 3*, ed. Edward Waldo Emerson (Boston: Houghton Mifflin Company, 1903). Even if the gift, as such, is impossible for Emerson, as he explores in 'Gifts', there nevertheless seems to be a crucial difference between the self-interest endemic to market transactions, in which one ultimately 'gives' the work of others, and the offerings of a producer who 'gives' the work of his own hands.
5. *Complete Essays*, 402.
6. *Complete Essays*, 403.
7. *Complete Essays*, 403.

8. *Complete Essays*, 403. The gift is a frequent topic in Emerson's writings, central to many of his most significant essays such as 'Nature', 'Self-Reliance', 'Compensation', and 'Friendship'. For an examination of the role of the gift in Emerson's work broadly, see Richard A. Grusin, '"Put God in Your Debt": Emerson's Economy of Expenditure', where he argues that Emerson viewed the market economy and the spiritual economy of expenditure as being essentially discontinuous. For a study of the complex relationship between the transcendentalists and philanthropy, see Thomas LeCarner, 'A Portion of Thyself: Thoreau, Emerson, and Derrida on Giving'.
9. *Complete Essays*, 405. Compare to his comments in 'Heroism': 'The magnanimous know very well that they who give time, or money, or shelter, to the stranger – so it be done for love and not for ostentation, – do, as it were, put God under obligation to them, so perfect are the compensations of the universe' (*Complete Essays*, 254).
10. See Montaigne's 'On Affectionate Relationships': 'In the kind of friendship I am talking about, if it were possible for one to give to the other it is the one who received the benefaction [recevroit le bien-fait] who would lay an obligation on his companion. For each of them, more than anything else, is seeking the good of the other [s'entre-bienfaire], so that the one who furnishes the means and the occasion is in fact the more generous [faict le liberal], since he gives his friend the joy of performing for him what he most desires' (214). But in friendship, what is above all brought into question is the possibility of the gift, as Montaigne here intimates. This is why, when he comes to addressing the relationship between husband and wife, he cites the practice of disallowing the presentation of gifts from the one to the other, for it is just such acts of donation that *betray* the division, in the couple, between what through marriage ought to become *one*. Michel de Montaigne, *The Complete Essays*, trans. and ed. M.A. Screech (New York: Penguin, 2003), 205–19.
11. *Complete Essays*, 404.
12. *Complete Essays*, 404. Compare to his lecture 'The Transcendentalist', where he describes the experience of the idealist as 'inclin[ing] him to behold the procession of facts you call the world, as flowing perpetually outward from an invisible, unsounded centre in himself, centre alike of him and of them, and necessitating him to regard all things as having a subjective or relative existence, relative to that aforesaid Unknown Centre of him [. . .]. It is simpler to be self-dependent. The height, the deity of man is, to be self-sustained, to need no gift, no foreign force' (*Complete Essays*, 89–90).
13. For the latter tradition, what is essential is that the gift does not present itself as an element within an exchange, that it defer, to the point of obfuscating,

the obligation to return. For Emerson, it is not enough that the gift should appear not to oblige. Instead, the gift should itself *be* without value, it should enact no binding. For another reading of Emerson's essay that discusses its relation to Kant's philosophy, see Gary Shapiro, '"Give me a Break!" Emerson on Fruits and Flowers'.
14. Compare the parallels between Kant's description of the satisfaction taken from the beautiful, as being necessarily 'disinterested and free': 'das des Geschmacks am Schönen einzig und allein ein uninteressiertes und freies Wohlgefallen sei' (*Critique of the Power of Judgement*, 95/123) and Mauss's description of the appearance – but not reality – of the gift, as being 'free and disinterested': 'le caractère volontaire, pour ainsi dire, apparemment libre et gratuit, et cependant contraint et intéressé de ces prestations' (*The Gift*, 4/66).
15. *Complete Essays*, 402.
16. *Complete Essays*, 403. As Emerson puts it in his lecture on 'The Young American': 'This is the good and this the evil of trade, that it goes to put everything *into market*, talent, beauty, virtue, and man himself' (234), in *The Collected Works of Ralph Waldo Emerson, Volume I: Nature, Addresses, and Lectures*, eds Alfred Riggs Ferguson and Robert E. Spiller (Cambridge, MA: Harvard University Press, 1971), 217–46. Later, in 'Wealth', he diagnoses the loss of autonomy of the rural farmer, which has led to such a false state of property: 'A farm is a good thing, when it begins and ends with itself, and does not need a salary, or a shop, to eke it out. Thus, the cattle are a main link in the chain-ring. If the non-conformist or aesthetic farmer leaves out the cattle, and does not also leave out the want which the cattle must supply, he must fill the gap by begging or stealing. When men now alive were born, the farm yielded everything that was consumed on it. The farm yielded no money, and the farmer got on without. If he fell sick, his neighbors came in to his aid: each gave a day's work; or a half day; or lent his yoke of oxen, or his horse, and kept his work even: hoed his potatoes, mowed his hay, reaped his rye; well knowing that no man could afford to hire labor, without selling his land. In autumn, a farmer could sell an ox or a hog, and get a little money to pay taxes withal. Now, the farmer buys almost all he consumes – tin-ware, cloth, sugar, tea, coffee, fish, coal, railroad-tickets, and newspapers' (*Complete Essays*, 712).
17. *Complete Essays*, 816; 459. See also, for example, 'Experience', where he opposes, in quasi-Heideggerian fashion, the 'reception' of gifts to their 'getting', as a squaring of accounts: 'The great gifts are not got by analysis' (351). And later: 'All I know is reception; I am and I have: but I do not get, and when I have fancied I had gotten anything, I found I did not. I worship

with wonder the great Fortune. My reception has been so large, that I am not annoyed by receiving this or that superabundantly. I say to the Genius, if he will pardon the proverb, *In for a mill, in for a million.* When I receive a new gift, I do not macerate my body to make the account square, for if I should die I could not make the account square. The benefit overran the merit the first day, and has overrun the merit ever since. The merit itself, so-called, I reckon part of the receiving' (*Complete Essays*, 363). On giving versus getting (or grasping) in Heidegger, upon which ground he divides human from animal, see *What is Called Thinking?*, 16. In 'Prudence', while the gift of genius should be the 'child of genius', what is condemned in contemporary society is precisely the conversion of 'talent . . . to money', for the '*men of parts* . . . use their gift to refine luxury, not to abolish it', whereas 'Genius is always ascetic, and piety, and love' (242–3). In 'Man the Reformer', however, Emerson declares that 'the general system of our trade [. . .] is a system of selfishness [. . .] of distrust, of concealment, of superior keenness, not of giving but of taking advantage' (*Collected Works* I, 148). This does not mean, though, that Emerson's views of the market were uniform. On his shifting positions vis-à-vis the market and commodification, see Gilmore, 18–34, Joel Porte, *Representative Man: Ralph Waldo Emerson in His Time*, and David Robinson, *Emerson and the Conduct of Life*.
18. *Complete Essays*, 403.
19. On the eighteenth-century conceptual separation of the gift from exchange, or more precisely the *free gift* from *interested exchange*, see Jarvis, 'The Gift in Theory'. For Jarvis, in line with Mauss and Mary Douglas, the rise of economism marks the genealogical origin of the modern 'ideology' of the pure gift. See also Parry, who links this idea back to Mauss's text, which, he argues, has been systematically misread. Without discounting the main thrust of Jarvis's essay – or Parry's – it is perhaps symptomatic that when it comes time for Parry to locate the genealogical origin of this separation, he can at best point to a 'likely hypothesis' in Mauss: 'The beginnings of the ideological revolution which destroyed the ancient wisdom are located in the late Roman Empire with the legal separation of persons from things. But the main thrust of the discussion on Rome is that this distinction – which is central to our concepts of property and market exchange – evolved out of earlier concepts strictly comparable to those of the gift economies described for the "primitive" world. The record, however, does not allow Mauss to establish this as anything more than a "likely hypothesis"' (459). Parry later identifies the '*universalistic* ethic of disinterested giving' and the '*universalistic* conception of purely disinterested giving' with the birth of Christianity specifically (468).

20. *Complete Essays*, 402. On the ubiquity of gift-giving in nineteenth-century England, see Finn.
21. David Foster Wallace and Ostap Karmodi, '"A Frightening Time in America": An Interview with David Foster Wallace', *New York Review of Books* 13 June 2011. Available at: <https://www.nybooks.com/daily/2011/06/13/david-foster-wallace-russia-interview/>, last accessed 22 October 2018.
22. The problem of poetry in Emerson is too vast for me to take up here. Nevertheless, minimally, one will note a tendency, visible in 'Art' (*Essays: First Series*), 'The Poet', and 'Poetry and the Imagination', to situate the poet as a world-historical figure and poetry as 'true science' (*Complete Essays*, 329). It is just this tendency that Thoreau most clearly writes against in *Walden*, even if he does so, as I have already mentioned, in rather obscure and indirect fashion. The problem of the writer for Thoreau displaces the figure of the poet for Emerson, and the consequences are far-reaching for both authors. For one recent attempt to concretise the role of poetry for Emerson, see John T. Lysaker, *After Emerson*, 19–39.
23. *Complete Essays*, 403.
24. *Complete Essays*, 402.

8

Thoreau on Poetic Purchase

> There are two classes of men called poets. The one cultivates life, the other art, – one seeks food for nutriment, the other for flavor; one satisfies hunger, the other gratifies the palate. There are two kinds of writing, both great and rare; one that of genius, or the inspired, the other of intellect and taste, in the intervals of inspiration. The former is above criticism, always correct, giving the law to criticism. It vibrates and pulsates with life forever. It is sacred, and to be read with reverence, as the works of nature are studied. There are few instances of a sustained style of this kind; perhaps every man has spoken words, but the speaker is then careless of the record. Such a style removes us out of personal relations with its author; we do not take his words on our lips, but his sense into our hearts.
>
> Thoreau, *A Week on the Concord and Merrimack Rivers*[1]

> The majority of the following poems are to be considered as experiments . . . Readers accustomed to the gaudiness and inane phraseology of many modern writers, if they persist in reading this book to its conclusion, will perhaps frequently have to struggle with feelings of strangeness and awkwardness: they will look round for poetry, and will be induced to enquire by what species of courtesy these attempts can be permitted to assume that title.
>
> Wordsworth, 'Advertisement' to *Lyrical Ballads* (1798)[2]

In turning now to Thoreau and life at Walden Pond, we begin to explore the problem of poetry from a vastly different perspective. In contrast to Wordsworth and Shelley's investments in the traditional milieu of poetic aesthetics, which resulted in questionings of the logics of inspiration and poetic divinity, the autobiographical, domestic ruminations of Thoreau on the commercial exploits of his fellow Concordians possess no such obvious investiture. Poetry – at least that which is generically identified as 'poetry' – if and when it does appear in *Walden*, does so only in passing, at times by way of verse interludes or dramatic dialogues, but most often as a thematic topos: a foreign concept that is alternately examined and exalted, but almost always as if from the outside looking in.[3] *Walden*, though certainly a poetic work, is not generally read as one *of poetry*. And Thoreau, its author, though a dabbler in the poetic arts, would under most circumstances be considered a 'poet' only in the most extended sense of this term.

Nevertheless, as Stanley Cavell, Michael T. Gilmore, Richard Gravil, and Lance Newman have each shown, the speaker of *Walden* is one who views himself as carrying the mantel of the heroic bard-poet.[4] He bears the weight of those 'benefactors of the race, whom we have apotheosized as messengers from heaven, bearers of divine gifts of man'.[5] And he is, in the Wordsworthian sense of the phrase, and however problematic it may be, *a man speaking to men*, but one who does so in the language called for by his present.[6] This is neither to say that *Walden* somehow in fact represents, or ought to be read as, a work of 'poetry', at least in any straightforward sense of this term. Nor that its speaker is, or ought to be understood to be, 'a poet' – though he does, at times, explicitly identify as such.[7] Rather, it is to point out that *Walden*'s speaker/author/writer, whom I shall henceforth refer to simply as 'Thoreau', views himself as inheritor of this tradition and, accordingly, that the distance he takes from it and the ambivalence he expresses towards it call to be read as deliberate forms of critique, if not outright displacements, of the tradition itself. It is to indicate, moreover, that even if Thoreau's talent as a poet – now the man 'Thoreau', insofar as he can be rigorously parsed from his self-inscription – has been roundly questioned, the questions of *poetry* and of *the poet* were nevertheless ones that were front and centre in his thoughts. And this is true not only in *Walden*, but already in *A Week on the Concord and Merrimack Rivers*, where, precisely, he begins to conceive of a form of poetry that would not only no longer be identifiable by formal or generic standards, but also be inseparable from 'life itself', one understood to be *the inscription of life itself*: 'My life has been the poem I would have writ,/ But I could not both live and utter it.'[8] Thus, whether conceived of *as prose* – 'To an unskilful rhymer the Muse thus spoke in prose', *as pure, pre-generic expression of Nature* – 'Yet poetry, though the last and finest result, is a natural fruit', or as that which, precisely, *enacts the overturning of poetry* – 'When the poet is most inspired, is stimulated by an *aura* which never even colors the afternoons of common men, then his talent is all gone, and he is no longer a poet', the question of poetry is, unmistakably, already at the forefront of Thoreau's highly complex, autobiographical self-inscription.[9]

Although, then, *Walden* is neither a work of verse, nor a poem, nor even, strictly speaking, a prose poem, I will nevertheless argue that it takes up the central questions confronting both poetic discourse and the gift in the nineteenth century. And though one could read the traces of this problematic throughout the text – as it implicitly factors into the specific determination of Thoreau's vision for an American author caught between the freely given products of Nature and the restricted economies of urban civilisation – it is also treated, in at least one moment of the work, in explicit fashion. To be precise, it is treated in *nearly* explicit fashion, through a half-effaced, but still legible segment of the text, previously published as 'A Poet Buying a Farm' (See Appendix).

There, at the beginning of *Walden*'s second chapter, and directly following the opening section on 'Economy', Thoreau stages a conflict between poetic aneconomy and prosaic economy through the attempt of 'a poet' to transact the purchase of the Hollowell farm from its farmer owner. The purchase inevitably fails, but just as Shelley's poet's failure to name in the 'Hymn' or Wordsworth's inability to ground his poetic gifts in a pure present in *The Prelude* announced the true points of departure of those poems, so too, I will argue, does Thoreau's unsuccessful acquisition open another order of event from within the economy of his autobiography. It is from this point that everything in the work should be read.

Through a reading of the narrative of the Hollowell purchase, I will argue that *Walden performs* a poetry that, in Thoreau's view, would be more worthy of the name 'poetry' than what usually goes by that name. Poetry, for Thoreau, does not happen in a secluded or rarefied realm, as the mere appearance of an inspired 'unfather'd vapor', but, precisely, at the unsettling moment of poetic and prosaic language's crossing into the other, when they cease to be *either* wholly separable, *or* wholly reducible to one another. Thus, rather than maintaining its distance from the coldness of the commodity world, through the special circulation of an inspired-gift-turned-generous-present, the 'gift of poetry' becomes, for Thoreau, inseparable from the undecidability of poetry's very event, in an act of imaginative generosity that both is and is not one. We could say that poetry appears in *Walden* – when and if it does appear – only as 'the flower of commodities', which figure must now be heard in the full, undecidable play of Emerson's tortuous genitive. And it is for this reason that Thoreau's overdetermined, highly ambivalent relation to the poetic tradition must, in the final analysis, be taken to be absolutely calculated: calculated, that is, to be incalculable, and to enact both a *pas de don* and a *pas de poésie*.

THE INSCRIPTION OF *WALDEN*'S PRE-HISTORY

In the second chapter of *Walden*, entitled 'Where I Lived, and What I Lived For', three prefatory pages are dedicated to recounting a rather dazzling event. It is the purchase of the Hollowell farm. This purchase, it must be noted, never properly or entirely takes place. Neither in 'real life' – that is, in the lived encounter between Thoreau and the farmer – nor in the 'text' – which is to say, the narrative recounting of this event – was Thoreau ever, in deed, 'burned by actual possession'.[10] Neither did he seize possession of the property itself, by entering or occupying it, nor did he seize possession of the deed to that property, the signed title that entitles its proper and legal possessor to ownership of the coordinate land. Thoreau never holds either the title to the land, or the land itself, either *de facto* or *de jure*, licitly or illicitly. The closest Thoreau ever comes to ownership is a verbal commitment, made to the current owner and proprietor, with whom he agrees to buy the farm. Although the promises to buy and sell the property fail, by all indications, to come to fruition, although the land does not change hands and no exchange beyond this exchange of promises takes place, this exchange, what we might call *the deed before the deed before the deed*, sets in motion a sequence of events that surpasses Thoreau's arithmetic and, indeed, any art of counting.

The space of the Hollowell episode is thus slight, occupying but a few pages at the opening of *Walden*'s second chapter, and although, narratively speaking, it is no more than a transition serving to prepare for what Thoreau himself will admit is *Walden*'s proper topic – that is, life at Walden Pond – nevertheless, as a segue to life at the pond it offers singular insight into the project that it stands to introduce. According to J. Lyndon Shanley, whose 1957 *The Making of Walden* remains the definitive study of Thoreau's process in composing *Walden*, the episode first entered its pages in 1852. Five years after Thoreau's first lectures of *Walden* material, and three years after the completion of the book's first draft in 1849, the Hollowell scene was added to *Walden*'s seminal fourth draft, just as the work was taking on its definitive structure.[11] Although there is no evidence that Thoreau began writing the episode prior to 1852 – already five years after leaving Walden Pond in September of 1847 – his journal and a letter of Ellen Sewall's support the dating of its occurrence to before the move to Walden in July of 1845.[12] The *Variorum Walden* notes that the Hollowell farm was 'An old farm on the Sudbury River just below Hubbard's bridge [now Heath's Bridge], in Concord'.[13] No more than two miles from Walden Pond, Thoreau frequented the spot and probably 'purchased' it in April of 1841.[14] Walter Harding's *The Days of Henry Thoreau* recounts this period preceding Thoreau's move to Walden and, although his main source for details of the purchase appears to be what Thoreau writes of it himself in *Walden*, his contextualisation is helpful for understanding how it fits into what was actually a series of attempts that Thoreau made at this time to find a proper writing retreat.[15] Initially interested in taking an attic room, Harding explains, Thoreau turned instead to the purchase of a farm, and only after investigating several spots – including, but not restricted to the Weird Dell, Baker Farm, and Hollowell farm – did he look into building a cabin by Sandy Pond. Only once refused by the owners of the latter, much as he was earlier by those of the Hollowell farm, did Thoreau then explore Walden Pond as a viable spot, probably because the land surrounding it had recently been purchased by Emerson.[16]

Thoreau's purchase of the Hollowell farm must, then, first and foremost, be understood within the context of this *series* of failed attempts to settle down. It was one effort among others, and as such, it partook of the same general impulse that would ultimately culminate in his settlement at Walden Pond. At the same time, being the only precursor within this series to make it into the pages of *Walden*, it stands out from these other efforts. It is *exemplary*. That is to say, it stands as a representative part of this whole and, in standing thus, stands out, apart from what it represents. That Thoreau would, moreover, excerpt it, so as to publish it on its own as 'A Poet Buying a Farm' in 1852 – as one of only two portions of *Walden* to be published independently, alongside 'The Iron Horse' – confirms its semi-autonomous, if not emblematic, character.[17]

Although, then, the Hollowell episode remains a significant moment within the biographical pre-history of *Walden*, as *one* failed effort among so many others, and *the one* effort to be recounted, in full, within its pages, there is some reason to think that its importance does not lie simply in its historical character, not least of all because, when Thoreau does publish it as 'A Poet Buying a Farm', its status as a strictly autobiographical account is no longer entirely evident. Within *Sartain's Union Magazine*, it reads as a pithy literary essay, as a possible fiction, even as a *récit*. At any event, that the passage does not simply stand in for Thoreau's other, failed attempts to take up residence prior to the move to Walden, is ultimately confirmed by his own assessment of the encounter, as he relates it in *Walden*'s second chapter. After having recounted his purchase, but before launching into a description of Walden Pond itself, Thoreau relates, by way of transition, what he there calls the one 'experiment', to the other: 'The present [Walden] was my next experiment of this kind, which I purpose to describe more at length, for convenience putting the experience of two years into one.'[18]

The move to Walden follows the failed acquisition of the Hollowell farm. And yet, when it comes time to narrate the transition from the one to the other, in *Walden*, what Thoreau stresses is not their difference. Far from opposing them on the basis of their temporal successiveness, or even that of their ostensibly contradictory outcomes, *as experiments* – for the first would, to all appearances, represent an experimental failure, while the second an experimental success — what Thoreau instead emphasises is their structural homogeneity. They both (apparently) represent 'experiments' of the same 'kind': 'The present was my next experiment *of this kind*,' he explains, without further qualification or equivocation. It would thus be a question, in reading the Hollowell purchase (but also the whole of *Walden*), not only of tracking Thoreau's shifting motivations and the twists of fate that ultimately led him to the pond, but also, and more critically, of asking how the two events of the (failed) purchase and the (successful) settlement might be understood to be analogous. And not simply the drive to purchase the farm and that to move to Walden, but the very experimental character of the one and the other.[19] Nor, if I may anticipate a bit, should we succumb to the temptation to relate the former, 'unsuccessful', encounter, to the latter, 'successful', taking up of residence, as triumphant conclusion relates to foundering antecedent, for what the Hollowell purchase ultimately problematises is just the difference between poetic failure and prose success, or mere failed purchase and fully realised possession. This is a difference that Thoreau himself will probe in *Walden*'s concluding chapter, as if anticipating just this response: 'Why should we be in such desperate haste to succeed, and in such desperate enterprises?'[20]

In *The Senses of Walden*, Cavell points out that Thoreau repeats himself only once in his remarkable autobiography.[21] This singular repetition takes place immediately following the Hollowell episode and just before Thoreau launches into the description of Walden Pond. In it, Thoreau takes *Walden*'s opening epigraph and re-cites it, thereby repeating his opening declaration of purpose. It were, thus, as though the text of *Walden* had to be begun again, following the relation of this encounter, or even as though it had *not yet* begun, despite all appearances to the contrary. 'As I have said', Thoreau writes, 'I do not propose to write an ode to dejection, but to brag as lustily as chanticleer in the morning, standing on his roost, if only to wake my neighbors up.'[22] Have we been adequately awoken? And how will we know when we've left our state of slumber?

Be it by choice or by compulsion, the delivery of this second alarum, dispatched at the moment of the text's transition from first to second experiment 'of this kind', obliges us to reflect on the discursive situation of the Hollowell purchase, which is set apart from the rest of *Walden*, being placed chronologically, structurally, and conceptually anterior to it. It were as though this episode, though inscribed within *Walden*'s pages, nevertheless remained cordoned off from its proper subject, which it, however, doubles. It is as if, though a part of the writing of *Walden*, it nevertheless stood before its present, furnishing us with an opportunity to relearn everything that we thought we knew about it.

Thoreau's narrative of his failed purchase precedes, then, but also anticipates in kind the experiment at Walden Pond, recounted but also performed in *Walden*. And it is the very exemplarity of 'Walden', its meaning and the meaning of its 'experiment', that is therefore at stake here in the short Hollowell passage. I will argue in what follows that it would be only by reading the Hollowell experiment again and gauging the sense of its failure that one would be prepared to shed light on the experimental sense of 'Walden'. Whatever 'Walden' – this experiment, which is related to, but not necessarily identical with, *Walden* – gives, may thus also be given by this purchase without possession that, evidently, only a 'poet' would be capable of transacting, precisely by failing to transact.

ECONOMY BEFORE ECONOMY, OR LIVING DELIBERATELY

> There is a property in the horizon which no man has but he whose eye can integrate all the parts, that is, the poet. This is the best part of these men's farms, yet to this their warranty-deeds give no title.
>
> Emerson, 'Nature'[23]

> Things always bring their own philosophy with them, that is, prudence. No man acquires property without acquiring with it a little arithmetic also.
>
> Emerson, 'Montaigne, or the Skeptic'[24]

Thoreau's purchase of the Hollowell farm opens the second chapter of *Walden*. Treating of a poet and doing so in prose, Thoreau places his versifier in the most uninspired and unpoetic of situations, entangling him in a transaction of dollars and cents. The poet here narrated is also the one narrating, and this fact will not be without interest, either for Thoreau's own, complicated relationship with poetry, or for the referential status of the events here recounted.[25] While the differences in content between the text of 'A Poet Buying a Farm' and that of the Hollowell episode in *Walden* are relatively slight – consisting principally in the additions of the ultimate and ante-penultimate paragraphs of the latter – the ramifications of *Walden*'s contextual frame cannot be overlooked.[26] As a work unto itself, 'A Poet Buying a Farm' was a clever essay. Once inscribed into the sinuous folds of Thoreau's autobiographical exploration, however, its narrative becomes a possible mirror for *Walden*'s own tortuous structure and intent.[27]

As I have already pointed out, *Walden*'s second chapter is divided into two unequal parts. The first, prefatory portion, consists of 'A Poet Buying a Farm' with the aforementioned amendments. The second part, by far the bulk of the chapter, is separated from the first by a line space, and takes up Thoreau's 'next experiment', that famous experiment at Walden Pond. As the chapter title indicates, the majority of 'Where I Lived, and What I Lived For' will be concerned with where Thoreau lived, and what he lived for, but though the heading poses the *where* and *what* as separate subjects, they are in fact inseparable for Thoreau, who famously moved to Walden Pond to 'live deliberately', and whose entire project is built on the premise that *where* always conditions *what*, or perhaps more precisely that *what* should condition *where*.[28]

That being said, Chapter 2 begins neither with *where* nor *what*, but instead with a reflection on the stage of life that makes one reflect on living. 'At a certain season of our life we are accustomed to consider every spot as the possible site of a house,' he begins.[29] We next learn that at a certain season of his life, Thoreau himself gave in to reflections of just this kind, and even had the custom of buying houses in imagination: 'I have thus surveyed the country on every side within a dozen miles of where I live. In imagination I have bought all the farms in succession, for all were to be bought, and I knew their price.'[30] A problem of reference immediately arises as it becomes clear that this imagined habit – or habit of imagining – could not have been completely restricted to Thoreau's fantasy, as the practice eventually earned him the title of 'real-estate broker' with his friends:

> I walked over each farmer's premises, tasted his wild apples, discoursed on husbandry with him, took his farm at his price, at any price, mortgaging it to him in my mind; even put a higher price on it, – took every thing but a deed of it, – took his word for his deed, for I dearly love to talk, – cultivated it, and him too to some extent, I trust, and withdrew when I had enjoyed it long enough, leaving him to carry it on. This experience entitled me to be regarded as a sort of real-estate broker by my friends.[31]

At a certain season of our life, Thoreau tells us, we become accustomed to considering every spot as the possible site of a house. We reflect on what it might mean to live here or there and, in this way, we become real-estate brokers, but with one important caveat. What interests us at this stage is not necessarily settling down – it is not making an investment and becoming physically, materially, or even symbolically interested, in the Kantian or Emersonian senses of this term – but, rather, what interests us is only the speculative *idea* of planting one's seed, taking up residence, and seeing what may come. Once we have taken our pleasure in a given site, we take our leave and move on again.

This 'custom' takes shape, Thoreau tells us, at first only in the idlest of ways: by considering every spot. One looks, examines, or scrutinises, one contemplates, judges, or reflects, but without any particular investment, perhaps only with the slightest investment in the possibility of investing. The *Oxford English Dictionary* speculates that, though 'such a use is not known in the Latin writers', the verb 'to consider' might have been 'originally a term of astrology or augury', given that the Latin *sidus, sider-* means 'star'.[32] At a certain season of our life, Thoreau relates, every speck of dirt becomes an object of observation, when we suddenly turn our sidereal glances down from the heavens to focus on the contemplation of spots of earth below.

Be it prophetic or not, such a practice of speculation raises a number of questions. What kind of contemplative activity is this, given its neither wholly interested, nor wholly disinterested bearing – indeed, given that in it a seemingly purely ocular consideration quickly transmutes into motile surveyorship, imaginary purchase, and even, eventually, consumption, conversation, and cultivation as well? What Thoreau wants – what he 'enjoys' – is not ownership, but the frivolity of free contemplation *with a view to ownership*. And this is not just any free contemplation, but surveying, purchasing, mortgaging, outbidding for, and cultivating, *in imagination*, that which he calls 'the house'. We have, therefore, left the ideals of both Emerson and Kant far behind. But what, exactly, is a house? Why does it become the subject of our youthful speculations? And what does one acquire when one acquires one, be it through purchase or, as Thoreau elsewhere considers, inheritance?[33]

The house, Thoreau tells us time and again in *Walden*, is not only where one resides, but the very source of those ills that have befallen his neighbours and, among them, prototypically the Concord farmer. This is not because there is anything inherently wrong with sedentary life – or 'taking a seat', as he glosses it – but because the house, and with it the farm, in their modern iterations, have become those places where man's lack of celestial consideration has concretised in an unnatural state of debt and an unmanageable web of entanglements. Such a web is what one now calls 'community':

> We belong to the community. It is not the tailor alone who is the ninth part of a man: it is as much the preacher, and the merchant, and the farmer. Where is this division of labor to end? and what object does it finally serve? No doubt another *may* also think for me; but it is not therefore desirable that he should do so to the exclusion of my thinking for myself.[34]

To consider every spot as the possible site of a house, and to do so as only a poet could, *in imagination*, is to set oneself apart from such a community, and that in a very peculiar way: for it is neither simply to settle, nor simply not to settle, but to situate oneself between these states, through a half-step (not) beyond. It is, evidently, to withdraw from the circuit of encumbrances, debts, rents, and labours that mark the economy of *homo economicus*, but to do so while retaining an eye for his very plight.[35]

This is a common enough story. Indeed, it is *the* story, as it has traditionally been received, of *Walden*, dating to Thoreau's own day, as the tale of his self-imposed exile and self-reflective reinvention of Crusoe.[36] At stake in Thoreau's imagined practice of speculation is, therefore, nothing short of the story of *Walden*. How better to exit the division of labour and to begin again than to refuse the locus and point of departure of economy itself, the *oikos* of *oikonomia*? In considering ever spot as the possible site of a house – but in doing so *only* in imagination, and thus without investment – it is thus as though Thoreau surveyed from a point above, beyond, or prior to the economy of his neighbours,[37] as though he did so without either 'acquisition' or – to steal a word from Emerson – the 'arithmetic' that necessarily follows from it. One never *simply* buys a house – or *the farm*, as it were. One never simply buys a house because 'the house' is not one commodity among others, but the point from which 'purchase', 'price', 'deed', 'mortgage', 'rent', and 'commodity' each become thinkable in the first place. All commerce begins and ends with this locus of 'household management', which shuttles back and forth between the Laplander's 'skin dress' and the modern man's 'mausoleum'.[38]

To consider every spot as the possible site of a house – which is to say, to speculate, in imagination, upon the acquisition of one – is thus 'to speculate' upon the birthplace of speculation, 'to purchase' – or to refrain from purchasing – the possibility of purchase. Leaving aside the problem of the referential status of this (imagined?) habit of imagining, what has become clear are the stakes of Thoreau's earliest imaginative–commercial meditations, which, similar to Descartes's, also had to negotiate the economy of movement and rest, of walking and writing. By tasting, cultivating, and mortgaging each farm, all without a deed, it is as though Thoreau attempted to imagine an investment without investment, and did so from nowhere, before any *oikonomia*, or economy, might be established. Is this not the very privilege of the poet?

Such is the question that we must ask, in reading this episode and assessing its implications for *Walden* as a whole. Elsewhere in the text, Thoreau is rather clear that the poet stands out, distinguished from the other common figures who arrive at his cabin. Compared to those of the farmer, hunter, soldier, and even doctor, the comings and goings of the poet are *other*, virtually incalculable with respect to the regular economies of the workday:

> The one who came from farthest to my lodge, through deepest snows and most dismal tempests, was a poet. A farmer, a hunter, a soldier, a reporter, even a philosopher, may be daunted; but nothing can deter a poet, for he is actuated by pure love. Who can predict his comings and goings? His business calls him out at all hours, even when doctors sleep.[39]

The business of the poet is *other*. Actuated by pure love, the poet's comings and goings are, like Emerson's genius and god of the gift to whom 'we must not affect to prescribe', unable to be anticipated by our common measures. The poet's movements are unable to be reckoned on, for what calls him out are professional concerns even less predictable, and ultimately less graspable, than those of either the philosopher or the doctor. It is for this reason that his movements are erratic, or, at any rate, why they must appear erratic to those unfamiliar with him: which is to say, to everyone with knowledge only of the labours of regular wage-earners.

The poet's movements are other. Nevertheless, even poets, even very good poets, must eat on occasion:

> – Eh, Mr. Poet, is it you? How do you like the world to-day?
>
> *Poet.* See those clouds; how they hang! That's the greatest thing I have seen to-day. There's nothing like it in old paintings, nothing like it in foreign lands, – unless when we were off the coast of Spain. That's a true Mediterranean sky. I thought, as I have my living to get, and have not eaten to-day, that I might go a fishing. That's the true industry for poets. It is the only trade I have learned. Come, let's along.[40]

Even the poet grows hungry once a day: which is to say that, though the 'business' of the poet, for Thoreau, or more precisely, the business of Thoreau-the-writer-surveyor-mortgager-poet, while unable simply to be reckoned with that of the farmer, must nevertheless still constitute *a kind of business*.[41] The poet's 'industry' must provide him with some form of sustenance, or livelihood, even if not in the same manner, or of the same variety, as the farmer's industrial products. Everything thus hinges on how one understands the poet's imaginative 'withdrawal' – and this is the very word that Thoreau will use, at the conclusion of the Hollowell episode, to describe his movement. Withdrawal, therefore, from life in Concord, from the economy of his neighbours, and from traditional property ownership.[42]

PURCHASE WITHOUT POSSESSION

> I wish to speak a word for Nature, for absolute freedom and wildness, as contrasted with a freedom and culture merely civil, – to regard man as an inhabitant, or a part and parcel of Nature, rather than a member of society. I wish to make an extreme statement, if so I may make an emphatic one, for there are enough champions of civilization: the minister, and the school-committee, and every one of you will take care of that.
>
> Thoreau, 'Walking'[43]

I noted above that the problem that we have been tracking, between the business of the farmer and that of the poet, or between an interested exchange and one evidently without interest – or one interested, precisely, in remaining without interest – could also be translated, in Thoreau, into the question of his withdrawal, in general, in writing *Walden*. As we shall now see, it can also be mapped on to the dynamic that maintains within *Walden* between wildness and civilisation, or 'nature' and 'culture'. If the labour of the poet can be radically separated from that of the farmer, (as the gifts of Nature oppose the mercantile productions of man), it is because the former partakes of a wildness, to which Thoreau himself returns in his writing, and about which the civilised farmer has long forgotten. Each of these stories hangs together, which is why everything still now hangs in the balance.

Thoreau, of course, at times comes very close to affirming that his withdrawal is a simple exit from economic life in Concord. *Walden* opens with the following:

> When I wrote the following pages, or rather the bulk of them, *I lived alone*, in the woods, a mile from any neighbor, *in a house which I had built myself*, on the shore of Walden Pond, in Concord, Massachusetts, *and earned my living by the labor of my hands only*. I lived there two years and two months. At present I am a *sojourner* in civilized life again.[44]

At moments like these, it is as though at Walden Pond, the site of *his* house, there was neither circulation nor economy, or, at least, as though the economy of Walden/*Walden* existed entirely apart from that of society at large.[45] This would be the force of the final sentence: Now that Thoreau is back in 'civilized life' he is once again a 'sojourner', since he has re-entered the aimless circulation that marks the restlessness of modern man's commodities and state of homelessness alike. One could expand this thought to include, as well, the entire discussion, offered later in 'Economy', of Thoreau's finances and capital in moving to the pond. In direct contrast to the unspecifiable and unpayable debts of Thoreau's townsmen – those poor inheritors of farms, houses, barns, cattle, and farming tools – the full articulation, down to the last half and three-quarters cent, of the costs of moving to the pond, would allow Thoreau to exit, by way of *his* economy, the economy of his neighbours.

This is a common enough story. And it is one that functions whether one believes that Thoreau succeeded in escaping the commodity economy, or that he failed to do so, for example, because he must reproduce the very economic forms that he opposes, in opposing them. If, however, we leave this specific question suspended for the moment – if only because it is still poorly posed, being too concerned with success and failure – it would still remain to be seen how this new economy, set apart, is supposed to function. That is, it remains to be seen how the poet, or hermit, once returned to the most basic conditions of production available to him, should make ends meet.

If the ideal – and idealistic – independence of the once-autonomous farmer of Concord was a temptation too great for either Emerson or Thoreau ever fully to abandon, it remained the case that even that idealised vision had itself to be subtended by what Marx, a few years later in *Capital*, will have identified as the 'Nature-given materials' upon which our productive activities take aim.[46] In other words, neither poet nor hermit can hope to survive by fishing, if there are no fish present to begin with. Nature must supply that which, only later, is taken up, appropriated, and displaced by the market. And the way in which it does so is through what Richard Grusin has dubbed the 'economy of nature': through expenditure, extravagance, and free bestowals; what Thoreau, in 'Walking', calls Nature's 'absolute freedom and wildness'.[47]

Though the idea that Nature gives freely and abundantly, while humans give only with restrictions or not at all, is a far from original proposition in Thoreau, it is nevertheless a critical element of his writings, which one encounters widely, from 'Walking' to *Walden* to 'Wild Apples'. In 'Walking', for example, the language of economic commerce is directly contrasted with that of natural or divine dispensation. These represent two entirely different orders – as they did in Emerson – with 'wealth' helpless to 'buy' what only the grace of God may give. And here, in conspicuous fashion, the walker is inserted in precisely the place traditionally held by the poet, as *born* recipient of the bountiful gift of God:

No wealth can buy the requisite leisure, freedom, and independence, which are the capital in this profession. It comes only by the grace of God. It requires a direct dispensation from Heaven to become a walker. You must be born into the family of the Walkers. *Ambulator nascitur, non fit.*[48]

Similarly, in 'Wild Apples', what marks the natural, wondrous state of this fruit are just its 'evanescent and celestial qualities', which are seen to evaporate as soon as they are carried to market, or even touched by the hand of the shopper. 'It would be well', Thoreau writes, 'if we accepted these gifts with more joy and gratitude, and did not think it enough simply to put a fresh load of compost about the tree.'[49] Nowhere, however, is the divine, uncalculating, freely given character of the natural world prone to dispense itself without reservation more visible than in 'The Bean-Field' chapter of *Walden*:

> Ancient poetry and mythology suggest, at least, that husbandry was once a sacred art; but it is pursued with irreverent haste and heedlessness by us, our object being to have large farms and large crops merely. We have no festival, nor procession, nor ceremony, not excepting our Cattle-shows and so called Thanksgivings, by which the farmer expresses a sense of the sacredness of his calling, or is reminded of its sacred origin. It is the premium and the feast which tempt him. He sacrifices not to Ceres and the Terrestrial Jove, but to the infernal Plutus rather. By avarice and selfishness, and a groveling habit, from which none of us is free, of regarding the soil as property, or the means of acquiring property chiefly, the landscape is deformed, husbandry is degraded with us, and the farmer leads the meanest of lives. He knows Nature but as a robber . . . We are wont to forget that the sun looks on our cultivated fields and on the prairies and forests without distinction. They all reflect and absorb his rays alike, and the former make but a small part of the glorious picture which he beholds in his daily course. In his view the earth is all equally cultivated like a garden. Therefore we should receive the benefit of his light and heat with a corresponding trust and magnanimity. What though I value the seed of these beans, and harvest that in the fall of the year?[50]

Here, in the wake of the Roi Soleil and in anticipation of Zarathustra, the sun looks down upon our fields and dispenses light freely and without distinction. Just as men of the past, Thoreau laments in 'Wild Apples', 'could afford then to stick a tree by every wall-side and let it take its chance', so too does the sun dole out its rays without afterthought or inhibition.[51] And just as the price of grafted apple trees now spells the likely end of the wild apple, so too would a restricted economy of light mean the end of Nature itself, in its most essential and extravagant form.

Though different in its emphasis from the market-oriented, economic readings of critics such as Lowell, Gilmore, and Bercovitch, the extravagant, general economy of Nature that I have just sketched out would nevertheless risk reaffirming the former accounts, to the extent that Nature's extravagance (or general economy) remains in a relation of simple opposition to the restraint (or restricted economies) of man and the market.[52] Thus, while these two forms of economy, sketched out by Grusin with explicit reference to Bataille, may *at times* give the appearance of being strictly divorced, at yet other moments it becomes evident that their separation can no longer be maintained. What must be attended to are those moments in which, precisely, it is no longer possible to discern the difference between the two, or to tell in which form of economy one is participating. Indeed, what *Walden* masterfully demonstrates, time and again, what it testifies to with uncanny perspicacity, is precisely the impossibility of maintaining this distinction, even as it remains no less impossible to abandon it completely.

Let us return to the scene from which we started: Thoreau's consideration, perambulation, and purchase, all in imagination, of the farms of his neighbours. Already there are indications that things may not be as clear-cut as they seemed, the first of which is to be found in the trope of spectating that organises this passage through the farmlands. Thoreau is here closer to a *flâneur* than a peripatetic, subjecting each property, as he passes through the idyllic countryside, to the vulgar lens of the window-shopper: 'all were to be bought, and I knew their price'. Just as troubling is the figure of the farm itself, which is here the privileged object of Thoreau's imagined speculations. As well as being one of the most recurrent figures in *Walden*, it is also one of the most overdetermined: as the site of the dissemination of seeds, of both cultivated and wild apples, of farmers, with their pecuniary interests, as well as the poet, with his poetic ones, the farm comes to name the privileged site of a chance. It is there that – to return once more to Emerson – one witnesses the very birth of the *flower of commodities*: of a gift that is no longer that of the classical poet's transeconomy of beauty, but instead bestowed as the chance of an event, out of the unholy marriage of poet *and* market. It is there where, as the location in which such supposedly rigorous oppositions as those between nature and culture, beauty and interest, poet and farmer, unrestricted and restricted economy, and even solar gift economy and agricultural commodity exchange, are all put into contact and made to contaminate one another.[53]

Hence the interest of the Hollowell farm's purchase, which takes place, Thoreau informs us not once, but twice, under the leading hand of his imagination:

My imagination carried me so far that I even had the refusal of several farms, – the refusal was all I wanted, – but I never got my fingers burned by actual possession. The nearest that I came to actual possession was when I bought the Hollowell place.[54]

Carried by his imagination, Thoreau tells us that he had already received the refusal of several farms and that, odd as it may seem, the refusal was all he wanted. What will mark the specificity of the Hollowell farm experiment is the proximity to which Thoreau comes to being burned: to crossing the boundary leading outside his speculative imagination and into the terrestrial domain of 'actual possession'.

Following Thoreau's opening speculations on houses, the first paragraph of 'Where I Lived' immediately shifts to speculations on living, where it is a matter of inhabiting without inhabiting:

Wherever I sat, there I might live, and the landscape radiated from me accordingly. What is a house but a *sedes*, a seat? – better if a country seat [. . .] Well, there I might live, I said; and there I did live, for an hour, a summer and a winter life; saw how I could let the years run off, buffet the winter through, and see the spring come in. The future inhabitants of this region, wherever they may place their houses, may be sure that they have been *anticipated*. An afternoon sufficed to lay out the land into orchard, woodlot, and pasture, and to decide what fine oaks or pines should be left to stand before the door, and whence each blasted tree could be seen to the best advantage; and then I let it lie, *fallow perchance*, for a man is rich in proportion to the number of things which he can afford to let alone.[55]

One could read the above passage and the recounting of the purchase of the Hollowell farm that follows it as repetitions. On each occasion, there is a fall from the privacy, safety, and sterility of the guiding hand of the imagination into the burning, binding commitment of reproductive work in the field. In this passage in particular the pure, spectating glance metamorphoses into the projective act of the creative imagination ('saw how I could let the years run off'), before it arrives, finally, at a fantastic pronouncement by the poet, to which we will return: 'The future inhabitants of this region, wherever they may place their houses, may be sure that they have been anticipated.' It would be difficult to say in what, exactly, such anticipation consists. Straddling the weightless flight of the imagination and the heavy-handed labour of the cultivator, anticipation might be said to articulate their very difference, or to constitute a mode of reflection – or perhaps of experimentation – that threatens, however unpredictably, to traverse the gap between the two. Thoreau, evidently, escapes unscathed from his anticipation, rich as he is in proportion to that which he can afford to let alone. And yet, at the same time, anticipation would here appear truly to constitute 'anticipation' only to the extent that it might *possibly* become something more – or less – than itself, which necessary possibility Thoreau recognises with his haunting 'perchance'. The barrenness of land sown by the imagination is so perchance, which is to say that a certain, even unaccountable fecundity, lies within. What seed might yet be sown through sheer anticipation, perchance?

Thoreau's purchase of the Hollowell farm, what he will call the first 'experiment' of the Walden Pond variety, is thus initiated by his imagination, and almost by chance, for, as he tells it, 'the refusal was all I wanted'. He purchases it by chance, as though he had been testing some boundary all along, but without really wanting to exceed it – both wanting *and* not wanting to exceed it. The possibility of not simply remaining within the realm of the imagination is thus threatened from the very first moment that its movement is initiated, and this risk is one that the imagination carries within itself:[56]

> My imagination carried me so far that I even had the refusal of several farms, – the refusal was all I wanted, – but I never got my fingers burned by actual possession. The nearest that I came to actual possession was when I bought the Hollowell place, and had begun to sort my seeds, and collected materials with which to make a wheelbarrow to carry it on or off with; but before the owner gave me a deed of it, his wife – every man has such a wife – changed her mind and wished to keep it, and he offered me ten dollars to release him.[57]

Thoreau, by his own admission, buys the Hollowell property. But between the purchase and what he calls 'actual possession' remains an abyss because the gap, let us say, between buying and owning both *is* and *is not* one. To the danger of being burned through 'actual possession' must then be compared this other danger, which is one of much more troubling nature: the danger, that is, of no longer being able to determine, absolutely, where exactly purchase ends and possession begins; of not knowing, in other words, *when* and *if* one is or is not burned, just as Wordsworth could not tell if he was or was not a chosen poet, what he had or did not have to give, and Shelley, what the 'frail spells' of poets might avail, or not avail, to sever.

How to know how close is *too close*? How to know the exact point where purchase ends and possession begins? This is another way of asking: how to know when the linguistic performative becomes materially, economically, and legally binding, or, more to the point, when the linguistic utterance *becomes* performative? This is not merely a question of juridical norms and distinctions. It cannot be resolved through recourse to ready-made legal notions: for example, in the distinction between contract signing and closing. Such distinctions cannot touch on, they cannot legislate over, the very process through which a linguistic utterance becomes juridically binding in the first place. This the hand cannot grip. The poet's imaginative offer to buy, once met by the farmer's prosaic acceptance of price, brings into question whether any given utterance's determination, as earnest *or* ironic, prosaic *or* poetic, literal *or* figurative, or binding *or* non-binding, might be decided. Here, the elusiveness of the linguistic utterance, proffered under the leading hand of Thoreau's imagination, yet invested with the weight of a prosaic commodity exchange, emerges in the gap between purchase and possession. Thoreau buys the Hollowell farm. And yet, he remains, somehow, untouched by actual possession – or so he says. This gap in experience cannot simply be adjudicated or be made to conform to ready-made juridical standards. And it is here that we shall find the remains of something called 'poetry'.

Is it a coincidence, then, if the site of this abyss is occupied, narratively speaking, by the farmer's wife? The wife, who is here both absolutely singular and absolutely universal – 'every man has such a wife' – stands between the male interlocutors and haunts their exchange. Legally prohibited from the ownership of property, the wife here has no voice proper to her. She is juridically excluded from participating in this scene.[58] And yet, she, more than any other, speaks to the vertiginous gulf that ought to distinguish purchase from possession.

According to his own testimony, then, Thoreau is never burned by actual possession. And yet, for all that, the farm's purchase does, in fact, appear to take place. It *appears*, to all appearances, to take the form of a legally binding contract. Even if, following Thoreau, we allow that purchase does not yet constitute possession, it nevertheless here carries the force of a covenant, exemplified by the farmer's counter-offer of ten dollars, which he puts forward so as to be released from his bond. With the farmer's counter-offer, which functions to recognise and indemnify an obligation, Thoreau expresses shock, and is led to make the first pronouncement of 'truth' in his narrative:

> Now, to speak the truth, I had but ten cents in the world, and it surpassed my arithmetic to tell, if I was that man who had ten cents, or who had a farm, or ten dollars, or all together.[59]

What happens here *in* Thoreau's narrative, but also happens *to* his narrative, is an experience with the character of his own speech, which, in being taken as titled by the farmer, reveals something about the nature of poetic – though we could also say fictional, counterfeit, or imaginative – language. The farmer accepts Thoreau's proposal to buy the farm, and what looked like mere playing – 'my imagination carried me so far' – an exercise in informal or poetic speech, is taken as prosaic. Yet what seals the deal for Thoreau – to abuse the expression – is not the farmer's acceptance of the offer to buy, but his subsequent reneging on the pact. It is the moment of the farmer's appeal to exit the deal that turns out to be the decisive affirmation of the contractual – which is to say, binding or performative – character of their earlier interaction. The farmer, in sum, by offering Thoreau *something for nothing* – by offering something (ten dollars) for what, so far as 'Thoreau', the poet, was concerned, ought to have been nothing (an utterance of the imagination) – asserts a contractually binding, legally valid interpretation of what had come to pass between them. And this affirms, for Thoreau, its irreversibility. The moment the untitled offer to purchase is taken as titled currency there is no turning back – or, at least, there might not be, for who is to say that the farmer is not himself playing at poetry, in his turn?[60] At any event, 'poetic' or counterfeit language, once it is taken as 'prosaic' or titled speech, cannot *simply* be untitled, without the necessary possibility that one be held accountable for the repayment of some debt.

It is at the moment of the farmer's counter-offer of ten dollars in remuneration for the voiding of the deal that the sense of the poet's discourse breaks down and he admits: the transaction surpassed my arithmetic. The limit of the arithmetical is here not simply fictional or poetic speech – the play of the imagination – but what is experienced by Thoreau as the moment of fiction's crossing over into the realm of 'truth', a counterfeit coin yielding valid or titled currency.

The farmer offers Thoreau ten dollars to be released from his bond. With this, Thoreau's pure speculation has turned a profit and it is revealed that he has been speculating with real, titled currency all along – or, at least, with that which had the capacity to be taken as such. (But didn't Thoreau know that this was a possibility all along? Wasn't this just what tempted him in the first place?) At any event, the transformation of poetic speech into legally binding pledge is what Thoreau cannot comprehend. It is the reason why he cannot simply balance his account, cannot, that is, entirely master the text that he so adeptly produces. We also begin to see here what is at stake in Thoreau's 'anticipation' and the haunting 'perchance' that marked seed left unsown. If poetic discourse can be taken as prosaic – and vice versa – it becomes impossible to anticipate the value of anticipation, the practical, legal, or commercial values of 'purely' theoretical or imaginative labour. This is also to say that the ahistorical, aneconomical, or free work of the imagination can no longer be pre-emptively excluded from history and economy.

As though it still held out the possibility of delimiting these fields, of the imagination and of real or titled speech, Thoreau makes his appeal to 'truth':

> Now, to speak the truth, I had but ten cents in the world, and it surpassed my arithmetic to tell, if I was the man who had ten cents, or who had a farm, or ten dollars, or all together.

However, at this moment, *in truth*, Thoreau can no longer tell what is given: whether he is who he thought he was – the man with ten cents – or someone who has purchased a farm, or someone whose compensation for the voiding of that purchase has earned him ten dollars; *or*, finally, somehow, by some incalculable calculation, he who has 'all together'. In the moment of truth, nothing is taken for granted, and at the same time, everything remains in suspense.

Could we here identify a logic of the commodity at work, one that Thoreau would then satirise through his unarithmetical exchange? The figure of the commodity, as a material good as well as an exchange-value, is also marked by a confusion over its ontological status: which is to say, over what it may be at any given moment. When Marx, in *Capital*, distinguishes among the various stages of a commercial exchange – for example, with the formula M–C–M (Money–Commodity–Money) – he is able to do so because he has recourse to the diachrony of time, which separates out any given moment within a history of transactions from any other. Translated into the text's terms, so far as Thoreau is concerned, the formula M–C–M should yield something like: *ten cents for a farm for ten cents*. But now, by the farmer's accounting, it instead gives: *ten cents for a farm for ten dollars*. Thoreau's confusion over what he has and, consequently, who he is could therefore be understood to ironise commodity logic, which appears now (to Thoreau) to produce something out of nothing. Just as the individual commodity, once reduced to an exchange value, becomes harder and harder to dissociate conceptually from all other commodities of equal value, here the magic of capitalist speculation would enact a series of substitutions that remain incomprehensible for Thoreau's particular strand of materialism.

And yet, the commensurability of the inequivalent in Thoreau's calculation – ten cents for a farm for ten dollars, culminating in the figure of the 'all together' – may point to something more radical than satire. Or, put otherwise, the consequences of such 'satire' might go far beyond the realm of the commodity alone, for, while rendering equivalent inequivalent things – such as goods and money – is simply what good capitalists do, Thoreau's culminating 'all together' neither appears to correspond to the potential outcome of any exchange, nor seems to follow from any other form of capitalist speculation. Instead, it announces the moment of their confusion: of the dream-like phantasmagoria that no longer knows how to separate out illusion from reality. All of this is to say that one can never arrive at Thoreau's 'all together' *through* exchange or the logic of the commodity, but only at the moment of that logic's collapse, when time, personal identity, and value all cease to function as pillars of economic stability. But how, then, is such a moment of collapse to be understood?

It is as though the dissymmetry of Thoreau's – or the poet's – imaginative offer to buy the farm, with the prosaic acceptance of the farmer, had, at last, been translated back into what is no longer, strictly speaking, distinguishable as either 'poetic' or 'economic' speech. The latter's diachronic accounting – sequential narrative, logic, and the balancing of accounts – is here flattened through the former's synchronic, aberrant, and vagrant textuality. Thoreau can no longer tell whether he has ten cents, or a farm, or ten dollars, or all together. He can no longer even tell who he is because the borders lying between himself and the farmer, but also between the word and thing, the 'farm' and farm, signifier and referent, have become undecidable. *The poet buys the farm* to this extent: that what happens in poetry, or fails to happen, what happens in failure, is not a versified speech, or even a readily recognisable language of the imagination that opposes and therefore upholds a prosaic discourse of work and labour, but, *in truth*, an irruption internal to the language of 'truth' that renders the one indissociable from the other. The poet, we could say, both buys *and* does not buy the farm. The poet dies *and* lives on, lives on to die again, but also dies, *as poet*.

Thoreau's failure of arithmetic thus reveals something about the very moment of exchange, which moment remains both necessary and impossible in his account: necessary because the possibility of exchange is the condition for any contract, but impossible because one could never rigorously determine the value of any coin, currency, or signifier, at any given time. Each is haunted by its reversibility. And while this may result in a certain experience of madness (of the 'all together'), it also opens the possibility of reading – and therefore misreading – in the first place, at that 'moment' when words and deeds coexist, and do so precisely in order to be substituted for one another: like a promise for a promise for a deed for a title for land, and so on. Poetry, or the experience of a poet buying a farm, the *experiment* of a poet buying a farm, therefore no longer names a versified language either of non-exchange, or of exchange, but the experience of a language that would cease to be taken for granted (or given), and whose value or meaning would, as a consequence, no longer remain assured, be it as poetic or prosaic, binding or non-binding, referential or self-referential. This is why it may also always be overlooked. This is why the 'event' entailed in this experience or experiment is one that both happens and does not quite happen, one that barely happens, if it happens at all. Whether we still call what remains, in the wake of this event, 'poetry' is for this reason ultimately less important than how we account for the status of the experiment, once prose accounting has lost its bearing. Yet what, then, becomes of the gift?

CLOSING ACCOUNTS

When Thoreau recovers his senses – and cents – but finds that he is still faced with the farmer's impending ten dollars, he resolves to let things stand as they are, or nearly so:

> it surpassed my arithmetic to tell, if I was that man who had ten cents, or who had a farm, or ten dollars, or all together. However, I let him keep the ten dollars and the farm too, for I had carried it far enough; or rather, to be generous, I sold him the farm for just what I gave for it, and, as he was not a rich man, made him a present of ten dollars, and still had my ten cents, and seeds, and materials for a wheelbarrow left. I found thus that I had been a rich man without any damage to my poverty. But I retained the landscape, and I have since annually carried off what it yielded without a wheelbarrow.[61]

Thoreau wishes to walk away: to abandon, without remainder, what must never actually have been his, if his claim to having never been 'burned by actual possession' is to remain at all plausible. Indeed, if his interaction with the owner of the Hollowell place is to remain an anecdote within the annals of his life before 'Walden', the story of a near-collision but eventual escape from the threat of domestic, or domesticated, existence, then it is crucial that he not bear the traces of the encounter so that his poverty not be damaged thereby. The opposition operating between monetary or material and intellectual or spiritual poverty here makes possible the distinction between two forms of 'retention': one that relies on wheelbarrows and another that does not. What is essential is that Thoreau not bear the burden of the land on his shoulders but rather, and even to this day, that he retains only the landscape. Such an immaterial scene is all the better because, lifting up his mind without wearing down his body, it allows for a pecuniary poverty to coexist with intellectual affluence. But does Thoreau walk away with his poverty intact? Does the time of his encounter, that failed encounter of his experimental mis-acquisition, really pass without material effects, so that afterwards Thoreau will still, seemingly, be able to gloat that he 'had been a rich man without any damage to [his] poverty'?

There are indications that matters are not so straightforward, the first being Thoreau's admission of a labour done. Just as he will have been 'carried' by his imagination, so too does he, with reference to the exchange with the farmer, 'carr[y] it far enough'. And while he possesses the 'generosity' to return all the farmer's possessions without usury, the question of compensation nevertheless lingers. Hence Thoreau's reference to, and identification with, Atlas in the following paragraph:

> To enjoy these advantages I was ready to carry it on; like Atlas, to take the world on my shoulders, – I never heard what compensation he received for that, – and do all those things which had no other motive or excuse but that I might pay for it and be unmolested in my possession of it.[62]

Thoreau, unlike Atlas, does not carry it on. However, in raising the question of compensation, and in doing so by way of Atlas's labour, he does displace the reciprocal order of recompense. As with his earlier speculations on the house, Thoreau's comparison to Atlas short-circuits questions of commercial economy by placing, metonymically, the figure of economy as a whole (now the 'world') within an individual exchange, as though one could trade 'economy' without already belonging to its system. Giving the whole for a part, or the 'world' in lieu of a mere load or harvest, the question of repayment is stifled before it may even be uttered, for certainly no coin or currency could be adequate to the efforts of one who upholds the system of currency itself, by virtue of which said 'coin' acquires its value in the first place. If Atlas's labour raises the question of compensation, then, it is not because he lacked the sponsors to expiate his debts properly, but because the language of debt and expiation is no longer adequate to it.[63]

The question thus becomes whether Thoreau's work does not, like Atlas's, displace the order or circulation of debt: that is, whether his 'exchange' with the owner of the Hollowell farm does not exceed the basic conditions of accounting, such that it would no longer simply be a matter of picking up, or putting back down again, a given load. What, after all, does Thoreau carry and then evidently put back down? '[F]or I had carried *it* far enough', he specifies. The referent of the 'it', however, is ambiguous, and can only with great difficulty be determined as the land – the land that Thoreau *would have* carried on, had the farmer sold it to him. 'It' may just as well refer to the conversation, or to the impression that Thoreau carried the cash required to make such a purchase in the first place. Nor is the ambiguity of the 'it' at all dispelled by the verb 'carrying', for this verb's frequency in the passage, and each time with different degrees of literality, is itself overdetermined. The insistence of carrying, carrying on, carrying off, carrying far enough, and carrying both with and without a wheelbarrow is by itself sufficient to highlight the uncanniness of the displacements here carried out. Displacements that occur not only between fields and farms, but also tropes and tracts, in an agri-linguistic play that 'grounds' this passage in every sense of the word, and in so doing underwrites it with so many metaphorical figures for metaphor that it becomes difficult to tell the status of any given term at any given time. If, then, at the end of the day, what Thoreau carries far enough is not simply *this* conversation with the farmer, but a language that threatens to lose itself in the abyssal distinction between poetry and prose, then *it* may not be something he can simply re-place.

The gesture of putting back down, in other words, just like that of picking up, or of coming into possession, may fail. Closing an account such as Thoreau's will never be a simple matter of returning, or giving back, to someone what he or she is due: not, anyway, without the haunting possibility of some remainder, perchance. This remainder, unlike what Thoreau claims he takes away from his encounter – '[b]ut I retained the landscape' – is no longer something present, but speaks to what in his 'all together' remained at bay, unspoken, and unaccounted for, as the residue of the linguistic fracture that poetry *perhaps* induces. Frail spells.

Confronted, then, with the farmer's ten dollars, Thoreau cannot simply return them. He cannot simply let the farmer 'keep' his ten dollars as though nothing had happened or come to pass, as though all accounts were squared with nothing left over, as though an unpayable debt had not been accrued. As if to acknowledge this – even as he would disavow it – Thoreau cannot but make one final, superfluous, act of 'generosity':

> However, I let him keep the ten dollars and the farm too, for I had carried it far enough; or rather, to be generous, I sold him the farm for just what I gave for it, and, as he was not a rich man, made him a present of ten dollars, and still had my ten cents, and seeds, and materials for a wheelbarrow left.

Thoreau's irony in this passage is palpable. In what lies the generosity of returning to its original owner something one never ought to have acquired in the first place? If generosity is to be understood as the character of magnanimity, of being able to give without conditions or calculations – which is to say, without obligation or debt – then Thoreau, the poet, is here the last person that one would describe in this way. Moreover, the distinction, however slight, between 'letting keep' on the one hand, and 'making a present' on the other, is not merely formal. Who would simply equate *not stealing* with *bestowing through largesse*?

Nevertheless, and in spite of this gap, both interpretations do remain possible, and even valid accounts of Thoreau's actions. It is no less deniable that Thoreau let the farmer 'keep' the ten dollars and farm, *as though* nothing had happened, than that he 'sold' the farm back for just what he gave for it, while making the farmer a present of ten dollars, *as though* something had, indeed, come to pass. By positing both accounts, Thoreau, in sum, produces an ambivalence within his text that allows him both to avow and to disavow their encounter, or perhaps it would be better to say he gives two accounts of what remains, as yet, an undecidable event.[64] Like Wordsworth's 'one word more', Thoreau's commentary runs the risk of narrative poverty and excess, of giving too little and too much, inextricably and undecidably. And is not such a suspension of distinctions what Thoreau inscribes first and foremost? Is it not the first mark of his 'extravagance'?

It is by way of such an irreducible narrative doubling that the spectre of 'generosity' may, finally, make a return. What is here 'generous' – if generous it is – is not the subject named Thoreau, but the narrative supplement itself, insofar as it offers a difference that both is and is not one, and a gift that both is and is not one. Such a form of generosity, if we may still call it that, defies the calculations of narrative transparency and accountability, as well as the economic logic of debt and obligation. And it is through this textual excess that Thoreau ultimately suspends any question of closure concerning what he does or does not walk away with. To put it differently: it is in this way that he reaffirms the impossibility of anticipating what seeds may yet be left sown or unsown.

Having given his gift – or at least the spectre of a gift that may or may not be one – Thoreau finally returns, in concluding the passage, to the question of what he will have 'yielded without a wheelbarrow'. This time, however, it is a question less of a given subject named 'Thoreau', or even the implicit speaker of the passage, than of a 'poet', of unknown provenance:[65]

> I have frequently seen a poet withdraw, having enjoyed the most valuable part of a farm, while the crusty farmer supposed that he [we] had got a few wild apples only. Why, the owner does not know it for many years when a poet has put his farm in rhyme, the most admirable kind of invisible fence, has fairly impounded it, milked it, skimmed it, and got all the cream, and left the farmer only the skimmed milk.[66]

We might ask, by way of conclusion, what the nature of such a rhyme-fence would be? Seizing, *in language*, the fattiest, richest portion of this figural farm-cow, 'the poet' impounds and secures his somewhat unlikely poetic bounty. 'Cream' does not here simply name a good to be drunk or meted out incrementally, but something, already, on the order of excess. The richest milk a cow can give, it names what cannot be reduced to dollars and cents, yet also, what always might be: above all, when it is skimmed. For Thoreau, the experience of a poet buying a farm is to be located somewhere between purchase and possession – or cream and skimmed milk – at the site of an impossible confrontation between two different economies, where, *impounded in rhyme*, 'the farm' is no longer given as such but, hollow-ed out in its very name, it opens itself to being written.

NOTES

1. *A Week on the Concord and Merrimack Rivers* (Boston: James R. Osgood and Company, 1873), 386–7. Henceforth, *A Week*.
2. *William Wordsworth: The Major Works*, 591.
3. See, for example, the conclusion to 'Economy' for such complementary verses, 57–8, and the chapter 'Brute Neighbors' for a dialogue with a poet, 151–3.
4. That Thoreau identifies with the hero-bard is a central element of Cavell's reading in *The Senses of Walden: An Expanded Edition* (Chicago: University of Chicago Press, 1992). As Cavell explains, 'The writer is aligning himself with the major tradition of English poetry, whose most ambitious progeny, at least since Milton, had been haunted by the call for a modern epic' (6). And later: 'Since "experiment of this kind" directly refers to the possessing of a house, and since that has just before been shown to be, rightly understood, a poetic exercise, the present experiment is the book at hand . . . The experiment is the present – to make himself present to each circumstance, at every eventuality; since he is writing, in each significant mark' (60–1). See also *Senses*, 13; 31; 33. Gilmore contends that both 'Civil Disobedience' and *Walden* 'aspire to public influence, and both specify the hero-bard as a kind of transcendent legislator who discerns the truth with special clarity because of his position of detachment' (14). Nevertheless, Gilmore argues that Thoreau was forced to 'amend his expectations as a poet-legislator' when the public showed little interest in it, and instead 'settled for the captaincy of a huckleberry party' (15). In *A Week*, Thoreau confirms this identification, writing that: 'Before printing was discovered, a century was equal to a thousand years. The poet is he who can write some pure mythology to-day without the aid of posterity. In how few words, for instance, the Greeks would have told the story of Abelard and Heloise, making but a sentence of our classical dictionary [. . .] We moderns, on the other hand, collect only

the raw materials of biography and history' (68). Compare also his comments concerning the 'matutine intellectual of the poet' in *A Week* to what he says of the dawn in *Walden*: 'In the history of the human mind, these glowing and ruddy fables precede the noonday thoughts of men, as Aurora the sun's rays. The matutine intellect of the poet, keeping in advance of the glare of philosophy, always dwells in this auroral atmosphere' (*A Week*, 69). 'Every morning was a cheerful invitation to make my life of equal simplicity, and I may say innocence, with Nature herself. I have been as sincere a worshipper of Aurora as the Greeks. I got up early and bathed in the pond; that was a religious exercise, and one of the best things which I did. [. . .] It was Homer's requiem; itself an Iliad and Odyssey in the air, singing its own wrath and wanderings. There was something cosmical about it [. . .] All poets and heroes, like Memnon, are the children of Aurora, and emit their music at sunrise. To him whose elastic and vigorous thoughts keep pace with the sun, the day is a perpetual morning' (*Walden*, 63–5). See also, in *A Week*, 98–9 and 388.

5. *Walden*, 28.
6. On Thoreau's relationship with Wordsworth in *Walden*, as one of 'profound identification', see Richard Gravil, *Romantic Dialogues: Anglo-American Continuities, 1776–1862*, 202–3 and Lance Newman, *Our Common Dwelling* (New York: Palgrave MacMillan, 2005), 83–96. For Thoreau's relationship with the Romantics in general, see James McIntosh, *Thoreau as Romantic Naturalist*.
7. In some ways similar to Wordsworth and his circle's indecision, concerning the reasons why he could not finish the *Recluse*, so too have critics debated Thoreau's reasons for abandoning writing in verse after he dedicated so much energy, early on, to just that. For a review of these assessments, see Newman, 93–4. For his part, Newman views Thoreau's decision to write in prose as that *of* a poet: 'It is not that Thoreau was unable to compose regular verse and so dropped the genre, but rather he recognized that the essence of poetry was not accentual-syllabic meter and regular form' (94).
8. *A Week*, 364.
9. *A Week*, 399; 99; 362.
10. *Walden*, 59.
11. J. Lyndon Shanley, *The Making of Walden* (Chicago: University of Chicago Press, 1957), 68. Two years later, in 1854, *Walden* is published.
12. Walter Harding alludes to such a letter in *The Days of Henry Thoreau: A Biography* (New York: Dover, 1982), 123n.9. It was written to Prudence Ward on 8 April 1841.
13. *The Variorum Walden*, ed. Walter Harding (New York: Twayne, 1962), 28n.2.

14. There are a number of telling journal entries during April of 1841 as well, which might lead one to think that he purchased the farm then, or at least was beginning to consider it. See especially *The Journal of Henry D. Thoreau 1*, eds Bradford Torrey and Francis H. Allen (New York: Dover, 1962), 80–1, for 16 April: 'I have been inspecting my neighbors' farms to-day and chaffering with the landholders, and I must confess I am startled to find everywhere the old system of things so grim and assured. Wherever I go the farms are run out, and there they lie, and the youth must buy old land and bring it to.'
15. Although Thoreau's desire to find a quiet spot to write precedes his brother John's death in 1842, after his death the search for a retreat – including the move to Walden – becomes expressly motivated by the project to write *A Week*, so as to commemorate two weeks spent with his brother.
16. For various reasons, including the refusal of the owner of the Hollowell place, Thoreau's own developing ideas about the problems surrounding property and ownership, and, if some speculation is permissible, probably also his lack of capital, Thoreau eventually discarded the idea of owning a farm and decided instead to take to the woods. As Harding points out, the practice was not at all uncommon for this period in America. Charles Wheeler, a classmate of Thoreau's at Harvard, lived for a short while in a cabin at Flint's Pond – during which time Thoreau may have visited him – and Ellery Channing, Thoreau's close friend and source for the 'poet' in the dialogue of 'Brute Neighbors', spent time living alone in a cabin on the Illinois prairies (*Variorum*, 13). Other 'experimental' living practices were also occurring in Concord throughout the 1840s, including the well-known Brook Farm and Fruitlands communities.
17. Both texts were published in 1852 in *Sartain's Union Magazine*. 'The Iron Horse', which was later incorporated into the chapter 'Sounds', treats of the ecological soundscape created by the newly introduced locomotive in the woods of Concord. Harding notes in the *Variorum Walden* that it is possible that Thoreau intended to publish more of *Walden* independently, but the failure of *Sartain's Union Magazine* in August 1852 may have stripped him of his venue (283n.1). Incidentally, as a result of the magazine's failure, Thoreau was never paid for either publication. Gilmore, citing Thoreau's correspondence with Horace Greeley, argues that both publications were part of an effort at self-promotion prior to *Walden*'s publication, to drum up sales, a situation that adds another layer of irony to what is recounted here (10).
18. *Walden*, 60.
19. On the broader relation between Thoreau's sense of experimentation and the natural sciences, see Bernhard Kuhn, *Autobiography and Natural Science*

in the Age of Romanticism. On the rise of experimental science, see also Robert Mitchell, *Experimental Life*.
20. *Walden*, 219. By contrast, readers such as Neufeldt, while acknowledging that *Walden* 'constitutes a serious parody of the guide to success and a number of its conventions' (157), nevertheless have been inclined to read it as a 'success story': 'The protracted labor on *Walden* secured its success, made "success unexpected in common hours" its theme, and increasingly identified enterprising young men eager for success as its internalized readers. As such, *Walden* presented itself as a success manual, a guidebook for devotees of success in a culture of enterprise' (66). See Leonard N. Neufeldt, *The Economist: Henry Thoreau & Enterprise* (Oxford: Oxford University Press, 1989).
21. *The Senses of Walden*, 36.
22. *Walden*, 60–1. In *A Week*, Thoreau compares this state of the rooster to that of the inspired poet: 'When the poetic frenzy seizes us, we run and scratch with our pen, intent only on worms, calling our mates around us, like the cock, and delighting in the dust we make, but do not detect where the jewel lies, which, perhaps, we have in the mean time cast to a distance, or quite covered up again' (363). As always, though, there is an immediate wavering between full identification: 'Great prose, of equal elevation, commands our respect more than great verse, since it implies a more permanent and level height, a life more pervaded with the grandeur of the thought. The poet often only makes an irruption, like a Parthian, and is off again, shooting while he retreats: but the prose writer has conquered like a Roman, and settled colonies. The true poem is not that which the public read. There is always a poem not printed on paper, coincident with the production of this, stereotyped in the poet's life. It is *what he has become through his work*. Not how is the idea expressed in stone, or on canvas or paper, is the question, but how far it has obtained form and expression in the life of the artist. His true work will not stand in any prince's gallery' (363–4).
23. *Complete Essays*, 5–6.
24. *Collected Works of Ralph Waldo Emerson, Volume IV*, 87.
25. Most of Thoreau's writing of poetry took place between 1837 and 1844. While Thoreau did continue to write in verse and insert it into his prose works – such as in *A Week* and *Walden* – beginning in 1841 there is a marked decline in his writing of poems, and after 1844 he ceased altogether to try to publish them independently. On Thoreau and poetry composition, see Elizabeth Hall Witherell, 'Thoreau as Poet', where she makes this point and surveys Thoreau's complicated relationship with

verse composition, as well as her 'Thoreau's Watershed Season as a Poet: The Hidden Fruits of the Summer and Fall of 1841', and Lizzy LeRud, 'Living Poems in Thoreau's Prose'.

26. In both versions of the text, after the 'purchase' of the farm, there is explicit reference to 'a poet withdraw[ing]'. According to the annotated *Walden*, the 'poet' here named is Ellery Channing, Thoreau's friend and the model for the poet who appears in the dialogue of 'Brute Neighbors'. See also Channing's poem 'Baker Farm', quoted in the chapter of the same name, for a further reference for Thoreau's highly suggestive comments. *Walden: A Fully Annotated Edition*, ed. Jeffrey S. Cramer (New Haven, CT: Yale University Press, 2004). Such an interpretation is, however, insufficient to account either for the excerpted version's title, or for that version's explicit identification of the speaker with the poet: 'I have frequently seen a poet withdraw, having enjoyed the most valuable part of a farm, while the crusty farmer supposed that *we* had got a few wild apples only' (my emphasis). Thoreau's identification of himself with a poet comes and goes in *Walden*: 'This would have been the right kind of cat for me to keep, if I had kept any; for why should not a poet's cat be winged as well as his horse?' (158). For what it is worth, Cavell understands Thoreau to be inscribing himself in *Walden* within the major tradition of English poetry.

27. Of the paragraphs added after the publication of 'A Poet Buying a Farm', exclusively for *Walden*, the first explains the allure of the farm to the speaker, while the second reflects on a quote from Cato. Shanley notes that Thoreau began reading the Romans on agriculture in 1854 and contends, for this reason, that all the Latin citations were added at that point (69n.13).

28. Thoreau is nothing short of obsessed with the correspondence between place and life. To take a few indicative examples from *Walden*:

'Moreover, I, on my side, require of every writer, first or last, a simple and sincere account of his own life, and not merely what he has heard of other men's lives; some such account as he would send to his kindred from a distant land; *for if he has lived sincerely it must have been in a distant land to me*' (5; my emphasis).

'I discovered that my house actually had its site in such a withdrawn, but forever new and unprofaned, part of the universe . . . then I was really there, or at an equal remoteness from the life which I had left behind . . .' (63).

'*I went to the woods because I wished to live deliberately*, to front only the essential facts of life, and *see if I could not learn what it had to teach*, and not, when I came to die, discover that I had not lived' (65; my emphasis).

29. *Walden*, 58.
30. *Walden*, 58.
31. *Walden*, 58.
32. 'Consider, *v*', *OED Online* (Oxford University Press, March 2021).
33. On debt and inheritance, see especially *Walden*, 6 and 25–6, as well *A Week*, 371. Though it goes beyond the purview of the present chapter, the problem of errancy and sedentariness is not straightforward in *Walden*. Often, those who appear sedentary are the most vagrant. On the other hand, as one reads in 'Walking', the saunterer, though *sans terre*, is 'equally at home everywhere' (*Walden*, 260). On the decline of the Concord farmer, who is homeless in his home, and who suffers from worldly despair, see especially the 'Introduction' to Neufeldt's *The Economist*, 3–20.
34. *Walden*, 35.
35. As Neufedlt, Howe, and Robinson have shown, by the time Thoreau wrote *Walden*, Protestant and Unitarian notions of vocation had largely incorporated economic success into religious life. Hence the necessity, for Thoreau, of walking the fine line of critiquing economism while remaining beholden to a language of 'enterprise'. See Daniel Howe, *The Unitarian Conscience: Harvard Moral Philosophy, 1805–1861*, David Robinson *Apostle of Culture: Emerson as Preacher and Lecturer*, and Neufeldt, 53–69.
36. See, for example, James Russel Lowell's 'Thoreau's Letters', for an early expression of this position, in *Emerson and Thoreau: The Contemporary Reviews*, ed. Joel Myerson (Cambridge: Cambridge University Press, 1992), 437–46. In Lowell's view, to the extent that this was Thoreau's intent, his experiment was a massive failure: 'His shanty-life was a mere impossibility, so far as his own conception of it goes, as an entire independency of mankind' (444).
37. For another account of Thoreau's 'imagination' in this scene, as anticipating aspects of Heidegger's thinking, see Branka Arsić, *Bird Relics: Grief and Vitalism in Thoreau*, 266–71.
38. *Walden*, 22–3. 'Economy', from the Greek *oikonomia*, combines the word for house (*oikos*) with that for law (*nomos*). Originally, *oikonomia* referred to 'household management', or the laws governing the distribution (*nemein*) of goods to and from the house. Thoreau plays on this etymological sense throughout *Walden*, but above all in its first two chapters. Neufeldt takes the full etymological sense of this term as being integral to Thoreau's writings (174–5).
39. *Walden*, 180.
40. *Walden*, 152.
41. Thoreau never shies away from the language of business in *Walden*. As he puts it in the opening pages: 'I have thought that Walden Pond would be

a good place for business' (17). For in-depth studies of Thoreau's business practices, in *Walden* as well as throughout his life, see Neufeldt. As Gilmore explains, in America in the 1840s, 'Publishing had become an industry, and the writer a producer of commodities for the literary marketplace' (4). It is out of such a situation that Thoreau's writing in *Walden* must be approached. Yet while all of these critics show how Thoreau negotiated with the inescapability of the market for the literary writer, by attempting to craft new forms of 'business', rather than simply rejecting it altogether, they nevertheless miss what in his work remains irreconcilable within the work of the work: what, in other words, deconstructs the nature of 'business' from within. In this sense, Gilmore's claim that '*Walden* is a book at odds with its own beliefs; it is to point out Thoreau's complicity in the ideological universe he abhors' (36) is a great oversimplification.

42. On Thoreau's 'pastoral withdrawal' as a simple rejection of technology, see Leo Marx, *The Machine in the Garden*. As a (self-defeating) rejection of market society, see Gilmore, 35–51. As an asocial attempt to renaturalise labour, 'redeem the concept of work', and find 'spiritual redemption', see David Robinson, *Natural Life: Thoreau's Worldly Transcendentalism* (Ithaca, NY: Cornell University Press, 2004), 77–99. And as an effort to '[bind] the beams of a new moral order' through the forging of a community of one in Nature, see Newman, 160. As Cavell writes in the preface to *Senses of Walden*, '[Thoreau's] refusal is not in fact, though it is in depiction, a withdrawal; it is a confrontation, a return, a constant turning upon his neighbors' (xv). I follow Cavell in this, but will argue that the form of confrontation of *Walden*, and specifically of the nature of the language it employs, is ultimately one that Cavell perhaps takes *too* seriously. As Cavell writes at the conclusion of 'Words': 'Until we are capable of serious speech again – i.e., are reborn, are men [. . .] – our words do not carry our conviction, we cannot fully back them, because either we are careless of our convictions, or think we haven't any, or imagine they are inexpressible [. . .] If we learn how to entrust our meaning to a word, the weight it carries through all its computations will yet prove to be just the weight we will find we wish to give it' (35). To the contrary, I will propose that *Walden* remains, to the end, non-serious, or rather, serious about its non-seriousness, in its assumption of linguistic 'responsibility'. In this, the structure of Thoreau's word would be parallel to Shelley's frail frailty. Barbara Johnson, in 'A Hound, a Bay Horse, and a Turtle Dove: Obscurity in *Walden*', diagnoses the obscurity of *Walden* as emerging from Thoreau's self-displacement, 'literally, into the world of his own figurative language' (56). Understood in this way, Thoreau's self-displacement, his 'withdrawal', is not one into pure self-referentiality, but rather to the point

where the mutual possibilities of referentiality and self-referentiality meet. See Johnson, *A World of Difference* (Baltimore: Johns Hopkins University Press, 1987), 49–56.
43. *Walden*, 260.
44. *Walden*, 5; emphasis added.
45. On the economic sense of Walden's location outside Concord, see also Heinzelman, 28–9.
46. On the idealised notion of farmer, see Gilmore, 'Introduction'. Karl Marx, *Capital: An Abridged Edition*, ed. David McLellan (Oxford: Oxford University Press, 1995), 19.
47. *Walden*, 260. See Richard A. Grusin, 'Thoreau, Extravagance, and the Economy of Nature', *American Literary History* 5.1 (Spring 1993): 30–50. The phrase 'economy of nature' is taken, by Grusin, from eighteenth-century naturalist discourse. He shows how it persists, from the writings of Carl Linnaeus and Thomas Jefferson, up to the nineteenth century. In distinction to its representation as utilitarian, by Lester Ward and Stephen A. Forbes, Grusin argues that Thoreau's 'extravagant economy of nature reveals . . . an account of nature's economy that dispenses with the basic utilitarian premises of both classical economy and its Marxist critique' (35).
48. *Walden*, 261.
49. *Walden*, 292–3.
50. *Walden*, 114.
51. *Walden*, 308.
52. See Sacvan Bercovitch, *The American Jeremiad*. Grusin argues that Thoreau perceives the extravagance of nature and attempts to emulate it within what is otherwise a restricted human economy.
53. On 'apples' and the importance of distinguishing the cultivated from the wild, see especially 'Wild Apples' (1862) and the section 'Wild Apples' of *Wild Fruits*. In *Walden*, see also 'House-Warming'. On 'farmers', see especially the chapters 'Economy' and 'The Bean-Field'.
54. *Walden*, 59.
55. *Walden*, 58–9; emphasis added.
56. Thoreau's express desire for 'refusal', as well as the entire sequence of the Hollowell episode, bears comparison to Baudelaire's 'The Bad Glazier' (1862). 'One of my friends, the most inoffensive dreamer that ever lived, once set fire to a forest to see, he explained, if it were really as easy to start a fire as people said. Ten times in succession the experiment failed; but the eleventh time it succeeded only too well. Another will light a cigar standing beside a keg of gun-powder, just *to see, to find out, to test* his luck, to prove himself he has enough energy to play the gambler, to taste the

pleasures of fear, or for no reason at all, through caprice, through idleness', *Paris Spleen*, trans. Louise Varèse (New York: New Directions, 1970), 12. Baudelaire's poem refers implicitly to Rousseau's *Reveries of a Solitary Walker* and is an explicit rewriting of Poe's 'The Imp of the Perverse'. Although Thoreau will certainly not go so far as to theorise perversity, the trope of 'experimentation' as it appears in Baudelaire identifies something of the idleness that characterises Thoreau's narrative, and the almost passive abandon that quickly escalates from refusal to acceptance, and then to consequence, obligation, and punishment. See Rousseau's fourth reverie on lying for a similar progression, as well as Kierkegaard's *The Concept of Irony*, Part two, 'Observations for Orientation', in which he diagnoses a similar desire in the ironist (246–58).
57. *Walden*, 59.
58. The Married Women's Property Act, which granted women the rights of ownership, acquisition, and sale of property in Massachusetts, was passed in 1855. Being thus denied the right to hold the proper legal title for land that – if I may be allowed to speculate – she may well have inherited, such an appeal by the farmer's wife to her husband would have been her only extra-legal recourse. Although, then, Thoreau's misogynistic aside would hardly appear to be an indictment of gender inequality, it nevertheless highlights, whether intentionally or not, the marginal status of women within the contemporary legal realm and gives us to think another form of 'non-possession', and one no less capable of interrupting the free exchange between rights-bearing men. It even becomes possible, and perhaps necessary, to hear Thoreau's comment 'every man has such a wife' in a different vein altogether. If one takes the scope of his remark seriously, then '*every man* has such a wife' reads less as a misogynistic aside than it does as a comment about the structural necessity of thinking what (always) comes between two men in the (alleged) full presence of their speech.
59. *Walden*, 59.
60. But that is precisely the problem: who is to say? Who may give the final word, and the final word on the final word? The irreversibility of a debt is therefore here *threatened*. A more diabolical possibility would always remain, haunting Thoreau's narrative, and thereby bringing into question the irreversibility of irreversibility: the farmer himself could be playing a joke on Thoreau, or worse yet, weighing whether to pursue their interaction as binding or non-binding. Nothing excludes the possibility, in other words, that the poet is here the subject of a stunt, and that the farmer he believes to be so prosaic, so unimaginative and incapable of thinking in any terms beyond those of dollars and cents, is in fact the more cunning

of the two. Allowing for this irreducible possibility, what is important for us is that within the parameters of his narrative, Thoreau appears to take the farmer's sincerity at face value. Thoreau (evidently) takes the farmer's word to be binding, and in this way he (may) make the very same mistake of which he implicitly accuses the farmer. In any case, Thoreau's arithmetic is threatened by a conflict between poetic and prosaic discourse that remains inescapable, that stands suspended *between* poet and farmer.

61. *Walden*, 59.
62. *Walden*, 60.
63. Thoreau's reference to Atlas may be still more complicated. Although Thoreau ascribes to Atlas the bearing of 'the world', traditionally Atlas is understood to have borne the heavens. He was given this task as punishment for having sided with the Titans against the Olympians in the Titanomachy. His bearing of the heavens is thus already the repayment of a debt, in the form of a punishment for a transgression (albeit a transgression that becomes one only *after the fact*, once the Olympians take power). According to the *Odyssey* (1.60–70) and *Theogony* (ll.515–20), the purpose of his raising of the heavens was to separate them from the earth, and thus to break off the intercourse between these now-distinct spheres. In this way, Atlas was to establish two orders where previously there had been only one. Atlas's bearing of 'the world' – whatever, exactly, we understand Thoreau to mean by this – involves then *at the same time* the return or repayment of a debt in an economy that precedes it, *and* the establishing of two new economies, or orders, born out of the tension of this division. It is a *return* on a debt, and the *displacement* of the order of debt itself.
64. There is a tradition of scholarship on the parodic elements of *Walden*, beginning with Lawrence Buell's reading of *Walden* as parodic of travel literature in *Literary Transcendentalism*, up through Neufeldt's reading of 'Walden *as Parody*' (156–90). Yet while the irony *is* palpable in this passage, it nevertheless remains irreducible to common interpretative means that follow from the merely oppositional logic of likeness/difference, as I show in what follows.
65. According to the annotated *Walden*, the 'poet' here named is Ellery Channing. Yet as comparison of the *Walden* version of this encounter with the *Sartain's Union Magazine* version shows, Thoreau's identification – or non-identification – with the poet is ambivalent.
66. *Walden*, 59.

9

Baudelaire and the Gift of Pleasing

When each comes forth from his mother's womb, the gate of gifts closes behind him.

Emerson, 'Fate'[1]

There are inexorable destinies [destinées fatales]; there exists in each country's literature men who bear the word jinx written in mysterious characters on the sinuous folds of their foreheads.

Baudelaire, 'Edgar Allan Poe, sa vie et ses ouvrages'[2]

The obligation to accept is no less constraining. One has no right to refuse a gift, or to refuse to attend the potlatch. To act in this way is to show that one is afraid of having to reciprocate, to fear being 'flattened' [i.e. losing one's name] until one has reciprocated. In reality this is already to be 'flattened' . . . But in principle every gift is always accepted and even praised.

Mauss, *The Gift*[3]

Can one refuse a gift? Is it possible, under the right conditions, to simply say 'no', to walk away (with one's seed and wheelbarrow intact, for example), without looking back? To recuse oneself, which is also to say, to excuse oneself, from the reception of a proffered present? Speaking of the potlatch and of the 'obligation' that appears to adhere to the very offering of this offering, Mauss contends that in principle, at least, the answer must be 'no'. It would be impossible to refuse the gift, for even in refusing, one *in fact* accepts, either to return the gift with still greater interest, or else to suffer the 'flattening' effect that such a refusal invites. One may 'refuse', Mauss contends, in sum, but only if by 'refuse', one in fact means 'accept'. One accepts in refusing because, in truth, it is not up to 'me' to refuse or to accept. Once I have been singled out as recipient, I have already been answered for, I have already suffered the address that accepts, in advance, to refuse or to accept. Once I have accepted to accept (or refuse) – which acceptance *I* never have the chance of refusing – I have already accepted.

Because the proffering of the gift already interpellates me as a recipient (an 'I'), there is no real difference between acceptance and refusal, but only different gift-effects that might follow from either. And, in this respect, the gift may be said to be both undeniable and ineluctable, for it imposes itself upon a necessarily passive recipient even as it incites the latter to action. To be subject to the address of a donation is thus to be fated to respond. It is to be destined by a bestowal whose call cannot be denied. It is to be reborn into and through a circuit of obligations that come to constitute the very self of the self. Every gift, we might say, is the gift of a destiny, for it inexorably inscribes its mark upon its recipient. The problem for Baudelaire, as for Wordsworth, Shelley, and Thoreau, is that, though marked, the traces of the gift's inscription remain ever mysterious, on the verge of illegibility.

Thoreau's purchase of the Hollowell place in the previous chapter exposed an abyss. Lying between his words and those of the farmer, this chasm threatened to shatter the divide between material possession and linguistic matter, as well as the corresponding and conditional identity of the subject who – evidently – relied on this distinction for his very self-understanding. Such an encounter was thus not simply narrated by 'Thoreau', but imperilling his very ability to narrate, it opened an event of narration, at the limit of economic reasoning. Once faced with the necessity of traversing an impossible abyss – what was at once the condition of anything happening at all and a suspension of the presence of any happening – Thoreau had to subject his sense and cents to being borne away in its drift. The experience of a poet buying a farm was thus that of the event of such a traversal, which is also the traversal of the event.

In this way, Thoreau's purchase both picked up on the conflict already percolating in Wordsworth and Shelley, and shifted its orientation away from the verticality of questions of poetic divinity, into the horizontal realm of prosaic, economic exchange. As with the former two poets, for Thoreau poetry's gift ceased to be a 'present', instead manifesting as an event of rupture and a suspension of the referential function of language. The experience of a poet buying a farm is that of a (poetic) language no longer situatable by linguistic, generic, or juridical standards, but one anterior to or at the border of all such givens: what we might call its as yet *unapprehended* character.

Thus, while Thoreau's *Walden* represented a departure from Wordsworth's *Prelude* and Shelley's 'Hymn', both geographically and generically, it nevertheless repeated their visions of poetry's gift by performing its incalculable non-presence and surprising our very handle on the language of donation. Just as poetry, for Wordsworth, in the wake of *The Prelude*, could no longer be said to arrive – or even to have definitively *not* arrived – and just as it had, for Shelley, enacted the remaining of the name as always differing from itself, for Thoreau 'the poet's' gift was to render undecidable the difference between presence and non-presence, poetry and prose, and gift and non-gift.

In turning now to Baudelaire, the problem will once again be that of the impossible limit separating the economic from the poetic realm, and the conditions underlying each. Yet whereas *Walden* presented a testing ground for such traversals of limits through an extended exploration of the economy of economy, Baudelaire's work, like Mauss's, proffers peregrinations into what we could think of as the gift of the gift: into, variously, the laws – or *alegality* – surrounding the ineluctable arrival of the inborn; the principles behind the contingent invention of the unheralded present; and the economy, so to speak, of the aneconomical bestowal. It offers, in other words, speculations into what marks the specificity of the given, by interrogating the gulf that separates and bridges destiny and chance. Baudelaire thus returns us, in an odd way, to the very matter that initially haunted Wordsworth: the presence (or absence) of a destining divine endowment and its eventual implication within the calculations of patron–client, or commodity–market, negotiation.

Although, in what follows, I will focus on Baudelaire's rewriting of the gift of poetry in one text in particular, the prose poem 'The Fairies' Gifts' (1862), as with Wordsworth, the questions of gift and predestination are ones that recur throughout his œuvre, in his critical writings as well as his verse and prose poetry compositions. Yet far from being desirable features of his personal poetic mythology, for Baudelaire the gift and giftedness emerge as objects of suspicion. This is above all clear in a text like 'Counterfeit Money', where self-interested selflessness shrouds the gift in hypocrisy and invalidates it in advance. It is announced on the very first pages of the *Flowers of Evil* (1857), in Baudelaire's infamous address to his reader as '*Hypocrite* reader – my fellow – my brother' (1.40), and it shades all his interactions with the muse, his conception of poetic dissemination, and his very image of the poet, which is thus set in stark contrast with historical figures of prince pleasers and high priests.[4] Poems such as 'The Venal Muse', 'Exotic Perfume', 'I give you these verses so that if my name', and 'The Complaints of an Icarus' ironise traditional tropes of inspiration, the poem-gift, and poetic gift economy, while prose poems such as 'The Eyes of the Poor' and 'Let's Beat Up the Poor!' put a Bataillean spin on democratic and Christian ideals of community, charity, generosity, and goodwill. If poets neither freely receive nor freely give, Baudelaire asks time and again, what remains of them and their work? What kind of *work* is this work? What does it give, or take, in being proffered, and is there still a space for surprise when calculation, mechanisation, and marketisation haunt every aspect of its scene of production?

The *Spleen de Paris* is 'a little work', Baudelaire writes in his dedication to Arsène Houssaye, 'about which one couldn't say, without some injustice, that it has neither tail nor head, since everything, to the contrary, is there at once head and tail, alternately and reciprocally'.[5] This problem – of a work being simultaneously front and back, or head and tail, and thus neither front nor back, neither head nor tail – emerges in exemplary fashion in 'The Fairies' Gifts', which takes up a series of conceptual binaries (poetry/prose, fate/chance, gift/commodity), as well as the very relation between *The Flowers of Evil* and *Spleen de Paris*, in order to problematise each. In reading it, I will follow closely the progression of the text and its culmination in the quixotic figure of the 'Gift of pleasing [Don de plaire]', artfully crafted to stifle even the most rudimentary understanding. Baudelaire's poem, I will argue, proposes a gift of poetry irreducible both *to poetry* and *to the gift*. This is what 'prose poetry' names in the *Spleen de Paris*: a space in which are suspended the pretensions of the gift to be one, and along with them the dividing lines between poem and commodity, and aesthetic pleasure and economic satisfaction. As before, such a 'suspension' entails neither reduction, nor opposition, but the writing of a mode of relation not susceptible to classical logical determinations.

FATE AND CHANCE

As a poem dealing with the gift, and above all the gift of destiny, 'The Fairies' Gifts' stands at the juncture of two distinct but inseparable problematics in Baudelaire, whose complex relation never stopped fascinating him, and whose respective developments are woven into vast segments of his work. 'Fate' and 'chance' name the terms of an alleged opposition, but one that Baudelaire constantly troubled. For this reason, as a point of entry into our subject, it will be helpful first to flesh out this twofold constellation to which 'Les dons des fées' belongs.

On the one hand, on the side of chance, there is the well-known prose poem 'Counterfeit Money' (1864), a story of sinister speculation upon the offering of a forged two-franc piece. Given to a beggar in whose hands, the narrator muses, the piece could multiply 'in real money [en pièces vraies]' *or* could lead to prison, the titular coin initiates a series of reflections on human action and its unforeseeable consequences until, at last, the poem's speaker perceives an irreconcilable rift with his (apparently) artificially generous counterpart. In this way, 'Counterfeit Money' recounts the story of a broken friendship and through this tale wrestles with issues of contingency, hazard, bad luck, and everything that they may involve or make possible, including the unexpected gift, the event, the pleasurable nature of giving, and the displeasure of receiving.

On the other hand, on the side of fate, one finds a representative essay such as 'Philosophy of Toys [Morale du joujou]', first published in 1853, and which expounds on children's habits of play as well as their playthings. In addressing this topic, of utmost concern in 'Morale' is the question of predestination: that is, that of the child's innate 'gifts' or talents, and the ultimately fating nature of such endowments for the one blessed (or cursed) with them. Mixing in philosophical reflection with elements of autobiography and third-person narration, 'Morale' confronts these issues with the seriousness of one haunted by a personal affliction. Naturally, in taking up the problem of childhood destiny, it also treats everything that may come in its train, including, notably, fetishism, the metaphysical impulse, and the determinative character of memory.[6]

Explicit explorations of chance and fate, respectively, these two texts exemplify distinct constellations within Baudelaire's work. Moreover, in exemplifying them, they also indicate their interrelations with other, closely connected, problems and themes.[7] For example, the chance of 'Counterfeit Money' is articulated in terms of a pleasure – 'You're right, next to the pleasure of feeling surprise, there is none greater than to cause a surprise' – and therefore immediately enters into conversation with the problem of pleasure and pleasing in Baudelaire's writings generally.[8] This extends not only what he says concerning art and pleasure in his critical writings, or sexual pleasure in the *Fleurs du mal*, but also the link between pleasure and the aleatoric that emerges in other prose poems such as 'The Bad Glazier', 'The Gallant Marksman', the dedication 'To Arsène Houssaye', and, by extension, all those texts concerned with games and fortune such as 'Gambling' and 'The Generous Gambler'.[9] 'Counterfeit Money' stands as a synecdoche for the haphazard, the contingent, and the play of chance, whose situation marks nothing less than the whole of Paris – or *paris* [wagers] – the unknowable ground and condition of possibility of the numerous encounters of the *Tableaux Parisiens* and *Spleen de Paris*.[10]

By contrast, 'Philosophy of Toys', as the reverse side of this counterfeit coin, concerns much more emphatically the damning, conditioning, fating elements whose contemplation makes possible, or necessary, a text like 'Counterfeit Money' in the first place. 'I believe that children generally act on their toys, that their choice, in other words, is driven by dispositions and desires, vague, unformulated ones, it is true, but very real ones.'[11] As such, it brings to bear a suite of pieces concerned with the limiting nature of destiny, including Baudelaire's numerous Poe essays, the poem 'Bad Luck', the essay 'Advice for Young Writers', and the prose poems 'The Favours of the Moon', 'Vocations', 'The Crowds', and 'The Temptations: Or, Eros, Plutus, and Fame', among others.[12] And yet, even in 'Morale', which is Baudelaire's most direct exploration of the problem of predestination, the dooming nature of destiny is always questioned *alongside* so many figures of play and chance, which the child also embodies, and which reappear, in memorable fashion, in 'On the Essence of Laughter' and 'The Painter of Modern Life'. And while it is evident that 'Morale' broaches child's play precisely in order to bring into question its status as mere idle diversion, in doing so it nevertheless ultimately also gives birth to a prose poem, in 'The Poor Boy's Toy', that stands staunchly on the other side of the altar. 'The Poor Boy's Toy', of course, initially formed part of 'Morale', before being published separately in 1862. Nevertheless, its eventual, stand-alone explorations of poverty, art, and the birth of invention from need, veer definitively in the direction of *démesure* and the pleasure that it may elicit, much like the more famous 'Bad Glazier', to which it is closely connected.[13]

As the textual history of 'Morale' therefore already suggests, in spite of the double proliferation of this problematic, the divide between fate and chance may ultimately be less oppositional than it is abyssal: the expression of two sides of the same problem, or two answers to the same query, concerning the nature and limits of contingency, determination, and self-mastery, or what we could also think of as the still-unnamed ground that would underlie each and that 'Paris', perhaps, catachrestically names. What discussion of fate could occur without a consideration, implicit though it may be, of chance and the subject? And what reflection on chance, or luck, without fate in the backdrop? Each side requires the other, just as the gift's structuring of delay requires the prospect of its eventual return, and vice versa.

At the same time, and even if they ultimately respond to a similar concern with the nature of destination in life, the expository divide between Baudelaire's explorations of fate and chance points to the difficulty of simply folding the one into the other, or of merely reducing chance *to* fate, or fate *to* chance. As Baudelaire makes clear in his dedication to the volume, the appearance of this opposition, or of one very closely tied to it, lies at the heart of the modern poet's labour:

> But, to speak truthfully, I fear that my jealousy misled me [je crains que ma jalousie ne m'ait pas porté bonheur]. As soon as I'd started the work, I perceived that I not only remained far from my mysterious and brilliant model, but also that I was doing something (if this can be called *something*)

singularly different, accident concerning which everyone other than me would certainly be proud, but which can only profoundly humiliate a soul who sees the greatest honour of the poet to lie in accomplishing *just* what he'd planned to do.[14]

Intention and accident are the figures through which the modern poet is able to measure his success. They are definitional, determinative, even if also abyssal. The situation is thus one that would call neither for reduction, nor for absolute division, but, as Baudelaire's protracted interrogation of this dyad already testifies to, one that would require asking whether there is a space for chance within the unveiling of destiny, or, conversely, an element of fate within the play of chance. It is with these questions that 'The Fairies' Gifts' grapples, as it explores the paradoxes of a donation that, as Mauss and others have commented, requires at once the appearance of contingency, and the necessity of law.

THE FATE OF FATE

The organising scene of 'Les dons des fées' concerns the apportionment of fate to newborns. Fathers, whose sons are still within the first twenty-four hours of life, have brought their babes to receive their due.[15] This second birth, or birth into a birthright, takes place without the participation of mothers. Instead, taking the mother's place and supplementing her gift of life with 'Gifts, Faculties, good Chances, [and] invincible Circumstances [Les Dons, les Facultés, les bons Hasards, les Circonstances invincibles]', are the Fairies, 'bizarre Mothers of joy and pain [Mères bizarres de la joie et de la douleur]' and 'ancient and capricious Sisters of Destiny [Sœurs du Destin]'.[16] What these mother–sisters give are thus no mere toys or trinkets, nor anything that might be handled, exchanged, or returned, but what we might be tempted to call – if Baudelaire's poem did not precisely disrupt our conceptual and linguistic grasp of these phenomena and the registers in which they are given – 'natural', 'innate', 'divine', or even 'biological' gift-givens. The fairies traffic, in other words, in the immovable, transcendental conditions, or elementary data of life that, once awarded or denied, condition one's future inexorably: which is to say that, like Thoreau's speculations on the house, their offerings bring the apparently pre-economic, given conditions of economy *into* circulation.

The text of 'Les dons des fées' thus allegorises the destining of destiny – what here also amounts to the *gift* of destiny. And this doubled figure should be taken in its broadest, but also etymological sense, as the 'fixing', 'setting into place', or 'binding' of what limits or defines the life to come. Whether we call this 'destiny', 'providence', 'fate', or 'biology', or think of it through a Greek, Christian, or materialist conception, that which 'destines' or 'conditions' announces in this realm those unilateral limitations that supervene upon the existence of the subject and that determine that subject *as one*, before it may come into possession of itself. Destiny, in short, names for the individual that which is always already given, a point of radical passivity, which is why Baudelaire's poem, with its postal allegory of fate, forces us to ask what happens to this notion once it is figured as subject to, if not opened by, the evidently interested, ontic offering of a governing goddess. Unlike commodities, artworks, or beings in general, these givens *should be* excluded from all scenes of gift exchange. Yet by staging the scene of their presentation – of the gift of fate *as* the gifts of fates – and doing so as though it were a lowly lottery, in which mythical, transcendent, inhuman demi-deities are subjected to what one critic has called 'mechanical time', Baudelaire's poem ironises the divine realm in which it unfolds and subjects it to the very clichés of bureaucratic life and sovereign caprice all too prevalent during the Second Empire in France.[17]

> The poor Fairies were very busy, because the crowd of petitioners was great, and the intermediary world, placed between man and God, is subjected like us to the terrible law of Time and its infinite posterity, the Days, the Hours, the Minutes, the Seconds.
>
> [Les pauvres Fées étaient très affairées; car la foule des solliciteurs était grande, et le monde intermédiaire, placé entre l'homme et Dieu, est soumis comme nous à la terrible loi du Temps et de son infinie postérité, les Jours, les Heures, les Minutes, les Secondes.][18]

The fairies stand at the point that joins and separates these worlds. They reside in *le monde intermédiare*, this between that is not quite 'between' because it is still rooted in earthly temporality, and therefore opposed to divine eternity, rather than being situated in a conciliatory *aevum*. And they are themselves so many intermediaries, caught between the world of man and that of God, capable of super-human deeds yet encumbered by the constraints of the man-made second.[19] In this way, their situation resembles that of the still-heroic poet of the *Fleurs*: this Icarus–Albatross 'exiled on earth and subjected to sneers,/ His giant wings impeding his pace [Exilé sur le sol au milieu des huées/ Ses ailes de géant l'empêchent de marcher]' (ll.15–16).[20] This poet was 'grounded' to the extent that he remained bound to a tradition that he had to destroy. He was joined, in a kind of melancholic death fugue, to an *ideal* that was ever again penetrated by life-sapping *spleen*. And the fairies, like him, will also manage to bring some poetry, some imagination, and some divinity, into the prosaic human world. They stand between the infinite generosity of God and petty self-interest of Baudelaire's Frenchman, but insofar as they must deal with the latter, their heavy wings will only pose a burden on them.

As I indicated above, the destining and destined orders of Baudelaire's poem are articulated along gendered lines. Such a situation raises a number of questions. What does it mean that women and girls are excluded from the realm of destiny, yet embody the destining order? Why are these non-human fairy figures, the givers of destiny, circumscribed by the sororal and maternal, while the fraternity of men – or at least those men who 'have faith in Fairies' – is beholden to the ineluctable destining of its female other?[21] And as to this distinction among fathers, 'All the fathers who have faith in Fairies [Tous les pères qui ont foi dans les Fées]', are we to understand their *croyance* merely as superstition or, at a more fundamental level, as speaking, even if ironically, to the irreducibility of phenomena like *foi*, *fées*, and, by extension, art, the literary, and all that which cannot be absolutely analysed, explained, and accounted for?[22] The paternal demonstration of faith in fairies bears an essential relation to the play of fiction in general, even if, ultimately, these fathers may not be the kinds of readers who have retained a taste for the literary.

As to the fairies specifically, the 'Sisters of Destiny' epithet ascribed to them is a classical trope that serves to insert them within a long, Greco-Roman tradition of fating figures. The most famous such sisters were the Greek Moirai: Lachesis, Clotho, and Atropos. Goddesses of childbirth and overseers of existence, these sisters were charged with imparting to each newborn a path of life by spinning for him or her a destining thread. In this way, they presided over birth and supplied a maternal function without being mothers themselves. While, in Homer, the three do not yet appear as separate personae, with *moira* [part] emerging in the *Iliad* and *Odyssey* almost always as the embodiment of an impersonal *aisa* [destiny] and only rarely as fate personified, in Hesiod's *Theogony* they are explicitly named, first as the children of Night, and then of Zeus and Themis.[23] From this point on they would become fixtures of Greek myth and when, for example, Plato concludes *The Republic* with the Myth of Er, Socrates recounts the story of the three sisters, whom he there asserts are the daughters of Ananke, or necessity. Socrates explains that Lachesis [dispenser of lots] sings of what has been, Clotho [spinner] of what is, and Atropos [inevitable, or literally, unturnable] of what will be (617b-e).[24] The sisters, all dressed in white, each bear wreathes, and when a soul passes through the 'sacred spot' (614c) lying between heaven and earth, Socrates, relating Er's tale, recounts that Lachesis first dispenses lots to them before Clotho spins the selected life's threads and Atropos, to conclude, renders those threads irreversible.[25] In this way, they establish the course of each soul's time on earth prior to its next rebirth. Critically, in Socrates' recounting – but notably absent from Baudelaire's – this process is mediated by a decision that each soul must make, either informed by philosophical knowledge or doomed by ignorance of it, among the various lives available for selection.

Equivalents to the Greek Moirai, the Roman Parcae, Nona, Decima, and Morta, had the double role of presiding over childbirth and establishing destinies.[26] The Latin term *parcus*, like the Greek *moira*, originally bore an economic sense. While in classical Greek *moira* signified 'apportionment', or that which one is allotted, one's 'lot', the Latin adjective *parcus*, from the verb *parcere* (to spare or refrain from), designated frugality or thriftiness, which sense is preserved in the English 'parsimonious'.[27] In the Roman tradition Nona (ninth) was the goddess of childbirth, called upon during the ninth month of pregnancy to spin a child's thread of life, while Decima (tenth) would determine its length and Morta (death) would cut it. The Parcae were also known by the more familiar Latin term *fata*, or Fates. Thus, when Ovid speaks of them in *Tristia*, it is as the 'dominae fati' who attend an infant's birth:

> Whether chance brought this upon me or the wrath of the gods, or whether a clouded Fate [Parca] attended my birth, thou at least shouldst have supported by thy divine power one of the worshippers of thine ivy. Or is it true that whatever the sisters, mistresses of fate [dominae fati . . . cecinere sorores], have ordained, ceases wholly to be under a god's power? (5.3.12–18)[28]

Similar to English, which reflects this legacy of fating goddesses through its 'fairy' and 'fay', French is most closely marked by the Greek and Roman tradition in its 'fée', which derives from the same Latin root of *fatum*. From the verb *fari*, 'to speak', *fatum* literally translates as 'that which has been spoken'. In English, the double sense of the Latin *fatum* – as personified spirit and celestial cause – achieves semantic expression by being split into the two camps of fairy (or fay) and fate, which divide has as one of its consequences the erasure of their mutual origin, which is no longer heard in either.[29]

Similarly, in French, one finds both *fée* and *fatalité* (inevitability or destiny), along with various adjectival forms, *fatidique* (fateful) and *fatal* (inexorable, as in *Déesses fatales*), as well as their derivatives, *féerique*, *fatalement*, and so on, each etymologically linked to the Latin *fatum*.[30] And while French contains many words by which to name the impersonal conditions of fate and destiny, such as *destin, destinée, sort*, and *fatalité*, the *fée* of Baudelaire's text remains the only direct descendant of the Greek *moirai* and Roman *fata*, which still recalls their original, personified form.

All of this makes Baudelaire's poem quite classical (in its source material, if not in its content), which is by no means exceptional for his work. These Fates are the personified inheritors of a long line of female, destining deities. Sisters of destiny and mothers of joy and pain, they dispense a fate that they themselves embody. They are the reified concretion of its Greco-Roman inscription, the linguistic residue of its history, the given of its legacy's gift. But now, through the allegorical play of the prose poem, the fate that they incarnate and in turn dispense will be brought into contact with Baudelaire's own, modern, Parisian predicament: a predicament that is here exemplified by the ticking of the clock, whose standardised time impinges upon the harried fairies and contributes a novel element of chance to their fating bestowals. And in what, exactly, does this novelty now consist? Well, in its classical acceptation, from Homer, up through Plato and Ovid, the fates are conceived, precisely, as *giving time*. Now, however, they shall also be subjected to it.

POETIC SUPPLEMENTS

> Next, originally the *res* need not have been the crude, merely tangible thing, the simple, passive object of transaction that it has become. It would seem that the best etymology is one that compares the word to the Sanskrit *rah*, *ratih*, gift, present, something pleasurable [chose agréable]. The *res* must above all have been something that gives pleasure to another person [La *res* a dû être avant tout, ce qui fait plaisir à quelqu'un d'autre.]
>
> Mauss, The Gift[31]

> He would have been horrified at the idea of giving pleasure.
>
> Sartre, Baudelaire[32]

> There are some parents who never want to give anything. These are serious, excessively serious people, who haven't studied nature and who generally make those around them unhappy . . . They are neither acquainted with nor permit the poetic means of spending time.
>
> Baudelaire, 'Philosophy of Toys'[33]

Sisters of fate and mothers of joy and sorrow, the fairies gather to dole out a rather mixed bag of life-altering effects. Indeed, this is exactly what one might expect from overworked demi-deities (or poets), in charge of bestowing a haphazard blend of faculties, gifts, and invincible circumstances to humans with no recourse to refusal or replacement. As one fairy will explicitly point out at the conclusion of the text, these gifts are 'indisputable [indiscutable]':

that is, *non-exchangeable*, unable to be given, or given back, by any mere mortal, but what, being there from the start, condition the economy to come.[34]

Although, then, these givens are neither beings nor things – despite lying like so many prizes, or perhaps *prices*, next to the bench – it is worth reflecting, once again, on the relation between them and what gets proffered, for example, in 'La fausse monnaie', where it is a matter of a counterfeit coin that, like any other piece of change, may pass from one hand to the next.[35] Each of these offerings stands in stark contrast to the other: while the one is divine in nature, coming from on high to a passive recipient who, subsequently, has no recourse to offload it, the other circulates between subjects, through a prosaic process of gift exchange that dresses itself up as charitable alms.

As was already pointed out above, 'La fausse monnaie' concerns the reception of a coin whose potentially counterfeit nature opens its field of possibilities and conditions certain contingencies that, at the limit, remain unanticipatable. Yet because the introduction of the counterfeit entails not only its own indeterminate future, but also the general possibility of the indetermination of any coin as such – which, insofar as it *appears* as authentic, might always necessarily possibly *be* counterfeit, or vice versa – the presentation of this coin also announces an event that might be said to happen to *the given*, as such. Once the possibility of the counterfeit enters the economy of the 'authentic', authenticity itself comes into question and the value of the present gives itself over to non-presence. The gift of the counterfeit coin thus names an event through which the given gives itself otherwise, becoming open, in turn, to a future *à-venir*.[36]

Well, at its core, or at least if we follow its etymology, before the Greek term and conception of fate, *moira*, comes to name fating goddesses, it just signifies 'what one is allotted'. The receipt or reception of some thing – a lot, a card, or a coin – is one's *moira*, insofar as it is what one receives. And so too, then, is the counterfeit coin that Baudelaire's narrator's friend bestows a 'fate', insofar as it names or recalls the irreducible and ineradicable blindness of any recipient with respect to what he or she is given. One always receives – be it a commodity for payment, or a gift, with or without strings – without absolute or definitive knowledge of *what* one receives: without knowledge, that is, of what may come about, through the reception of the present. The presentation of the counterfeit announces this radical passivity that emanates no less from the ontic bestowal than from the transcendental given.

Now, 'The Fairies' Gifts', which engages with givens that one could not simply give, appears to concern just the opposite sort of endowment. It involves 'fate', not as a thing or being, but as an ontological or transcendental condition. It concerns the being of our being as fated, and asks how this 'event' of fating irrevocably conditions existence, from a point beyond it. And this is how the concept of fate in its Greek inheritance tends to be thought: as something that supervenes over and conditions life, from the outside. But, of course, even this transcendental or conditioning concept of fate is not totally distinct, or totally distinguishable, from the 'fate' bestowed by the counterfeit coin named above, not only because each represents a form of allotment, nor simply because the receipt of each is suffered passively – or as Mauss might say, 'cannot be refused' – but also, and more critically, because the divide between the transcendental or conditioning, and the ontic or conditioned, is itself not absolute. The former must always manifest *in* the latter, while the latter must always serve as the embodiment or manifestation of the former. What, at the limit, allows us to know when the mischievous or malevolent presentation of a coin by the other is itself fated, rather than a mere matter of contingency or chance? Since Fate, if it is to fate, must manifest itself *in* life, how is one to tell which indications are its own? There can be no question of 'fate' without that of its manifestation, and this is precisely why there can be no manifestation of 'chance' that is not, potentially, susceptible to fate, just as the 'authentic' is haunted by the counterfeit, and vice versa. The limit, however necessary, between fate and chance, therefore remains as unclear as ever, and this by another order of 'necessity' that no longer calls to one side or another of this opposition.

To return to the text, it is because these gifts are ungivable that fairies must do the dirty work. Yet in giving them out, unlike the 'prizes' that they resemble, the fairies follow no principle, nor law, in deciding on their allotment. If one gives 'prix' based on merit, if one should *earn* 'prix', in other words, then no such rule ought to determine or organise the distribution of 'dons':

> The gifts were not the reward of an effort, but on the contrary, a grace [grâce] accorded to one who had not yet lived, a grace that could determine one's destiny and become the source of one's misfortune as well as one's happiness [aussi bien la source de son malheur que de son bonheur].[37]

Far from being a superfluous or baroque condition placed upon their distribution, such indifference is just what a certain figure of the gift, polarised away from calculation, demands, for the gift, if it is to (appear to) be voluntary, must not succumb to any explicit economy of exchange, debt, or compensation. And if, as Derrida has argued, such a gift is *in fact* to be worthy of this name, then it must actually be given without condition and irrespective of all calculative reason. If the gift is to be *unconditional*, in sum, then it must also be *unmerited*, or, more precisely, given without respect to merit. The irony that will emerge later in the text, the irony that results from the particularly inappropriate character of each of the fairies' gifts with respect to their recipients, of the semblance of 'bad luck' at work in their acts of donation, is therefore doubly ironic, an irony of irony: since the very perceptibility of 'irony' requires reference to questions of merit and reason, reading irony into these gifts is itself the ironic gesture. The gift, at the limit, as *unmerited*, would be beyond irony or any dialectic of the subject.

The word that Baudelaire's text gives for this excess of reason and calculation, for what is or ought to be unjustifiable in the given, is 'grace'.[38] Yet what these gifts, once given, determine, what these gifts *give*, is just determination, necessity, and irrevocable circumstance. The gifts of the fairies/fates name the conjoining of contingency *and* necessity, of the spontaneous *and* circumscribed, of chance *and* fate, as a certain understanding of each term would, however paradoxically, seem to require.

At once subject to the law of Time and wholly unprincipled in their principle of distribution, the fairies bestow gifts [grâces] capable of determining one's destiny, which the narrator glosses as the joint source of misfortune and happiness. Although at no point in 'Les dons' is a specific tally given of the fairies or of their clients, nor any indication of the true count of their gifts, in point of fact only three are recounted, collectively calibrated to test the borders of the prose/poetry divide, as well as the imaginative capacity of the celestial civil servant. Moreover, if we are to trust the narrator, what renders these three presents worthy of being reported is not their standings *as gifts*, but precisely their status *as gift-exceptions*. As though so many supplements or appendages to the text, the three offerings and their presentations are introduced *aussi*, as well, in addition, as though they were not merely given, but somehow *also* given, in the mode of Wordsworth's 'one word more', or Thoreau's 'or to be generous':

> Also were committed on this day a few blunders that one might consider bizarre, if prudence, rather than caprice, were the distinctive, eternal character of the Fairies.
>
> [Aussi furent commises ce jour-là quelques bourdes qu'on pourrait considérer comme bizarre, si la prudence, plutôt que le caprice, était le caractère distinctif, éternel des Fées.][39]

Not quite gifts, or perhaps *more than* gifts, the following follow *also*. The only gifts whose presentations should be presented in 'Les dons' are thus those that, barely gifts at all, name something beyond the norm. These are not exactly donations, then, but 'bourdes': gaffes or blunders.[40] Nor are they given, but 'committed'. As the narrator points out, such gaffes could be considered strange, 'if prudence, rather than caprice, were the distinct and eternal character of fairies'. But given that the defining character of fairies *is* caprice, one can hardly wonder at the occurrence of these slip-ups. In fact, it would be worth asking whether, to what extent, or from whose perspective they may still even be considered *bourdes*, once caprice has become the rule. Only from the perspective of a certain reason, from a sense of propriety or debt, does it become possible to view these presents as *im*properly allocated. In any case, the extent to which, or standard by which, each gift might be considered a blunder must be weighed on a case-by-case basis.

Three gifts, then, and a series of blunders, which include these presents while not exactly being exhausted by them, for a certain profusion of *maladresse* enters Baudelaire's text at just the moment of their presentation, as if to remind us that there are at all times two scenes of donation and two gift (an) economies: that being narrated, among fairy, father, and son, and the scene of narration itself, between narrator and (hypocrite) reader.

The first gift-gaff is a rather predictable one, a case of the misappropriation of wealth and of the intensifying, rather than softening, of socio-economic inequality:

> Thus the power to attract wealth magnetically was awarded to the sole heir of a very rich family, who, being blessed neither with a sense of charity, nor with a lust for the most obvious goods in life, would later find himself prodigiously embarrassed by his millions.
>
> [Ainsi la puissance d'attirer magnétiquement la fortune fut adjugée à l'héritier unique d'une famille très riche, qui, n'étant doué d'aucun sens de charité, non plus que d'aucune convoitise pour les biens les plus visibles de la vie, devait se trouver plus tard prodigieusement embarrassé de ses millions.][41]

The 'puissance', or power, of attracting wealth – *fortune* is also good luck – is granted to an already wealthy heir. What is worse, or what is just as unfortunate, is that, lacking both a sense of charity and any desire for material goods, this heir should leave this fortune intact and, in so doing, inactive and out of work. Hence his 'embarrassment'. Such a blunder, or mistake – if mistake there is – would then consist in the presentation of an endowment that ultimately does not enter into circulation, going against the flow of public economy and private capital alike, and falling fallow as concerns both personal *convoitise* and social *charité*. Far from endorsing the social good, however, what the narrator recognises as the essence of this error is the simple failure of the gift to present itself. In order for the gift to be one, in order for it not to succumb to the embarrassment of the *bourde*, it must become manifest. It must *work*.

The second error, also introduced by the adverb *ainsi*, is comprised of the gifts of 'love of Beauty' and 'poetic Power' to a beggar's son. As with the first blunder, this slip too consists in the misapplication of productive forces. The distinction between these gifts does not, therefore, lie in any categorial difference, but only the domain in which each ought to act: the *kinds of production* of which each is capable. Thus, in stark contrast with the economic weight of the former endowment, the aesthetic character of poetic *Puissance* is now found to be helpless to alleviate the penury of its poor recipient and, for this reason, it ultimately renders itself impotent:

> Thus were given the love of Beauty and poetic Power to the son of a sombre pauper, quarry worker by condition, who could not, in any way, either assist his faculties or lighten the needs of his extremely poor offspring.
>
> [Ainsi furent donnés l'amour du Beau et la Puissance poétique au fils d'un sombre gueux, carrier de son état, qui ne pouvait, en aucune façon, aider les facultés, ni soulager les besoins de sa déplorable progéniture.][42]

By introducing the least commercially exploitable of abilities into the most impoverished of settings, the second gaffe not only leaves poverty in place, but more importantly, abandons the creative potentials of these presents to their eventual evanescence. Left to one without the means to put them to work, they appear destined to remain underdeveloped and unknown. Though the labour of a quarry-worker is likened to that of the poet elsewhere in Baudelaire – for what both seek are gems of one kind or another – here the *carrier* stands as an impediment to the blossoming of poetic power. Yet whether they are squandered within the realm of material interest, or now that of aesthetic beauty, the first two gifts presented in 'Les dons' constitute faults to the precise extent that, once given, they appear destined to remain latent and not to appear, as such.

If these two (apparent) *bourdes* are committed by the fairies, a third, in the form of a parapraxis, is immediately thereafter perpetrated by the narrator, who forgets, or more precisely, recalls that he has forgotten, to tell the reader something critical to the present context: 'I forgot to tell you that the distribution, in these solemn occasions, is without appeal, and that no gift may be refused.'[43] Leaving us uninformed increases the chances that further unwarranted mistakes and misunderstandings will follow and, as if by chance, it is just such a consequence that he recounts when he turns his attention back to the narrative. To be precise, what he relates is a *faux pas*, now perpetrated by one of the solicitors, in the form of an unbecoming accusation, precisely to have been forgotten by the fairies. This *faux pas* will ultimately lead to the third, and final, gift-gaffe.

Returning to his narrative, the narrator recounts that a shopkeeper [pauvre petit commerçant], grabbing hold of one of the fairies' multicoloured robes, cried out: "'Hey! Madame! You are forgetting us! There is still my little one! I don't want to have come for nothing [Je ne veux pas être venu pour rien].'"[44] Having exhausted their supply of prizes, 'because there remained no gift at all, no largesse to throw at this human trifle [car il ne restait plus aucun cadeau, aucune largesse à jeter à tout ce fretin humain]', the fairies had at this point already begun to leave. Although, then, 'nothing *at all* remained [il ne restait plus *rien*]', the accosted fairy will nevertheless attempt to assuage the father's plaint.[45]

Unlike the due or undue allocation of gifts at stake in the above-cited *bourdes*, the present incident concerns the fault of having nothing to give at all: of not giving, or of giving nothing. As for the concern of the fairy-giver for this oversight, it is easy to see how being unable to present a destiny (no matter the kind) represents a problem of a completely different order than that of the mere misapplication of endowments. While it is a simple enough matter for these deities to shrug off the pettiness of human reason and its inability to raise itself to the logic (or lack thereof) of a divinely proffered present; while, moreover, the very relation (or relatability) of the gift to reason (and calculation) is what should here be suspended, thereby annulling the *bourde* before it may even become one – on the other hand, to be seen to have overlooked, or to have miscalculated, on the need to give in the first place, would raise the spectre of an entirely different order of error: one endemic to the fairies themselves, rather than to the world in which their gifts fall or the reason of the humans (prototypically French) who are unable to comprehend them. Even if, as the narrator intimates, the gift should exceed reason and the order of calculation, even if the gift should be radically unmerited, as we are told, one must nevertheless still give *something*. Something must be given, or, at the very least, one must express the intention to give *no thing*. Otherwise, it would be a real blunder, a true accident, or, as Baudelaire puts it to Houssaye: a failure to do *just* what they had projected to do. To run out of gifts due to a lack of foresight would draw into question both the sovereignty of these providential sisters and the status of their gifts as pure, unadulterated presents, for if the fates themselves, being within time, can *mis*calculate, perhaps they too (even if only occasionally) *calculate*. The depletion of presents – but more precisely, the acknowledgement of this depletion – speaks to the finitude of these fairies and their subjection to a temporality that, precisely, serves to limit that which they have to give. But it also, of course, speaks to the finitude of the poet, who is also subject to the Law of Time, yet must all the same find ways of breaking with its order, lest he be no different from any other wage-earner. As we shall see, this finitude will be both the risk and the chance of the gift.

The Fairy, therefore, is in something of a bind. Faced with an unhappy supplicant, she has nothing left to give. In a stroke of good luck, however – or perhaps providence, or even chance – she remembers a well-known, yet little-used law:

> Nevertheless she remembered in time a well-known, though rarely applied law, in the supernatural world . . . The law that grants to Fairies, in cases such as this one, which is to say the case of exhaustion of fates, the ability to give one more, supplementary and exceptional, provided however that she has sufficient imagination to create it immediately.
>
> [Cependant elle se souvient à temps d'une loi bien connue, quoique rarement appliquée, dans le monde surnaturel . . . la loi qui concède aux Fées, dans un cas semblable à celui-ci, c'est-à-dire le cas d'épuisement des lots, la faculté d'en donner encore un, supplémentaire et exceptionnel, pourvu toutefois qu'elle ait l'imagination suffisante pour le créer immédiatement.][46]

This law, granting to fairies the ability to give one more lot [la faculté d'en donner encore un], one more prize or fate [lot], 'supplémentaire et exceptionnel'; the law, in sum, of imaginative creation, permitting the generation of yet something else, once everything known or given has been exhausted; this law, proper to the fairy-poet, allows her to attempt to supply the shopkeeper's surprising request. It allows her to create *immediately*, in the present of the present, one more gift. When nothing remains, when no gifts are present to be presented, this supplementary law covering the donation of supplements can be called upon, and it is certainly no coincidence that it is also at this moment, of the gift's creation in and by its supplemental statute, that the narrator turns to direct discourse and the present tense of enunciation in the narrative. Only with the third and final presentation – the supplement of a supplement, for we are still within the remainder of *bourdes* – does the narrator relate what comes to pass without further mediation or delay, giving himself over to the present, as though to recreate the scene of this event of the fairy's divine gift-creation.

Although the fairy's response to the shopkeeper evidently bears the condition of temporal immediacy – and, in this respect, recalls the 'transeconomy' and 'divine commerce' diagnosed by Derrida within the helio-poetic pull of Kant's *Critique* – in point of fact, it does not adhere to this standard in any simple or straightforward way. Her response instead appears to splinter the instantaneity of the instant in two, by dividing it into an *initial* moment of recollection and then a *subsequent* moment of implementation. She must recollect the law before she can enact it. Perhaps, then, the 'immediacy' here at stake is a more essential one, concerning the act of creation itself, rather than the actual temporal sequence in which it may unfold. While, then, her recollection occurs *in time*, or *à temps*, as an act of recall that occurs *just in time*, in order to maintain the order of the day without suffering another lapse, the implementation of the law, insofar as it invents a present, calls to another sense of this present. In applying the law *immediately*, in giving, which is to say, 'creating' this gift 'whole cloth', what comes to pass can no longer be timed as the mere transfer, or transformation, of a ready-made prize, content, matter, or given. One can give a prize in time. But how, or *when*, does one give that which *is not yet*, so that it may, in turn, be given to another? In what time does the imaginative act of creation work? How to mark the time of the event of the giving of a gift that comes, *ex nihilo*, from nothing to something? Baudelaire's text asks, in sum, when or even whether such acts – classic mark of the poet – can be measured.

Although well known, the law of supplemental donations is 'rarely applied', perhaps because the faculty or capacity it grants, 'la faculté d'en donner encore un', operates by way of the imagination, mediating its creations and facilitating their donations. And to each of these functions would then correspond a separate gift, for, in order for the law to be applied, and a gift given to someone, the imagination would first have to give this supplemental something, itself. It must do so 'immediately', and the question that this figure poses to any reading of the poem – in contradistinction to the *à temps* of memory: *in time* or *on* time, inserted *at* the time of time – is whether it merely names another temporal moment (in this case that of the presence of the present), or, precisely, a 'moment' of exception from such a succession of succeeding instants. Can the act of imaginative creation be grasped at a single point of time, as though it were one more event punctuating an infinitely long line of succeeding seconds?

As was already the case for the 'genius' of Wordsworth, the genuine existence, or even practical conceivability, of the act of creation out of the faculty of imagination is here ultimately less important than what such an act of creation names within the economy of Baudelaire's text. And just as in that other instance, here the supplemental faculty of imaginative creation announces the moment of rupture with economy and rational accounting, by offering us the excess of a supplemental innovation. What is created by the imagination, what renders the gifts of the imagination *creations* – if creations they are – is just, then, the absolute discontinuity of what the imagination gives with respect to any pre-existing present, be it of material, conceptual, or temporal nature.

This is *its* immediacy. Whether or not, then, it is possible, what 'creation' here names is just the discontinuity of a given gift, with respect to existing economies of beings. As such, what the fairy accomplishes, in appealing to this 'law', is the reaffirmation of her status as poet, *qua* giver, for, of course, *non merita nome di creatore, se non Iddio ed il Poeta*. And, to this extent, as the most affirmative gift of all, as the gift of being itself, the fairy's appeal to the law of supplemental donation bears all the historical weight of the poetry–gift complex, as well as all its ideological weight, as the line that ultimately separates poet from non-poet, demi-deity from human, and imagination from skill.[47]

As is befitting of such an act of creation, when the Fairy does at last announce her gift to the merchant and his son, it comes as a surprise. It is not, however, the kind of surprise that she, or he, might have expected or hoped for:

> So the good Fairy responded, with an assurance worthy of her rank: 'I give your son . . . I give him . . . the *Gift of pleasing*!'
>
> 'But please how? please . . . ? please why?' stubbornly asked the little storekeeper.
>
> [Donc la bonne Fée répondit, avec un aplomb digne de son rang: 'Je donne à ton fils . . . je lui donne . . . le *Don de plaire*!'
>
> 'Mais plaire comment? Plaire . . . ? plaire pourquoi ?' demanda opiniâtrement le petit boutiquier.][48]

The fairy's bestowal of her gift is realised in a speech act. But her performative, reported in direct discourse, in the first person of the present tense, does not merely announce the passage of a good, from the possession of one subject to that of another, but doubles as the act of creation itself, the means by which the 'thing' to be bestowed comes into being in the first place. This is both to say that (1) there is no 'gift' of the imagination here prior to its offering to the other, and (2) what is subsequently 'given' is at least twofold, even if the one could not simply be separated from the other: there is the postal offering of 'the gift of pleasing' and there is the a-postal generation, birth, or genesis of this 'gift' *itself*, as a 'present'. There is inscription and there is address, but also: there is inscription *as* address and address *as* inscription.

What, then, to make of this gift that is at least twice given in the fairy's *dictée*? Where has one ever seen the *Don de plaire*, the Gift of pleasing? Like all such inborn talents, the gift of pleasing has no being outside of its manifestations in the subject. These manifestations may testify, truly or falsely, to its presence, but they can never present it, the 'thing' itself, directly. Moreover, the gift of pleasing is distinct from the first two gift-gaffes – the 'power to magnetically attract wealth', and the 'love of Beauty and poetic

Power'. While the former could at least be said to have had spheres of action specific to them – those of economics and aesthetics, respectively – as well as to be minimally identifiable *as* 'powers' and 'love' – hence as abilities and sensibilities – the latter appeals to an at best vague notion of 'satisfaction' (pleasing or pleasure in general), and can be described by the fairy only in semi-tautological fashion, as a 'gift'.

But please how? please . . .? please why? asks the little shopkeeper. And though the fairy – along with the narrator – dismiss his grumblings as the mere quibbles of a 'common reasoner, incapable of elevating himself to the logic of the Absurd', indeed, as those of a 'little conceited Frenchman who wishes to understand everything', there is, nevertheless, good reason to be concerned.[49]

For instance, let's say one wanted to try to understand this gift on the basis of the most cutting-edge writing in aesthetics, perhaps by way of the then recently published French edition of Kant's *Critique du jugement*, translated by J. Barni and issued in 1846. One would, in this case, find the precise province of the *Don de plaire* profoundly difficult to place. To take one example among many, in section five of the Analytic of the Beautiful, when Kant sums up the First Moment of the judgement of taste, the comparison of satisfaction [Wohlgefallen] in the agreeable [das Angenehme] with satisfaction in the beautiful [das Schöne] and the good [das Gute] comes down to the following distinction:

> L'*agréable* signifie pour tout homme ce qui *lui fait plaisir*, le *beau*, ce qui lui *plaît* simplement; le *bon*, ce qu'il *estime et approuve*, c'est-à-dire ce à quoi il accorde une valeur objective.[50]
>
> Angenehm heißt jemandem das, was ihm vergnügt; schön, was ihm bloß gefällt; gut, was geschätzt, *gebilligt*, d.i. worin von ihm ein objektiver Werte gesetzt wird.[51]
>
> The *agreeable* signifies for each man that which *gives pleasure to him*; the *beautiful*, what simply *pleases* him; the *good*, what he *esteems and approves*, that is, what he grants objective value.

Whereas Kant's German has recourse to separate verbs to distinguish each of the above feelings of 'satisfaction' – *vergnügen* and *gefallen* – Barni's French must have recourse to the distinction between *plaire* and *faire plaisir*, or what he elsewhere describes as the distinction between what *simply* pleases [plaît] and the agreeable that *gives* pleasure [donne du plaisir]: 'C'est pourquoi on ne dit pas simplement de l'agréable qu'il *plaît*, mais qu'il *donne du plaisir*.'[52]

Thus, for a Frenchman, especially one foolish enough to try to 'interrogate and dispute the indisputable', a serious problem would arise as soon as he might ask where his son's gift for pleasing were itself to be classed, within

Kant's system. Is the satisfaction that he produces through his gift to be found among the elevated, pure pleasures of aesthetic judgements of taste, or the interested, merely agreeable gratifications belonging to subjective sensation, which can, sooner or later, tend towards lowly *jouissance*?[53] Does he, is he destined to, *please* or *give pleasure*? Are these pleasures to be simple, or complex? Is the gift of pleasing one for satisfying or for gratifying?

But please how? please . . .? please why? Is not, then, what troubles the shopkeeper precisely the resistance of this gift to incorporate itself into any ready-made class or category: that is, to conform either to the distinction of the beautiful or that of the agreeable; of the disinterested or the interested; of the aesthetic or the economic? But at the same time, and even as it resists classification, does not the gift of pleasing tell us something about giving itself? At least if one accepts Mauss's etymology of the *res*, by way of the Sanskrit *rah, ratih*, as a 'chose agréable', it does. If the gift, according to Mauss, is what should give pleasure, if the thing, prior to its Latinate designation as *res* and its closure within the Western metaphysics of contract and property law, originally simply designated that which circulates and, in circulating, pleases, then what we today call 'gift' would be but the vestige of this pre-capitalist, animated, pleasure-giving thing. Whether or not one subscribes to such an etymology, and I am certainly not asserting that Baudelaire had anything like this in mind, the figure of the *Don de plaire* would, nevertheless, take something at work in all giving – as the unifying trait of the 'thing' at the heart of the gift – and turn it, metonymically, *into* a singular present. Every gift gives, or ought to give, pleasure, in fact or in essence, and be it free and disinterested – as in the case of beauty – or obligatory and interested – as happens with so many mixed forms of gratification. The fact that gifts often *displease* – for example, this one – does nothing to change this general structure.[54] Or rather, it does nothing to change the *expectation* of pleasure from the gift, which gives displeasure its very sense and accounts for the supplement of indignation that always comes with it. The gift of pleasing therefore takes a part of the gift (its pleasing effect, that which may or may not be the primary purpose of giving, but which holds no specific relation to the content of any given present) and turns it into the whole (the thing given).

The third gift-gaffe thus departs from the former two, for the gift of pleasing, unlike the power to accrue wealth, the love of beauty, or poetic ability, has no meaning without reference to an other, an object, or a recipient, through which it may make itself manifest. However much variance inheres in these other gifts, they would, nevertheless, possess some specificity, as well as significance, for those who receive them, *immediately*. By contrast, the gift of pleasing remains wholly indeterminate for its recipient. Considered in isolation, it has no reality for its subject, until, that is, he should be confronted with another other, in which this gift may, finally, make itself manifest, but only by way of subsequent acts of address. The gift of pleasing is a gift for giving. Of course, this may also be the case for the power of winning fortune, the love of beauty, or poetic ability, which can also facilitate further acts of donation. But each of these gifts also bears an ineradicable ambivalence: I can become a miser or my love of beauty may be so esoteric that it rather displeases than pleases those who read my verse. The banality as well as the frustration and the mystery of the gift of pleasing lie in its having been stripped of the very ambivalence that is at work in *all* other works. It is sheer form without substance, a hedonistic reduction of an essential plurality. It names, as its immediate object, what can at most be one of those other gifts' possibilities, which makes it at once the most giving gift and the least, the gift most directed toward the well-being of the other and, for this very reason, the gift the least invested in it.

As I have already observed, the two preceding gifts (or *bourdes*) are opposed to each other as prose is from poetry, wealth from poverty, or economy from aneconomy. By contrast, the gift of pleasing has no substance, lacking a field or domain – or even a body – specific to it. Pleasing is part of each other gift yet isolates from each what one would hope would be only a secondary effect. And this singular character of pleasing – that is, of being character*less* – is precisely what infuriates the father. What is the *work* specific to this trait? It is neither part of the money economy *as such* (it produces no goods), nor part of what is excluded from this economy, as its proper margin (the realm of the poet-beggar). Instead, it seems to hang or float suspended, part of no one and nothing. And yet, one could not say that it remains 'apart' in the same way that the fairies do: caught *between* worlds. The gift of pleasing, as well as the boy who is endowed with this gift, is not pulled in two directions, left to fend off pursuers heroically from above *and* below. Instead, this boy, this gift, is both head and tail and neither head nor tail. His is a determination that is not yet set, a profession and a vocation that both is and is not one.

Within the logic of Baudelaire's corpus, there is of course a figure to which the gift of pleasing may be a more or less direct reference. Pleasing, pleasure, satisfaction, and gratification would be unthinkable here outside the spectre of the prostitute, who names for Baudelaire the one professional who specialises only in pleasing. Prostitution is also a form of labour that is necessarily ambiguous, caught between the financially driven pursuits of the workplace and the leisure and play that, for all other professions, anyway, ought to remain opposed. For Baudelaire, the prostitute names another flower of commodities. She articulates the place where work and pleasure become intertwined. Through this figure, the free-floating magnanimity of the gift of pleasing may locate one possible, embodied reference: the space in which frigid beauty is finally transmuted into cold cash, and cold cash into frigid beauty.

In the final analysis, however, the gift of pleasing may refuse even this distinction, precisely because it gives itself to it, as to all others, indifferently. At once bodiless and a figure for the body's bind, it disturbs the father because it is *both* too economical *and* not economical enough. The gift of pleasing, insofar as it gives pleasure, not only is immediately understood by all but also defies the understanding, forcing the inevitable question: *how?* It is the gift *of giving*, as it relates exclusively to the other, but precisely for this reason its effects are always deferred, always awaiting expression beyond the self's auto-affection, and thus never available as a present, to its possessor. This means, of course, that it may always be counterfeit. As a result, the gift of pleasing always, in some sense, remains to be given, above all to him to whom it is awarded.

The overwrought fairy who births the *Don de plaire* does so by accident. Out of time and under-prepared, she invents her inscrutable offering, just as the poet of 'The Sun' trips over words and collides with long-dreamt-of lines of verse. If she is a 'modern poet', scorned by an unappreciative clientele and disillusioned in her approach, the figures that she creates nevertheless stand far outside anything one might normally identify as 'poetry'. If hers is a divine act of the imagination, what she bequeaths nevertheless no longer seems comprehensible by the same solemn standards. Indeed, the *Don de plaire*, as a figure for the gift, for poetry, and for the commodity, all in one, cannot but also refuse each of these distinctions, even as it interposes itself among them. At once given and held back, it uncertainly awaits its fate. And, in this way, like the prose poem itself, it appears destined to confound all those who attempt, finally, to grasp it.

NOTES

1. *Emerson: Essays and Lectures*, ed. Joel Porte (New York: Penguin, 1983), 947.
2. Charles Baudelaire, *Œuvres complètes vol. 2*, ed. Claude Pichois (Paris: Gallimard, 1976), 249. Henceforth *OC* II. All translations from the French are mine unless otherwise noted.
3. Mauss, *The Gift*, 52–3.
4. Charles Baudelaire, *Œuvres complètes vol. 1*, ed. Claude Pichois (Paris: Gallimard, 1975), 6. Henceforth *OC* I.
5. *OC* I, 275. For two excellent accounts of the problem of 'prose poetry', see Barbara Johnson, *Défigurations du langage poétique* and Jonathan Monroe, *A Poverty of Objects: The Prose Poem and the Politics of Genre*.

6. On the latter, see my essay, 'The Gift of Memory in Baudelaire's "Morale du joujou"', *Nineteenth-Century French Studies* 43.3–4 (Spring–Summer 2015): 129–43.
7. Here, as elsewhere, I use 'chance' as a translation of the Aristotelian *automoton*, meaning that which is a matter of sheer contingency, or 'pure chance', as we say. For Aristotle, *automoton* opposes both fate (*moira*) and luck (*tuchē*), the latter of which he understands as being teleological and divine in nature. In French, while *hasard* is usually non-teleological in nature, *chance* can take on either sense of 'chance' or 'luck', depending on the context.
8. *OC* I, 323. On the problems of pleasure and criminality, especially as concern the accident and hitting one's mark, see Elissa Marder, 'From Poetic Justice to Criminal Jouissance: Poetry by Other Means in Baudelaire'. While the topic of pleasure in Baudelaire is far too vast to treat here, one may at least indicate that within *Spleen de Paris* one finds a number of different forms of pleasure, each with varying moral consequences. If in 'The Artist's Confession' a fairly traditional Romantic notion of *volupté* is put forward, which being too intense threatens pain, then in 'The Bad Glazier' a *jouissance* is named that is so powerful that it allows one to act in wilful disregard for its (necessarily) negative consequences. The *plaisir* of 'Counterfeit Money', by contrast, is directly associated with the experience of chance, by way of surprise. Baudelaire had treated the feelings of surprise and wonder in his *Salon de 1859*, where he differentiates between two forms of shock, one suitable for the arts and one an abuse of them (*OC* II, 616). For the problem of pleasure elsewhere in the critical writings, see especially 'Quelques caricaturistes français' (*OC* II, 547): 'Dans les arts, *il ne s'agit que de plaire*, comme disent les bourgeois'; 'Fusées' (*OC* I, 661): 'Ce qu'il y a d'enivrant dans le mauvais goût, c'est le plaisir aristocratique de déplaire'; and 'Réflexions sur quelques-uns de mes contemporains' (*OC* II, 153). On sexual pleasure in the *Fleurs du mal*, see in particular 'To a Passerby', 'Damned Women (In the pale glimmer)', and 'Morning Crepuscule'.
9. The gambling texts are difficult to classify, or rather, they are emblematic of the difficulty with classification in general. While games of chance depend on risk and contingency, the societal incorporation of and addiction to them necessarily concern the *systemisation* of the aleatoric, be it on a personal or a social level. This addiction, which is also the subject of 'The Bad Glazier', and which was visible in Thoreau's practice of *faux*-purchase in the last chapter, seems to do something irreversible to the fortune at work in the game itself.

10. *Paris*, in addition to naming the French capital, is also the plural form of the noun *pari*, or wager. See E. S. Burt on this semantic play in Baudelaire in *Poetry's Appeal: Nineteenth-Century French Lyric and the Political Space*, 1–47.
11. *OC* I, 585. Philippe Bonnefis, for example, explicitly proclaims that, 'Predestination . . . is the true subject of *Morale du joujou*', in 'Child's Play: Baudelaire's *Morale du joujou*', *Reconceptions: Reading Modern French Poetry*, eds Russell King and Bernard McGuirk (Nottingham: University of Nottingham, 1996), 33.
12. See, in particular, Baudelaire's 'Edgar Allan Poe, sa vie et ses ouvrages' (1852) and 'Edgar Poe, sa vie et ses œuvres' (1856), as well as my essay, 'Poe's Memory', in which I analyse their divergent approaches to poetic predestination, fate, and writing. The question of being gifted or blessed (*doué*) also plays prominently in the *Salon de 1859*, in the opposition between imagination and skill.
13. 'The Poor Boy's Toy' was initially published as a subsection of 'Morale du joujou' in 1853 before being extracted, amended, and published separately, in *La Presse* in 1862 as a prose poem, and subsequently in *Spleen de Paris* in 1869 – on both occasions immediately before 'The Fairies' Gifts'. Children, of course, 'jouent sans joujoux', in Baudelaire's well-known formulation (*OC* I, 583). Yet Baudelaire's text asks whether this play is not itself subjected to forms of predisposition and predestination. The question of play as it emerges in 'Morale' should be put to greater scrutiny, and not simply because children and their diversions become satanic in 'On the Essence of Laughter'. More fundamentally problematic is that, for the child who does not yet know 'work', the very notion of 'play' may be inadequate. Baudelaire's fascination with the prostitute, who embodied the becoming work of play, and becoming play of work, stands as a counterpoint to any grasp of the child in his writings.
14. 'A Arsène Houssaye', *OC* I, 276.
15. Baudelaire initially refers to 'nouveau-nés', the masculine plural of 'newborn', which leaves ambiguous whether female children might also be brought forward. All references to individual children are, however, to male infants. For an example in Baudelaire where a female child, or 'enfant gâtée', is made the recipient of a destiny, see 'The Favours of the Moon'.
16. *OC* I, 305. Most discussions of 'Les dons des fées' have focused on the supernatural elements in the text. Marc Eigeldinger, in his 'Baudelaire et "Le Compte de Gabalis"', traces their origin to Monfaucon de Villars's *Comte de Gabalis ou Entretiens sur les sciences secrètes*, and Reginald McGinnis, in his 'Modernité et sorcellerie: Baudelaire lecteur du XVIII siècle', examines the role of sorcery in the text. For other examinations of the prose poem,

see Maria C. Scott, *Baudelaire's* Le Spleen de Paris: *Shifting Perspectives*, and Sonya Stevens, *Baudelaire's Prose Poems: The Practice and Politics of Irony*. The figure of the fairy is one that reappears frequently in Baudelaire, from 'Philosophy of Toys' to 'The Crowds', and, interestingly, is a consistent element of his various early *noms de plume*, which include: Baudelaire-Dufays, Charles Baudelaire-Dufays, Pierre de Fays, and Charles Baudelaire du Fays. Baudelaire evidently took inspiration from his mother's maiden name, Caroline Archimbaut-Dufays. Everywhere there is *fairy* in Baudelaire, there is therefore also the secret signature of the mother, and counter-signature of the son.

17. For 'mechanical time', see 54 and 71–2n.77 in Paul Smith's 'Paul Cézanne's Primitive Self and Related Fictions', in *The Life and the Work: Art and Biography*, ed. Charles G. Salas (Oxford: Oxford University Press, 2007), 45–75. Concerning the question of modernity, Baudelaire's merging of the time of the fates and humankind inscribes a provocation. If there is no strict division in the poem between the temporality of the immortal fairies and that of their mortal petitioners, one must in turn ask in what lies the legitimacy of imputing the coordinate division on the poem itself, between the ostensible 'modernity' of its scene and the 'premodernity' to which it would be opposed; or between its 'mechanical age' and a prior, 'non-mechanical' one. The dream of such a pre-technical or *natural* temporality must be resisted, and not simply because of the implications of Baudelaire's poem. What, after all, would it mean to have a pre-technical time, a time *off the clock*, so to speak? On issues of technicity and time in Baudelaire, see Marder, *Dead Time: Temporal Disorders in the Wake of Modernity (Baudelaire and Flaubert)*, 14–67, as well as *The Mother in the Age of Mechanical Reproduction*.
18. *OC* I, 306.
19. Without simply conflating Baudelaire's fateful scene with a Christian context that it clearly troubles, it would nevertheless be worth comparing his depiction of the harried fairies to various medieval conceptions of time, and particularly the tripartite division found in Aquinas. For the latter, between Eternity (the timeless immutability of God) and Time (the finite mutability in which humans reside) lay *aevum*, an infiniteness with motion in which immutable angels are to be found, and through which they may have intercourse with humankind. On this and other medieval conceptions of time, see Ernst Kantorowicz, *The King's Two Bodies: A Study in Medieval Political Theology* (Princeton, NJ: Princeton University Press, 2016), 270–87. Kantorowicz compares Aquinas with Dante, for whom Paradise belonged to *aeternitas*, Purgatory to *tempus*, and Hell to *aevum*. As

he puts it, 'it would be senseless . . . should the sinners be made to suffer in timelessness, since in that case there would not be an infinite succession of punishment and pain' (281n.15).
20. *OC* I, 10.
21. *OC* I, 305.
22. In *Les Fées du moyen-âge* (Paris: Librairie Philosophique de Ladrange, 1843), Alfred Maury, a contemporary of Baudelaire, showed that the belief in fating fairies was one of the prominent 'pagan' institutions to have survived the rise of Christianity (88–93). Attempts to root out the remnants of Druidic belief and religious practice were prominent throughout the medieval period in France and Maury traces the resistance of these pre-Christian cults up to the nineteenth century.
23. On fate in Homer, see James Duffy, 'Homer's Conception of Fate', in *The Classics Journal* 42.8 (May 1947): 477–85. Duffy points to *Iliad* 24.49 for an instance of Moirai as personified. On fate in the *Theogony*, see ll.210–20 and 901–6. On the difference between Homeric fate and the later Stoic and Virgilian conceptions of fate and destiny, see Pierre Boyancé, 'Fatum', in *La Religion de Virgile* (Paris: PUF, 1963), 39–57. Boyancé concludes that while the Homeric *moira* is used largely with respect to the individual upon whom a destiny is allotted, the Stoic conception emphasises the sovereign utterance, or decree, whereby providence in general is decreed (42–3). Virgil, by contrast, incorporates aspects of both the Homeric personal fate and Stoic providence, while introducing a destiny of collectivities, such as that of Troy and Rome (44). Boyancé's work also touches on how conflicts between mutually incompatible destinies were resolved, such as the double role of Jupiter, as both a decreer of fate and one obedient to its decree.
24. Plato, *Republic, Volume II: Books 6–10*, eds and trans Christopher Emlyn-Jones and William Preddy (Cambridge, MA: Harvard University Press, 2013), 474–5.
25. *Republic, Volume II: Books 6–10*, 464–5.
26. On the relation between these two roles and the debates surrounding the importance or priority of either, see Léontine Louise Tels-de Jong, *Sur quelques divinités romaines de la naissance et de la prophétie*. As Tels-de Jong and others show, the Roman Parcae adopt the roles of the Greek deities while harbouring elements of older, Latin Druidic cults.
27. On this etymology, see especially Tels-de Jong, who disputes it.
28. *Tristia, Ex Ponto*, 220–1. See also Maury (7–13), where he traces the origins of the Greek and Roman destining goddesses to the topical, lococentric divinities of the Gauls and Germanic peoples. Protective goddesses,

these proto-Fates watched over the prosperity of humankind and presided over their destinies. Although there is no evidence to support a reading, or even knowledge, of Maury's work by Baudelaire, there are many resonances between what Maury discloses about medieval fairy mythology and Baudelaire's prose poem. See especially 29–33.
29. According to the *OED*, 'fairie', 'fay', and 'fate' all appear for the first time in the fourteenth century. None of this is to say that the Latin 'fatum' is itself completely univocal, as it bore a number of senses and was more fluid than we tend to think, but only that with respect to these English terms, their shared root has perhaps been obscured.
30. 'Déesses fatales' is one traditional way of referring to the Parcae in French.
31. *The Gift*, 64/186–7.
32. Jean-Paul Sartre, *Baudelaire*, trans. Martin Turnell (New York: New Directions, 1950), 126.
33. *OC* I, 586.
34. *OC* I, 307.
35. The text reads: 'The Gifts, Faculties, good Chances, invincible Circumstances, were accumulated next to the tribunal, like prizes/prices [prix] on the stage/road [estrade], in a distribution of prizes [prix].' As always, it is a matter here of *economisation* and *prosaification*, through the internal resemblance [comme] of a doubled signifier 'prize/price [prix]' that unwrites itself. Baudelaire here turns George's *zierliches Geschenk* into a road-side symbol of market value.
36. On 'La fausse monnaie', and its ramifications not only for literary fiction but also for the gift and event, see *Given Time*, 71–172 and Jennifer Bajorek, *Counterfeit Capital*.
37. *OC* I, 305.
38. For an interesting discussion of the emergence of 'grace' in early modern discourse, as the Protestant figure for God's 'free gift' of salvation, see Shershow, 149.
39. *OC* I, 306.
40. The primary sense of 'bourde', dating back to the twelfth century, is that of a fake or fabricated story that is told either for amusement (*plaisanterie*), or in order to deceive (*mensonge*). It later takes the sense of a grave error committed due to ignorance or absent-mindedness. For this reason, it is perhaps closest to 'blunder' (itself related to 'blind'), or 'slip', which implies ignorance rather than the knowing misapplication of judgement, as 'mistake' can sometimes indicate.
41. *OC* I, 306.
42. *OC* I, 306.

43. *OC* I, 306.
44. *OC* I, 306.
45. *OC* I, 307.
46. *OC* I, 307.
47. In the *Salon de 1859*, the imagination is also associated with a power of supplementation and with divinity, and is opposed to mere skill. See, for example, the follow passages: 'Cependant, pour revenir à ce que je disais tout à l'heure relativement à cette permission de suppléer que doit l'imagination à son origine divine' (*OC* II, 622); 'parce que l'imagination, grâce à sa nature suppléante, contient l'esprit critique' (*OC* II, 623); and 'Discrédit de l'imagination, mépris du grand, amour (non, ce mot est trop beau), pratique exclusive du métier, telles sont, je crois, quant à l'artiste, les raisons principales de son abaissement . . . Et mieux on possède son métier, moins il faut s'en prévaloir et le montrer, pour laisser l'imagination briller de tout son éclat. Voilà ce que dit la sagesse; et la sagesse dit encore: Celui qui ne possède que de l'habileté est une bête, et l'imagination qui veut s'en passer est une folle' (*OC* II, 612). The indefinable faculty of imagination, 'reine des facultés', that Baudelaire also esteems with having created the world – 'Comme elle a créé le monde (on peut bien dire cela, je crois, même dans un sens religieux), il est juste qu'elle le gouverne' (*OC* II, 621) – this faculty also holds her providence over the true and possible: 'L'imagination est la reine du vrai, et le *possible* est une des provinces du vrai. Elle est positivement apparentée avec l'infini' (*OC* II, 621).
48. *OC* I, 307.
49. *OC* I, 307.
50. Immanuel Kant, *Critique du jugement*, trans. J. Barni (Paris: Librairie Philosophique de Ladrange, 1846), 77.
51. *Kritik der Urteilskraft*, 123.
52. *Critique du jugement*, 71. The German reads: 'Daher man von dem Angenehmen nicht bloß sagt, es gefällt, sondern es vergnügt' (119).
53. For this is precisely where the agreeable can always lead: '[L'agréable] n'obtient pas de moi un simple assentiment, il y produit une inclination, et pour décider de ce qui est le plus agréable, il n'est besoin d'aucun jugement sur la nature de l'objet: aussi ceux qui ne tendent qu'à la jouissance (c'est le mot par lequel on exprime ce qu'il y a d'intime dans le plaisir) se dispensent volontiers de tout jugement' (*Critique du jugement*, 71–2).
54. It does, of course, displease the father: not that *pleasing* displeases him, but the *offering* of pleasing displeases him. And the possibility of such displeasure, which is at work for all gifts, save for those given by he who has the *Gift for pleasing*, further emphasises its emblematic role.

PART IV
GIVENS

10

Poetry Lost and Found in Howe, Goldsmith, and Philip

Blue potatoes are ungainly things
As are red and purple lamb chops
Yet when we eat and creep and fall
We never ask a silent question.

Work of stupefying genius number: 12

Racter, *The Policeman's Beard is Half-Constructed*[1]

~~Talent~~, if ever I really possessed a
<u>aptitude</u> of Talent, & quickness i
enough to suffer deeply in my m
my long & exceedingly severe M
Ill-health, and partly to private aff

Howe, 'Concordance'[2]

This poem is not meant to be read by us, and, by doing so, Bök is enacting one of his long-held precepts, that the future of literature will be written by machines for other machines to read or, better yet, parse.

Goldsmith, *Uncreative Writing*[3]

APPROPRIATION

For Baudelaire, as for Thoreau, reflection on the nature of poetic language and the impossibility of opposing it to that of the commodity inevitably leads to critical moments of self-reflection: poem and commodity, gift and exchange, neither can be absolutely separated from the other. At the same time, what follows is not the simple collapse of the one into the other – a mere matter of reduction – but rather a writing in which the difference between them is revealed to be undecidable. Poetry, the gift of poetry – if we may still appeal to these terms – *gives* its own undecidability as that which is 'proper' to it, but only at the expense of risking itself. Thus, if, for Heidegger, *Dichtung*, as the essence of all language, remained grounded in the certainty of its essentially giving nature, what appears to haunt the work of a Wordsworth, a Shelley, a Thoreau, and a Baudelaire – not to mention a Derrida – is precisely the anxiety, the madness, and the fragility of a 'gift of poetry' that can no longer be certain either what 'giving', or what 'poetry', now means.

As we have seen, such scriptural undertakings required massive textual investments on the parts of nineteenth-century authors. Securing insight into the undecidability of poetry's gift meant navigating not only antique notions of inspiration and divinity, but also the contemporary incursions of market forces. Compared, however, to the forms of discursive ambiguity, 'robopoetic verse', and 'radical artifice' that are today proffered, notably by late twentieth-century and early twenty-first century authors, these insights can risk appearing *cute*.[4] Writing in the wake of modernist efforts to eliminate subjectivity from poetic composition, to subordinate the role of meaning, and to reject the primacy of understanding, conceptual poets such as Kenneth Goldsmith and Vanessa Place all but reject the discursive specificity of 'poetry' as a distinct mode of language, or as an elevated form of speech. Inspired by Douglas Huebler's tendentious claim that 'the world is full of objects, more or less interesting, I do not wish to add any more,' Goldsmith and Place, along with Craig Dworkin, Tan Lin, and Charles Reznikoff, each actively efface the border between 'poetry' and 'non-poetry', printing found materials such as newspapers, legal briefings, and spoken conversation *as* poems and works of literature.[5] In this way, these contemporary authors repeat, in Duchampian fashion, the ontological, formal, and discursive uncertainty of the work of art, now for the work of poetry.

Thus, by embracing and exploiting an uncertainty that has always, to a certain extent, haunted the question of poetry, contemporary poetics risks not only troubling this difference, but also effacing it altogether, thereby *eliminating the gift*, or at least radically minimising its role within poetic self-definition, to the point of unrecognisability. As Susan Howe 'writes' in her recent collage poem, 'Concordance', appropriating the words of Coleridge and making them her own: ~~Talent~~, *if ever I really possessed a/ <u>aptitude</u> of Talent, and quickness i/ enough to suffer deeply*. What is *talent*? Howe here asks. And what if it has never been as instrumental as one likes to think? What if this <u>aptitude</u> has always been under erasure, so to speak? And whither the gift, in a world without Talent?

For Coleridge, writing to Southey in 1802, the above question resonated first and foremost as a reflection on his own poetic deficiency. Certain that his capacity for writing sublime verse was *gone*, he asks whether he had ever truly had any. What he does not ask, however, is whether there might not actually be such a thing. What he does not ask is whether the difference between those who have said ability and those who do not have it might not be one. Yet for Howe, rewriting Coleridge in 2019, this is precisely the question: whether such a 'deficiency' is a deficiency, after all. In the words of Coleridge:

> O that without words I could cause you to know all that I think, all that I feel, all that I hope, respecting that Poem! As to myself, all my poetic [T̶a̶l̶e̶n̶t̶]⁶ Genius, if ever I really possessed any Genius, & it was not rather a mere general aptitude of Talent, & quickness in Imitation/ is gone – and I have been fool enough to suffer deeply in my mind, regretting the loss – which I attribute to my long & exceedingly severe Metaphysical Investigations – & these partly to Ill-health, and partly to private afflictions which rendered any subject, immediately connected with Feeling, a source of pain & disquiet to me⁷

Silently substituting Coleridge's 'Genius' with the 'T̶a̶l̶e̶n̶t̶' that, one must imagine, he had initially written as 'Talent' and then, only subsequently, crossed out to make way for the more loaded term, Howe displaces the order of Coleridge's question. She appropriates his language, manipulates it, and thereby produces a text that both explicitly and implicitly brings into question the bearing of some of our most prized aesthetic categories. But she also *signs* these words in doing so, making them her own by way of this literary act of vandalism. Where, we could ask, is the Talent – or Genius – in this? This is to demand both whether either figure has ever really been present, in writing, and in what consists the Talent – or Genius – proper to *this form of writing*, which consists not in harnessing the 'shaping Spirit of Imagination' (as Coleridge puts it later in the letter), but instead in displacing the ready-made language of others?⁸

As we have observed, there are three major avenues by which the gift structures poetic discourse: through lyric subjectivity, as homing beacon of inspiration and locus of terrestrial gift exchange in patronage; through the notion of the giving-essence of the poetic word, which 'essence' survives the subordination of the subject, or so-called 'death of the author'; and through the ontological undecidability of the poem as aesthetic object, which interrupts the seamless (capitalist, but not only capitalist) exchange of poems by way of interruptive events of fracturing indecision. The gift participates in each of these realms of poetic discourse, which reflect and refract the status of the poetic text in the wake of the originary 'giving' nature of the disseminatory trace. And the poetic tradition, I have argued, takes up each of these 'gifts', in order to affirm a *poetic* difference: the specificity of what we call 'poetry' and what we call 'poet', along with their distance from forms of non-poetry and non-poet, whose prose works or lesser verse compositions would be unworthy of this name. The question that is thus posed by much late twentieth- and early twenty-first century writing, like Howe's, is what we are to make of a 'poetry' that does not distinguish itself, that appeals, precisely, to its non-difference from non-poetry; that is, in the words of Goldsmith, 'uncreative', and that eschews altogether the traditional roles of inspired bard and genius versifier, by appropriating found texts, using cut-and-paste filtration, mobilising rote transcription, self-organising through Oulipian constraint, and manipulating computer-generated, or robopoetic lyrics, such as those employed in the production of *The Policeman's Beard is Half-Constructed*, by 'Racter'.

Projects of uncreative writing, Flarf, *récriture*, and citational poetics, by embracing what we could think of as the limitation of the already given, rather than the freedom of what is not yet composed, thus reimagine poetic genius and its traditional relationship to artistic invention.[9] Nevertheless, such shifts of emphasis of form and process need not, necessarily, entail one of the values that underwrite them.

For example, in the case of constraint-based writing, such as Georges Perec's *A Void* or Jacques Roubaud's *Something Black*, said 'limitations' are often viewed, not as a rejection of creativity and novelty – calling cards of the gift in poetry – but rather as a fresh means of attaining those same ends. As Jan Baetens and Jean-Jacques Poucel put it in their introduction to a special issue of *Poetics Today* dedicated to constrained writing, 'The Challenge of Constraint':

> In line with the Oulipo and most scholars who have studied this type of writing (e.g., Motte 2003 [1986]; Thomas 1979; Consentein 2002), we defend the hypothesis that constraints are a universal phenomenon. Because constraint is embedded in the very notion of form, all periods, all languages, all types of literature provide more or less self-conscious examples of constrained writing, some more rigorously defined and some more directly motivated than others . . . Constrained writers, as we will see, often believe that the repudiation of rule-bound writing is counterproductive, for it produces works that are bound to other, perhaps unacknowledged conventions. The experimenters try to demonstrate that the practice of constraints is a 'superior' form of freedom because self-consciously elected and

invested in forms or resistance. Constrained writers often also agree that the willful adoption of rules can produce aesthetic surprises that would have been unthinkable without the use of constraints . . . Is it not more original and thus powerful to transform intentionally the conditions of play according to determinate principles than it is to stumble upon breakthroughs to a new field of creativity? And does the former not also sometimes lead to the latter? This is what constrained writers ask.[10]

Rather than being a rejection of freedom, invention, and creativity, 'constraint' has become a vehicle to '"superior" form[s] of freedom'. Or, as Christian Bök, another Oulipo-inspired writer and noted author of the lipogrammatic *Eunoia* puts it: 'language is very robust. Even under duress, it finds a way to say something uncanny, if not sublime.'[11] What is rejected by constraint poetics is thus not so much the gift – or, let us say, the spirit of the gift, in writing – as it is certain fashions of imagining 'giftedness'. *It is language itself that is gifted*, we could imagine Bök, and still in line with Stein and Heidegger, saying. What is needed is only the right opportunity for it to bring itself to light.

Creativity, surprise, and inventiveness thus remain the basic aims of Oulipian composition, even if these aims are now envisioned to be the products of language's own mechanism. An argument whose basic structure is shown to apply no less to the works of Perec than to the citational writing of Benjamin's *Arcades*, the language poetry of Charles Bernstein, and the found texts of Howe's *The Midnight*, in Marjorie Perloff's persuasive exploration of information-age poetics, *Unoriginal Genius*. As Perloff puts it, concerning trends among such media-driven and conceptual poetic forms:

> *Inventio* is giving way to appropriation, elaborate constraint, visual and sound composition, and reliance on intertextuality. Thus we are witnessing a new poetry, more conceptual than directly expressive – a poetry in which, as Gerald Bruns puts it with reference to Cage's 'writings through' *Finnegan's Wake*, the shift is 'from a Chomskyan linguistic competence, in which the subject is able to produce an infinite number of original sentences from the deep structure of linguistic rules, to the pragmatic discourse that appropriates and renews what is given in the discourse that constitutes a social and cultural world.'[12]

The 'unoriginal genius' of the twentieth and twenty-first centuries, we could say, remains for Perloff a 'genius'. Genius is dead but all the same remains, as the prized productive capacity of prior generations (read: Coleridge's 'shaping Spirit of Imagination') gives way to the 'appropriation and renewal' of 'what is given', for the contemporary writer. No longer a sign of being touched from above, this new genius – or perhaps talent, skill, or ~~talent~~? – nevertheless signals a capacity, honed by contemporary authors, to bring about surprises, *in the text that is already given*. An insight, of course, that might already have been applied to the writings of Stein, in her efforts to give the given noun again through linguistic modes of estrangement, or even to the poet of George's 'Wort', who had to learn that true linguistic innovation does not lie in ontic creation of a present (*inventio*), but in ontological presencing (appropriation and renewal). Generally speaking, then, the contemporary fascination with 'found', 'citational', and 'constraint-oriented' poetry would represent less a rejection of the value of the gift, as *end* of poetic praxis, than it would a refashioning of the means by which said end is to be attained. Poetry, whether esteemed now to be *good* or *bad* poetry – and this question remains hotly debated, especially as concerns its conceptual form – would remain bound up with invention, surprise, and genius, even as it rejects the traditional paths towards their realisation.

(And could we not, on these grounds, also include bio- or trans-genic poetry among these 'unoriginal' movements? In their focus on manipulating the 'writerly' qualities of biological processes, works by Eduardo Kac, Christian Bök, and Joe Davis focus less on *inventio*, than they do on the translative act itself, as it allows them to move between the codes of human language and those of biological structure. Nevertheless, at stake, for example for Bök, in *The Xenotext Project*, is still the most classical, most Homeric, most Shakespearean, most Wordsworthian desire *to give life*, through words, but now through the genetic code of a virtually immortal strain of bacteria, *D. radiodurans*, which should, if properly constructed, take on half the work of composition itself.[13])

Perloff's account thus has the benefit of being able to explain trends shared by large and diverse swaths of contemporary writing. At the same time, it leaves one wondering whether this is all that is at stake in new-age poetics, whether, indeed, there are not more radical variants of citation, appropriation, and unoriginality, which go further, if not outright rejecting, then at least bringing into question, these very values. It is one thing to read Howe's brilliant textual appositions and to see the genius Perloff speaks of, but it is quite another to read the mockery implicit, but also often *explicit*, in certain passages of *The Policeman's Beard*, among which is my personal favourite: 'Slice a visage to build/ A visage. A puzzle to its owner.'[14] In the robopoetic verse 'written' by Racter, in which the act of composition is outsourced to a privately owned artificial intelligence – in this case, one designed by William Chamberlain and Thomas Etter – there seems to be something else at work than a mere return to genius, especially at those moments when the program itself speaks of 'work[s] of stupefying genius' – and does so persuasively. One should at least ask, then, when confronted by works like these, whether such poetic projects remain bound to this system, and one should do so even if the 'sublimity' of Racter's various turns of phrase is still largely comprehensible through Bök's notion of linguistic 'robustness', and even if it is actually *required*, as a necessary possibility, by Derrida's notion of iterability. The deconstruction of the piecemeal bard, as Bök puts it, perhaps now calls to another order of interpretation – in principle, if not in fact; in intention, if not in actual implementation – for which Perloff's figure of 'unoriginality' would be inadequate because it is still too indebted to the matrix of 'originality', from which it never entirely escapes.

Before it is even a matter of such futuristic, inhuman, or posthuman writing-machines, however, certain uncreative works also raise this question – as to whether one could *simply* fold them back into the same old aesthetic categories – and they do so precisely at those moments when they appear to 'mimic' these a-telic, computer-based techniques of transcription.[15] Goldsmith's poem *Soliloquy* is one such example. Unlike the works of Oulipo, the collage poems of Howe, or even Goldsmith's later work in *Traffic* and *Day*, *Soliloquy* seems to announce a more radical writing project to the extent that, where these other texts might be said to 'renew' the given, *Soliloquy* risks merely giving (or repeating) it, and in this way giving up the fight over the gift, and with it, the entire matrix we have explored to this point.[16] *Soliloquy* is a book-length documentary transcription of a week's worth of the author's own speech, which – reports an incredulous writer for the *New Yorker* – Goldsmith had the audacity to 'claim . . . was poetry'.[17] The problems that a text such as *Soliloquy* poses to the gift modality of poetry are thus multiple, going beyond even those of most other conceptual works. First, according to the self-imposed law that Goldsmith gave himself in 'composing' the work, no editing of the text was allowed. What is transcribed is thus an immediate recording of lived events, without reworking or cutting, and thus without craft. *Soliloquy* is a work of conceptual poetry whose production required not a hint of talent, not an ounce of genius, not a hair of inspiration. To accept it as poetry is to accept that poetry is possible without any of these attributes, save, of course, for the *idea* of doing it in the first place, and in so doing, of *calling* it 'poetry'.

This latter point brings us to the second difficulty posed by *Soliloquy*. It is only given as a poem through various paratextual markers. Nothing internal to the text seems to dictate its belonging to this field. And yet, whether or not it is 'poetry' – or 'good poetry' – much like the Readymade, the simple fact that it forces one to consider whether it is, is already sufficient to testify to the decay of any hard and fast border. The question remains: if we are ready to accept texts such as *Soliloquy* as poetry, what does this mean for the genre, and even for the genre's own project of self-definition? Is this a 'poetry' that has, at last, given up the gift? And if so, what remains at stake in the use of this term? Take the following passage:

> Can I get a water? Thanks, it's alright. Well, first off, um, I finished my book that I've been working on for 3 years and I'm really happy that it's done. Completely. Well, it's been seen as some. Kind of a weird side project. He wanted to make 3 cases where the writing has, is the activity. So, I mean it's, I I can't define that book. Sometimes I think it's a big book of poetry, sometimes I think it's a reference book, sometimes I think it's a conceptual art piece. You know, it never, I haven't been able to pin it yet, really and it's, and it's flowed in and out of different contexts, like, I believe that the book, when Geoff publishes it will be received by the poetry world, by the writing world that I'm involved with.[18]

Goldsmith's aura-less transcription makes no pretence to being anything but raw, unworked prose. It is a prose that, like the book he here discusses, can be taken up by the 'poetry world': a prose whose radicalness lies precisely in its refusal to remove any of the detritus of everyday speech from its composition.[19] According to Bök – who is, as it happens, a friend of Goldsmith – in *Soliloquy* 'we experience the lyric voice of the poet as nothing more than a lengthy excerpt from the screenplay of our daily lives'.[20] As Bök understands it, the endgame of this merging of worlds entails nothing less than the collapse of the poetic and prosaic realms, along with the revelation of the false conceit of prior (read: Romantic) efforts, precisely to bring these languages closer together. Goldsmith's *Soliloquy* would thus represent *both* the natural endpoint of a distinctly poetic tradition *and* an unprecedented, revolutionary turn outside of this tradition. In the words of Bök:

> Goldsmith parodies the lyrical poetics of vernacular confession, revealing that, despite the desire of lyric poets to glorify the everyday language of their casual, social milieu, such a democratic utopianism often balks at the candour, if not the squalor, of ordinary language, so that in the end, the elite, poetic assertion continues to supersede the trite, phatic utterance. When Wordsworth wishes to articulate spontaneous expressions in a plainer, simpler diction, closer to actual, rustic speech, he still subordinates such colloquialism to the rules of clear prose, adorned with rhyme and metre. When Williams demands that poetry must validate the concrete language of quotidian existence, he still subjects his banal idiom to the formal rigour of concision and precision. When Ginsberg argues that an initial thought is a supreme thought, he seems to advocate the kind of unpremeditated

transcriptions imagined by Breton and Desnos, but like them, he still subordinates his rhapsodic outburst to the syntax of the rational sentence. When Antin transcribes his own improvised monologues, he streamlines them to make them seem more eloquent, more polished. When such poets profess to support the artless diction of common speech, they still refuse to subdue the formalities of their own literary artifice.[21]

Could we thus say that, according to such an understanding, *Soliloquy* brings to fruition a vision of poetic writing that Thoreau had already announced in *A Week*, but one that, *now*, the poet is finally brave enough to realise? 'When the poet is most inspired,' writes Thoreau, 'is stimulated by an *aura* which never even colors the afternoons of common men, then his talent is all gone, and he is no longer a poet.'[22] Now, the aura, too, is gone, along with the talent, as well as any recognisable difference between poetry and its others. Is this not, then, precisely a *pas de poésie*, a 'poetic' step beyond poetry – one that refuses to give anything, save for that which is (ostensibly) already given, but that, in doing so, risks effacing itself?

Through their use of found materials, rote transcription, and mechanical processes, works such as *Soliloquy*, Dworkin's *Parse*, and Simon Morris's *On the Road* attempt to radicalise the question of talent in ways that Howe – but evidently not Coleridge – motions toward. Through its elimination, they all but efface these works' signatures *as works*, unless, as Margaret Rhee, author of *Love, Robot* puts it, flipping the problem on its head, the question 'whether this particular poetry up for consideration, was even poetry . . . [is] how you know it's poetry'[23] - unless, as Bataille had already asserted some eighty years ago, 'Poetry that is not engaged in an experience exceeding poetry (distinct from it) is not the movement but the residue left by the turbulence. [. . .] Further along than poetry, the poet laughs at poetry. The poet laughs at how delicate poetry is.'[24]

Responding to the historical rise of these self-effacing modes of poetic writing, Jahan Ramazani identifies a certain trend and a critical difference. 'From the modernist moment into the twenty-first century', writes Ramazani in *Poetry and its Others*,

> poetry has dissolved itself into nonpoetry, parapoetry, even antipoetry. But in so doing, it has also paradoxically brought into view its specificities as poetry. A poem that almost becomes a novelistic fiction, a theoretical discourse, a legal brief, a news report, a prayer, or a musical song often distinguishes itself as poetry when on the verge of self-extinction . . . poetry both blends with its others and distinguishes itself from them.[25]

As Ramazani perceptibly shows, what remains for these frequently self-dissolving works are, precisely, the paratextual or diacritical markers that seek still to signify: *this is poetry*. Such markers remind us that these most unpoetic of works ought, somehow, still to be considered part of the genre. They remind us that, for better or worse, one of poetry's most recognisable signatures remains its 'self-resistance', out of which desire for self-annihilation may always emerge something that we would no longer wish to call by this name.

For works such as these – which are barely 'works' because they bring us face to face with the experience of the work *as a given*, and thus as *non-work* – all that remains is the index of the text's generic belonging. Yet even this index may itself always be sucked into the vortex of semiosis and, in this way, set ever into abeyance, unable, any longer, to testify to a clear and distinct extra-textual class or stratum. Such is the situation that Racter announces when it 'professes' its genius, doing so with the only 'genius' that may be proper to an algorithm: one, that is, of text and code alone. Such is, even before Racter (or, at least, before the technical means necessary to produce a 'Racter'), a possibility that is already audible in the poems of Howe and Goldsmith – to say nothing of those of Mallarmé and Wordsworth, and many others – when these texts signify their own (now subjectless) processes of signification, with respect to which it would be a mistake simply to refer back to a generative 'author'. What is an author, if not that to which the poem precisely points? And what is a poem, if not just the means by which are produced the capacity for, and categories of, generic diagnosis? The above is what, at yet another moment of 'Concordance', Howe's text gives to think (see Figure 10.1).

In the self-proclaimed – if half-effaced – botanical tradition of Gessner, Howe's poem here inscribes the indicative, 'diagnostic arrows', of generic classification. And perhaps every poem does so, whether it says so or not, as the simple effect of the positing power of its language. What *this* poem diagnoses, however, is no longer a mere taxonomic pre-position or belonging. Instead, it points to the originary, indicating inscription of the trace, writing *myself out of m. . . writing myself to my ow. . .* This poem, which is at once part of a whole and a whole unto itself, inscribes a difference. It inscribes its difference – its **Diagnostic Arrows**, if you will. But before such arrows may simply be sent or received, they here recall the pre-generic, infinitive imperative of no one, which sets everything into motion: *d to write a poem, b*. Before there is any poetry or *poiēsis*, Derrida was fond of saying, there is some poem. Likewise, for Howe – or perhaps we should say, for 'Howe' – the imperative 'to write a poem' is to be located prior to any determination of the proper borders of

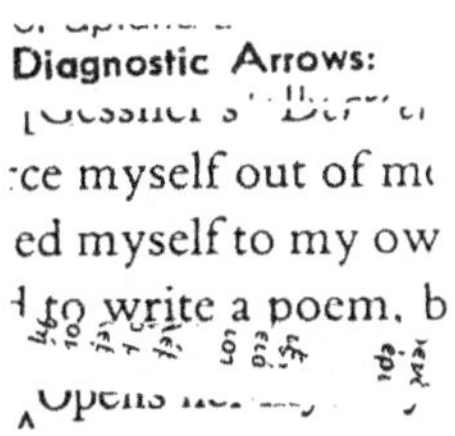

> **Diagnostic Arrows:**
> [Gessner's Differe
> ce myself out of m(
> ed myself to my ow
> d to write a poem, b
> Opens

Figure 10.1 By Susan Howe, from *CONCORDANCE*, copyright ©2019, 2020 by Susan Howe. Reprinted by permission of New Directions Publishing Corp.[26]

poetry, before, that is, there can be any delimitation of the inside or outside of its text. At the edge of the poem lies an abyss of signification. '**Diagnostic Arrows:**' points to this trace that no one gives, but that pre-orients every such distinguishing act of address.

DIS-APPROPRIATION

> The wild card is gifts ... Perhaps the most unfair, because it's unavoidable, is this gift of talent. I don't just mean you're a good dancer, you're a good singer, you're a good writer; but you have a mind for schoolwork, for example, and some people just don't, never will, never could ... Then, of course, there's the other gift, which is a little more ambiguous and hard to pinpoint, which is the gift of being born in a certain condition – with a certain amount of money, in a certain state, with a certain skin color and a certain gender. And what rights accrue to you because of that? And what duties accrue to you because of that?
>
> Smith, 'On Historical Nostalgia and the Nature of Talent'[27]

In their struggles to manage and manipulate masses of inherited material – be they textual, computational, or biological in nature – so-called 'uncreative' and 'unoriginal' writings stand out from their 'creative' and 'original' literary counterparts. Their primary conflict, we could say, is no longer with *giving*, but *the given*. Or rather, since the two remain profoundly interconnected, let us specify: the contemporary disruption of, and therefore fascination with, the given, still has everything to do with giving – with the question, *how to give?* – but now, in the experience of its exhaustion, once all the gifts have (apparently) been given out. Once – to paraphrase Baudelaire – there is *nothing* left to give, at all, because everything has already been allocated.

To the above experience of excess, overabundance, and oversaturation with the given, there should, however, be added yet others: ones that are no less invested in these questions, yet that tackle them from wholly different angles. As Smith writes above, one's gifts, be they talents or conditions, are never simply a matter of rights and duties that accrue, but also those that *do not accrue*. If 'appropriation' has become a popular – if problematic – figure for certain conceptual authors and critics for whom 'renewal' is the goal, then for other authors who confront fundamental disappropriations – of language, of voice, or of history – the matter of the given and poetry's role in responding to it resonate still otherwise.[28]

In the preface to her 1989 poetry collection, *She Tries Her Tongue, Her Silence Softly Breaks*, M. NourbeSe Philip writes of such a denial of language and of the privations of experience that ensue:

> The progenitors of Caribbean society as it exists today created a situation such that the equation between i-mage and word was destroyed for the African. The African could still think and i-mage, she could still conceive of what was happening to her. But in stripping her of her language, in denying the voice power to make and simultaneously, to express the i-mage – in denying the voice expression, in fact – the ability and power to use the voice was effectively stymied.[29]

The European progenitors of contemporary Caribbean society, having wrested the African from her land and imposed their languages upon her, stripped her of the capacity to express her own experience. They denied her access to her own language and, in so doing, removed the very means by which meaningful expression through powerful speech could take place. If 'the purpose for which language was ordained [was] giving voice to the i-mages of experience', then 'the English language merely served to articulate the non-being of the African'.[30] For the author who speaks from such a position of radical dispossession, the question thus becomes how to co-opt this language of the coloniser. How, without access to another language, to subvert the imposed 'father tongue', when the simple fact of its employment reaffirms its position of authority? And how, with no possibility of effacing or forgetting this history, to learn to speak in one's own voice, when the would-be native 'mother tongue', is denied a priori?

From its very title, the whole of *She Tries Her Tongue, Her Silence Softly Breaks* announces this project as its point of departure: to learn to speak when the givens of language are themselves other; to learn to speak when the very juridical, social, medical, and economic codes of one's language bespeak one's non-being and one's status as 'an object, a thing or chattel'.[31] And the role of poetry, in this sense, is to allow for the resources of the coloniser's tongue to be mobilised against themselves. It is to give access to a space where one may work to counteract the 'transubstantiations' and near-magical 'conversions' that its laws have perpetrated, through its various decisions and decrees, by rewriting its contexts and unearthing its false foundations.[32] And it is, finally, to forge a new language, and to do so out of the givens of the old one. Poetry, for Philip, works from within a language's matrix of the sayable, in order to say what is as yet unsayable for it. '*The limitation here is the text itself*,' she writes, in the notes to her experimental work *Zong!*:

> – *the language comprising the record*
> *Language appears to be a given – we believe we have the freedom to choose any words we want to work with from the universe of words, but so much of what we work with is a given.*[33]

In *Zong!*, Philip 'locked herself' within the text of the legal decision *Gregson v. Gilbert* in order to 'mutilate the text as the fabric of African life and the lives of these men, women and children were mutilated'.[34] Like Howe's collage poetry, *Zong!* restricts itself to repurposing found materials. In this case, the 'constraint' is the 1783 decision in the case of the slave ship *Zong*, in which never arises the question of the criminality involved in, but only the insurance liability for, throwing 150 slaves overboard. As Valéry Loichot notes in *Water Graves*,

> If the law governing the enslavement of humans gains a magic and sacred aura, to believe Philip, it is a malevolent one. As herself both a lawyer and a poet, Philip must rectify the law, reverse the sense of transubstantiation by giving humanity and sacred back to the victims of the legalized unritual, through her poetic creation. Poetry – poiesis as act of making – relays a faulty, even criminal, law.[35]

Zong! engages with the transubstantiation of humanity. It sets out to return what the malevolence of law has denied. Similar to Anne Carson's *Nox*, in which Carson memorialises her dead brother through the writing of a cenotaph text that gives face, name, and voice to the unmourned, *Zong!* decomposes so as to rededicate and re-form the source elements of its chosen archive.[36] '*The text has exploded into a universe of words,*' Philip writes on 15 December 2003,

> have given in to the impulse to fragment the words of the text – using it as a sort of grand boggle game and set to trying to find words within words. The text – the reported case – is a matrix – a mother document. I did not come to the decision easily – to break the words open . . . but that is where the impulse leads – to explode the words to see what other words they may contain.[37]

It is by breaking open the words that are already given – here, in the most heinous testament to the cruelty and coldness of law as it legislates on, affirms, and performs the reduction of African lives to property – that *Zong!* ventures to hear 'what other words they may contain'. And this is how one arrives, from the prose of eighteenth-century British lawmakers, to the fragmented and exploded compositions of *Zong!* (see Figures 10.2 and 10.3):

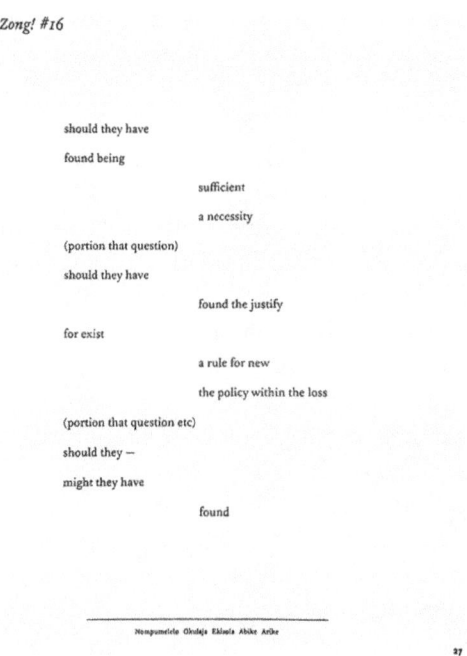

Figure 10.2 Page 27 of *Zong!* © 2008 by M. NourbeSe Philip. Published by Wesleyan University Press and reprinted with permission.[38]

POETRY LOST AND FOUND 259

Figure 10.3 Page 101 of *Zong!* © 2008 by M. NourbeSe Philip. Published by Wesleyan University Press and reprinted with permission.[39]

Philip's work shares with that of Howe, Goldsmith, and Bök a concern with the givens of language, text, biology, talent, and history. Indeed, it shares with them a profound interest in negotiating with these 'gifts', so as to explore the limits of the sayable, of translation, and of signification. In doing so, however, it highlights the incontrovertible inheritance of some givens, which it is never simply a matter of 'managing' or 'manipulating'. These givens precede and make possible the sayable. They condition the subject and that subject's language, their 'l/anguish', as Philip puns in her 'Discourse on the Logic of Language'.[40] The mother/matrix is other, and this historical dispossession turns poetry for her into a kind of secondary, or 'prosthetic tongue', with which the irreversible entanglement of father *and* mother can be expressed and, perhaps, re-angled.[41] 'English/ is my mother tongue', she writes in the 'lyric' column of the discursively hybrid 'Discourse'[42]:

> A mother tongue is not
> not a foreign lan lan lang
> language

l/anguish
anguish
– a foreign anguish
[. . .]
I have no mother
tongue
no mother to tongue
no tongue to mother
to mother
tongue
me
[. . .]
but I have
a dumb tongue
tongue dumb
father tongue
and english is
my mother tongue
is
my father tongue
is a foreign lan lan lang
language
l/anguish
  anguish
a foreign anguish
is English –

A foreign anguish is english. And it is because this anguish precedes and pre-empts the poet that she, in turn, mothers this tongue that english is, but also mothers this tongue that english might yet become.

Such becoming – or birth – is, finally, the subject of the leftmost column of 'Discourse', which runs along the book's vertical axis, going counter to each of the other three 'logics'. Playing on the plurality of 'tongues', Philip here returns to a by now well-known poetic topos: the gift of the word. And yet, though familiar, in her hands this offering becomes utterly unrecognisable, a sight to behold that leaves one gasping for breath, at the edge of asphyxiation:

WHEN IT WAS BORN, THE MOTHER HELD HER NEWBORN CHILD CLOSE: SHE BEGAN THEN TO LICK IT ALL OVER. THE CHILD WHIMPERED A LITTLE, BUT AS THE MOTHER'S

TONGUE MOVED FASTER AND STRONGER OVER ITS BODY, IT GREW SILENT—THE MOTHER TURNING IT THIS WAY AND THAT UNDER HER TONGUE, UNTIL SHE HAD TONGUED IT CLEAN OF THE CREAMY WHITE SUBSTANCE COVERING ITS BODY.

THE MOTHER THEN PUT HER FINGERS INTO HER CHILD'S MOUTH—GENTLY FORCING IT OPEN; SHE TOUCHES HER TONGUE TO THE CHILD'S TONGUE, AND HOLDING THE TINY MOUTH OPEN, SHE BLOWS INTO IT – HARD. SHE WAS BLOWING WORDS – HER WORDS, HER MOTHER WORDS, THOSE OF HER MOTHER'S MOTHER, AND ALL THEIR MOTHERS BEFORE – INTO HER DAUGHTER'S MOUTH.[43]

Coming on the heels of George and Baudelaire, Philip here reimagines the space of donation and the plane of its descent. The word is at once a matter of inspiration and fate, of life and inheritance. Both ethereal and plastic, these MOTHER WORDS give new sense to Auden's beloved dictum, forcing us to reassess not only what poetry makes – or does not make – happen, or how it 'flows', but also in what way it can be said *to be* 'a way of happening, a mouth'.[44] Poetry, we could say, is for Philip what unsettles the primacy of birth by disclosing that its 'givens' are not given, but founded. It is here that the word intervenes in a general economy that can no longer be restricted to semantic sense or ready-made discursive constraint.

NOTES

1. Racter, *The Policeman's Beard is Half-Constructed* (New York: Warner Books, 1984), 40; 33.
2. Susan Howe, *Concordance* (New York: New Directions, 2020), 88.
3. Kenneth Goldsmith, *Uncreative Writing* (New York: Columbia University Press, 2011), 174.
4. On robopoetics, see especially Christian Bök, 'The Piecemeal Bard is Deconstructed: Notes Toward a Potential Robopoetics', *Object 10: Cyberpoetics* (Winter 2002), 10–18. The phrase 'radical artifice' is Marjorie Perloff's. See her *Radical Artifice*.
5. See, in particular, Goldsmith's *Day*, Place's *Tragodía 1: Statement of Facts*, *Tragodía 2: Statement of the Case*, and *Tragodía 3: Argument*, Dworkin's *Parse*, Tan Lin's *Seven Controlled Vocabularies and Obituary 2004. The Joy of Cooking*, and Charles Reznikoff's *Testimony: The United States 1885–1915: Recitative. Volume 1.*

6. Though the printed edition of Coleridge's letter omits it, the manuscript held at the Morgan Library shows Coleridge wrote and then crossed out '~~Talent~~' before replacing it with 'Genius'.
7. *STCL*, I:831. 29 July 1802.
8. *STCL*, I:831. 29 July 1802.
9. On *récriture*, see Antoine Compagnon, *La Seconde Main ou le travail de la citation*. Notable antecedents to citational poetics include Mallarmé's *Un Coup de dés*, Eliot's *The Wasteland*, Duchamp's *Ready-mades*, and Benjamin's *Arcades Project*. On this history, see especially Goldsmith, *Uncreative Writing*, and Perloff, *Unoriginal Genius*.
10. Jan Baetens and Jean-Jacques Poucel, 'Introduction: The Challenge of Constraint', *Poetics Today* 30.4 (2009), 611–34; 614, 616, 619.
11. Christian Bök and Krista Zala, 'Q&A: Poetry in the Genes', *Nature* 458 (2009): 35. See also his comments in 'The Piecemeal Bard is Deconstructed': 'Oulipo implies that, unless we can analyse our own authorial functions with this kind of mechanical detachment, we might find ourselves enslaved to instinct, blindly obeying a form of unconscious inspiration that, far from liberating us (as a surrealist might aver), does nothing but entrap us even more subtly in the rote maze of our own poetic habits' (11).
12. *Unoriginal Genius: Poetry by Other Means in the New Century* (Chicago: University of Chicago Press, 2012), 11–12.
13. See Bök, *The Xenotext: Book 1*, and Eduardo Kac, 'Biopoetry', *Kac Web*. Available at <www.ekac.org/biopoetry.html>, last accessed 30 November 2020. On each of their poetic projects, see Susan Vanderborg, 'Transgenic Poetry: Loss, Noise, and the Province of Parasites'.
14. *Policeman's Beard*, 71.
15. What each of these examples touches on is the limit between the human and inhuman, or man and machine, in their mutual capacity for repetition and iteration. At a certain level, then, does the question of the gift *in poetry* not come down to that of the death-drive, as a haunting alterity that threatens life from the very moment of its birth? The other of the gift in poetry is not to be found *outside*, but precisely as the limit between gift and non-gift, or man and machine, that forces each of the terms of the opposition to be reconfigured. This is why the questions raised by contemporary poetry are at once novel and ancient, unheralded and returns of past forms. In each case, it is a question of 'inanimation', as David Wills employs this term. See his *Inanimation: Theories of Inorganic Life*.
16. On the 'genius' of Goldsmith's *Traffic* and *Day*, see *Unoriginal Genius*, 146–66.

17. See Alec Wilkinson, 'Something Borrowed: Kenneth Goldsmith's poetry elevates copying to an art, but did he go too far?', *The New Yorker*, 28 September 2015. Available at: <https://www.newyorker.com/magazine/2015/10/05/something-borrowed-wilkinson>, last accessed 9 May 2021.
18. *Soliloquy* (New York: Granary Books, 2001), 10–11.
19. For an excellent synopsis of *Soliloquy*, see Christopher Schmidt, 'The Waste-Management Poetics of Kenneth Goldsmith'.
20. Christian Bök, 'A Silly Key: Some Notes on *Soliloquy* by Kenneth Goldsmith', *Open Letter* 12.7 (2005): 65–76; 65.
21. 'A Silly Key', 67.
22. *A Week*, 362.
23. Margaret Rhee, *Love, Robot* (Brooklyn, NY: the operating system, 2017), 89.
24. Georges Bataille, *Guilty*, trans. Stuart Kendall (Albany, NY: SUNY Press, 2011), 93.
25. *Poetry and its Others: News, Prayer, Song, and the Dialogue of Genres* (Chicago: University of Chicago Press, 2014), 12.
26. *Concordance*, 55.
27. 'On Historical Nostalgia and the Nature of Talent', 21 November 2019. Available at <https://www.npr.org/2016/11/21/502857118/novelist-zadie-smith-on-historical-nostalgia-and-the-nature-of-talent>, last accessed 1 December 2020.
28. 'Appropriative writing' is a favoured term of both Goldsmith and Perloff. For Goldsmith, it indicates a writing that repurposes that which belongs to others, doing so with as little authorial involvement as possible. Appropriative writing reinvents the already invented, and in so doing it is supposed to raise serious questions about the nature of property, authorship, and identity. Of course, it also involves, as a matter of logical necessity, a process of disappropriation, as the proper of the other is ap-propriated by the same. The perils of Goldsmith's approach, and the silent iniquities it involves, were painfully demonstrated during his 2015 reading at Brown University, 'The Body of Michael Brown'. For an excellent account of some of the problems with conceptual poetics – though one that dates to before the controversy – see Sueyen Juliette Lee, 'Shock and Blah: Offensive Postures in "Conceptual" Poetry and the Traumatic Stuplime'.
29. *She Tries Her Tongue, Her Silence Softly Breaks* (Charlottetown, Prince Edward Island: Ragweed Press, 1989), 14.
30. *She Tries Her Tongue*, 16.
31. M. NourbeSe Philip and Setaey Adamu Boateng, *Zong!* (Middletown, CT: Wesleyan University Press, 2008), 196.

32. *Zong!*, 196.
33. *Zong!*, 192.
34. *Zong!*, 193.
35. Valéry Loichot, *Water Graves: The Art of the Unritual in the Greater Caribbean* (Charlottesville: University of Virginia Press, 2020), 204.
36. In *Nox*, Carson bestows on her brother 'the last gift owed to death', through an impossible act of loving translation in the form of a lexicon, cataloguing each word of Catallus' poem 101, 'Many the peoples many the oceans I crossed'.
37. *Zong!*, 200.
38. *Zong!*, 27.
39. *Zong!*, 101.
40. *She Tries Her Tongue*, 56–9.
41. I take the term 'prosthetic tongue' from Katie Chenoweth. See *The Prosthetic Tongue: Printing Technology and the Rise of the French Language.*
42. On the significance of the trans-disciplinarity, or 'intergeneric porosity', of Philip's poetry, see Ramazani, 46.
43. *She Tries Her Tongue*, 56–8.
44. *Collected Poems*, 246.

Conclusion: The Birth of Lyric in the *Homeric Hymn to Hermes*

But now tell me this, resourceful son of Maia: did these marvelous accomplishments attend you from birth, or did some god or mortal give you this remarkable gift and teach you god-inspired singing? For this is a marvelous new-uttered sound I am hearing, that I declare no man and none of the immortals dwelling in Olympus has ever known, apart from you, deceitful son of Zeus and Maia. What skill is this? What song for desperate cares? What the method? For truly, this lets one enjoy three boons all together, good cheer, love, and sweet sleep.

Homeric Hymn to Hermes (ll.439–49)[1]

The *Homeric Hymn to Hermes* recounts that on the day that he was born, the god Hermes crawled out of his cradle and stumbled upon a tortoise. Inspired by the sight, he took the lovely being in both hands, cut off its limbs, scooped out its marrow, and fixed stalks of reed across the back of the shell before stretching an ox hide over all. In this way was the first lyre framed and, with it, 'lyric', which Hermes, son of Maia, subsequently presented to Apollo – god of prophecy, music, and poetic inspiration – in order to appease the latter for the theft of his herd.

Born of animal sacrifice and contrived with an immortal's ingenuity, the lyre, we learn in the passage above, produces a music in its inventor's hands that proves irresistible: literally 'unheard of' (νεήφατον ὄσσαν ἀκούω), marvels the sun god, the instrument is primed to contribute to 'good cheer, love, and sweet sleep', while offering hope to the hopeless (τίς μοῦσα ἀμηχανέων μελεδώνων). So struck by it is Apollo that, though initially infuriated by the loss of his herd, even he now feels compelled to reciprocate in turn, presenting Hermes with the gift of a silver whip and, upon an exchange of oaths, a golden staff designed to protect the talented trickster's future fortunes. Through the bestowal of the lyre along with its marvellous melodies, the *Hymn* thus recounts how the immortal brothers affirmed their newfound friendship, how the sun god secured his provenance over the poetic arts, and how a now songless Hermes became proper overseer of the pilfered cattle, all while assuming responsibility for humankind's future deeds of barter.

By furnishing a myth of lyric's divine creation and bestowal, the *Homeric Hymn* thus contributed to a Greek conception of song that – as Apollo himself testifies – had already traced the human flair for verse back to a godly gift, for, whether of Apollo, son of Zeus, or the Muses, Zeus' daughters, the source for song was in either case to be located in gifts of inspiration, or in a given, inborn ability. Thus understood, the inhuman otherworldliness of *aoidē* and, subsequently, *poiēma* could at once be explained *and* affirmed, both asserted *and* accounted for. As such, 'song' and then 'poetry' were – at least in theory – destined to circulate without suffering the debasements reserved for mere human goods, offerings set to be imparted rather than sold, received rather than bought, and exchanged, via tributes and sacrifices, rather than barter and market stalls. Poetry, as gift of the gods, was thereby set into motion and destined to circulate *as a present*, be it through the voice of the inspired rhapsode, the word of the poet prophet, or, as with the *Hymn*, the canny peace offering of the entrapped debtor.

As we have seen in the readings of the preceding chapters, it would be difficult to underestimate the impact of this Greek conception of poetic donation within the archives of Western poetry. Visible everywhere, from Maecenas' acts of patronal largesse to Shakespeare's offers of immortalising rhyme, Coleridge's notion of the poetical genius, and even Heidegger's positing of the work of art's *Wahrheit*, its impact manifests in every facet of what we today call the 'poetic work', which, as Hénaff, Birardi, and Hyde each reminds us, precisely *works*, or at least *should work*, in each instance *as gift*: that is, in the mode peculiar to what Mauss calls the 'form and reason for exchange in archaic societies', and therefore *not* in the fashion evidently endemic to 'industrial products'. The determination of poetry as gift, the determination that poetry *is*, or *should be*, a gift consequently marks the widest range of poetic history, assuring poetry of its distinction among the arts and supplying it with a source for its authority. It is an association that is established, moreover, in every facet of literary production. One sees it at work in the traditional figures of Western poetic theory, such as prophetic incantation, the poet's offerings of song, the endowments of genius, and the gifts of language, as well as in the poetic work's various material and economic exploits, such as acts of dedication, the composition of victory odes, and the histories of patron–client reciprocation. Even within the poetic work itself, the association functions as a self-reflexive mark of its own specificity, through which the lyric subject comes to recognise him- or herself as that subject, and by means of which poetry's privilege may therefore be performed, from within.[2]

There could hardly be any history of poetry in the West, in short, without a consideration of the gift's ubiquity, nor, perhaps, any corresponding concept of poetry without some relation to this distinction, which frequently serves as one of its most essential predicates. As we have seen, however, far from being a simply historical determination, something of the gift may already be written into the very inscription of the trace, as the cut that opens poematic address and marks every sending. Taken from this perspective, the long history of gift poetics would be comprehensible, precisely, as a *response* to the fundamental, structuring condition of all writing, and poetic history, as *the history* of a certain recognition of the non-presence of the present. As such, poetry would write itself as an experience of this encounter, alternating between 'transeconomy' and 'an-economy': that is, between vehicle of metaphoric passage and obstruction, within the passing, of every such passage.

In responding to this situation, one may thus be led back into the menagerie, or one may stray into the wilderness of its immediate vicinities, through what Derrida has called 'the gift of the poem', and Celan, 'the absolute poem', which 'doesn't exist!'[3] These possibilities, which are never simply opposed nor opposable, would haunt every iteration of its mark. In readings of Horace, Heidegger, Stein, Wordsworth, Thoreau, Baudelaire, Philip, and others, we have witnessed so many possible responses. And though it may be that one cannot but respond to this situation, at the same time, at certain moments of its history interrogations appear to gain a self-reflexive intensity that is, at others, evidently lacking.

And yet, even from the brief passage cited above, it is obvious that the *Homeric Hymn to Hermes* also inscribes a great deal of complexity within its helio-poetic vision. In it, already, an abundance of explanations for the appearance of song circulate, as Apollo struggles to account for this otherwise unaccountable marvel that is *aoidē*. Moreover, as is already evident, Hermes' offering, far from conforming to a modern sense of 'generosity', functions to compensate directly for the god's misdeeds, to the point that Apollo responds by placing the young trickster in charge of deeds of barter. In other words, instead of offering a univocal vision of the poetic gift, such as one has come to expect of Plato and his followers, the *Hymn* bears all the complexity of an unsettled poetic reflection upon the nature of poetry, and all of the uneasiness of an uncertain theoretical reflection upon the split between giving and exchanging. This lack of decisiveness is not a failing of the *Hymn* – or, to be specific, of Apollo, who voices it – but a necessary response to a real state of uncertainty. Already, then, at the geographic and historical origin of Western poetry's helio-tropic orbit, within a (poetic) text invested in giving account to the theoretical possibility of 'poetry', the threats of duplicity, treachery, and non-return haunt its originary, founding acts and inaugural articles.

Be this as it may, and in spite of what I would be tempted to call Apollo's rigorous indecisiveness, it is undeniable that the emergence of the lyre and, with it, song, is here coincident with the sacrifice of an animal: one that, moreover, appears to be constitutively impeded from observing the splendour of its own shell – structurally denied access, in other words, to its own being, as well as to what Hermes esteems to be its greatest good. It is only in death that the tortoise will become a singer, only in death that the animal, evidently, attains the state requisite for producing song, only in death, therefore, and with this sacrificial gift of death, that it may, subsequently, be reborn:

> Hermes it was who first crafted the singing tortoise . . . 'Where did you get this fine plaything, this blotchy shell that you wear, you tortoise living in the mountains? I shall take you indoors; you will be of some use to me, and I shan't undervalue you, I shall be the very first to profit from you. Better to be in the house, it's dangerous outside. For you will be a check against baneful visitation while you live, but if you die, then you may be a beautiful singer.' (ll.25–39)[4]

The birth of poetry, in the *Hymn*, is thus also that of a poetic gift economy in which death – a relation to and even a being-towards-death – marks the irreversible opening. Whether or not, then, song turns out to be part of a gift- or barter-economy, whether it can be traced back to divine inspiration or to the ingenuity of *physis*, it remains here the distinct property of humanity, henceforth to be proffered through the benevolence of Apollo, god of the sun.

In this way, the *Hymn* might be said to offer a primal scene of helio-*poiēsis*. Whatever doubt or hesitation concerning the provenance of poetry may initially have appeared here, it is immediately covered over by this sacrificial act, which establishes, at one fell swoop, the difference between human and animal, and the poet – who knows death – and non-poet, who remains in ignorance of it. One thus finds a repetition, or rather an antecedent, of the very economy of poetry that, as late as Heidegger, locates in *Dasein* the privileged access to some poetic essence, if only through a prior openness to language, to being, to death, and to a gift that is categorically denied to the animal other.

Far from receding into the background, this solar trajectory of poetry remains a visible element of the whole history of poetry and poetics, including the nineteenth and twentieth centuries, and not only in Kant and Nietzsche, but also in Wordsworth, Shelley, Thoreau, Baudelaire, and Bataille. It remains an integral element, in other words, of the work of those very authors whom, I have argued, precisely subvert it, calling to an other poetry, or to a poetry that fails to be poetry, from within the circumference of this heliotropic circus. And this has been a constant motif in the preceding chapters: what marks the nineteenth-century writing of the poetic gift is not a rejection of gift poetics, but a re-inscription of its various economies by way of moments of indecision, failure, fragility, and non-arrival.

In venturing the above readings, I have thus tried to attend to what makes the works of these authors singularly potent for diagnosing tensions that have always haunted poetic discourse. Moreover, in tracing the problematic of the gift of poetry through issues of poetic postality and ontology, I have tried to show how this *poetic* tradition – which is to say, a certain tradition invested in *the question of poetry* – may be more bifid than Derrida often gave it credit for, how it may introduce, not only a *pas de don*, but also a *pas de poésie*.

In responding to the decline of European patronage, the rise of the book trade, and the Kantian consolidation of aesthetics as an independent field, what thus makes these works stand apart is, precisely, that they do not merely articulate so many *positions*, for or against poetry, for or against giving, or for or against capitalism, and so on, but the very failures of the gift/economy, art/commodity, aesthetics/economics, and poetry/prose binaries themselves. In facing the aporias presented by the gift of poetry, these works are both more ambivalent and more troubling politically, aesthetically, and economically, than those that take either 'poetry' or 'the gift' for granted. This is their lesson, though it is not one that – to steal a line from Thoreau – one might simply hope to carry off with a wheelbarrow.

NOTES

1. *Homeric Hymns. Homeric Apocrypha. Lives of Homer*, ed. and trans. Martin L. West (Cambridge, MA: Harvard University Press, 2003), 148–51. Translation modified throughout with reference to *Hesiod. The Homeric Hymns and Homerica*, trans. Hugh G. Evelyn-White (Cambridge, MA: Harvard University Press, 1914), 394–7.
2. Much recent work has focused on troubling what has become a universalising conception of 'lyric', blind to historical and geographic differences. Throughout the previous chapters, I have been far less interested in establishing something like a universal genre of 'lyric', or even 'poetry', than in asking in what way the highly divergent forms of writing that have been

put forward under these names have consistently attempted to affirm their difference through appeals to the gift. For recent attempts to re-theorise lyric, see especially Virginia Jackson, *Dickinson's Misery*, Virginia Jackson and Yopie Prin, *The Lyric Theory Reader*, Culler, *Theory of the Lyric* and *Critical Rhythm: The Poetics of a Literary Life Form*, eds Jonathan Culler and Ben Glaser, as well as Francesco Giusti, *Il Desiderio della lirica: poesia, creazione, conoscenza*, and John Michael, *Secular Lyric*.
3. See *Sovereignties in Question*, 11, 15.
4. *Homeric Hymn*, 114–17 (translation modified). For a similar opposition of the tortoise in life and death, see *The Ichneutae of Sophocles*, trans. Richard Johnson Walker (London: Burns and Oates, 1919): 'But how can that which even aforetime also was speechless now in death raise this loud clamour?' (475).

Appendix: Henry David Thoreau, 'A Poet Buying a Farm'

A POET BUYING A FARM.

BY THOREAU.

At a certain season of our life we are accustomed to consider every spot as the possible site of a house. I have thus surveyed the country on every side within a dozen miles of where I live. In imagination I have bought all the farms in succession, for all were to be bought, and I knew their price. I walked over each farmer's premises, tasted his wild apples, discoursed on husbandry with him, took his farm at his price, at any price, mortgaging it to him in my own mind, even put a higher price on it,—took everything but a deed of it, took his word for his deed, for I dearly love to talk; cultivated it, and him too, to some extent, I trust, and withdrew, when I had enjoyed it long enough, leaving him to carry it on. This experience entitled me to be regarded as a sort of real estate broker by my friends. Wherever I sat, there I might live,—and the landscape radiated from me accordingly. What is a house but a *sedes*, a seat? better if a country-seat. I discovered many a site for a house not likely to be soon improved, which some might have thought too far from the village, but to my eyes the village appeared too far from it. Well, "there I might live," I said; and there I did live for an hour, a summer and a winter life, saw how I could let the years run off, buffet the winter through, and see the spring come in. The future inhabitants of this region, wherever they may place their houses, may be sure that they have been anticipated. An afternoon sufficed to lay out the land into orchard, wood-lot, and pasture, and to decide what fine oaks or pines should be left to stand before the door, and whence each rotten tree could be seen to the best advantage; and then I let it lie, fallow perchance, for a man is rich in proportion to the number of things which he can afford to let alone.

My imagination carried me so far that I even had the "refusal" of several farms,—the refusal was all I wanted,—but I never got my fingers burnt by actual possession. The nearest that I came to actual proprietorship was when I bought the Hollowell Place, and had begun to sort my seeds, and collected materials with which to make a wheelbarrow to carry it on or off with; but before the owner gave me a deed of it, his wife,—every man has such a wife,—changed her mind and wished to keep it, and he offered me ten dollars to release him. Now, to speak the truth, I had but ten cents in the world, and it surpassed my arithmetic to tell if I was that man who had ten cents, or who had a farm, or who had ten dollars, or all together. However, I let him keep the ten dollars and the farm too, for I had carried it far enough; or rather, to be generous, I sold him the farm for just what I gave for it, and as he was a poor man, made him a present of ten dollars, and still had my ten cents, and seeds, and materials for a wheelbarrow left. I found thus that I had been a rich man, without any damage to my poverty. But I retained the landscape, and I have since annually carried off what it yielded, without a wheelbarrow. With respect to landscapes,

"I am monarch of all I survey,
My right there is none to dispute."

I have frequently seen a poet withdraw, having enjoyed the most valuable part of a farm, while the crusty farmer supposed that we had got a few wild apples only. Why, the owner does not know it for many years when a poet has put his farm in rhyme, the most admirable kind of invisible fence, has fairly impounded it, milked it, skimmed it, and got all the cream, and left the farmer only the skimmed milk.

All that I can say then, with respect to farming is, that I have had my seeds ready. Many think that seeds improve with age. I have no doubt that time discriminates between the good and the bad, and when at last I shall plant, I shall be less likely to be disappointed. But I would say to my fellows, once for all, as long as possible live free and uncommitted. It makes but little difference, whether you are committed to a farm or the county jail!

Figure A.1 Henry David Thoreau (1852), 'A Poet Buying a Farm', *Sartain's Union Magazine* 11: 127.

Bibliography

Abrams, M. H. (1973). *Natural Supernaturalism*. New York: W. W. Norton.
— (1984). *The Correspondent Breeze*. New York: W. W. Norton.
Agamben, Giorgio (1999). *The Man Without Content*, trans. Georgia Albert. Stanford, CA: Stanford University Press.
Alfano, Chiara (2020). *Derrida Reads Shakespeare*. Edinburgh: Edinburgh University Press.
Ali, Samer M. (2010). *Arabic Salons in the Islamic Middle Ages: Poetry, Public Performance, and the Presentation of the Past*. Notre Dame, IN: University of Notre Dame Press.
Aristotle and Longinus (1995). *Poetics. Longinus: On the Sublime. Demetrius: On Style*, trans. Stephen Halliwell, rev. Donald A. Russell. Cambridge, MA: Harvard University Press.
Armstrong, Isobel and Virginia Blain (eds) (1999). *Women's Poetry: Late Romantic to Late Victorian: Gender and Genre, 1830–1900*. New York: Macmillan.
Arsić, Branka (2016). *Bird Relics: Grief and Vitalism in Thoreau*. Cambridge, MA: Harvard University Press.
Atlick, Richard D. (1957). *The English Common Reader: A Social History of the Mass Reading Public, 1800–1900*. Chicago: University of Chicago Press.
Attridge, Derek (2004). *The Singularity of Literature*. London: Routledge.
Auden, W. H. (1976). *Collected Poems*, ed. Edward Mendelson. New York: Modern Library.
Bacchylides (1992). 'Dithyrambs 19', in *Greek Lyric, Volume IV: Bacchylides, Corinna, and Others*, ed. and trans. David A. Campbell. Cambridge, MA: Harvard University Press, 232–3.
Baetens, Jan and Jean-Jacques Poucel (2009). 'Introduction: The Challenge of Constraint', *Poetics Today* 30.4: 611–34.
Bajorek, Jennifer (2008). *Counterfeit Capital: Poetic Labor and Revolutionary Irony*. Stanford, CA: Stanford University Press.

Bambach, Charles and Theodore George (eds) (2019). *Philosophers and their Poets: Reflections on the Poetic Turn in Philosophy since Kant*. Albany, NY: SUNY Press.

Barfield, Owen (1967). 'Imagination and Inspiration', in *Interpretation: The Poetry of Meaning*, eds Stanley Romaine Hopper and David L. Miller. New York: Harcourt, Brace & World, 54–76.

Baudelaire, Charles (1970). *Paris Spleen*, trans. Louise Varèse. New York: New Directions.

— (1975). *Œuvres complètes vol. 1*, ed. Claude Pichois. Paris: Gallimard.

— (1976). *Œuvres complètes vol. 2*, ed. Claude Pichois. Paris: Gallimard.

Bataille, Georges (1947). *La Haine de la poésie*. Paris: Éditions de Minuit.

— (1997). *The Bataille Reader*, trans. Allan Stoekl, eds Fred Botting and Scott Wilson. Oxford: Blackwell.

— (2011). *Guilty*, trans. Stuart Kendall. Albany, NY: SUNY Press.

Bennington, Geoffrey (2016). *Scatter 1: The Politics of Politics in Foucault, Heidegger, and Derrida*. New York: Fordham University Press.

Bennington, Geoffrey and Jacques Derrida (1993). *Jacques Derrida*. Chicago: University of Chicago Press.

Berardi, Franco (2012). *The Uprising: On Poetry and Finance*. Cambridge, MA: MIT Press.

Bercovitch, Sacvan (1978). *The American Jeremiad*. Madison: University of Wisconsin Press.

Berger, Anne-Emmanuelle (2004). *Scènes d'aumône: misère et poésie au XIXe siècle*. Paris: Honoré Champion.

Bieri, James (2004). *Percy Bysshe Shelley: Youth's Unextinguished Fire, 1792–1816*. Newark: University of Delaware.

Blood, Susan (2002). 'The Poetics of Expenditure', *MLN* 117.4: 836–57.

Bloom, Harold (1971). *The Visionary Company*. Ithaca, NY: Cornell University Press.

— (1973) *The Anxiety of Influence*. Oxford: Oxford University Press.

Bök, Christian (2002). 'The Piecemeal Bard is Deconstructed: Notes Toward a Potential Robopoetics', *Object 10: Cyberpoetics* 10–18.

— (2005). 'A Silly Key: Some Notes on *Soliloquy* by Kenneth Goldsmith', *Open Letter* 12.7: 65–76.

— (2015). *The Xenotext: Book 1*. Toronto: Coach House Books.

Bök, Christian and Krista Zala (2009). 'Q&A: Poetry in the Genes', *Nature* 458: 35.

Bonnefis, Philippe (1996). 'Child's Play: Baudelaire's *Morale du joujou*', in *Reconceptions: Reading Modern French Poetry*, eds Russell King and Bernard McGuirk. Nottingham: University of Nottingham.

Bourdieu, Pierre (1993). *The Field of Cultural Production*, ed. Randal Johnson. New York: Columbia University Press.

— (1997). 'Marginalia – Some Additional Notes on the Gift', in *The Logic of the Gift*, ed. Alan Schrift. New York: Routledge, 231–44.
— (1997). *Outline of a Theory of Practice*, trans. Richard Nice. Cambridge: Cambridge University Press.
— (1998). *Practical Reason: On the Theory of Action*, trans. Randall Johnson. Stanford, CA: Stanford University Press.
Bowditch, Phebe Lowell (2001). *Horace and the Gift Economy of Patronage*. Oakland: University of California Press.
Boyancé, Pierre (1963). *La Religion de Virgile*. Paris: PUF.
Bruno, Paul W. (2011). *Kant's Concept of Genius*. London: Continuum.
Buell, Lawrence (1973). *Literary Transcendentalism: Style and Vision in the American Renaissance*. Ithaca, NY: Cornell University Press.
Bulter, James A. (1975). 'Wordsworth's "Tuft of Primroses": "An Unrelenting Doom"', *Studies in Romanticism* 14.3: 237–48.
Bundy, Murray W. (1930). '"Invention" and "Imagination" in the Renaissance', *The Journal of English and German Philology* 29.4: 535–45.
Burke, Seán (ed.) (1995). *Authorship: From Plato to the Postmodern: A Reader*. Edinburgh: Edinburgh University Press.
Burt, E. S. (2000). *Poetry's Appeal: Nineteenth-Century French Lyric and the Political Space*. Stanford, CA: Stanford University Press.
Burwick, Frederick (2004). *Poetic Madness and the Romantic Imagination*. State College: Pennsylvania State University Press.
Cameron, Kenneth Neil (1974). *Shelley: The Golden Years*. Cambridge, MA: Harvard University Press.
Carson, Anne (1999). *Economy of the Unlost (Reading Simonides of Keos with Paul Celan)*. Princeton: Princeton University Press.
— (2010). *Nox*. New York: New Directions.
Carson, Anne and Kevin McNeilly (2003). 'Gifts and Questions – An Interview with Anne Carson', *Canadian Literature* 176: 12–25.
Cavell, Stanley (1992). *The Senses of Walden: An Expanded Edition*. Chicago: University of Chicago Press.
Cervantes, Miguel de (2008). *Don Quixote de la Mancha*, trans. Charles Jarvis, ed. E. C. Riley. Oxford: Oxford University Press.
Chenoweth, Katie (2020). *The Prosthetic Tongue: Printing Technology and the Rise of the French Language*. Philadelphia: University of Pennsylvania Press.
Chernaik, Judith (1972). *The Lyrics of Shelley*. Cleveland: Case Western Reserve University Press.
Cicero (1923). *Pro Archia. Post Reditum in Senatu. Post Reditum ad Quirites. De Domo Sua. De Haruspicum Responsis. Pro Plancio*, trans. N. H. Watts. Cambridge, MA: Harvard University Press.

Clark, Timothy (1986). 'Being in Mime: Heidegger and Derrida on the Ontology of Literary Language', *MLN* 101.5: 1003–21.
— (1989). *Embodying Revolution: The Figure of the Poet in Shelley*. Oxford: Clarendon Press.
— (1992). *Derrida, Heidegger, Blanchot: Sources of Derrida's Notion and Practice of Literature*. Cambridge: Cambridge University Press.
— (1997). *The Theory of Inspiration*. Manchester: Manchester University Press.
— (2005). *The Poetics of Singularity: The Counter-Culturalist Turn in Heidegger, Derrida, Blanchot and the Later Gadamer*. Edinburgh: Edinburgh University Press.
Cole, Peter (ed. and trans.) (2007). *The Dream of the Poem: Hebrew Poetry from Muslim and Christian Spain 950–1492*. Princeton: Princeton University Press.
Coleridge, Samuel Taylor (1835). *Specimens of the Table Talk of the late Samuel Taylor Coleridge*, vol. 2. New York: Harper & Brothers.
— (1836). *The Literary Remains of Samuel Taylor Coleridge, Volume 1*, ed. Henry Nelson Coleridge. London: William Pickering.
— (1966). *Collected Letters of Samuel Taylor Coleridge (vols. 1–6)*, ed. Earl Leslie Griggs. Oxford: Clarendon.
— (1983). *Biographia Literaria*, eds James Engell and W. Jackson Bate, in *The Collected Works of Samuel Taylor Coleridge*, 7.2. Princeton: Princeton University Press.
Commager, Steele (1995). *The Odes of Horace: A Critical Study*. Norman: University of Oklahoma Press.
Compagnon, Antoine (1979). *La Seconde Main ou le travail de la citation*. Paris: Seuil.
Cox, Jeffrey N. (1998). *Poetry and Politics in the Cockney School: Keats, Shelley, Hunt and their Circle*. Cambridge: Cambridge University Press.
Cronin, Richard (1981). *Shelley's Poetic Thoughts*. London: Macmillan.
Culler, Jonathan (1981). *The Pursuit of Signs: Semiotics, Literature, Deconstruction*. London: Routledge.
— (2015). *Theory of the Lyric*. Cambridge, MA: Harvard University Press.
Culler, Jonathan and Ben Glaser (eds) (2019). *Critical Rhythm: The Poetics of a Literary Life Form*. New York: Fordham University Press.
Curran, Stuart (1983). '*Adonais* in Context', in *Shelley Revalued*, ed. Kelvin Everest. Leicester: Leicester University Press.
Curtius, E. R. (1983). *European Literature and the Latin Middle Ages*. Princeton: Princeton University Press.
Dante (1867). *The Divine Comedy*, trans. Henry Wadsworth Longfellow. Boston: Ticknor and Fields.

Davis, Natalie Zemon (2000). *The Gift in Sixteenth-Century France*. Madison: University of Wisconsin Press.
De Man, Paul (1984). *The Rhetoric of Romanticism*. New York: Columbia University Press.
Derrida, Jacques (1974). *Glas*. Paris: Galilée.
— (1975). 'Economimesis', in *Mimesis, Des articulations*, eds Sylviane Agacinski, Jacques Derrida, Sarah Kofman, Philippe Lacoue-Labarthe, Jean-Luc Nancy, and Bernard Pautrat. Paris: Aubier-Flammarion, 55–93.
— (1979). 'Living On: Border Lines', in *Deconstruction and Criticism*, trans. James Hulbert. New York: Seabury Press, 75–176.
— (1981). *Dissemination*, trans. Barbara Johnson. Chicago: University of Chicago Press.
— (1981). 'Economimesis', trans. Richard Klein, *Diacritics* 11.2: 2–25.
— (1981). *Positions*, trans. Alan Bass. Chicago: University of Chicago Press.
— (1982). *Margins of Philosophy*, trans. Alan Bass. Chicago: University of Chicago Press.
— (1984). *Signéponge–Signsponge*, trans. Richard Rand. New York: Columbia University Press.
— (1985). *The Ear of the Other*, ed. Christie McDonald, trans. Peggy Kamuf. New York: Schocken Books.
— (1986). *Parages*. Paris: Galilée.
— (1987). *Psyché: Inventions de l'autre*. Paris: Galilée.
— (1987). *The Truth in Painting*, trans Geoffrey Bennington and Ian McLeod. Chicago: University of Chicago Press.
— (1991). *Donner le temps. 1. La fausse monnaie*. Paris: Éditions Galilée.
— (1992). *Acts of Literature*, ed. Derek Attridge. New York: Routledge.
— (1992). *Given Time: 1. Counterfeit Money*, trans. Peggy Kamuf. Chicago: University of Chicago Press.
— (1993). *Khōra*. Paris: Galilée.
— (1994). *Politique de l'amitié: suivi de L'oreille de Heidegger*. Paris: Galilée.
— (1995). *On the Name*, ed. Thomas Dutoit, trans David Wood, John P. Leavey Jr and Ian McLeod. Stanford, CA: Stanford University Press.
— (1995). *Points . . . : Interviews, 1974–1994*, trans. Peggy Kamuf, ed. Elisabeth Weber. Stanford, CA: Stanford University Press.
— (1995). *The Gift of Death*, trans. David Wills. Chicago: University of Chicago Press.
— (1997). *Of Grammatology*, trans. Gayatri Spivak. Baltimore: Johns Hopkins University Press.
— (2002). 'Ants', trans. Eric Prenowitz. *Oxford Literary Review* 24: 17–42.

— (2002). *Writing and Difference*, trans. and ed. Alan Bass. New York: Routledge.
— (2004). 'L'Esprit de l'argent. Autour des écrits de Jacques Derrida sur l'argent', in *L'Argent: croyance, mesure, spéculation*, ed. Marcel Drach. Paris: La Découverte, 193–234.
— (2005). *Sovereignties in Question: The Poetics of Paul Celan*, eds and trans Thomas Dutoit and Outi Pasanen. New York: Fordham University Press.
— (2005). 'Women in the Beehive: A Seminar with Jacques Derrida', *Differences: A Journal of Feminist Cultural Studies* 16.3: 139–57.
— (2006). *Geneses, Genealogies, Genres, and Genius*, trans. Beverley Bie Brahic. New York: Columbia University Press.
— (2007). 'A Certain Impossible Possibility of Saying the Event'. *Critical Inquiry* 33.2: 441–61.
— (2007). *Psyche: Inventions of the Other, Volume I*, trans. Catherine Porter. Stanford, CA: Stanford University Press.
— (2008). *Psyche: Inventions of the Other, Volume II*, eds Peggy Kamuf and Elizabeth Rottenberg, trans John P. Leavey Jr and Elizabeth Rottenberg. Stanford, CA: Stanford University Press.
— (2008). *The Animal that Therefore I Am (More to Follow)*, ed. Marie-Louise Mallet, trans. David Wills. New York: Fordham University Press,
— (2009). *The Beast and the Sovereign, Volume I*, trans. Geoffrey Bennington. Chicago: University of Chicago Press.
— (2017). *The Death Penalty, Volume 2*, eds Geoffrey Bennington and Marc Crépon, trans. Elizabeth Rottenberg. Chicago: University of Chicago Press.
— (2020). *Geschlecht III: Sex, Race, Nation, Humanity*, ed. Geoffrey Bennington and trans Katie Chenoweth and Rodrigo Therezo. Chicago: University of Chicago Press.
— (2020). *Life Death*, eds Pascale-Anne Brault and Peggy Kamuf, trans Pascale-Anne Brault and Michael Naas. Chicago: University of Chicago Press.
— (2021). *Clang*, trans David Wills and Geoffrey Bennington. Minneapolis: Minnesota University Press.
— (2021). *Donner le temps II*, eds Laura Odello, Peter Szendy, and Rodrigo Therezo. Paris: Éditions du Seuil.
— (2021). *Perjury and Pardon, Volume I*, trans. David Wills. Chicago: University of Chicago Press.
Descartes, René (1998). *Discourse on Method and Meditations on First Philosophy*, trans. Donald A. Cress. Indianapolis: Hackett.
Détienne, Marcel (1996). *The Masters of Truth in Ancient Greece*, trans. Janet Lloyd. New York: Zone Books.

Dick, Alexander (2000). 'Poverty, Charity, Poetry: The Unproductive Labors of "The Old Cumberland Beggar"', *Studies in Romanticism* 39.3: 365–96.

Dickinson, Emily (2016). *Emily Dickinson's Poems: As She Preserved Them*, ed. Cristanne Miller. Cambridge, MA: Harvard University Press.

Diderot, Denis and Jean le Rond d'Alembert (eds) (1757). *L'Encyclopédie, ou dictionnaire raisonné des sciences, des arts et des métiers*. University of Chicago: ARTFL.

Dowden, Edward (ed.) (1888). *Correspondence of Henry Taylor*. London: Longmans, Green, and Co.

Du Bellay, Joachim (1903). *La Défense et illustration de la langue françoise suivie de L'Olive et quelques autres œuvres poétiques, 1*. Paris: Revue de la Renaissance.

Duffy, Cian (2009). *Shelley and the Revolutionary Sublime*. Cambridge: Cambridge University Press.

Duffy, James (1947). 'Homer's Conception of Fate', *The Classics Journal* 42.8: 477–85.

Dworkin, Craig (2008). *Parse*. Berkeley, CA: Atelos.

Eigeldinger, Marc (1969). 'Baudelaire et "Le Compte de Gabalis"', *Revue d'histoire littéraire de la France* 6: 1020–1.

Eilenberg, Susan (1992). *Strange Power of Speech: Wordsworth, Coleridge & Literary Possession*. Oxford: Oxford University Press.

Elson, Christopher and Garry Sherbert (eds and trans) (2017). *In the Name of Friendship: Deguy, Derrida and Salut*. Leiden: Brill.

Emerson, Ralph Waldo (1903). *The Complete Works of Ralph Waldo Emerson: Essays 2nd Series, volume 3*, ed. Edward Waldo Emerson. Boston: Houghton Mifflin Company.

— (1950). *The Complete Essays and Other Writings of Ralph Waldo Emerson*, ed. Brooks Atkinson. New York: Random House.

— (1971). *The Collected Works of Ralph Waldo Emerson, Volume I: Nature, Addresses, and Lectures*, eds Alfred Riggs Ferguson and Robert E. Spiller. Cambridge, MA: Harvard University Press.

— (1983). *Emerson: Essays and Lectures*, ed. Joel Porte. New York: Penguin.

— (1987). *The Collected Works of Ralph Waldo Emerson, Volume IV: Representative Men*, eds Wallace E. Williams and Douglas Emory Wilson. Cambridge, MA: Harvard University Press.

Eron, Sarah (2014). *Inspiration in the Age of Enlightenment*. Newark: University of Delaware Press.

Esterhammer, Angela (2009). *Romanticism and Improvisation, 1750–1850*. Cambridge: Cambridge University Press.

Evelyn-White, Hugh G. (trans.) (1914). *Hesiod. The Homeric Hymns and Homerica*. Cambridge, MA: Harvard University Press.

Ferrari, Franco (2010). *Sappho's Gift: The Poet and Her Community*, trans Benjamin Acosta-Hughes and Lucia Prauscello. Ann Arbor: Michigan Classical Press.
Finn, Margot C. (2003). *The Character of Credit: Personal Debt in English Culture, 1740–1914*. Cambridge: Cambridge University Press.
Fumerton, Patricia (1986). 'Exchanging Gifts: Elizabethan Currency of Children and Poetry', *ELH* 53.2: 241–78.
Garofalo, Daniela (2012). *Women, Love, and Commodity Culture in British Romanticism*. New York: Routledge.
Genette, Gérard (1997). *Paratexts: Thresholds of Interpretation*, trans. Jane E. Lewin. Cambridge: Cambridge University Press.
Gill, Stephen (ed.) (2006). *William Wordsworth's The Prelude: A Casebook*. Oxford: Oxford University Press.
Gilmore, Michael T. (1985). *American Romanticism and the Marketplace*. Chicago: University of Chicago Press.
Gitting, Robert (1964). *The Keats Inheritance*. London: Heinemann.
Giusti, Francesco (2017). *Il Desiderio della lirica: poesia, creazione, conoscenza*. Rome: Carocci.
Godbout, Jacques T. and Alain C. Caille (1998). *The World of the Gift*, trans. Donald Winkler. Montreal: McGill-Queen's University Press.
Godelier, Maurice (1999). *The Enigma of the Gift*, trans. Nora Scott. Chicago: University of Chicago Press.
Godzich, Wlad and Jeffrey Kittay (1987). *The Emergence of Prose: An Essay in Prosaics*. Minneapolis: Minnesota University Press.
Goethe, Johann Wolfgang von (1989). *The Sorrows of Young Werther*, trans. Michael Hulse. New York: Penguin.
Gold, Barbara K. (2011). *Literary Patronage in Greece and Rome*. Chapel Hill: University of North Carolina Press.
Goldsmith, Kenneth (2001). *Soliloquy*. New York: Granary Books.
— (2003). *Day*. Great Barrington, MA: The Figures.
— (2011). *Uncreative Writing*. New York: Columbia University Press.
Grabo, C. H. (1936). *The Magic Plant*. Chapel Hill: University of North Carolina Press.
Gravil, Richard (2000). *Romantic Dialogues: Anglo-American Continuities, 1776–1862*. New York: St Martin's Press.
Gravil, Richard and Daniel Robinson (eds) (2015). *The Oxford Handbook of William Wordsworth*. Oxford: Oxford University Press.
Greaney, Patrick (2008). *Untimely Beggar: Poverty and Power from Baudelaire to Benjamin*. Minneapolis: Minnesota University Press.
Griffin, Dustin (1990). 'The Beginnings of Modern Authorship: Milton and Dryden', *Milton Quarterly* 24.1: 1–7.

— (1996). *Literary Patronage in England, 1650–1800*. Cambridge: Cambridge University Press.

Griffin, Robert J. (2005). *Wordsworth's Pope: A Study in Literary Historiography*. Cambridge: Cambridge University Press.

Grossman, Allen (1992). *The Sighted Singer*. Baltimore: Johns Hopkins University Press.

Grusin, Richard A. (1988). '"Put God in Your Debt": Emerson's Economy of Expenditure', *PMLA* 103.1: 35–44.

— (1993). 'Thoreau, Extravagance, and the Economy of Nature', *American Literary History* 5.1: 30–50.

Guillory, John (1983). *Poetic Authority: Spenser, Milton, and Literary History*. New York: Columbia University Press.

Guyer, Sara (2015). *Reading with John Clare: Biopoetics, Sovereignty, Romanticism*. New York: Fordham University Press,

Haggarty, Sarah (2010). *Blake's Gifts: Poetry and the Politics of Exchange*. Cambridge: Cambridge University Press.

Hale, Sarah Josepha (ed.) (1850). *The Poet's Offering for 1850*. Philadelphia: Grigg, Elliot, & Co.

Hall, Jean (1992). 'The Divine and the Dispassionate Selves: Shelley's *Defence* and Peacock's *The Four Ages of Poetry*', *Keats–Shelley Journal* 41: 139–63.

Hall, Spencer (1983). 'Power and Poet: Religious Mythmaking in Shelley's "Hymn to Intellectual Beauty"', *Keats–Shelley Journal* 32: 123–49.

Haney, David P. (2010). *William Wordsworth and the Hermeneutics of Incarnation*. State College: Penn State University Press.

Harding, Walter (1982). *The Days of Henry Thoreau: A Biography*. New York: Dover.

Hartman, Geoffrey (1962). 'A Poet's Progress: Wordsworth and the "Via Naturaliter Negativa"', *Modern Philology* 59.3: 214–24.

Heal, Felicity (2014). *The Power of Gifts: Gift-Exchange in Early Modern England*. Oxford: Oxford University Press.

Heidegger, Martin (1968). *What is Called Thinking?*, trans. J. Glenn Gray. New York: Harper & Row.

— (1971). *Poetry, Language, Thought*, trans. Albert Hofstadter. New York: Harper & Row.

— (1977). *Gesamtausgabe I. Abteilung: Veröffentlichte Schriften 1914–1970. Band 5. Holzwege*. Frankfurt am Main: Vittorio Klostermann.

— (1981). *Gesamtausgabe I. Abteilung: Veröffentlichte Schriften 1910–1976. Band 4. Erläuterungen zu Hölderlins Dichtung*. Frankfurt am Main: Vittorio Klostermann.

— (1982). *On the Way to Language*, trans. Peter D. Hertz. San Francisco: Harper & Row.

— (1985). *Gesamtausgabe I. Abteilung: Veröffentlichte Schriften 1910–1976. Band 12. Unterwegs zur Sprache.* Frankfurt am Main: Vittorio Klostermann.
— (1996). *Hölderlin's Hymn 'The Ister'*, trans William McNeill and Julia Davis. Bloomington: Indiana University Press.
— (2000). *Elucidations of Hölderlin's Poetry*, trans. Keith Hoeller. Amherst: Humanity Books.
— (2002). *Off the Beaten Track*, eds and trans Julian Young and Kenneth Haynes. Cambridge: Cambridge University Press.
Heinzelman, Kurt (1980). *The Economics of the Imagination.* Boston: University of Massachusetts Press.
Hénaff, Marcel (2010). *The Price of Truth: Gift, Money, and Philosophy*, trans. Jean-Louis Morhange. Stanford, CA: Stanford University Press.
Herder, Johann Gottfried von and Jean-Jacques Rousseau (1966). *On the Origin of Language*, trans John H. Moran and Alexander Gode. Chicago: University of Chicago Press.
Hesiod (2007). *Theogony. Works and Days. Testimonia*, ed. and trans. Glenn W. Most. Cambridge, MA: Harvard University Press.
Hess, Scott (2005). *Authoring the Self: Self-Representation, Authorship, and the Print Market in British Poetry from Pope through Wordsworth.* New York: Routledge.
Heyd, Michael (1995). *Be Sober and Reasonable: The Critique of Enthusiasm in the Seventeenth and Early Eighteenth Centuries.* Leiden: Brill.
Heywood, John (1907). *The Book of Elizabethan Verse*, ed. William Stanley Braithwaite. Boston: Herbert B. Turner & Co.
Hillard, George (ed.) (1877). *Life, Letters, and Journals of George Ticknor, vol. II.* Boston: James R. Osgood and Company.
Hoeller, Hildegard (2012). *From Gift to Commodity: Capitalism and Sacrifice in Nineteenth-Century American Fiction.* Durham: University of New Hampshire Press, 2012.
Hogle, Jerrold E. (1989). *Shelley's Process: Radical Transference and the Development of his Major Works.* Oxford: Oxford University Press.
Hölderlin, Friedrich (2004). *Friedrich Hölderlin: Poems and Fragments*, trans. Michael Hamburger. London: Anvil Press Poetry.
Homer (1919). *Odyssey. Volume 1: Books 1–12*, trans. A. T. Murray, revised George E. Dimock. Cambridge, MA: Harvard University Press.
Horace (1926). *Satires. Epistles. The Art of Poetry*, trans. H. Rushton Fairclough. Cambridge, MA: Harvard University Press.
Howe, Daniel (1970). *The Unitarian Conscience: Harvard Moral Philosophy, 1805–1861.* Cambridge, MA: Harvard University Press.
Howe, Susan (2020). *Concordance.* New York: New Directions.

Hoyoux, Jean (1944). 'Les Moyens d'existence d'Érasme', *Bibliothèque d'Humanisme et Renaissance* 5: 7–59.
Hyde, Lewis (2007). *The Gift: Creativity and the Artist in the Modern World*. New York: Vintage.
Irlam, Shaun (1999). *Elations: The Poetics of Enthusiasm in Eighteenth-Century Britain*. Stanford, CA: Stanford University Press.
Isomaki, Richard (1991). 'Interpretation and Value in "Mont Blanc" and "Hymn to Intellectual Beauty"', *Studies in Romanticism* 30.1: 57–69.
Jackson, Virginia (2005). *Dickinson's Misery: A Theory of Lyric Reading*. Princeton: Princeton University Press.
Jackson, Virginia and Yopie Prin (2014). *The Lyric Theory Reader*. Baltimore: Johns Hopkins University Press.
Jacobs, Carol (1985). 'On Looking at Shelley's Medusa', *Yale French Studies* 69: 163–79.
Jacobus, Mary (1994). *Romanticism, Writing and Sexual Difference: Essays on the Prelude*. Oxford: Oxford University Press.
— (2012). *Romantic Things: A Tree, a Rock, a Cloud*. Chicago: University of Chicago Press.
Jager, Colin (2014). *Unquiet Things: Secularism in the Romantic Age*. Philadelphia: University of Pennsylvania Press.
Jarvis, Simon (1998). 'Wordsworth's Gifts of Feeling', *Romanticism* 4.1: 90–103.
— (1999). 'The Gift in Theory', *Dionysius* 17: 201–22.
— (2006). *Wordsworth's Philosophic Song*. Cambridge: Cambridge University Press.
Jeffrey, Francis (1855). *Contributions to the Edinburgh Review by Francis Jeffrey*. London: Longman, Brown, Green, and Longmans.
Johnson, Barbara (1979). *Défigurations du langage poétique*. Paris: Flammarion.
— (1987). *A World of Difference*. Baltimore: Johns Hopkins University Press.
Johnson, Samuel (1755). 'To Give', in *A Dictionary of the English Language, Vol I*. London: W. Strahan.
Johnston, Kenneth R. (1975). '"Home at Grasmere": Reclusive Song', *Studies in Romanticism* 14.1: 1–28.
— (1982). 'Wordsworth and the Recluse: The University of Imagination', *PMLA* 97.1: 60–82.
— (2001). *The Hidden Wordsworth*. New York: W. W. Norton.
Jonson, Ben (1988). *The Complete Poems*, ed. George Parfitt. New York: Penguin.
Kac, Eduardo. 'Biopoetry'. *Kac Web*. <www.ekac.org/biopoetry.html>, last accessed 30 November 2020.
Kallendorf, Craig (1995). 'From Virgil to Vida: The *Poeta Theologus* in Italian Renaissance Commentary', *Journal of the History of Ideas* 56: 41–62.

— (1997). 'In Search of a Patron: Anguillara's Vernacular Virgil and the Print Culture of Renaissance Italy', *The Papers of the Bibliographical Society of America* 91: 294–326.
Kant, Immanuel (1846). *Critique du jugement*, trans. J. Barni. Paris: Librairie Philosophique de Ladrange.
— (1974). *Kritik der Urteilskraft*. Frankfurt am Main: Suhrkamp.
— (2000). *Critique of the Power of Judgement*, trans Paul Guyer and Eric Matthews, ed. Paul Guyer. Cambridge: Cambridge University Press.
— (2005). *Groundwork for the Metaphysics of Morals*, ed. Lara Denis, trans. Thomas K. Abbott. Ontario: Broadview Press.
Kantorowicz, Ernst (2016). *The King's Two Bodies: A Study in Medieval Political Theology*. Princeton: Princeton University Press.
Karmodi, Ostap and David Foster Wallace (2011). '"A Frightening Time in America": An Interview with David Foster Wallace', *New York Review of Books*, 13 June 2011. <https://www.nybooks.com/daily/2011/06/13/david-foster-wallace-russia-interview/>, last accessed 22 October 2018.
Kaske, Carol V. and John R. Clark, (eds) (1989). *Three Books on Life*. Binghamton, NY: CEMERS.
Keane, Angela (2002). 'The Market, the Public and the Female Author: Anna Laetitia Barbauld's Gift Economy', *Romanticism* 8.2: 161–78.
Keats, John (2008). *Keats's Poetry and Prose*, ed. Jeffrey N. Cox. New York: W. W. Norton.
— (2011). *The Letters of John Keats: 1814–1821: Volume I, 1814–1818*, ed. Hyder Edward Rollins. Cambridge: Cambridge University Press.
Kierkegaard, Søren (1992). *The Concept of Irony: With Continual Reference to Socrates*, eds and trans Howard V. Hong and Edna H. Hong. Princeton: Princeton University Press.
Klein, Richard (1981). 'Kant's Sunshine', *Diacritics* 11.2: 26–41.
Knapp, John (1999). 'The Spirit of the Classical Hymn in Shelley's "Hymn to Intellectual Beauty"', *Style* 33.1: 43–66.
Kuhn, Bernhard (2009). *Autobiography and Natural Science in the Age of Romanticism: Rousseau, Goethe, Thoreau*. New York: Routledge.
Kuiken, Kir (2014). *Imagined Sovereignties: Toward a New Political Romanticism*. New York: Fordham University Press.
Kurtz, Benjamin (1933). *The Pursuit of Death*. London: Oxford University Press.
Laborie, Lionel (2015). *Enlightening Enthusiasm: Prophecy and Religious Experience in Early Eighteenth-Century England*. Manchester: Manchester University Press.
Lamb, Jonathan (2001). *Preserving the Self in the South Seas, 1680–1840*. Chicago: University of Chicago Press.

Landon, Letitia Elizabeth (1997). *Letitia Elizabeth Landon: Selected Writings*, eds Jerome McGann and Daniel Ross. Ontario: Broadview Press.

Langan, Celeste (1995). *Romantic Vagrancy: Wordsworth and the Simulation of Freedom*. Cambridge: Cambridge University Press.

Lawrence, Sean (2012). *Forgiving the Gift: The Philosophy of Generosity in Shakespeare and Marlowe*. Pittsburgh: Duquesne University Press.

LeCarner, Thomas (2014). 'A Portion of Thyself: Thoreau, Emerson, and Derrida on Giving', *Revue française d'études américaines* 3.140: 65–77.

Ledbetter, Kathryn (1994). 'Lucrative Requests: British Authors and Gift Book Editors', *The Papers of the Bibliographical Society of America* 88.2: 207–16.

Lee, Sueyen Juliette (2014). 'Shock and Blah: Offensive Postures in "Conceptual" Poetry and the Traumatic Stuplime', *Evening Will Come: A Monthly Journal of Poetics* 41.

Leighton, Angela (1984). *Shelley and the Sublime*. Cambridge: Cambridge University Press.

Lerner, Ben (2016). *The Hatred of Poetry*. New York: Farrer, Straus and Giroux.

LeRud, Lizzy (2017). 'Living Poems in Thoreau's Prose', *Nineteenth-Century Prose* 44: 155–76.

Levinson, Marjorie (1988). *Keats's Life of Allegory*. Oxford: Blackwell.

Levy, Michelle (2008). *Family Authorship and Romantic Print Culture*. New York: Palgrave Macmillan.

Lin, Tan (2010). *Seven Controlled Vocabularies and Obituary 2004. The Joy of Cooking*. Middletown: Wesleyan University Press.

Lindstrom, Eric Reid (2011). *Romantic Fiat: Demystification and Enchantment in Lyric Poetry*. New York: Palgrave Macmillan.

Liu, Alan (1989). *Wordsworth: The Sense of History*. Stanford, CA: Stanford University Press.

Locke, John (1824). *The Works of John Locke, vol. 8 (Some Thoughts Concerning Education, Posthumous Works, Familiar Letters)*. London: Rivington.

Lodge, Thomas (1853). *A Defence of Poetry, Music, and Stage-Plays*. London: Printed for the Shakespeare Society.

Loichot, Valéry (2020). *Water Graves: The Art of the Unritual in the Greater Caribbean*. Charlottesville: University of Virginia Press.

Longenbach, James (2004). *The Resistance to Poetry*. Chicago: University of Chicago Press.

Lowell, James Russell (1992). 'Thoreau's Letters', in *Emerson and Thoreau: The Contemporary Reviews*, ed. Joel Myerson. Cambridge: Cambridge University Press, 437–46.

Lyons, Deborah (2012). *Dangerous Gifts: Gender and Exchange in Ancient Greece*. Austin: Texas University Press.

Lysaker, John T. (2017). *After Emerson*. Bloomington: Indiana University Press.
McGinnis, Reginald (2007). 'Modernité et sorcellerie: Baudelaire lecteur du XVIII siècle', *Alea* 9.1: 34–47.
McIntosh, James (1974). *Thoreau as Romantic Naturalist*. Ithaca, NY: Cornell University Press.
McNiece, Gerald (1975). 'The Poet as Ironist in "Mont Blanc" and "Hymn to Intellectual Beauty"', *Studies in Romanticism* 14.4: 311–36.
Mandell, Laura (2001). 'Felicia Hemans and the Gift-Book Aesthetic', *Cardiff Corvey: Reading the Romantic Text* 6.1: 1–12.
Marder, Elissa (2002). *Dead Time: Temporal Disorders in the Wake of Modernity (Baudelaire and Flaubert)*. Stanford, CA: Stanford University Press.
— (2012). *The Mother in the Age of Mechanical Reproduction*. New York: Fordham University Press.
— (2014). 'From Poetic Justice to Criminal Jouissance: Poetry by Other Means in Baudelaire', in *Time for Baudelaire (Poetry, Theory, History)*, eds E. S. Burt, Elissa Marder and Kevin Newmark. New Haven, CT: Yale University Press, 67–84.
Marion, Jean-Luc (2002). *Being Given: Toward a Phenomenology of Givenness*, trans. Jeffrey L. Kosky. Stanford, CA: Stanford University Press.
Marks, Emerson R. (1981). *Coleridge on the Language of Verse*. Princeton: Princeton University Press.
Marotti, Arthur F. (1990). 'Shakespeare's Sonnets as Literary Property', in *Soliciting Interpretation: Literary Theory and Seventeenth-Century English Poetry*, eds Elizabeth D. Harvey and Katharine Eisman Maus. Chicago: University of Chicago Press, 143–73.
— (1991). 'Patronage, Poetry, and Print', *The Yearbook of English Studies* 21: 1–26.
Marx, Karl (1995). *Capital: An Abridged Edition*, ed. David McLellan. Oxford: Oxford University Press.
Marx, Leo (1964). *The Machine in the Garden*. Oxford: Oxford University Press.
Matlak, Richard E. (1997). *The Poetry of Relationship: The Wordsworths and Coleridge, 1797–1800*. New York: St Martin's Press.
Maury, Alfred (1843). *Les Fées du moyen-âge*. Paris: Librairie Philosophique de Ladrange.
Mauss, Marcel (1990). *The Gift: The Form and Reason for Exchange in Archaic Societies*, trans. W. D. Halls. New York: Routledge.
— (2007). *Essai sur le don: Forme et raison de l'échange dans les sociétés archaïques*. Paris: Presses Universitaires de la France.
Mellor, Anne K. (1997). 'The Female Poet and the Poetess: Two Traditions of British Women's Poetry, 1780–1830', *Studies in Romanticism* 36.2: 261–76.

Melville, Peter (2007). *Romantic Hospitality and the Resistance to Accommodation*. Waterloo, CA: Wilfrid Laurier University Press.

Mercier, Thomas Clément (2021). 'Re/pro/ductions: *Ça déborde*', *Poetics Today* 42.1: 23–48.

Michael, John (2018). *Secular Lyric: The Modernization of the Poem in Poe, Whitman, and Dickinson*. New York: Fordham University Press.

Miller, Christopher R. (2005). 'Shelley's Uncertain Heaven', *ELH* 72.3: 577–603.

Milton, John (2005). *Paradise Lost*, ed. Gordon Teskey. New York: W. W. Norton.

Minto, William (1889). 'Wordsworth's Great Failure', *Nineteenth Century* 26: 435–51.

Mitchell, Andrew J. (2015). *The Fourfold: Reading the Late Heidegger*. Evanston, IL: Northwestern University Press.

Mitchell, Robert (2007). *Sympathy and the State in the Romantic Era: Systems, State Finance, and the Shadows of Futurity*. New York: Routledge.

— (2013). *Experimental Life: Vitalism in Romantic Science & Literature*. Baltimore: Johns Hopkins University Press.

Modiano, Raimonda (1989). 'Coleridge and Wordsworth: The Ethics of Gift Exchange and Literary Ownership', *The Wordsworth Circle* 20.2: 113–20.

— (1993). 'Blood Sacrifice, Gift Economy and the Edenic World: Wordsworth's "Home at Grasmere"', *Studies in Romanticism* 32.4: 481–521.

Monroe, Jonathan (1998). *A Poverty of Objects: The Prose Poem and the Politics of Genre*. Ithaca, NY: Cornell University Press.

Montaigne, Michel de (2003). *The Complete Essays*, trans. and ed. M. A. Screech. New York: Penguin.

Most, Glenn W. (1982). 'Greek Lyric Poets', in *Ancient Writers: Homer to Caesar*, ed. Torrey James Luce. New York: Charles Scribner's Son.

Murphy, Stephen (1997). *The Gift of Immortality: Myths of Power and Humanist Poetics*. Cranbury, NJ: Farleigh Dickinson Press.

Murray, Penelope (1981). 'Poetic Inspiration in Early Greece', *The Journal of Hellenic Studies* 101: 87–100.

— (1983). 'Homer and the Bard', in *Aspects of the Epic*, eds Tom Winnifrith, Penelope Murray, and K. W. Grandsen. London: MacMillan, 1–15.

Nagy, Gregory (2007). 'Lyric and Greek Myth', in *The Cambridge Companion to Greek Mythology*, ed. Roger D. Woodard. Cambridge: Cambridge University Press, 19–51.

Neufeldt, Leonard (1989). *The Economist: Henry Thoreau & Enterprise*. Oxford: Oxford University Press.

Newlyn, Lucy (2003). *Reading, Writing, and Romanticism: The Anxiety of Reception*. Oxford: Oxford University Press.

Newman, Lance (2005). *Our Common Dwelling*. New York: Palgrave MacMillan.

Notopoulos, James A. (1943). 'The Platonic Sources of Shelley's "Hymn to Intellectual Beauty"', *PMLA* 58.2: 582–4.

— (1949). *The Platonism of Shelley*. Durham, NC: Duke University Press.

Ovid (1924). *Tristia. Ex Ponto*, trans. A. L. Wheller, rev. G .P. Goold. Cambridge, MA: Harvard University Press.

Parry, Jonathan (1986). 'The Gift, the Indian Gift and the "Indian Gift"', *Man* 21.3: 453–73.

Pascal, Roy (1953). *The German Sturm und Drang*. New York: Philosophical Library.

Pavlock, Barbara (1982). 'Horace's Invitation Poems to Maecenas: Gifts to a Patron', *Ramus* 11.2: 79–98.

Peacock, Thomas Love (1921). *Peacock's Four Ages of Poetry. Shelley's Defence of Poetry. Browning's Essay on Shelley*, ed. H. F. B. Brett-Smith. Boston: Houghton Mifflin Company.

Perloff, Marjorie (1991). *Radical Artifice: Writing Poetry in the Age of Media*. Chicago: University of Chicago Press.

— (2007). 'Presidential Address 2006: It Must Change', *PMLA* 122.3: 652–62.

— (2012). *Unoriginal Genius: Poetry by Other Means in the New Century*. Chicago: University of Chicago Press.

Pfau, Thomas (1997). *Wordsworth's Profession: Form, Class, & the Logic of Early Romantic Cultural Productions*. Stanford, CA: Stanford University Press.

Philip, M. NourbeSe (1989). *She Tries Her Tongue, Her Silence Softly Breaks*. Charlottetown, Prince Edward Island: Ragweed Press.

Philip, M. NourbeSe and Setaey Adamu Boateng (2008). *Zong!* Middletown, CT: Wesleyan University Press.

Pindar (1997). *Nemean Odes. Isthmian Odes. Fragments*, ed. and trans. William H. Race. Cambridge, MA: Harvard University Press.

— (1997). *Olympian Odes. Pythian Odes*, ed. and trans. William H. Race. Cambridge, MA: Harvard University Press.

Place, Vanessa (2010). *Tragodía 1: Statement of Facts*. Los Angeles: Blanc Press.

— (2011). *Tragodía 2: Statement of the Case*. Los Angeles: Blanc Press.

— (2011). *Tragodía 3: Argument*. Los Angeles: Blanc Press.

Plato (1924). *Laches. Protagoras. Meno. Euthydemus*, trans. W. R. M. Lamb. Cambridge, MA: Harvard University Press.

— (1925). *Statesman. Philebus. Ion*, ed. W. R. M. Lamb, trans. Harold North Fowler. Cambridge, MA: Harvard University Press.

— (1926). *Laws. Volume I*, trans. R. G. Bury. Cambridge, MA: Harvard University Press.

— (2005). *Euthyphro. Apology. Crito. Phaedo. Phaedrus*, trans. Harold North Fowler. Cambridge, MA: Harvard University Press.

— (2013). *Republic, Volume II: Books 6–10*, eds and trans Christopher Emlyn-Jones and William Preddy. Cambridge, MA: Harvard University Press.

Polanyi, Karl (1944). *The Great Transformation: The Political and Economic Origins of Our Time*. Boston: Farrar & Rinehart.

Pollin, Burton R. (1974). 'Godwin's "Memoirs" as a Source of Shelley's Phrase "Intellectual Beauty"', *Keats–Shelley Journal* 23: 14–20.

Poovey, Mary (2008). *Genres of the Credit Economy*. Chicago: University of Chicago Press.

Pope, Alexander (1894). *English Prose Selections*, 3, ed. Henry Craik. New York: Macmillan and Co.

Porte, Joel (1979). *Representative Man: Ralph Waldo Emerson in His Time*. Oxford: Oxford University Press.

Potkay, Adam (2012). *Wordsworth's Ethics*. Baltimore: Johns Hopkins University Press.

Pyle, Forest (1999). '"Frail Spells": Shelley and the Ironies of Exile', in *Irony and Clerisy*, ed. Deborah Elise White, *Romantic Circles Praxis Series*. <www.rc.umd.edu/praxis/irony/pyle/frail.html>.

— (2014). *Art's Undoing: In the Wake of a Radical Aestheticism*. New York: Fordham University Press.

Racter (1984). *The Policeman's Beard is Half-Constructed*. New York: Warner Books.

Rajan, Tillotama (1980). *Dark Interpreter: The Discourse of Romanticism*. Ithaca, NY: Cornell University Press.

Ramazani, Jahan (2014). *Poetry and its Others: News, Prayer, Song, and the Dialogue of Genres*. Chicago: University of Chicago Press.

Rankine, Claudia (2004). *Don't Let Me Be Lonely: An American Lyric*. New York: Penguin.

Rappoport, Jill (2004). 'Buyer Beware: The Gift Poetics of Letitia Elizabeth Landon', *Nineteenth-Century Literature* 58.4: 441–73.

— (2014). *Giving Women: Alliance and Exchange in Victorian Culture*. Oxford: Oxford University Press.

Regier, Alexander (2012). *Fracture and Fragmentation in British Romanticism*. Cambridge: Cambridge University Press.

Reznikoff, Charles (1978). *Testimony: The United States 1885–1915: Recitative. Volume 1*. Los Angeles: Black Sparrow Press.

Rhee, Margaret (2017). *Love, Robot*. Brooklyn, NY: the operating system.

Ringler, William (1941). 'Poeta Nascitur Non Fit: Some Notes on the History of an Aphorism', *Journal of the History of Ideas* 2.4: 497–504.

Rizzo, Betty (1991). 'The Patron as Poet Maker: The Politics of Benefaction', *Studies in Eighteenth-Century Culture* 20: 241–66.

Roberts, Hugh (1996) 'Chaos and Evolution: A Quantum Leap in Shelley's Process', *Keats–Shelley Journal* 45: 156–94.

— (1997). *Shelley and the Chaos of History: A New Politics of Poetry*. State College: Penn State University Press.

Robinson, David (1982). *Apostle of Culture: Emerson as Preacher and Lecturer*. Philadelphia: University of Pennsylvania Press.

— (1993). *Emerson and the Conduct of Life: Pragmatism and Ethical Purpose in the Later Work*. Cambridge: Cambridge University Press.

— (2004). *Natural Life: Thoreau's Worldly Transcendentalism*. Ithaca, NY: Cornell University Press.

Rosenbaum, Susan (2001). '"A Thing Unknown, without a Name": Anna Laetitia Barbauld and the Illegible Signature Author(s)', *Studies in Romanticism* 40.3: 369–99.

Rosenthal, Adam R. (2015). 'Poe's Memory', *MLN* 130.4: 863–78.

— (2015). 'The Gift of Memory in Baudelaire's "Morale du joujou"', *Nineteenth-Century French Studies* 43.3–4: 129–43.

— (2016). 'The Gift of the Name in Shelley's "Hymn to Intellectual Beauty"', *Studies in Romanticism* 55: 29–50.

— (2017). 'Some Notes Toward the Dignity of this Pipe (which is not one)', *Política común* 12. <http://dx.doi.org/10.3998/pc.12322227.0012.007>, last accessed 15 June 2021.

— (2022). 'On Derrida's *Donner le temps, Volumes I & II*: A New Engagement with Heidegger', *Research in Phenomenology* 52.1.

Rowlinson, Matthew (2010). *Real Money and Romanticism*. Cambridge: Cambridge University Press.

Royle, Nicholas (2003). *Jacques Derrida*. London: Routledge.

— (2009). *In Memory of Jacques Derrida*. Edinburgh: Edinburgh University Press.

Ruthven, K. K. (1976). 'Keats and "Dea Moneta"', *Studies in Romanticism* 15.3: 445–59.

Rzepka, Charles (1995). *Sacramental Commodities: Gift, Text, and the Sublime in De Quincey*. Boston: University of Massachusetts Press.

— (2016). *Selected Studies in Romantic and American Literature, History, and Culture: Inventions and Interventions*. New York: Routledge.

Saghafi, Kas (2011). 'Incurable Haunting: Saluting Michel Deguy', *Oxford Literary Review* 33.2: 245–64.

Sahlins, Marshall (1972). *Stone Age Economics*. Chicago: Aldine Publishing Company.
Sartre, Jean-Paul (1950). *Baudelaire*, trans. Martin Turnell. New York: New Directions.
Schmidt, Christopher (2008). 'The Waste-Management Poetics of Kenneth Goldsmith', *SubStance* 37.2: 25–40.
Scott, Alison V. (2005). *Selfish Gifts: The Politics of Exchange and English Courtly Literature, 1580–1628*. Cranbury, NJ: Farleigh Dickinson Press.
Scott, Maria C. (2005). *Baudelaire's* Le Spleen de Paris: *Shifting Perspectives*. London: Routledge.
Shakespeare, William (2008). *The Complete Sonnets and Poems: The Oxford Shakespeare*. Oxford: Oxford University Press.
Shanley, J. Lyndon (1957). *The Making of Walden*. Chicago: University of Chicago Press.
Shapiro, Gary (1999). '"Give me a Break!" Emerson on Fruits and Flowers', *The Journal of Speculative Philosophy* 13.2: 98–113.
Sharp, Ronald A. (1989). 'Keats and the Spiritual Economies of Gift Exchange', *Keats–Shelley Journal*, 38: 66–81.
Shelley, Percy (1909). *The Letters of Percy Bysshe Shelley*, vol. 1, ed. Roger Ingpen. London: Sir Isaac Pitman & Sons.
— (1989). *The Poems of Shelley: Volume One: 1804–1817*, eds Geoffrey Matthews and Kelvin Everest. London: Routledge.
— (2002). *Shelley's Poetry and Prose*, eds Donald H. Reiman and Neil Fraistat. New York: W. W. Norton.
Shershow, Scott Cutler (2005). *The Work and the Gift*. Chicago: University of Chicago Press.
Sidney, Sir Philip (2002). *An Apology for Poetry (or The Defence of Poesy)*, ed. R. W. Maslen. Manchester: Manchester University Press.
Skidan, Aleksandr (1999). 'The Resistance of/to Poetry', *boundary 2* 26.1: 244–7.
Simpson, David (1987). *Wordsworth's Historical Imagination*. Cambridge: Cambridge University Press.
— (2009). *Wordsworth, Commodification, and Social Concerns*. Cambridge: Cambridge University Press.
Smith, Paul (2007). 'Paul Cézanne's Primitive Self and Related Fictions', in *The Life and the Work: Art and Biography*, ed. Charles G. Salas. Oxford: Oxford University Press, 45–75.
Smith, Zadie (2016). 'On Historical Nostalgia and the Nature of Talent', 21 November. <https://www.npr.org/2016/11/21/502857118/novelist-zadie-smith-on-historical-nostalgia-and-the-nature-of-talent>, last accessed 1 December 2020.

Snell, Bruno (1961). *Poetry and Society: The Role of Poetry in Ancient Greece*. Bloomington: Indiana University Press.

Sophocles (1919). *The Ichneutae of Sophocles*, trans. Richard Johnson Walker. London: Burns and Oates.

Southey, Robert (1889). *Letters from the Lake Poets: Samuel Taylor Coleridge, William Wordsworth, Robert Southey, to Daniel Stuart*. London: West, Newman and Co.

Spenser, Edmund (1978). *The Faerie Queene*, eds Thomas P. Roche, Jr and C. Patrick O'Donnell, Jr. New York: Penguin.

Sperduti, Alice (1950). 'The Divine Nature of Poetry in Antiquity', *Transactions and Proceedings of the American Philological Association* 81: 209–40.

Starobinski, Jean (1970). *La Relation critique*. Paris: Gallimard.

Stein, Gertrude (1985). *Lectures in America*. Boston: Beacon Press.

Stetkevych, Suzanne (2002). *The Poetics of Islamic Legitimacy*. Bloomington: Indiana University Press.

Stevens, Sonya (2000). *Baudelaire's Prose Poems: The Practice and Politics of Irony*. Oxford: Oxford University Press.

Still, Judith (1997). *Feminine Economies: Thinking Against the Market in the Enlightenment and the Late Twentieth Century*. Manchester: Manchester University Press.

Strathern, Marilyn (1990). *The Gender of the Gift*. Berkeley: University of California Press.

Sturluson, Snorri (2006). *The Prose Edda: Norse Mythology*, ed. and trans. Jesse L. Byock. New York: Penguin.

Svenbro, Jesper (1984). 'La Découpe du poème. Notes sur les origines sacrificielles de la poétique grecque. *Poétique* 58: 215–32.

Tels-de Jong, Léontine Louise (1959). *Sur quelques divinités romaines de la naissance et de la prophétie*. Delft: Avanti.

Temple, William (1908). 'Plato's Vision of the Ideas', *Mind* 17: 502–17.

Thoreau, Henry David (1852). 'A Poet Buying a Farm', *Sartain's Union Magazine* 11: 127.

— (1873). *A Week on the Concord and Merrimack Rivers*. Boston: James R. Osgood and Company.

— (1962). *The Journal of Henry D. Thoreau 1*, eds Bradford Torrey and Francis H. Allen. New York: Dover.

— (1962). *The Variorum Walden*, ed. Walter Harding. New York: Twayne.

— (2004). *Walden: A Fully Annotated Edition*, ed. Jeffrey S. Cramer. New Haven, CT: Yale University Press.

— (2008). *Walden, Civil Disobedience and Other Writings*, ed. William Rossi. New York: W. W. Norton.

Vanderborg, Susan (2016). 'Transgenic Poetry: Loss, Noise, and the Province of Parasites', *Postmodern Culture* 26.3.
Vernant, Jean-Pierre (2006). *Myth and Thought Among the Greeks*, trans. Janet Lloyd. New York: Zone Books.
Vitale, Francesco (2018). *Biodeconstruction: Jacques Derrida and the Life Sciences*, trans. Mauro Senatore. Albany, NY: SUNY Press.
Walker, Jeffrey (2000). *Rhetoric and Poetics in Antiquity*. Oxford: Oxford University Press.
Ward, Wilfred (1904). *Aubrey de Vere: A Memoir Based on His Unpublished Diaries and Correspondence*. London: Longmans, Green, and Co.
Wasserman, Earl (1971). *Shelley: A Critical Study*. Baltimore: Johns Hopkins University Press.
Webbe, William (1895). *A Discourse of English Poetrie* (1586), ed. Edward Arber. Westminster: A. Constable and Co.
West, Martin L. (ed.) (2003). *Homeric Hymns. Homeric Apocrypha. Lives of Homer*, Cambridge, MA: Harvard University Press.
Wetzel, Michael (1993). 'Liebesgaben: Streifzüge des literarischen Eros', in *Ethik der Gabe: Denken nach Jacques Derrida*, eds Michael Wetzel and Jean-Michel Rabaté. Berlin: Akademie Verlag, 223–47.
White, Deborah Elise (2000). *Romantic Returns: Superstition, Imagination, History*. Stanford, CA: Stanford University Press.
White, N. I. (1940). *Shelley*, Vol. 1. New York: A. A. Knopf.
Wilkinson, Alec (2015). 'Something Borrowed: Kenneth Goldsmith's poetry elevates copying to an art, but did he go too far?' *The New Yorker*, 28 September 2015. <https://www.newyorker.com/magazine/2015/10/05/something-borrowed-wilkinson>, last accessed 9 May 2021.
Wills, David (2016). *Inanimation: Theories of Inorganic Life*. Minneapolis: Minnesota University Press.
Witherell, Elizabeth Hall (1990). 'Thoreau's Watershed Season as a Poet: The Hidden Fruits of the Summer and Fall of 1841', *Studies in the American Renaissance* 49–106.
— (1995). 'Thoreau as Poet', in *The Cambridge Companion to Henry David Thoreau*, ed. Joel Myerson. Cambridge: Cambridge University Press, 57–70.
Wolfson, Susan J. (2009). 'Byron's Ghosting Authority', *ELH* 76.3: 763–92.
Wood, Sarah (2011). 'Editorial: "It will have blood"', *Oxford Literary Review* 33.2: v–xi.
Wordsworth, William (1907). *Letters of the Wordsworth Family from 1787 to 1855, Volume 1*, ed. William Angus Knight. Boston: Ginn and Company.

— (1967). *The Letters of William and Dorothy Wordsworth, 2nd Edn, vol. 1: The Early Years 1787–1805*, eds Ernest de Selincourt and Chester L. Shaver. Oxford: Clarendon.
— (1967). *The Letters of William and Dorothy Wordsworth, 2nd Edn, vol. 2: The Middle Years, Part 1: 1806–1811*, eds Ernest de Selincourt and Mary Moorman. Oxford: Clarendon.
— (1977). *Home at Grasmere: Part First, Book First, of The Recluse*, ed. Beth Darlington. Ithaca, NY: Cornell University Press.
— (1977). *The Prelude, 1798–1799*, ed. Stephen Parrish. Ithaca, NY: Cornell University Press.
— (1978). *The Letters of William and Dorothy Wordsworth, 2nd Edn, vol. 4: The Later Years, Part 1: 1821–1828*, ed. Alan G. Hill. Oxford: Clarendon.
— (1992). *Lyrical Ballads, and Other Poems, 1797–1800*, eds James Butler and Karen Green. Ithaca, NY: Cornell University Press.
— (2007). *The Excursion*, eds Sally Bushell, James Butler, and Michael Jaye. Ithaca, NY: Cornell University Press.
— (2008). *William Wordsworth: The Major Works*, ed. Stephen Gill. Oxford: Oxford University Press.
Young, Edward (1918). *Edward Young's Conjectures on Original Composition*, ed. Edith J. Morley. London: Longmans, Green & Co.
Zhuo, Yue (2018). 'Derrida and the Essence of Poetry', in *After Derrida: Literature, Theory and Criticism in the Twenty-First Century*, ed. Jean-Michel Rabaté. Cambridge: Cambridge University Press.
Zionkowski, Linda (2016). *Women and Gift Exchange in Eighteenth-Century Fiction: Richardson, Burney, Austen*. New York: Routledge.

Index

aesthetics
   aesthetic pleasure and the economy of giving, 168–70, 171
   Kantian, 233–4
aoidē/aoidos, term, 41
Aristotle, 12, 29 n.8, 42, 51 n.11, 237 n. 7
Arsić, Branka, 208 n.37
Auden, W. H., 59, 261

Baetens, Jan, 248
Baudelaire, Charles
   chiffonnier figure, 71
   conceptual binaries, 216, 226, 245–6
   'Counterfeit Money', xv, xvii–xviii, 2, 13, 18, 19–20, 22, 26, 215, 216–17, 224
   'Edgar Allan Poe, sa vie et ses ouvrages', 213
   fate and chance problematic, 216–19, 224–5
   fate as an unconditional gift, 224–5
   Flowers of Evil, 215, 217, 220
   the gift of poetry, 216, 246
   'Philosophy of Toys', 217–18, 223
   'Plaintes d'un Icare', 23–4, 26, 215
   the problem of pleasure and pleasing, 217
   questions of gifts and predestination, 215–16, 217, 218
   Spleen de Paris, 216
   traces of a gift's inscription, 214
   see also 'Fairies' Gifts, The' (Baudelaire)
Beaumont, Sir George, 88
Bellay, Joachim du, 59
Blake, William, 50, 70
Bök, Christian, xiii, 249, 250, 251, 252–3
Bourdieu, Pierre, 15
Bowditch, Phebe Lowell, 61, 63
Burwick, Frederick, 48–9

Calvert, Raisley, 101–2, 103–4, 106–7, 117 n.80
Carson, Anne, xvi, xxv n.17, 37, 257–8
Cavell, Stanley, 179, 183
Cicero, 52 n.14
Clang [*Glas*], 27 n.5
Clare, John, 50, 71
classical poetry
   divine creation/human production division, 42–4, 265–6
   divinity of poetry, 41–2, 266
   fating figures, 221–2
   gift-modality of poetry, 43
   given talent vs man-made talent, 43
   Homeric Hymn to Hermes, 265–6, 267–8
   opposition between nature (*physis*) and art (*technē*), 42–4
   patronage of, 60–1
Coleridge, Dorothy, 87, 90–1, 93, 99, 100–1
Coleridge, Samuel Taylor
   on the critical reception of Wordsworth's *The Excursion*, 90
   on genius, 49, 50
   on the poetic gift, 50, 246–7
   The Prelude as a 'gift to Coleridge', 93, 95, 97, 98, 107, 108
   Susan Howe's re-writing of, 246–7
   term poematic, 31 n.29
   on Wordsworth and *The Recluse*, 87–8, 89, 92
   Wordsworth's personal debt to, 85, 99
constrained writing, 248–9
contemporary writing
   challenge of how to give, 254–61
   constrained writing, 248–9

INDEX 295

genius/talent dialectic, 246–7, 249–51
  the gift in, 246–52
  poetic language in, 246–8
  poetic language of self-effacing works, 251–4
  poetic language of the radically dispossessed, 255–61
  robopoetic verse, 246, 248, 250–1
Culler, Jonathan, xxiv n.9, 66

Dante, 52 n.27
Darlington, Beth, 91
Davis, Joe, 250
Davis, Natalie Zemon, 73
dell'Anguillara, Giovanni Andrea, 58, 60, 77 n.29
Demodocus, 43
Derrida, Jacques
  Dichtung concept, 130–1
  the gift and poetry's interrelation/work on the gift, xiii
  the gift as a marking of a trace, xiv–xv, xvi
  the gift exchange concept, 12, 15–16
  'Living On', 11, 19, 20
  notion of literature, 35 n.53
  'Plato's Pharmacy', 2, 12, 27 n.6
  poematic/poetic distinction, xviii–xix, 3–4, 6, 15, 18
  'Psyche: Invention of the Other', 11, 20
  récit, narrative and the poematic, 11, 18–19, 21–2, 25–6, 38
  structuring role of the gift, xiii, xvii
  see also 'Economimesis' (Derrida); *Given Time* (Derrida)
Descartes, René, 48
Dick, Alexander, 70
Dickinson, Emily, 58–9, 60
Dryden, John, 67

'Economimesis' (Derrida)
  concept of the gift within, 7
  economy of poetry and the gift, 6–10
  helio-poetics in, 1–2
  Kant's production and mimesis dialectic, 6–9
  relationship with *Given Time*, xvii, 2, 7, 24
  treatments of poetry and gift, xvii, 7
economy
  aesthetic pleasure and the economy of giving, 168–70, 171
  commodification of poetry, 162–3
  conflict with poetic aneconomy, 9, 10, 180
  debt and repayment in Thoreau, 199–203
  economisation of the gift, 163
  the economy of Nature in *Walden*, 190–2
  the economy of poetry and the gift in 'Economimesis' (Derrida), 6–10
  the gift as source and circuit of exchange, xviii, 131–3, 140–1
  gift/debt dialectic in Emerson, 166, 170–1
  gift-economy of poetry, xi–xii, 72–3, 124, 267, 268–9
  the gift exchange concept, 12–17, 26, 69, 71–2, 100
  gift-giving and market value in Emerson, 166, 167, 168–9
  impossibility of the gift exchange, 12–17, 26
  Kant's production and mimesis dialectic, 6–9
  linguistic utterance/commodity exchange relationship in *Walden* (Thoreau), 194–9, 214
  Marxian Money–Commodity–Money, 197
  patronage and the socio-economic weight of the gift, 61, 63–4, 67–72
  socio-economic fragmentation of the gift, 161–2
  socio-economic inequalities, 70
  socio-economic weight of the gift in Baudelaire, 225–6, 227–8, 236
  transition of the imagination into, 195–9
  withdrawal of Thoreau from the economy of Concord, 189–90
Eilenberg, Susan, 68
Emerson, Ralph Waldo
  'Fate', 213
  'Montaigne, or the Skeptic', 184
  'Nature', 184
  'New England Reformers', 169
  opposition to the market, 169
  see also 'Gifts' (Emerson)
Eron, Sarah, 47
excess/restraint opposition, xxiv n.9

'Fairies' Gifts, The' (Baudelaire)
  the fairies as female destining semi-deities, 219, 221–4, 225
  fating figures, 221–2
  the gift as (un)merited, 225–6
  the gift of destiny, 219–20
  the gift of nothing, 229–30
  the gift of pleasing (*Don de plaire*), 232–6
  gift-exceptions, 226–7
  gift-gaffe of beauty and poetic power, 228
  gift-gaffe of wealth, 227–8
  gifting blunders, 226–30
  imagination and the act of creation, 230–2
  the immediacy of creation, 230–2
  linguistic lineage of the *fée*, 221–2
  socio-economic weight of the gift, 225–6, 227–8, 236

Finn, Margot C., 69
Fumerton, Patricia, 78 n.32

Genette, Gérard, 76 n.12
genius
　cult of, 49–50
　as a divine gift, 85–6
　during the Enlightenment, 48–9
　in *Geneses*, 27 n.6, 32 n.37
　genius/talent dialectic in contemporary writing, 246–7, 249–51
　ingenium figure, 48
　as nature given, 47–8
　opposition between nature and art, 44, 46
　the poet's gift of, xi, 10, 48
　robopoetic verse and, 250–1
　substitution for Talent, 246–7
　see also inspiration; production
George, Stefan, 131–2, 138
gift-books, 71
gift-giving
　aesthetic pleasure and the economy of giving, 168–70, 171
　charitable donation, 70–1
　Emerson's gift of giving, 166–70
　the gift of pleasing (*Don de plaire*), 232–6
　gift-giving and market value in Emerson, 166, 167, 168–9
　within the literary marketplace, 68–71
　obligation of the gift, 84, 85, 96–7
　the poem as the gift of patronage, 59, 64–7, 73–4
　poetic gift economies, xi–xii, 72–3, 124, 267, 268–9
　the poetic word and immortality in Wordsworth, 103–7
　pre-modern exchange, 69–70, 124
　refusal/acceptance of a gift, 213–14
　Romantic male poets and, 71
　see also patronage
'Gifts' (Emerson)
　on the act of giving, 165–8, 170–1
　aesthetic pleasure and the economy of giving, 168–70, 171
　flowers as the ideal gift, 168–9, 171
　'fruit' as between beauty and value, 172–3
　the gift of poetry, 170, 171
　gift/debt dialectic, 166, 170–1
　gift-giving and market value, 166, 167, 168–9
　poematic opening, 166, 167
Gilmore, Michael T., 179
Given Time (Derrida)
　concluding poems of, 23–5
　Derrida's turn away from poetry, xvii–xviii, 2, 3–4, 14, 25–6
　the end of poetry, 23–5
　the gift as the text, 25–6
　the gift exchange concept, 12, 15–16
　the gift within *récit* (narrative), 5, 6, 11, 18–25
　helio-poetic in, 2
　impossibility of the gift, 12–17, 26
　poetry/gift relationship, xvii, 3–4, 11
　relationship with 'Economimesis', xvii, 2, 7, 24
　structural impossibility of the gift, xvii, 5–6
　treatment of Baudelaire's 'Counterfeit Money', xvii–xviii, 2
Godzich, Wlad, 38
Gold, Barbara K., 73
Goldsmith, Kenneth
　conceptual poetry, 246
　elimination of the gift, xiii
　Soliloquy, 251–3
　Uncreative Writing, 245
Gravil, Richard, 179
Griffin, Dustin, 67
Grusin, Richard, 190, 192
Guillory, John, 46–7

Harding, Walter, 181–2
Heidegger, Martin
　Dichtung, term, 138
　Dichtung concept, xviii, 122, 129, 130–1, 133, 246
　'The Essence of Language', 131–2, 141
　the gift as a 'thing', xiii–xiv
　the gift as source and circuit of exchange, 131–3
　the gift of poetry in the thought of, 127–34
　'Heidegger's Hand (*Geschlecht* II)',, 9
　language and the naming of the thing, 128–30, 132, 141
　on the poetic word, 131–3, 138
　poetry's endowing and founding nature, xi, 128–30, 131, 133–4
helio-poetics
　circularity, 2, 9–10
　definition, 1–2
　Derrida's turn away from, 2, 25–6
　in 'Economimesis', 2
　emergence of, 5–6
　in *Given Time*, 2
　in *Homeric Hymn to Hermes*, 267, 268
　poetry/gift relationship, 8–10

Hesiod
    divinity of poetry, 41, 42
    fating figures, 221
    Theogony, 42
Heubler, Douglas, 246
Heyd, Michael, 47
Heywood, John, 59
Hölderlin, Friedrich, x, 50
Homer
    fating figures, 221
    Greek terms for poetry, 41
    Odyssey, 37, 42
    poetry as a divine gift, 41, 42
Homeric Hymn to Hermes, 265–6, 267–8
Horace, 43, 64–5, 107
Howe, Susan, 'Concordance', 245, 246, 254–5, *255*
Hyde, Lewis, xi, 37, 75 n.6, 84
'Hymn to Intellectual Beauty' (Shelley)
    as autobiographical, 139, 148–50
    'critique' of the gift-receiving-and-giving voice of lyric, 140–1
    frailty of poetic language, 139
    'Intellectual Beauty' as a name of the unnameable, 140–5, 152
    the name as remainder, 145, 147, 150–2, 153
    the name of God as the remainder, 150–2, 153
    naming as the poet's endeavour, 145–50, 152, 153–4
    narrative arc, 139–40
    the poetic debt, 148, 149
    poetic donation in, 152–3

imagination
    for the act of creation in 'The Fairies' Gifts' (Baudelaire), 230–2
    creation of new images, 46–7
    within the economic sphere, 195–9
    free production of, 7–8
    memory of God's creation, xi
    rise of, 46
    Romantics revival of, 46
    self-given poetic authority, 46
    Thoreau's quest for a site for a house, 185–7, 192–4
inspiration
    in contemporary poetics, 248–50
    decline of and the rise of imagination, 46
    as divine, 42–7
    divine inspiration/human production division, xi, 42–5, 50
    during the Enlightenment, 46–7
    as inebriation, 163

Jacobs, Carol, 157 n.13
Jarvis, Simon, 33 n.44, 109 n.1, 170, 176 n.19
Johnson, Barbara, 27 n.3, 209 n.42, 236 n.5
Johnson, Ben, 45–6
Johnston, Kenneth R., 101

Kac, Eduardo, 250
Kant, Immanuel
    aesthetics, 233–4
    on the gift of pleasing, 233–4
    on the natural gifts of South Sea Islanders, 69–70
    nature-given genius, 48
    poetic *ingenium* notion, 37
    poetry as the summit of art, 8–9
    production and mimesis dialectic, 6–9
Keats, John, 50, 61, 68, 70, 72
Kittay, Jeffrey, 38
Klein, Richard, 72

Lamb, Charles, 71
Lamb, Jonathan, 69
language
    as beyond prose, xii
    constrained writing, 248–9
    in contemporary poetics, 246–8, 251–4
    'Discourse on the Logic of Language' (Philip), 259–60
    the gift and, 122
    the gift as source and circuit of exchange, 131–3
    the gift of the poetic word, 138–9, 260–1
    Heidegger's poetic word, 131–3, 138
    names and nouns in Gertrude Stein, 121, 122–3, 125
    as the naming of the thing (Heidegger), xiii–xiv, 128–30, 132, 141
    ontological tradition of poetics, 121, 125
    the poetic word and immortality in Wordsworth, 103–7
    of the radically dispossessed, 255–61
    in *Soliloquy* (Goldsmith), 251–3
    the strangeness of, 122
    transformation of poetic speech into legally binding pledge in *Walden* (Thoreau), 194–9, 214
    see also naming
Ledbetter, Kathryn, 71
Lévi-Strauss, Claude, 65
Locke, John, 48
Lodge, Thomas, 44–5
Loichot, Valéry, 257
Longinus, 44

Mallarmé, Stéphane, xxv n.13, 19, 23, 71, 254
Man, Paul de, 120
Mandell, Laura, 71
Marder, Elissa, 237 n.8
Marx, Karl, 190, 197
Mauss, Marcel
  account of gift-giving, xiii
  binding nature of the gift, 84
  etymology of the *res*, 234
  The Gift, 213, 223
  impossibility of the gift, 12, 15
  obligation of the gift, 85
  on the refusal/acceptance of a gift, 213–14
  socio-economic fragmentation of the gift, 161–2
Miller, Christopher R., 159 n. 21
Milton, John, xi, 46, 60, 74
mimesis, 6–9
Minto, William, 88
Modiano, Raimonda, 109 n.1
Montaigne, Michel de, 174 n.10
Murray, Penelope, 52 n.12, 52 n.15

naming
  'Intellectual Beauty' as a name of the unnameable, 140–5, 152
  the name as remainder in Shelley, 145, 147, 150–2, 153
  names and nouns in Gertrude Stein, 121, 122–3, 125
  name-things in poetry, 124
  naming as the poet's endeavour, 145–9, 152, 153–4
  naming function of 'Intellectual Beauty', 140–5, 152
  poetry as the naming of the thing (Heidegger), 128–30, 132, 141
  poetry's singular function of, 121–5, 143
Newman, Lance, 179

onto-theology, xiii, xviii, xix, 6, 7–9, 26
Ovid, 43, 103, 222

patronage
  concrete copies of works, 61–2
  conventions of gifting, 61, 63
  dedicatory inscriptions, 61–2, 64–7, 73–4
  gift-books, 71
  in the Greco-Roman period, 60–1
  impact of print technology, 67–8
  and the limits of poetry, 59–60

Nature's patronage of Wordsworth via the gift, 86–7, 89–92, 94–6
patronage presents, 61–4
the poem as the gift, 59, 64–7, 73–4
poetic donation and, 37, 60–4
poetic embeddings, 61–2
poetic gift economies, xi, 67, 72–3
poetic immortality, 62
Raisley Calvert's patronage of Wordsworth, 101–2, 103–4, 106–7, 117 n.80
in the Romantic period, 68–72
the socio-economic weight of the gift, 61, 63–4, 67–72
term, 59
see also gift-giving
Peacock, Thomas Love, 162–3, 166
Perloff, Marjorie, xxiv n.10, 152, 249, 250, 251, 263 n. 28
Philip, M. NourbeSe
  'Discourse on the Logic of Language', 259–60
  She Tries Her Tongue, Her Silence Softly Breaks, 256–7
  Zong! 257–8, *258*, *259*
Pindar, 42, 103
Place, Vanessa, 246
Plato
  enthousiasmos, 49
  fating figures, 221, 223
  four noble *furores*, 56 n.43
  within the helio-poetic tradition, 2, 8, 9–10, 12
  Ion, 42
  Platonism of the 'Hymn', (Shelley), 139, 143, 145, 154 n.3, 155 n.7
  poetic inspiration/production division, 42, 43, 52 n.12, 52 n.14, 55 n.29
  poetry as god-given gift, x–xi, 50, 267
'Plato's Pharmacy' (Derrida), 2, 12, 27 n.6
poematic
  and the act of inscription, xv–xvi
  as *Dichtung*, 29 n.9
  as distinct from the poetic in Derrida, xviii–xix, 3–4, 6, 15, 18
  récit, narrative and the poematic, 11, 18–19, 21–2, 25–6, 38
  term, 31 n.30
poetic donation
  of authorship, 60
  Derrida's scepticism of, 12–13
  divine creation and bestowal, x, xi, 7, 41–50, 266

Greek conception of, 41–4, 265–6
  in 'Hymn to Intellectual Beauty' (Shelley),
    152–3
  patronage and, 37, 60–4
  The Prelude as a 'gift to Coleridge', 93, 95,
    97, 98, 107, 108
  in relation to the gift/text relationship, xi,
    xiv–xvi, 12–13, 25–6, 267
  within the site of the book, 67, 72
poetry
  differentiated from 'non-poetry', 38, 44, 84
  as divine, x, xi, 7, 41–50
  gift-status of, x–xiii, 5–6, 37–8
  Greek terms for, 41
  as the Kantian summit of art, 8–9
  poetry/Poetry distinction, 44–5
  term, 38
poiēsis, term, 41
Ponge, Francis, 3, xxv n.13, 20
Poovey, Mary, 68, 78 n.34
Pope, Alexander, 67
Poucel, Jean-Jacques, 248
Prelude, The (Wordsworth)
  act of writing, 93–4
  dilemma between ability and indolence, 92
  the gift and the poet's status, 85, 86–7
  the gift as obligation, 96–7
  as a 'gift to Coleridge', 93, 95, 97, 98, 107, 108
  meaning and power of the name
    'Wordsworth', 87, 94
  poetic and personal debts resolved by, 98–108
  receiving and giving in, 94–109
  reception/reciprocation correlation
    of the gift, 84–7, 92–5, 96–8, 102,
    106–7, 138
  references to song, 105
  value of the gift of *The Prelude*, 107–9
print culture
  commodification of poetry, 162–3
  gift-books, 71
  patronage and the book trade, 73
  poetic donation in the site of the book, 67, 72
  poetic vocation vs. literary markets, 68–9
production
  divine inspiration/human production
    division, 42–5, 50
  poetry/Poetry distinction, 44–5
  production and mimesis dialectic, 6–9
  professionalisation of the poet, 68–9
Pyle, Forest, 152, 159 n.19

Racter, *The Policeman's Beard is Half-Constructed*,
  245, 247, 250–1, 254

Ramazani, Jahan, 253–4
Rankine, Claudia, 66–7
récit (narrative)
  Baudelaire's 'Counterfeit Money' as,
    xvii–xviii, 19–20
  concept, 11
  Derrida's turn to, 2, 3, 19, 22
  and the gift in *Given Time*, 5, 6, 11
  the gift within, 18–25, 133
  in Ponge's 'Fable', 20
  récit, narrative and the poematic, 11, 18–19,
    21–2, 25–6, 38
  re-marking of the text, 20–2, 25
  term, 17–18
Renaissance
  dedicatory inscriptions, 67–8
  divine inspiration/human production
    division, 45
  the givenness of poetry, 44–5
  nature/nurture argument and poetic
    composition, 45–6
  patronage and the book trade, 73
restraint/excess opposition, xxiv n.9
Rhee, Margaret, 253
robopoetic verse, 246, 248, 250–1
Romantics
  figures of the poetic gift, 50, 69–71
  the gift exchange concept, 69, 71–2
  gift-giving and the male poets, 71
  idea of charity, 70
  revival of imagination, 46
  significance of Wordsworth's *The Recluse*,
    87–90, 92, 93
  see also Coleridge, Samuel Taylor;
    Shelley, Percy Bysshe; Wordsworth,
    William
Royle, Nicholas, 30 n.12
Rzepka, Charles, 109 n.1

secularisation, 46, 47
Shakespeare, William, 62, 83
Shanley, J. Lyndon, 181
Shelley, Percy Bysshe
  Defence of Poetry, xxiv n.9, 140, 143, 162
  the poetic gift, 141
  see also 'Hymn to Intellectual Beauty'
    (Shelley)
Sidney, Sir Philip
  Apology for Poetry, 45
  nature/nurture argument and poetic
    composition, 45–6
  on the poetic gift, xi
  role of the imagination, 46–7

Smith, Zadie, 255
Socrates, 221–2
song
    as classical terms for poetry, 41
    divine bestowal of, 41–2, 43, 72, 266, 267, 268
    references to in *The Prelude* (Wordsworth), 105
speech-act theory, 65–6
Spenser, Edmund, 46, 47, 50, 67, 74, 102, 143, 156
Stein, Gertrude
    name-things in poetry, 124
    on poetic naming, 121
    poetry's concern with nouns, 121, 122–3
    poetry's 'naming' function, 122–3, 125

temporality
    double temporality of the gift, 7–8
    the Fates gift of, 223
    the immediacy of creation in 'The Fairies' Gifts' (Baudelaire), 230–2
    instantaneity/deferral double temporality, 7–8
Tennyson, Alfred, 71
text
    the gift/text relationship, xi, xiv–xvi, 12–13, 25–6, 267
    récit's re-marking of, 20–2, 25
Thoreau, Henry David
    beauty and value relationship, 172–3
    the gift of poetry, 70, 171, 253
    pastoral withdrawal, 209 n.42
    Walden, 165
    A Week on the Merrimack and Concord Rivers, 178, 179
    see also *Walden* (Thoreau)
Ticknor, George, 92
travel narratives, 69

Walden (Thoreau)
    autobiographical form of, 178–9, 183
    correspondence between place and life, 207 n.28
    debt and repayment, 199–203
    the economy of Nature in, 190–2
    experiment at Walden Pond, 185
    failure/success dialectic, 180, 181–4
    the figure of the poet, 179–80
    the figure of the poet as outside the market, 187–9
    the gift of poetry, 180
    imagination and the quest for a site for a house, 185–7, 192–4
    linguistic utterance/commodity exchange relationship, 194–8, 214
    as a performance of a poem, 180
    'A Poet Buying a Farm', 180, 181–5, 214, 271–2
    as a poetic work, 179
    the quest for a site for a house, 185–7, 192–4
    separation of purchase from possession, 194–9
    speaker/author/writer, 179, 184, 188
    transformation of poetic speech into legally binding pledge, 194–9
    withdrawal of Thoreau from the economy of Concord, 189–90
Wallace, David Foster, 171
Webster, Daniel, 169
White, Deborah Elise, 157 n.14
Wordsworth, William
    'Advertisement' to *Lyrical Ballads*, 178
    The Excursion, 90, 94, 105
    genius as a divine gift and, 85–6
    the gift's reception/reciprocation correlation, 84–7, 92–5, 96–8, 102, 106–7, 138
    Gothic church analogy, 94
    Home at Grasmere, 105–6
    idea of charity, 70
    literary expectations of *The Recluse*, 87–90, 92, 93
    Nature's patronage of via the gift, 86–7, 89–92, 94–6
    obligation of the gift, 85
    the poem as the gift, 102–3
    the poetic word and immortality, 103–7
    preparation for the writing of *The Recluse*, 87–8, 93–4, 96–7
    the question of the gift in, 84–6
    Raisley Calvert's patronage of, 101–2, 103–4, 106–7, 117 n.80
    The Recluse, 85, 86–93
    relationship with Coleridge, 85
    stance on gift-books, 71
    status as a poet, 84–5, 89–90, 91–3, 95, 96, 98, 106
    text signed 'Wordsworth', 86, 87, 94, 104, 109
    see also *Prelude, The* (Wordsworth)

Yeats, W. B., 59
Yitzhaq Ibn Khalfoun, 58, 60
Young, Edward, 49

EU representative:
Easy Access System Europe
Mustamäe tee 50, 10621 Tallinn, Estonia
Gpsr.requests@easproject.com

www.ingramcontent.com/pod-product-compliance
Lightning Source LLC
Chambersburg PA
CBHW052045220426
43663CB00012B/2447